COMMENTARIES ON AMERICAN LAW

By James Kent

Volume I

LAW BOOKS

CLAITOR'S PUBLISHING DIVISION
Baton Rouge, La.

This edition of
Commentaries on American Law
is an unabridged republication of the
first edition published in New York between
1826 and 1830.

Vol. I paper ISBN # 0-87511-702-3
Vol. I hardbound ISBN # 0-87511-707-4
Vols. I-IV paper ISBN # 0-87511-706-6
Vols. I-IV hardbound ISBN # 0-87511-711-2

Published and for sale by:
Claitor's Publishing Division
3165 S. Acadian Thwy.,
P.O. Box 3333
Baton Rouge, LA 70821
All Rights Reserved

Manufactured in the United States of America

COMMENTARIES ON AMERICAN LAW

Volume I

COMMENTARIES

ON

AMERICAN LAW.

BY JAMES KENT.

VOLUME I.

NEW-YORK:

PUBLISHED BY O. HALSTED,
Law Buildings, Nassau-street.

1826.

Southern District of New-York, ss.

BE IT REMEMBERED, That on the twenty-fifth day of November, A. D. 1826, in the fifty-first year of the Independence of the United States of America, James Kent, of (L. S.) the said district, hath deposited in this office the title of a book, the right whereof he claims as author, in the words following, to wit:

"Commentaries on American Law. By James Kent. Volume I."

In conformity to the act of Congress of the United States, entitled, "An act for the encouragement of learning, by securing the copies of maps, charts, and books, to the authors and proprietors of such copies, during the time therein mentioned." And also to an act, entitled, "An act supplementary to an act, entitled, an act for the encouragement of learning, by securing the copies of maps, charts, and books, to the authors and proprietors of such copies, during the times therein mentioned, and extending the benefits thereof to the arts of designing, engraving, and etching historical and other prints."

JAMES DILL,
Clerk of the Southern District of New-York.

Clayton & Van Norden, Printers,
64 Pine-street.

PREFACE.

HAVING retired from public office in the summer of 1823, I had the honour to receive the appointment of Professor of Law in Columbia College. The trustees of that institution have repeatedly given me the most liberal and encouraging proofs of their respect and confidence, and of which I shall ever retain a grateful recollection. A similar appointment was received from them in the year 1793, and this renewed mark of their approbation determined me to employ the entire leisure in which I found myself, in further endeavours to discharge the debt which, according to Lord Bacon, every man owes to his profession. I was strongly induced to accept the trust from the want of occupation; being apprehensive that the sudden cessation of my habitual employment,[a] and the contrast between the discussions of the forum, and the solitude of

---

[a] I was appointed Recorder of New-York in March, 1797, and, from that time until August, 1823, was constantly employed in judicial duties.

retirement, might be unpropitious to my health and spirits, and cast a premature shade over the happiness of declining years.

The following Lectures are the fruit of the acceptance of that trust; and in the performance of my collegiate duty, I had the satisfaction to meet a collection of interesting young gentlemen of fine talents and pure character, who placed themselves under my instruction, and in whose future welfare a deep interest is felt.

Having been encouraged to suppose that the publication of the Lectures might render them more extensively useful, I have been induced to submit the present volume to the notice of students, and of the junior members of the profession, for whose use they were originally compiled. Another volume is wanting to embrace all the material parts of the Lectures which have been composed. It will treat, at large, and in an elementary manner, of the law of property, and of personal rights, and commercial contracts; and will be prepareed for the press in the course of the ensuing year, unless in the mean time there should be reason to apprehend, that another volume would be trespassing too far upon the patience and indulgence of the public.

NEW-YORK, NOVEMBER 23d, 1826.

CONTENTS.

PART I.

OF THE LAW OF NATIONS.

                                                              Page

LECTURE I.—Of the Foundation and History of the Law of Nations, - - - - - - - - - - - - - - - - - - - 1

LECTURE II.—Of the Rights and Duties of Nations in a State of Peace, - - - - - - - - - - - - - - - - - 21

LECTURE III.—Of the Declaration, and other early measures of a state of War, - - - - - - - - - - - - - - 45

LECTURE IV.—Of the various kinds of Property liable to Capture, 69

LECTURE V.—Of the Rights of Belligerent Nations in relation to each other, - - - - - - - - - - - - - - - 85

LECTURE VI.—Of the general Rights and Duties of Neutral Nations, - - - - - - - - - - - - - - - - - - 107

LECTURE VII.—Of Restrictions upon Neutral Trade, - - - - - 124

LECTURE VIII.—Of Truces, Passports, and Treaties of Peace, 149

LECTURE IX.—Of Offences against the Law of Nations, - - - - 169

PART II.

OF THE GOVERNMENT AND CONSTITUTIONAL JURISPRUDENCE OF THE UNITED STATES.

LECTURE X.—Of the History of the American Union, - - - - - - 189

LECTURE XI.—Of Congress, - - - - - - - - - - - - - - - - - - 207

LECTURE XII.—Of Judicial Constructions of the Powers of Congress, - - - - - - - - - - - - - - - - - - 229

CONTENTS.

Page
LECTURE XIII.—Of the President, - - - - - - - - - - - - - - - - 255
LECTURE XIV.—Of the Judiciary Department, - - - - - - - - - 275
LECTURE XV.—Of the Original and Appellate Jurisdiction of the Supreme Court, - - - - - - - - - - - - 293
LECTURE XVI.—Of the Jurisdiction of the Federal Courts in respect to the Common Law, and in respect to parties, - - - - - - - - - - - - - - - 311
LECTURE XVII.—Of the District and Territorial Courts of the United States, - - - - - - - - - - - - - - - - 331
LECTURE XVIII.—Of the Concurrent Jurisdiction of the State Governments, - - - - - - - - - - - - - - - - 363
LECTURE XIX.—Of Constitutional Restrictions on the Powers of the several States, - - - - - - - - - - - - 381

PART III.

OF THE VARIOUS SOURCES OF THE MUNICIPAL LAW OF THE SEVERAL STATES.

LECTURE XX.—Of Statute Law, - - - - - - - - - - - - - - - - - - 419
LECTURE XXI.—Of Reports of Judicial Decisions, - - - - - - - 439
LECTURE XXII.—Of the principal Publications on the Common Law, - 465
LECTURE XXIII.—Of the Civil Law, - - - - - - - - - - - - - - - 481

COMMENTARIES

ON

AMERICAN LAW.

PART I.

OF THE LAW OF NATIONS.

LECTURE I.

OF THE FOUNDATION AND HISTORY OF THE LAW OF NATIONS.

When the United States ceased to be a part of the British empire, and assumed the character of an independent nation, they became subject to that system of rules which reason, morality, and custom had established among the civilized nations of Europe, as their public law. During the war of the American revolution, Congress claimed cognizance of all matters arising upon the law of nations, and they professed obedience to that law, "according to the general usages of Europe."[a] By this law we are to understand that code of public instruction, which defines the rights and prescribes the duties of nations, in their intercourse with each other. The faithful observance of this law is essential to national character, and to the happiness of mankind. According to the observation of the President de Montesquieu,[b] it is founded on the principle, that different nations ought to do each other as much good in peace,

---

a Ordinance of the 4th December, 1781, relative to maritime captures. *Journals of Congress*, vol. vii. 185.

b *L'Esprit des Loix*, b. 1. c. 3.

and as little harm in war, as possible, without injury to their true interests. But, as the precepts of this code are not defined in every case with perfect precision, and as nations have no common civil tribunal to resort to for the interpretation and execution of this law, it is often very difficult to ascertain, to the satisfaction of the parties concerned, its precise injunctions and extent; and a still greater difficulty is the want of adequate pacific means to secure obedience to its dictates.

There has been a difference of opinion among writers, concerning the foundations of this law. It has been considered by some as a mere system of positive institutions, founded upon consent and usage; while others have insisted that the law of nations was essentially the same as the law of nature, applied to the conduct of nations, in the character of moral persons, susceptible of obligation and laws. We are not to adopt either of these theories as exclusively true. The most useful and practical part of the law of nations is, no doubt, instituted or positive law, founded on usage, consent, and agreement. But it would be improper to separate this law entirely from natural jurisprudence, and not to consider it as deriving much of its force, and dignity, and sanction, from the same principles of right reason, and the same view of the nature and constitution of man, from which the science of morality is deduced. There is a natural and a positive law of nations. By the former, every state, in its relations with other states, is bound to conduct itself with justice, good faith, and benevolence; and this application of the law of nature has been called by Vattel, the necessary law of nations, because nations are bound by the law of nature to observe it; and it is termed by others, the internal law of nations, because it is obligatory upon them in point of conscience.[a]

We ought not, therefore, to separate the science of public law from that of ethics, nor to encourage the dangerous

---

[a] *Vattel*, Prelim. sec. 7.

suggestion, that governments are not as strictly bound by the obligations of truth, justice, and humanity, in relation to other powers, as they are in the management of their own local concerns. States, or bodies politic, are to be considered as moral persons, having a public will, capable and free to do right and wrong, inasmuch as they are collections of individuals, each of whom carries with him into the service of the community, the same binding law of morality and religion which ought to control his conduct in private life. The law of nations is a complex system, composed of various ingredients. It consists of general principles of right and justice, equally suitable to the government of individuals in a state of natural equality, and to the relation and conduct of nations; of a collection of usages and customs, the growth of civilization and commerce; and of a code of conventional or positive law.[a] In the absence of these latter regulations, the intercourse and conduct of nations are to be governed by principles fairly to be deduced from the rights and duties of nations, and the nature of moral obligation; and we have the authority of the lawyers of antiquity, and of some of the first masters in the modern school of public law, for placing the moral obligation of nations and of individuals on similar grounds, and for considering individual and national morality as parts of one and the same science.

The law of nations, so far as it is founded on the principles of natural law, is equally binding in every age, and upon all mankind. But the Christian nations of Europe, and their descendants on this side of the Atlantic, by the vast superiority of their attainments in arts, and science, and commerce, as well as in policy and government; and, above all, by the brighter light, the more certain truths, and the more definite sanction, which Christianity has communicated to the ethical jurisprudence of the ancients, have established a law of nations peculiar to themselves. They form together a community of

---

[a] 2 *Mason*, 448. Story, J.

nations, united by religion, manners, morals, humanity, and science, and united also by the mutual advantages of commercial intercourse, by the habit of forming alliances and treaties with each other, of interchanging ambassadors, and of studying and recognising the same writers and systems of public law.

After devoting the present lecture to a cursory view of the history of the law of nations, I shall enter upon the examination of the European and American code of international law, and endeavour to collect, with accuracy, its leading principles, and to discuss their practical details.

The law of nations, as understood by the European world, and by us, is the offspring of modern times. The most refined states among the ancients seem to have had no conception of the moral obligations of justice and humanity between nations, and there was no such thing in existence as the science of international law. They regarded strangers and enemies as nearly synonymous, and considered foreign persons and property as lawful prize. Their laws of war and peace were barbarous and deplorable. So little were mankind accustomed to regard the rights of persons or property, or to perceive the value and beauty of public order, that in the most enlightened ages of the Grecian republics, piracy was regarded as an honourable employment. There were powerful Grecian states that avowed the practice of piracy; and the fleets of Athens, the best disciplined and most respectable naval force in all antiquity, were exceedingly addicted to piratical excursions. It was the received opinion, that Greeks were bound to no duties, nor by any moral law, without compact, and that prisoners taken in war had no rights, and might lawfully be put to death, or sold into perpetual slavery, with their wives and children.[a]

---

[a] *Mitford's History of Greece*, 8vo. edit. vol. ii. 352. vol. vi. 107. 185. *et passim*. *Ward's Enquiry into the History of the Law of Nations*, vol. i. 177—183. *Goguet's Origine des Loix*, &c. part ii. b. 5. *Grotius*, b. iii. c. 7. *Justin's Hist*. l. 43. c. 3. *Potter's Antiquities of Greece*, b. iii. c. 10. & 12. b. iv. c. 21.

There were, however, many feeble efforts, and some successful examples, to be met with in Grecian history in favour of national justice. The object of the Amphictyonic Council was to institute a law of nations among the Greeks, and to check violence and settle contests between Grecian states by a pacific adjustment. It was also a law of nations among them, and one which was very religiously observed, to allow to the vanquished the privilege of burying their own dead, and to grant the requisite truce for that purpose. Some of the states had public ministers resident at the courts of others,[a] and there were some distinguished instances of great humanity shown to prisoners of war. During a cessation of arms in the course of the Peloponnesian war, Athens and Sparta agreed to an exchange or mutual surrender of prisoners.[b] The sound judgment and profound reflections of Aristotle, naturally raised his sense of right above the atrocious maxims and practices of his age, and he perceived the injustice of that doctrine of Grecian policy, that, by the laws of war, the vanquished became the absolute property of the victor. "Wise men," he observed, "entertained different opinions upon that subject. Some considered superiority as a proof of virtue, because it is its natural effect, and they asserted it to be just that the victors should be masters of the vanquished; whilst others denied the force of the argument, and maintained that nothing could be truly just which was inconsistent with humanity."[c] He then proceeded to weaken by argument the false foundations on which the law of slavery, by means of capture in war, was established; and though he does not write on the subject very distinctly or forcibly, it seems to be quite apparent that his convictions were on that side.

The Romans exhibited much stronger proofs than the Greeks of the influence of regular law, and there was a marked difference between those nations in their intercourse

---

a Mitford's History, vol. 5. 378—9.   *b Thucyd.* l. 5. c. 18.
c Gillies' Aristotle, vol. 2. 35, 36.

with foreign powers. It was a principle of the Roman government, that none but a sworn soldier could lawfully fight the enemy; and in many instances the Romans showed that they excelled the Greeks, by the possession of a sterner and better sense of justice. The institution of a college of heralds, and the fecial law, were proofs of a people considerably advanced in the cultivation of the law of nations as a science; and yet with what little attention *they* were accustomed to listen to the voice of justice and humanity, appears but too plainly from their haughty triumphs, their cunning interpretation of treaties, their continual violation of justice, their cruel rules of war, and the whole series of their wonderful successes, in the steady progress of the conquest of the world. The perusal of Livy's magnificent History of the rise and progress of the Roman power, excites our constant admiration of the vigour, the skill, the valour, and the fortitude of the Roman people, yet, notwithstanding the splendour of the story, and the attractive simplicity of the writer, no reader of taste and principle can well avoid feeling a thorough detestation of the fierce spirit of conquest which it displays, and of the barbarous international law and customs of the ancients.

A purer system of public morals was cultivated, and insensibly gained ground, in the Roman state. The cruelties of Marius in the Jugurthan war, when he put part of the inhabitants of a Numidian town to the sword, and sold the rest for slaves, were declared by Sallust[a] to be a proceeding *contra jus belli*. At the zenith of the Roman power, the enlarged and philosophical mind of Cicero was struck with extreme disgust, at the excesses in which his countrymen indulged their military spirit. He justly discerned that mankind were not intended, by the law and constitution of their nature, as rational and social beings, to live in eternal enmity with each other; and he recommends, in one of the most beautiful and perfect ethical codes to be met with

---

[a] *Sal. Jug.* ch. 91.

among the remains of the ancients, the virtues of humanity, liberality, and justice, towards other people, as being founded in the universal law of nature. Their ancestors, he observed, considered that man as an enemy whom they regarded merely as a foreigner, and to deny to strangers the use and protection of the city, would be inhuman. To overturn justice by plundering others, tended to destroy civil society, to violate the law of nature, and the institutions of Heaven; and by some of the most happy illustrations, as well as by some of the most pathetic examples, Cicero vindicated the truth, and inculcated the value of the precept, that nothing was truly useful which was not honest.[a] In the latter ages of the Roman empire, when their municipal law became highly cultivated, and adorned by philosophy and science, the law of nations was recognised as part of the natural reason of mankind. *Quod vero naturalis ratio inter omnes homines constituit, id apud omnes gentes peræque custoditur, vocatur que jus gentium, quasi quo jure omnes gentes utantur.*[b] The Roman law was destined to attain the honourable distinction of becoming a national guide to future ages, and to be appealed to by modern tribunals and writers, in cases in which usage and positive law were silent, as one authoritative evidence of the decisions of the law of nations.

It must be admitted, however, that the sages from whose works the pandects were compiled, speak very indistinctly and imperfectly on the subject of national law. They must be read with much discrimination, as Grotius observed,[c] for they often call that the law of nations which prevailed, and perhaps by casual consent, among some nations only, and many things which belonged to the law of nations they treated indiscriminately with matters of mere municipal law. The Roman jurisprudence, in its most cultivated state, was a very imperfect transcript of the precepts of na-

---

a *Off.* b. 3. sec. 5, 6, 7. 11.   b *Dig.* 1. 1. 9.   *Inst.* 1. 2. 1.
c *Proleg.* sec. 53.

tural justice, on the subject of national duty. It retained strong traces of ancient rudeness, from the want of the Christian system of morals, and the civilizing restraints of commerce. We find the barbarous doctrine still asserted, that prisoners of war became slaves *jure gentium*,[a] and even in respect to foreign nations with whom the Romans were at peace, but had no particular alliance, it is laid down in the Digests, that whoever passed from one country to the other became immediately a slave. *Nam si cum gente aliqua neque amicitiam, neque hospitium, neque fœdus amicitiæ causa factum habemus: hi hostes quidem non sunt. Quod autem eo nostro ad eos pervenit, illorum fit: et liber homo noster ab eis captus, servus fit, et eorum. Idemque si ab illis ad nos aliquid perveniat.*[b] It is impossible to conceive of a rule of national law more directly calculated to destroy all commercial intercourse, and to maintain eternal enmity between nations.

The irruption of the northern tribes of Scythia and Germany, overturned all that was gained by the Roman law, annihilated every restraint, and all sense of national obligation, and civil society relapsed into the violence and confusion of the barbarous ages. Mankind seemed to be doomed to live once more in constant distrust or hostility, and to regard a stranger and an enemy as almost the same. Piracy, rapine, and ferocious warfare, deformed the annals of Europe. The manners of nations were barbarous, and their maxims of war cruel. Slavery was considered as a lawful consequence of captivity. Mr. Barrington[c] has cited the laws of the Wisigoths, Saxons, Sicilians, and Bavarians, as restraining by the severest penalties, the plunder of shipwrecked goods, and the abuse of shipwrecked seamen, and as extending the rights of hospitality to strangers. But, not-

---

[a] *Inst.* 1. 3, 4. *Dig.* lib. 1. tit. 5. sec. 5. and lib. 49. tit. 15. ch. 12. sec. 1.

[b] *Dig.* 49. 15. 5. 2.

[c] Observations on the Statutes, chiefly the more ancient, pa. 22.

withstanding a few efforts of this kind to introduce order and justice, and though municipal law had undergone great improvement, the law of nations remained in the rudest and most uncultivated state, down to the period of the 16th century. In many instances, shipwrecked strangers were made prisoners and sold as slaves, without exciting any complaint, or offending any public sense of justice. Numerous cases occurred of acts of the grossest perfidy and cruelty towards strangers and enemies. Prisoners were put to death for their gallantry and brave defence in war. There was no reliance upon the word and honour of men in power. Reprisals and private war were in constant activity. Instances were frequent of the violation of embassies, of the murder of hostages, the imprisonment of guests, and the killing of heralds. The victor in war had his option in dealing with his prisoners, either to put them to death, or reduce them to slavery, or exact an exorbitant ransom for their deliverance. So late as the time of Cardinal Richlieu, it was held to be the right of all nations to arrest strangers who came into the country without a safe conduct.[a]

The Emperor Charlemagne made distinguished efforts to improve the condition of Europe, by the introduction of order, and the propagation of Christianity; and we have cheering examples, during the darkness of the middle ages, of some recognition of public law, by means of alliances, and the submission of disputes to the arbitrament of a neutral power.[b] Mr. Ward enumerates five institutions, existing about the period of the eleventh century, which made a deep impression upon Europe, and contributed in a very essential degree to improve the law of nations. These institutions were. the feudal system, the concurrence of Europe in one form of religious worship and government, the

---

[a] *Ward's History of the Law of Nations,* ch. 7, 8, 9.
[b] *Ib.* vol. i. 322—328.

establishment of chivalry, the negotiations and treaties forming the conventional law of Europe, and the settlement of a scale of political rank and precedency.

Of all these causes of reformation, the most weight is, perhaps, to be attributed to the intimate alliance of the great powers as one Christian community. The influence of Christianity was very efficient towards the introduction of a better and more enlightened sense of right and justice among the governments of Europe. It taught the duty of benevolence to strangers, of humanity to the vanquished, of the obligation of good faith, and of the sin of murder, revenge, and rapacity. The history of Europe, during the early periods of modern history, abounds with interesting and strong cases, to show the authority of the church over turbulent princes and fierce warriors, and the effect of that authority in meliorating manners, checking violence, and introducing a system of morals which inculcated peace, moderation, and justice. The church had its councils or convocations of the clergy, which formed the nations professing Christianity into a connexion resembling a federal alliance, and those councils sometimes settled the titles and claims of princes, and regulated the temporal affairs of the Christian powers. The confederacy of the Christian nations was bound together by a sense of common duty and interest, in respect to the rest of mankind. It became a general principle of belief and action, that it was not only a right, but a duty, to reduce to obedience, for the sake of conversion, every people who professed a religious faith different from their own. To make war upon infidels was, for many ages, a conspicuous part of European public law; and this gross perversion of the doctrines and spirit of Christianity, had at least one propitious effect upon the Christian powers, inasmuch as it led to the cultivation of peace and union between them, and to a more free and civilized intercourse. The notion that it was lawful to invade and subdue Mahometan and Pagan countries, continued very long to sway the minds of men; and it was not until after the age of Grotius and Bacon, that this error was entirely eradicated. Lord Coke[a] held, that an alliance for mutual defence was unlawful between Christians and Turks; and Grotius was very cautious as to the admission of the lawfulness of alliances with infidels, and he had no doubt that all Christian nations were bound to assist one another against the attacks of infidels.[b] Even Lord Bacon[c] thought it a matter of so much doubt, as to propound it seriously as a question, whether a war with infidels was not first in order of dignity, and to be preferred to all other just temporal quarrels; and whether a war with infidels might not be undertaken merely for the propagation of the Christian faith, without other cause of hostility.

The influence of chivalry had a very beneficial effect upon the laws of war. It introduced declarations of war by heralds, and to attack an enemy by surprise was deemed cowardly and dishonourable. It dictated humane treatment to the vanquished, courtesy to enemies, and the virtues of fidelity, honour, and magnanimity in every species of warfare.

The introduction and study of the civil law must also have contributed largely to more correct and liberal views of the rights and duties of nations. It was impossible that such a refined and wise system of municipal and ethical jurisprudence as the Roman law, could have been taught in universities and schools, and illustrated by a succession of eminent civilians, who were worthy of being associated with the Roman sages, without at the same time producing a great effect upon the public mind. The very existence of such a grand monument of the embodied wisdom of the ancients, when once it became to be known and examined, must have shed a broad stream of light upon the feudal institutions, and the public councils of the European nations. We accordingly find that the rules of the civil law became to be applied to the government of national rights, and they have

---

a 4 *Inst.* 155.   *b Grotius,* b. 2. c. 15. sec. 11, 12.
c Bacon's Works, vol. iii. 472. 492.

contributed very materially to the erection of the modern international law of Europe. From the 13th to the 16th century, all controversies between nations were adjudged by the rules of the civil law.

The influence of treaties, conventions, and commercial associations, had a still more direct and visible influence in the formation of the great modern code of public law. They gave a new character to the law of nations, and rendered it more and more of a positive or instituted code. Commercial ordinances and conventions contributed greatly to improve and refine public law, and the intercourse of nations, by protecting the persons and property of merchants in cases of shipwreck, and against piracy, and against seizure, and arrest upon the breaking out of war. Auxiliary treaties were tolerated, by which one nation was allowed to be an enemy to a certain extent only. Thus, if, in time of peace, a defensive treaty had been made between one of the parties to a subsequent war, and a third power, by which a certain number of troops were to be furnished in case of war, a compliance with this engagement implicated the auxiliary as a party to the war, *only so far* as her contingent was concerned. The nations of Europe had advanced to this extent in diplomatic science, as early as the beginning of the 13th century, and such a refinement was totally unknown to the ancients. Treaties of subsidy showed also the progress of the law of nations. The troops of one nation, to a definite extent, could be hired for the service of one of the belligerents, without affording ground for hostility with the community which supplied the specific aid. The rights of commerce began to be regarded as under the protection of the law of nations, and Queen Elizabeth complained of the Spaniards, that they had prohibited commerce in the Indian seas contrary to that law.

The efforts that were made, upon the revival of commerce, to suppress piracy, and protect shipwrecked property, show a returning sense of the value, and of the obligations of national justice. The case of shipwrecks may be cited, and dwelt upon for a moment, as a particular and strong instance of the feeble beginnings, the slow and interrupted progress, and final and triumphant success, of the principles of public right. Valin[a] imputes the barbarous custom of plundering shipwrecked property, not merely to the ordinary cupidity for gain, but to a more particular and peculiar cause. The earliest navigators were almost all pirates, and the inhabitants of the coasts were constantly armed against their depredations, and whenever they had the misfortune to be shipwrecked, they were pursued with a vindictive spirit, and deemed just objects of punishment. The practice of plundering shipwrecks has been traced to the Rhodians, and from them it passed to the Romans; and the efforts to restrain it were very feeble and gradual, and mixed with much positive injustice. The goods cast ashore first belonged to the fortunate occupant, and then they were considered as belonging to the state. This change from private to public appropriation of the property, rendered a returning sense of right and duty more natural and easy. The Emperors Hadrian and Antoninus had the honour of having first renounced the claim to shipwrecked property, in favour of the rightful owner. But the inhuman customs on this subject were too deeply rooted to be eradicated by the wisdom and vigilance of the Roman lawgivers. The laws in favour of the unfortunate were disregarded by succeeding emperors, and when the empire itself was overturned by the northern barbarians, the laws of humanity on this subject were swept away in the tempest, and the continual depredations of the Saxons and Normans, induced the inhabitants of the western coasts of Europe, to treat all navigators who were thrown by the perils of the sea upon their shores, as pirates, and to punish them as such, without inquiry or discrimination.

The Emperor Andronicus Comnenus, who reigned at Constantinople in 1183, made great efforts to repress this inhuman practice. His edict was worthy of the highest

---

[a] Com. sur. Ord. tom. 2. 579—587.

praise, but it ceased to be put in execution after his death. Pillage had become an inveterate moral pestilence. It required something more effectual than papal bulls, and the excommunication of the church, to stop the evil. The revival of commerce, and with it a sense of the value of order, commercial ordinances, and particular conventions and treaties between sovereigns, contributed gradually to suppress this criminal practice, by rendering the regulations on that subject a branch of the public law of nations. Valin says, it was reserved to the ordinances of Lewis XIV. to put the finishing stroke towards the extinction of this species of piracy, by declaring that shipwrecked persons and property were placed under the special protection and safeguard of the crown, and the punishment of death without hope of pardon, was pronounced against the guilty.

The progress of moderation and humanity in the treatment of prisoners, is to be imputed to the influence of conventional law, establishing a general and indiscriminate exchange of prisoners, rank for rank, and giving protection to cartel ships for that purpose. It is a practice of no very ancient introduction among the states of Europe, and it was not of very familiar use in the age of Grotius, and it succeeded the elder practice of ransom. From the extracts which Dr. Robinson[a] gives from Bellus, who was a judge or assessor in the armies of Charles V. and Philip II., he concludes, that no practice so general, and so favourable to the conduct of prisoners, as a public exchange in time of war, was known in the 16th century. The private interest of the captor in his prisoner, continued through that period; and the practice of ransom, founded on the right of property, claimed by the captor, succeeded to the Greek and Roman practice of killing prisoners, or selling them as slaves.

The custom of admitting resident ministers at each sovereign's court, was another important improvement in the security and facility of national intercourse; and this led to

---

a 3 *Rob. Rep.* Appendix A.

the settlement of a great question, which was very frequently discussed in the 15th and 16th centuries, concerning the inviolability of ambassadors. It came at last to be a definitive principle of public law, that ambassadors were exempted from all local jurisdiction, civil and criminal; though Lord Coke considered the law in his day to be, that if an ambassador committed any crime which was not merely *malum prohibitum*, he lost his privilege and dignity as an ambassador, and might be punished as any other private alien, and that he was even bound to answer civilly for his contracts that were good *jure gentium*.[a]

Thus stood the law of nations at the age of Grotius. It had been rescued, to a very considerable extent, from the cruel usages and practices of the northern barbarians. It had been restored to some degree of science and civility by the influence of Christianity, the study of the Roman law, and the spirit of commerce. It had grown greatly in value and efficacy, from the intimate connexion and constant intercourse of the modern nations of Europe, who were derived from a common origin, and were governed by similar institutions, manners, laws, and religion. But it was still in a state of extreme disorder, and its principles were but little known, and less observed. It consisted of a series of undigested precedents, without order or authority. Grotius has, therefore, been justly considered as the father of the law of nations; and he arose like a splendid luminary, dispelling darkness and confusion, and imparting light, and guides, and security, to the intercourse of nations. It is said that Lord Bacon first suggested the necessity of such a work as that of Grotius, reducing the law of nations to the certainty and precision of a regular science. Grotius has himself fully explained the reasons which led him to undertake his necessary, and most useful, and immortal work.[b] He found the sentiment universally prevalent, not only among the vulgar, but among men of reputed wisdom and learning, that war was

---

a 4 *Inst.* 153.   *b Proleg. De Jur. Bel.*

a stranger to all justice, and that no commonwealth could be governed without injustice. The saying of Euphemus in Thucydides, he perceived to be in almost every one's mouth, that nothing which was useful was unjust. Many persons, who were friends to justice in private life, made no account of it in a whole nation, and did not consider it as applicable to rulers. He perceived a horrible licentiousness and cruelty in war, throughout the Christian world, of which barbarians might be ashamed. When men took up arms, there was no longer any reverence for law either human or divine, and it seemed as if some malignant fury was sent forth into the world, with a general license for the commission of all manner of wickedness and crime.[a]

The object of Grotius was to correct these false theories and pernicious maxims, by showing a community of sentiment among the wise and learned of all nations and ages, in favour of the natural law of morality. He likewise undertook to show that justice was of perpetual obligation, and essential to the well being of every society, and that the great commonwealth of nations stood in need of law, and the observance of faith, and the practice of justice. His object was to digest in one systematic code, the principles of public right, and to supply authorities for almost every case in the conduct of nations; and he had the honour of reducing the law of nations to a system, and of producing a work which has been resorted to as the standard of authority in every succeeding age. The more it is studied, the more will our admiration be excited at the consummate execution of the plan, and the genius and erudition of the author. There was no system of the kind extant, that had been produced by the ancient philosophers of Greece, or by the primitive Christians. The work of Aristotle on the rights of war, and the writings of the Romans on their fecial law, had not survived the wreck of ancient literature; and the treatises of some learned moderns on public law, were

---

[a] *Proleg.* sec. 2. and 28.

most imperfect, and exceedingly defective in illustrations from history, and in omitting to place their decisions upon the true foundations of equity and justice.* Grotius, therefore, went purposely into the details of history and the usages of nations, and he resorted to the testimony of philosophers, historians, orators, poets, civilians, and divines, because they were the materials out of which the science of morality was formed; and when many men, at different times and places, unanimously affirmed the same thing for truth, it ought to be ascribed to some universal cause. His unsparing citation of authorities, in support of what the present age may consider very plain and undisputed truths, has been censured by many persons as detracting from the value of the work. On the other hand, the support that he gave to those truths, by the concurrent testimony of all nations and ages, has been justly supposed to contribute to that reverence for the principles of international justice, which has since distinguished the European nations.

Among the disciples of Grotius, Puffendorf has always held the first rank. His work went more at large into the principles of natural law, and combined the science of ethics with what may be more strictly called the law of nations. It is copious in detail, but of very little practical value in teaching us what the law of nations is at this day. It is rather a treatise on moral philosophy than on international law; and the same thing may be said of the works of Wolfius, Burlamaqui, and Rutherforth. The Summary of the Law of Nations, by Professor Martens, is a treatise of greater practical utility, but it is only a very partial view of the system, being confined to the customary and conventional law of the modern nations of Europe. Bynkershoeck's treatise on the law of war, has always been received as of great authority, on that particular branch of the science of the law of nations, and the subject is ably and copiously discussed. The work is replete with practical illustration,

---

a Proleg. of Grot. sec. 36, 37, 38.

though too exclusive in its references to the ordinances of his own country, to render his authority very unquestionable. The most popular, and the most elegant writer on the law of nations, is Vattel, whose method has been greatly admired. He has been cited, for the last half century, more freely than any one of the public jurists; but he is very deficient in philosophical precision. His topics are loosely, and often tediously and diffusively discussed, and he is not sufficiently supported by the authority of precedents, which constitute the foundation of the positive law of nations. There is no one work which combines, in just proportions, and with entire satisfaction, an accurate and comprehensive view of the necessary and of the instituted law of nations, and in which principles are sufficiently supported by argument, authority, and examples. Since the age of Grotius, the code of war has been vastly enlarged and improved, and its rights better defined, and its severities greatly mitigated. The rights of maritime capture, the principles of the law of prize, and the duties and privileges of neutrals, have grown into very important titles in the system of national law. We now appeal to more accurate, more authentic, more precise, and more commanding evidence of the rules of public law, by a reference to the decisions of those tribunals, to whom, in every country, the administration of that branch of jurisprudence is specially intrusted. We likewise appeal to the official documents and ordinances of particular states, which have professed to reduce into a systematic code, for the direction of their own tribunals, and for the information of foreign powers, the law of nations, on those points which relate particularly to the rights of commerce, and the duties of neutrality. But in the absence of higher and more authoritative sanctions, the ordinances of foreign states, the opinions of eminent statesmen, and the writings of distinguished jurists, are regarded as of great consideration on questions not settled by conventional law. In cases where the principal jurists agree, the presumption will be very great in favour of the solidity of their maxims; and no civilized nation, that does not arrogantly set all ordinary law and justice at defiance, will venture to disregard the uniform sense of the established writers on international law. England and the United States have been equally disposed to acknowledge the authority of the works of jurists, writing professedly on public law, and the binding force of the general usage and practice of nations, and the still greater respect due to judicial decisions recognising and enforcing the law of nations. In all our foreign negotiations, and domestic discussions of questions of national law, we have paid the most implicit respect to the practice of Europe, and the opinions of her most distinguished civilians. In England, the report, made in 1753, to the king, in answer to the Prussian memorial, is very satisfactory evidence of the obedience shown to the great standing authorities on the law of nations, to which I have alluded. And in a case which came before Lord Mansfield, in 1764, in the K. B.[a] he referred to a decision of Lord Talbot, who had declared that the law of nations was to be collected from the practice of different nations, and the authority of writers; and who had argued from such authorities as Grotius, Barbeyrac, Bynkershoeck, Wiquefort, &c. in a case where British authority was silent. The most celebrated collections and codes of maritime law, such as the *Consolato del Mare*, the laws of Oleron, the laws of the Hanseatic league, and, above all, the marine ordinances of Lewis XIV., are also referred to, as containing the most authentic evidence of the immemorial and customary law of Europe.

The dignity and importance of this branch of jurisprudence, cannot fail to recommend it to the deep attention of the student; and a thorough knowledge of its principles is necessary to lawyers and statesmen, and highly ornamental to every scholar, who wishes to be adorned with the accomplishments of various learning. Many questions arise in the course of commercial transactions, which require for their solution an accurate acquaintance with the conven-

---

[a] Triquet v. Bath, 3 Burr. 1478.

tional law of Europe, and the general doctrines of the prize tribunals. Though we may remain in peace, there is always war raging in some part of the globe, and we have at the present moment[a] neutral rights to exact, and neutral duties to perform, in the course of our Mediterranean trade, and in the trade to the Brazils, and along the shores of the Pacific. A comprehensive and scientific knowledge of international law is highly necessary, not only to lawyers practising in our commercial ports, but to every gentleman who is animated by liberal views, and a generous ambition to assume stations of high public trust. It would be exceedingly to the discredit of any person who should be called to take a share in the councils of the nation, if he should be found deficient in all the great leading principles of this law; and I think I cannot be mistaken in considering the elementary learning of the law of nations, as not only an essential part of the education of an American lawyer, but as proper to be academically taught. My object, therefore, in some succeeding lectures, will be to discuss all the leading points arising upon the rights and duties of nations, in the several relations of peace, of war, and of neutrality.

---

[a] November, 1824.

LECTURE II.

OF THE RIGHTS AND DUTIES OF NATIONS IN A STATE OF PEACE.

A VIEW of the external rights and duties of nations in peace, will lead us to examine the grounds of national independence, the extent of territorial jurisdiction, the rights of embassy, and of commercial intercourse.

Nations are equal in respect to each other, and entitled to claim equal consideration for their rights, whatever may be their relative dimensions or strength, or however greatly they may differ in government, religion, or manners. This perfect equality, and entire independence of all distinct states, is a fundamental principle of public law. It is a necessary consequence of this equality, that each nation has a right to govern itself as it may think proper, and no one nation is entitled to dictate a form of government, or religion, or a course of internal policy, to another. No state is entitled to take cognizance or notice of the domestic administration of another state, or of what passes within it as between the government and its own subjects.[a] The Spaniards, as Vattel observes, violated all rules of right, when they set up a tribunal of their own to judge the Inca of Peru according to their laws. If he had broken the law of nations in respect to them, they would have had a right to punish him; but when they undertook to judge of the merits of his own interior administration, and to try and punish him for

---

[a] *Grotius de Jure belli et pacis*, b. 1. c. 3. sec. 8. *Vattel, Droit des Gens*, b. 2. c. 4. sec. 54. *Rutherforth's Inst.* b. 2. c. 9.

acts committed in the course of it, they were guilty of the grossest injustice. No nation had a contention within itself, but the ancient Romans, with their usual insolence, immediately interfered, and with profound duplicity pretended to take part with the oppressed for the sake of justice, though in reality for the purpose of dominion. It was by a violation of the right of national independence, that they artfully dissolved the Achæan league, and decreed that each member of the confederacy should be governed by its own laws, independent of the general authority.[a] But so surprisingly loose and inaccurate were the theories of the ancients on the subject of national independence, that the Greeks seem never to have questioned the right of one state to interfere in the internal concerns of another.[b] We have several instances within time of memory, of unwarrantable and flagrant violations of the independence of nations. The interference of Russia, Prussia, and Austria, in the internal government of Poland, and first dismembering it of large portions of its territory, and then finally overturning its constitution, and destroying its existence as an independent power, was an aggravated abuse of national right. There were several cases which preceded, or which arose during the violence of the French revolution, which were unjustifiable invasions of the rights of independent nations, to prescribe their own forms of government, and to deal in their discretion with their own domestic concerns. Among other instances, we may refer to the invasion of Holland by the Prussian arms in 1787, and of France by the Prussian arms in 1792, and of wars fomented or declared against all monarchical forms of government, by the French rulers, during the earlier and more intemperate stages of their revolution. We may cite, also, the invasion of Naples by Austria in 1821, and the still more recent invasion of Spain by France,

---

a *Livy*, b. 38. c. 30. *Florus*, b. 2. c. 7. *Montesq. Consid. sur les Causes de la Grand. des Rom.* ch. 6.

b *Mitford's Hist. of Greece*, vol. 5. 127.

under the pretext of putting down a dangerous spirit of internal revolution and reform, as instances of the same violation of the absolute equality and independence of nations.

Every nation has an undoubted right to provide for its own safety, and to take due precaution against distant as well as impending danger.[a] A rational fear is said to be a justifiable cause of war. *Posse vicinum impediri, ne in suo solo, sine alia causa suaque evidenti utilitate, muni mentum nobis propinquum extruat, aut aliud quid faciat, unde justa formido periculi oriatur.*[b] The danger must be great, distinct, and imminent, and not rest on vague and uncertain suspicion. The British government officially declared to the allied powers in 1821,[c] that no government was more prepared than their own, " to uphold the right of any state or states to interfere where their own security or essential interests were seriously endangered by the internal transactions of another state. That the assumption of the right was only to be justified by the strongest necessity, and to be limited and regulated thereby. That it could not receive a general and indiscriminate application to all revolutionary movements, without reference to their immediate bearing upon some particular state or states; that its exercise was an exception to general principles of the greatest value and importance, and as one that only properly grows out of the circumstances of the special case ; and exceptions of this description could never, without the utmost danger, be so far reduced to rule, as to be incorporated into the ordinary diplomacy of states, or into the institutes of the law of nations."

The limitation to the right of interference with the internal concerns of other states, was defined in this instance with uncommon precision ; and no form of civil government which a nation may think proper to prescribe for itself, can

---

a *Vattel*, b. 2. c. 4. sec. 49, 50.
b *Huber de Jure civitatis*, lib. 3. c. 7. sec. 4.
c *Lord Castlereagh's circular despatch of January* 19, 1821.

be admitted to create a case of necessity justifying an interference by force; for a nation, under any form of civil policy which it may choose to adopt, is competent to preserve its faith, and to maintain the relations of peace and amity with other powers.

It is sometimes a very grave question, when and how far one nation has a right to assist the subjects of another, who have revolted, and implored that assistance. It is said,[a] that assistance may be afforded consistently with the law of nations, in extreme cases, as when rulers have violated the principles of the social compact, and given just cause to their subjects to consider themselves discharged from their allegiance. Vattel mentions the case of the Prince of Orange as a justifiable interference, because the tyranny of James II. had compelled the English nation to rise in their defence, and to call for his assistance. The right of interposition must depend upon the special circumstances of the case. It is not susceptible of precise limitations, and is extremely delicate in the application. It must be submitted to the guidance of eminent discretion, and controlled by the principles of justice and sound policy. It would clearly be a violation of the law of nations, to invite subjects to revolt who were under actual obedience, however just their complaints; or to endeavour to produce discontents, violence, and rebellion, in neighbouring states, and under colour of a generous assistance, to consummate projects of ambition and dominion. The most unexceptionable precedents are those in which the interference did not take place until the new states had actually been established, and sufficient means and spirit had been displayed to excite a confidence in their stability. The assistance that England gave to the United Netherlands when they were struggling against Spain, and the assistance that France gave to this country during the war of our revolution, were justifiable acts, founded in wisdom and policy. And it is not to be doubted that

---

a *Vattel*, b. 2. c. 4. sec. 56. *Rutherforth*, b. 2. c. 9.

the government of the United States had a perfect right, in the year 1822, to consider the Spanish provinces in South America as legitimate powers, which had attained sufficient solidity and strength to be entitled to the rights and privileges belonging to independent states.[a]

Nations are at liberty to use their own resources in such manner, and to apply them to such public purposes, as they may deem best, provided they do not violate the perfect rights of other nations, nor endanger their safety, nor infringe the indispensable duties of humanity. They may contract alliances with particular nations, and grant or withhold particular privileges, in their discretion. By positive engagements of this kind, a new class of rights and duties are created, which forms the conventional law of nations, and constitutes the most diffusive, and, generally, the most important branch of public jurisprudence. And it is well to be understood, at a period when alterations in the constitutions of governments, and revolutions in states, are familiar, that it is a clear position of the law of nations, that treaties are not affected, nor positive obligations of any kind with other powers, or with creditors, weakened, by any such mutations. A state neither loses any of its rights, nor is discharged from any of its duties, by a change in the form of its civil government. The body-politic is still the same, though it may have a different organ of communication.[b] So, if a state should be divided in respect to territory, its rights and obligations are not impaired, and if they have not been apportioned by special agreement, those rights are to be enjoyed, and those obligations fulfilled, by all the parts in common.[c]

The extent of jurisdiction over the adjoining seas, is often

---

[a] *President's Message to Congress of 8th of March*, 1822, *and act of Congress of 4th of May*, 1822, ch. 52.

[b] *Burlamaqui, Nat. and Pol. Law*, vol. 2. part 4. ch. 9. sec. 16. *Rutherforth's Institutes*, b. 2. ch. 10.

[c] *Rutherforth, ub. sup.*

a question of difficulty and of dubious right. As far as a nation can conveniently occupy, and that occupancy is acquired by prior possession or treaty, the jurisdiction is exclusive. Navigable rivers which flow through a territory, and the sea coast adjoining it, and the navigable waters included in bays, and between headlands and arms of the sea, belong to the sovereign of the adjoining territory, as being necessary to the safety of the nation, and to the undisturbed use of the neighbouring shores.[a] The open sea is not capable of being possessed as private property. The free use of the ocean for navigation and fishing, is common to all mankind, and the public jurists generally and explicitly deny that the main ocean can ever be appropriated. The subjects of all nations meet there, in time of peace, on a footing of entire equality and independence. No nation has any right of jurisdiction at sea, except it be over the persons of its own subjects, in its own vessels; and so far, territorial jurisdiction may be considered as preserved, for the vessels of a nation are, in many respects, considered as portions of its territory, and persons on board are protected and governed by the law of the country to which the vessel belongs.[b] This jurisdiction is confined to the ship; and no one ship has a right to prohibit the approach of another at sea, or to draw round her a line of territorial jurisdiction, within which no other is at liberty to intrude. Every vessel, in time of peace, has a right to consult its own safety and convenience, and to pursue its own course and business, without being disturbed, and without having violated the rights of others.[c] As to narrow seas, and waters approaching the land, there have been many and sharp controversies among the European nations, concerning the claim for exclusive dominion. The

---

[a] *Grotius*, b. 2. c. 2. sec. 12—c. 3. sec. 7. *Puff.* b. 3. c. 3. sec. 4— b. 4. c. 5. sec. 3 and 3. *Vattel*, b. 1. ch. 22, 23.

[b] *Grotius*, b. 2. c. 3. sec. 10 and 13. *Rutherforth*, b. 2. c. 9. *Vattel*, b. 1. c. 19. sec. 216. 2 *Barnwell & Cresswell*, 448, Forbes v Cochrane.

[c] The Marianna Flora, 11 *Wheaton*, 38.

questions arising on this claim are not very clearly defined and settled, and extravagant pretensions are occasionally put forward. The subject abounds in curious and interesting discussions, and, fortunately for the peace of mankind, they are, at the present day, matters rather of speculative curiosity than of use.

Grotius published his *Mare Liberum*, against the Portuguese claim to an exclusive trade to the Indies, through the South Atlantic and Indian Oceans, and he shows that the sea was not capable of private dominion. He vindicates the free navigation of the ocean, and the right of commerce between nations, and justly exposes the folly and absurdity of the Portuguese claim. Selden's *Mare Clausum* was intended to be an answer to the doctrine of Grotius, and he undertook to prove, by the laws, usages and opinions of all nations, ancient and modern, that the sea was, in point of fact, capable of private dominion, and he poured a flood of learning over the subject. He fell far short of his great rival in the force and beauty of his argument, but he entirely surpassed him in the extent and variety of his citations and researches. Having established the fact, that most nations had conceded that the sea was capable of private dominion, he showed by numerous documents and records, that the English nation had always asserted and enjoyed a supremacy over the surrounding or narrow seas, and that this claim had been recognised by all the neighbouring nations. Sir Matthew Hale considered the title of the king to the narrow seas adjoining the coasts of England, to have been abundantly proved by the treatise of Selden, and Butler speaks of it as a work of profound erudition.[a] Bynkershoeck has also written a treatise on the same contested subject, in which he concedes to Selden much of his argument, and admits that the sea was susceptible of dominion, though he denies the title of the English, on the ground of a want of uninterrupted possession. He said there was no instance, at that

---

[a] *Harg. Law Tracts.* 10. *Co. Litt.* lib. 3. n. 205.

time, in which the sea was subject to any particular sovereign, where the surrounding territory did not belong to him.^a

The claim of dominion to close or narrow seas, is still the theme of discussion and controversy. Puffendorf^b admits, that in a narrow sea the dominion of it may belong to the sovereigns of the adjoining shores. Vattel also^c lays down the position, that the various uses to which the sea contiguous to the coast may be applied, render it justly the subject of property. People fish there, and draw from it shells, pearls, amber, &c.; and who can doubt, he observes, that the pearl fisheries of Bahram and Ceylon may not be lawfully enjoyed as property? Chitty, in his late work on *commercial law*,^d has entered into an elaborate vindication of the British title to the four seas, surrounding the British islands, and known by the name of the British seas, and, consequently, to the exclusive right of fishing, and of controlling the navigation of foreigners therein. On the other hand, Sir Wm. Scott, in the case of the *Twee Gebroeders*,^e did not treat the claim of territory to contiguous portions of the sea with much indulgence. He said, the general inclination of the law was against it; for in the sea, out of the reach of cannon shot, universal use was presumed, in like manner as a common use in rivers flowing through conterminous states was presumed; and yet, in both cases, there might, by legal possibility, exist a peculiar property, excluding the universal, or the common use. The claim of Russia to sovereignty over the Pacific ocean north of the 51st degree of latitude, as a close sea, was considered by our government, in 1822, to be against the rights of other

---

a *Dissertatio de Dominio Maris. Bynk. opera. tom.* 2. 124.
b *Droit de la Nat. et Gens.* lib. 4. ch. 5. sec. 5—10.
c B. 1. ch. 23.
d Vol. 1. 88—102.
e 3 *Rob. Adm.* 336.

nations.ᵃ It it difficult to draw any precise or determinate conclusion, amidst the variety of opinions, as to the distance to which a state may lawfully extend its exclusive dominion over the sea adjoining its territories, and beyond those portions of the sea which are embraced by harbours, gulfs, bays, and estuaries, and over which its jurisdiction unquestionably extends.ᵇ All that can reasonably be asserted is, that the dominion of the sovereign of the shore over the contiguous sea, extends as far as is requisite for his safety, and for some lawful end. A more extended dominion must rest entirely upon force, and maritime supremacy. According to the current of modern authority, the general territorial jurisdiction extends into the sea as far as cannon shot will reach, and no farther, and this is usually calculated to be a marine league; and the Congress of the United States have recognised this limitation, by authorizing the District Courts to take cognizance of all captures made within a marine league of the American shores.ᶜ The executive authority of this country, in 1793, considered the whole of Delaware bay to be within our territorial jurisdiction; and it rested its claim upon those authorities which admit that gulfs, channels, and arms of the sea, belong to the people with whose lands they are encompassed; and it was intimated that the law of nations would justify the United States in attaching to their coasts an extent into the sea, beyond the reach of cannon shot.ᵈ Considering the great extent of the line of the American coasts, we have a right to claim for fiscal and defensive regulations, a liberal extension of maritime jurisdiction; and it would not be unreasonable, as I apprehend, to assume, for domestic purposes connected with

---

a *Mr. Adams' Letter to the Russian Minister, March 30th,* 1822.
b *Azuni on the Maritime Law of Europe,* vol. 1. p. 206.
c *Bynk. Q. Pub. J.* c. 8. *Vattel,* b. 1. c. 23. sec. 289. *Act of Congress, June 5th,* 1794, ch. 50.
d *Opinion of the Attorney General concerning the seizure of the ship Grange, dated* 14th *of May,* 1793, *and the Letter of the Secretary of State to the French Minister, of* 15th *of May,* 1793.

our safety and welfare, the control of the waters on our coasts, though included within lines stretching from quite distant headlands, as, for instance, from Cape Ann to Cape Cod, and from Nantucket to Montauck Point, and from that point to the capes of the Delaware, and from the south cape of Florida to the Mississippi. It is certain that our government would be disposed to view with some uneasiness and sensibility, in the case of war between other maritime powers, the use of the waters of our coast, far beyond the reach of cannon shot, as cruising ground for belligerent purposes. In 1793, our government thought they were entitled, in reason, to as broad a margin of protected navigation, as any nation whatever, though at that time they did not positively insist beyond the distance of a marine league from the sea shores;[a] and, in 1806, our government thought it would not be unreasonable, considering the extent of the United States, the shoalness of their coast, and the natural indication furnished by the well defined path of the Gulf Stream, to expect an immunity from belligerent warfare, for the space between that limit and the American shore. At least it ought to be insisted, that the extent of the neutral immunity should correspond with the claims maintained by Great Britain around her own territory, and that no belligerent right should be exercised within " the chambers formed by headlands, or any where at sea within the distance of four leagues, or from a right line from one headland to another.[b] In the case of the *Little Belt*, which was cruising many miles from shore between Cape Henry and Cape Hatteras, our government laid stress on the circumstance that she was " hovering on our coasts," and it was contended on the part of the United States, that they had a right to know the national character of armed ships in such a situation, and that it was a right immediately connected with our

---

[a] Mr. Jefferson's *Letter to M. Genet, November 8th*, 1793.
[b] Mr. Madison's *Letter to Messrs. Monroe and Pinckney*, dated May 17th, 1806.

tranquility and peace. It was further observed, that all nations exercise the right, and none with more rigour, or at a greater distance from the coast, than Great Britain, and none on more justifiable grounds than the United States.*a* 'There can be but little doubt, that as the United States advance in commerce and naval strength, our government will be disposed more and more to feel and acknowledge the justice and policy of the British claim to supremacy over the narrow seas adjacent to the British isles, because we shall stand in need of similar accommodation and means of security.

It was declared, in the case of *Le Louis*,*b* that maritime states claim, upon a principle just in itself, and temperately applied, a right of visitation and inquiry within those parts of the ocean adjoining to their shores. They were to be considered as parts of the territory for various domestic purposes, and the right was admitted by the curtesy of nations. The English hovering laws were founded upon that right. The statute of 9 Geo. II. c. 35, prohibited foreign goods to be transhipped, within four leagues of the coast, without payment of duties; and the act of Congress of March 2d, 1799, ch. 128, sec. 25, 26, 27. 99, contained the same prohibition; and the exercise of jurisdiction, to that distance, for the safety and protection of the revenue laws, was declared by the Supreme Court, in *Church* v. *Hubbard*,*c* to be conformable to the laws and usages of nations.

As the end of the law of nations is the happiness and perfection of the general society of mankind, it enjoins upon every nation the punctual observation of benevolence and good will, as well as of justice, towards its neighbours.*d* This is equally the policy and the duty of nations. They ought to promote a free intercourse for commercial purposes, in

---

a Mr. Monroe's *Letter to Mr. Foster, October 11th, 1811, and President's Message, November 5th, 1811.*
b 2 *Dodson's Adm. Rep.* 245.
c 2 *Cranch*, 187.
d *Vattel's Prelim.* sec. 12, 13. b. 2. ch. 1. sec. 2, 3.

order to supply each other's wants, and promote each other's prosperity. The variety of climates and productions on the surface of the globe, and the facility of communication, by means of rivers, lakes, and the ocean, invite to a liberal commerce, as agreeable to the law of nature, and extremely conducive to national amity, industry, and happiness.[a] The numerous wants of civilized life, can only be supplied by mutual exchange between nations of the peculiar productions of each; and who that is familiar with the English classics, has not dwelt with delight on the description of the extent and blessings of English commerce, which Addison has given with such graceful simplicity, and such enchanting elegance, in one of the *Spectator's* visits to the Royal Exchange?[b] But, as every nation has the right, and is disposed to exercise it, of judging for itself, in respect to the policy and extent of its commercial arrangements, the general freedom of trade, however reasonably and strongly it may be inculcated in the modern school of political economy, is but an imperfect right, and necessarily subject to such regulations and restrictions, as each nation may think proper to prescribe for itself. Every state may monopolize as much as it pleases of its own internal and colonial trade, or grant to other nations, with whom it deals, such distinctions and particular privileges as it may deem conducive to its interest.[c] The celebrated English navigation act of Charles II. contained nothing, said Martens, contrary to the law of nations, notwithstanding it was very embarrassing to other countries. When the United States put an entire stop to their commerce with all the world, in December, 1807, by laying a general embargo on their trade, without distinction as to nation, or limit as to time, no other power complained of it, and the foreign government most affected by it, and against whose interests it

---

[a] *Vattel*, b. 2. c. 2. sec. 21.   [b] *Spectator*, vol. 1. No. 69.
[c] *Puff.* b. 4. c. 5. sec. 10.   *Vattel*, b. 1. c. 8. sec. 92. 97. *Martens' Summary of the Law of Nations*, 146. 148. 1 *Chitty on Commercial Law*, 76—81.

was more immediately directed, declared to our government,^a that, as a municipal regulation, foreign states had no concern with it, and that the British government did not conceive that they had the right, or the pretension, to make any complaint of it, and that they had made none.

No nation has a right, in time of peace, to interfere with, or interrupt, any commerce which is lawful by the law of nations, and carried on between other independent powers, or between different members of the same state. The claim of the Portuguese, in the height of their maritime power in India, to exclude all other European people from commerce with Asia, was contrary to national law, and a just cause of war. Vattel called it a pretension no less iniquitous than chimerical.[b] The recent attempt of Russia to appropriate to herself an exclusive trade in the North Pacific, met with a prompt resistance on the part of this country; and the government of the United States claimed for its citizens, the right to carry on trade with the aboriginal natives, on the north-west coast of America, without the territorial jurisdiction of other nations, even in arms and ammunitions of war.[c]

Treaties of commerce, defining and establishing the rights and extent of commercial intercourse, have been found to be of great utility; and they occupy a very important title in the code of national law. They were considered, even two centuries ago, to be so conducive to the public welfare, as to overcome the bigotry of the times; and Lord Coke[d] admitted them to be one of the four kinds of national compacts that might, lawfully, be made with infidels. They have multiplied exceedingly within the last century, for it has been found by experience, that the general liberty of trade, resting solely on principles of common right, benevolence, and sound policy, was too vague and precarious to be consistent with the safety of the extended intercourse and

---

a Mr. Canning's Letter to Mr. Pinkney, Sept. 23d, 1808.
b b. 2. c. 2. sec. 24.
c Mr. Adams' Letter to the Russian Minister, March 30th, 1822.
d 4 Inst. 155.

complicated interests of great commercial states. Every nation may enter into such commercial treaties, and grant such special privileges, as they think proper; and no nation, to whom the like privileges are not conceded, has a right to take offence, provided those treaties do not affect their perfect rights. A state may enter into a treaty, by which it grants exclusive privileges to one nation, and deprives itself of the liberty to grant similar privileges to any other. Thus, Portugal, in 1703, by her treaty with England, gave her the monopoly of her wine trade; and the Dutch, formerly, by a treaty with Ceylon, engrossed the cinnamon trade, and, latterly, they have monopolized the trade of Japan.^a These are matters of strict legal right; but it is, nevertheless, in a moral sense, the duty of every nation to deal kindly, and liberally, and impartially towards all mankind, and not to bind itself by treaty with one nation, in contravention of those general duties which the law of nature dictates to be due to the rest of the world.

Every nation is bound, in time of peace, to grant a passage, for lawful purposes, over their lands, rivers, and seas, to the people of other states, whenever it can be permitted without inconvenience; and burthensome conditions ought not to be annexed to the transit of persons and property. If, however, any government deems the introduction of foreigners, or their merchandise, injurious to those interests of their own people which they are bound to protect and promote, they are at liberty to withhold the indulgence. The entry of foreigners and their effects is not an absolute right, but only one of imperfect obligation, and it is subject to the discretion of the government which tolerates it.^b The state may even levy a tax or toll upon the persons and property of strangers *in transitu*, provided the same be a rea-

---

a 1 *Chitty on Commercial Law*, 40, 41, 42.

b *Puff.* b. 3. ch. 3. sec. 5, 6, 7. *Rutherforth*, b. 2. ch. 9. *Vattel*, b. 2. c. 7. sec. 94—c. 8. sec. 100—c. 9. sec. 123. 130—c. 10. sec. 132. 1 *Chitty*, 84—89.

sonable charge, by way of recompense for the expense which the accommodation creates.[a] These things are now generally settled in commercial treaties, by which it is usually stipulated, that there shall be free navigation and commerce between the nations, and a free entry to persons and property, subject to the ordinary revenue and police laws of the country, and to the special terms and conditions prescribed by the treaty.

A nation possessing only the upper parts of a navigable river, is entitled to descend to the sea without being embarrassed by useless and oppressive duties or regulations. It is doubtless a right of imperfect obligation, but one that cannot justly be withheld without good cause. When Spain, in the year 1792, owned the mouth, and both banks of the lower Mississippi, and the United States the left bank of the upper portion of the same, it was strongly contended on the part of the United States, that by the law of nature and nations, we were entitled to the navigation of that river to the sea, subject only to such modifications as Spain might reasonably deem necessary for her safety and fiscal accommodation. It was further contended, that the right to the end, carried with it, as an incident, the right to the means requisite to attain the end; such, for instance, as the right to moor vessels to the shore, and to land in cases of necessity. The same clear right of the United States to the free navigation of the Mississippi through the territories of Spain to the ocean, was asserted by the Congress under the confederation.[b] The claim in that case, with the qualifications annexed to it, was well grounded on the principles and authorities of the law of nations.[c]

---

a *Rutherforth*, b. 2. ch. 9. *Vattel*, b. 2. c. 10. sec. 134. 1 *Chitty*, 103—106.

b *Instructions given to Mr. Jay in* 1780. *Resolution of Congress of September*, 1788. *Report of the Secretary of State to the President, March* 18, 1792.

c *Grotius*, lib. 2. c. 2. sec. 11, 12, 13. 15.—c. 3. sec. 12. *Puff*. lib. 3. c. 3. sec. 5, 6. 8. *Vattel*, b. 1. sec. 292.—b. 2. sec. 127. 129. 132.

When foreigners are admitted into a state upon free and liberal terms, the public faith becomes pledged for their protection. The courts of justice ought to be freely open to them to resort to for the redress of their grievances. But strangers are equally bound with natives, to obedience to the laws of the country during the time they sojourn in it, and they are equally amenable for infractions of the law. It has sometimes been made a question, how far one government was bound by the law of nations, and, independent of treaty, to surrender, upon demand, fugitives from justice, who, having committed crimes in one country, flee to another for shelter. It is declared by the public jurists,[a] that every state is bound to deny an asylum to criminals, and upon application and due examination of the case, to surrender the fugitive to the foreign state where the crime was committed. The language of the authorities is clear and explicit, and the law and usage of nations rest on the plainest principles of justice. It is the duty of the government to surrender up fugitives upon demand, after the civil magistrate shall have ascertained the existence of reasonable grounds for the charge, and sufficient to put the accused upon his trial. The guilty party cannot be tried and punished by any other jurisdiction than the one whose laws have been violated, and, therefore, the duty of surrendering him applies as well to the case of the subjects of the state surrendering, as to the case of subjects of the power demanding the fugitive. The only difficulty, in the absence of positive agreement, consists in drawing the line between the class of offences to which the usage of nations does, and to which it does not apply, inasmuch as it is understood, in practice, to apply only to crimes of great atrocity, or deeply affecting the public safety. The act of the legislature of New-York, of the 5th of April, 1822, ch. 148. gave facility to the surren-

---

[a] *Grotius*, b. 2. ch. 21. sec. 3, 4, 5. and *Heineccius's Com.* h. t. *Burlamaqui*, part 4. c. 3. sec. 19. *Rutherforth*, b. 2. c. 9. *Vattel*, b. 2. ch. 6. sec. 76. 77.

der of fugitives, by authorizing the Governor, in his discretion, on requisition from a foreign government, to surrender up fugitives charged with murder, forgery, larceny, or other crimes, which, by the laws of this state, were punishable with death, or imprisonment in the state prison; provided the evidence of criminality was sufficient, by our laws, to detain the party for trial on a like charge. Such a legislative provision was requisite, for the judicial power can do no more than to cause the fugitive to be arrested and detained, until sufficient means and opportunity have been afforded for the discharge of this duty, to the proper organ of communication with the power that makes the demand.

The European nations, in early periods of modern history, made provision by treaty for the mutual surrender of criminals seeking refuge from justice. Treaties of this kind were made between England and Scotland in 1174, and England and France in 1303, and France and Savoy in 1378, and the last treaty made special provision for the surrender of criminals, though they should happen to be subjects of the state to which they had fled. Mr. Ward[a] considers these treaties as evidence of the advancement of society in regularity and order.

Ambassadors form an exception to the general case of foreigners resident in the country, and they are exempted absolutely from all allegiance, and from all responsibility to the laws of the country to which they are deputed. As they are representatives of their sovereigns, and requisite for negotiations and friendly intercourse, their persons, by the consent of all nations, have been deemed inviolable; and the instances are rare in which popular passions, or perfidious policy, have violated this immunity. Some very honourable examples of respect for the rights of ambassadors, even when their privileges would seem in justice to have been forfeited on account of the gross abuse of them,

---

[a] *Hist. of the Law of Nations.* vol. 2. 818—820.

are to be met with in the ancient Roman annals, notwithstanding the extreme arrogance of their pretensions, and the intemperance of their military spirit.*a* If, however, ambassadors should be so regardless of their duty, and of the object of their privilege, as to insult, or openly attack the laws or government of the nation to whom they are sent, their functions may be suspended by a refusal to treat with them, or application can be made to their own sovereign for their recall, or they may be dismissed, and required to depart within a reasonable time. We have had instances within our own times, of all these modes of dealing with ministers who had given offence, and it is not to be denied, that every government has a perfect right to judge for itself whether the language or conduct of a foreign minister be admissible. The writers on public law go still further, and allow force to be applied to confine or send away an ambassador, when the safety of the state, which is superior to all other considerations, absolutely requires it, arising either from the violence of his conduct, or the influence and danger of his machinations. This is all that can be done, for ambassadors cannot, in any case, be made amenable to the civil or criminal jurisdiction of the country; and this has been the settled rule of public law ever since the attempt made in the reign of Elizabeth to subject the Scotch ambassador to criminal jurisdiction, and the learned discussions which that case excited.*b* By fiction of law, an ambassador is considered as if he were out of the territory of the foreign power; and it is an implied agreement among nations, that the ambassador, while he resides within the foreign state, shall be considered as a member of his own country, and the government he represents has exclusive cognizance of his conduct, and control of his person. The attendants and effects of the ambassador are under his pro-

---

a Livy, b. 2. c. 4. b. 30. c. 25.

b Vattel, b. 4. c. 7. sec. 97—103. *Ward's History*, vol. 2. p. 486—552.

tection and privilege, and equally exempt from the foreign jurisdiction, though there are strong instances in which their inviolability has been denied and invaded.[a] The distinction between ambassadors, ministers plenipotentiary, and envoys extraordinary, relates to diplomatic precedence and etiquette, and not to their essential powers and privileges.[b]

A government may, in its discretion, lawfully refuse to receive an ambassador, and without affording any just cause for war, though the act would, probably, excite unfriendly dispositions, unless accompanied with conciliatory explanations. The refusal may be upon the ground of the ambassador's bad character, or former offensive conduct, or because the special subject of the embassy is not proper, or not convenient for discussion.[c] A state may also be divided and distracted by civil wars, so as to render it inexpedient to acknowledge the supremacy of either party. Bynkershoeck says,[d] that this right of sending ambassadors belongs to the ruling party, in whom *stet rei agendi potestas*. This is placing the right where all foreign governments place it, in the government *de facto*, which is in the actual exercise of power; but the government to whom the ambassador is sent, may exercise its discretion in receiving, or refusing to receive him.

It sometimes becomes a grave question, in national discussions, how far the sovereign is bound by the act of his minister. This will depend upon the nature and terms of his authority. It is now the usual course for every government to reserve to itself the right to ratify or dissent from the treaty agreed to by its ambassador. A general letter of credence is the ordinary letter of attorney, or credential of the minister; and it is not understood to confer a power

---

[a] *Rutherforth*, b. 2. c. 9. *Ward's History*, vol. 2, 552, 3.
[b] *Martens*, p. 201—207. *Vattel*, b. 4. c. 6.
[c] *Rutherforth*, b. 2. c. 9.
[d] *Quæst. J. Pub.* lib. 2. c. 3.

upon the minister to bind his sovereign conclusively. To do so important an act would require a distinct and full power, containing an express authority to bind the principal definitively, without the right of review, or the necessity of ratification on his part. This is not the ordinary or prudent course of business. Ministers always act under instructions, which are confidential, and which, it is admitted, they are not bound to disclose;[a] and it is a well grounded custom, as Vattel observes,[b] that any engagement which the minister shall enter into is of no force among sovereigns, unless ratified by his principal. This is now the usage, although the treaty may have been signed by plenipotentiaries.[c]

Consuls are commercial agents, appointed to reside in the sea ports of foreign countries, with a commission to watch over the commercial rights and privileges of the nation deputing them. The establishment of consuls is one of the most useful of modern commercial institutions. They were first appointed about the 12th century, in the opulent states of Italy, such as Pisa, Lucca, Genoa, and Venice, and their origin has been ascribed to the necessity for extraordinary assistance in those branches of commerce formerly carried on with barbarous and uncivilized nations.[d] The utility of such a mercantile officer has been perceived and felt by all trading nations, and the Mediterranean trade, in particular, stands highly in need of such accredited agents.[e] Consuls have been multiplied and extended to every part of the world, where navigation and commerce can successfully penetrate, and their duties and privileges are now generally limited and defined in treaties of commerce, or by the statute regulations of the country which they represent. In

---

a *Wicquefort's L'Amb.* tom. 1. sec. 14. *Martens*, p. 217.
b B. 4. c. 6. sec. 77.
c The Eliza Ann, 1 *Dodson's Adm. Rep.* 244.
d 1 *Chitty on Commercial Law*, 48, 49.
e *Jackson on the Commerce of the Mediterranean*, p. 30. ch. 4.

some places, they have been invested with judicial powers over the disputes between their own merchants in foreign ports; but in the commercial treaties made by Great Britain, there is rarely any stipulation for clothing them with judicial authority, except in treaties with the Barbary powers; and in England it has been held, that a consul is not strictly a judicial officer, and they have there no judicial power.[a] It has been urged by some writers, as a matter highly expedient, to establish rules requiring merchants abroad to submit their disputes to the judicial authority of their own consuls, particularly with reference to shipping concerns. But no government can invest its consuls with judicial power over their own subjects, in a foreign country, without the consent of the government of the foreign country, founded on treaty; and there is no instance, in any nation of Europe, of the admission of any criminal jurisdiction in foreign consuls. The laws of the United States, on the subject of consuls and vice-consuls,[b] specially authorize them to receive the protests of masters and others, relating to American commerce, and they declare that their consular certificates, under seal, shall receive faith and credit in the courts of the United States. It is likewise made their duty, where the laws of the country permit, to administer on the personal estates of American citizens, dying within their consulates, and leaving no legal representative, and to take charge of and secure the effects of stranded American vessels, in the absence of the master, owner, or consignee; and they are bound to provide for destitute seamen, within their consulates, and to send them, at the public expense, to the United States. These particular powers and duties are similar to those prescribed to British consuls, and to consuls under the consular convention between the United States and France, in 1788; and they are in accordance with the usages of nations, and are

---

[a] 3 *Taunton*, 162. 1 *Chitty*, 50, 51.

[b] *Acts of Congress of 14th April*, 1792, ch. 24, *and of Feb.* 28. 1803, ch. 62.

not to be construed to the exclusion of others, resulting from the nature of the consular appointment.[a] The former consular convention between France and this country, allowed consuls to exercise police over all vessels of their respective nations, " within the interior of the vessels," and to exercise a species of civil jurisdiction, by determining disputes concerning wages, and between the masters and crews of vessels belonging to their own country. The jurisdiction claimed under the consular convention with France, was merely voluntary, and altogether exclusive of any coercive authority;[b] and we have no treaty at present which concedes even such consular functions. The doctrine of our courts is,[c] that a foreign consul, duly recognised by our government, may assert and defend, as a competent party, the rights of property of the individuals of his nation, in the courts of the United States, and may institute suits for that purpose, without any special authority from the party for whose benefit he acts. But the court, in that case, said, that they could not go so far as to recognise a right in a vice-consul to receive actual restitution of the property, or its proceeds, without showing some specific power, for the purpose, from the party in interest.

No nation is bound to receive a foreign consul, unless it has agreed to do so by treaty, and the refusal is no violation of the peace and amity between the nations. Consuls are to be approved and admitted in the usual form, and if any consul be guilty of illegal or improper conduct, he is liable to have his *exequatur*, or written recognition of his character, revoked, and to be punished according to the laws of the country in which he is consul; or he may be sent back to his own country, at the discretion of the government which he has offended. The French consuls are forbidden to be concerned in commerce, and, by the act of Congress

---

[a] 1 *Beawes' L. M.* tit. Consuls, p. 292, 293.
[b] Mr. *Pickering* to Mr. *Pinckney, January* 16th, 1797.
[c] Case of the Bello Corrunes, 6 *Wheaton*, 168.

of February 28th, 1803, American consuls residing on the Barbary coast, are forbidden also; but British and American consuls are generally at liberty to be concerned in trade; and in such cases the character of consul does not give any protection to that of merchant, when these characters are united in the same person.[a] Though the functions of consul would seem to require, that he should not be a subject of the state in which he resides, yet the practice of the maritime powers is quite lax on this point, and it is usual, and thought most convenient, to appoint subjects of the foreign country to be consuls at its ports.

A consul is not such a public minister as to be entitled to the privileges appertaining to that character, nor is he under the special protection of the law of nations. He is entitled to privileges to a certain extent, such as for safe conduct, but he is not entitled to the *jus gentium*. Vattel thinks,[b] that his functions require that he should be independent of the ordinary criminal jurisdiction of the country, and that he ought not to be molested, unless he violates the law of nations by some enormous crime; and that if guilty of any crime, he ought to be sent home to be punished. But no such immunities have been conferred on consuls by the modern practice of nations; and it may be considered as settled law, that consuls do not enjoy the protection of the law of nations any more than other persons who enter the country under a safe conduct. In civil and criminal cases they are equally subject to the laws of the country in which they reside.[c] The same doctrine declared by the public jurists, has been frequently laid down in the English and

---

[a] *Beawes' L. M.* vol. 1. tit. Consuls, p. 291. 1 *Chitty*, 57, 58. 3 *Rob. Adm. Rep.* 27, The Indian Chief.

[b] B. 2. c. 2. sec. 34.

[c] *Wicquefort's L'Amb.*, b. 1. c. 5. *Bynk. de foro legat.* c. 10. *Marten's Summ.* b. 4. c. 3. sec. 3.

American courts of justice.[a] It seems, however, from some decisions in France mentioned by Mr. Warden,[b] that foreign consuls cannot be prosecuted before a French tribunal for acts done by them in France by order of their government, and with the authorization of the French government, and that in general a consul cannot be prosecuted without the previous consent of his government. Consular privileges are much less extensive in Christian than in Mahometan countries. In the latter they cannot be imprisoned for any cause whatever, except by demanding justice against them of the Porte,[c] and they partake very considerably of the character of resident ministers. They are diplomatic agents under the name of consuls, and enjoy the rights and privileges which the Ottoman Porte recognises in relation to the foreign ministers resident at Constantinople. By treaty an entire immunity is usually given to the persons, domestics, and effects of the resident consuls, and no consuls reside with the Barbary states but under the protection of treaties.[d]

Considering the importance of the consular functions, and the activity which is required of them in all great maritime ports, and the approach which consuls make to the efficacy and dignity of diplomatic characters, it was a wise provision in the constitution of the United States, which gave to the Supreme Court original jurisdiction in all cases affecting consuls. as well as ambassadors and other public ministers, and the federal jurisdiction is understood to be exclusive of the state courts.[e]

---

[a] Viveash v. Becker, 3 *Maule & Selw.* 284. Clarke v. Cretico, 1 *Taunton*, 106. United States v. Ravara, 2 *Dallas*, 297. The Commonwealth v. Korsloff, 5 *Serg. & Raw.* 545. 1 *Chitty*, 70.
[b] *On Consuls*, p. 108—116.
[c] 1 *Chitty*, 71.
[d] *Shaler's Sketches of Algiers*, p. 39. 307.
[e] 5 *Serg. & Raw.* 545.

LECTURE III.

OF THE DECLARATION, AND OTHER EARLY MEASURES OF A STATE OF WAR.

In the last Lecture, we considered the principal rights and duties of nations in a state of peace; and if those duties were generally and duly fulfilled, a new order of things would arise, and shed a brighter light over the history of human affairs. Peace is said to be the natural state of man, and war is undertaken for the sake of peace, which is its only lawful end and purpose.[a] War, to use the language of Lord Bacon,[b] is one of the highest trials of right; for, as princes and states acknowledge no superior upon earth, they put themselves upon the justice of God by an appeal to arms. The history of mankind is an almost uninterrupted narration of a state of war, and it gives colour to the extravagant theory of Hobbes,[c] who maintains, that the natural state of man is a state of war of all against all; and it adds plausibility to the conclusions of those other writers, who, having known and studied the Indian character, insist, that continual war is the natural instinct and appetite of man in a savage state. It is, doubtless, true, that a sincere disposition for peace, and a just appreciation of its blessings, are the natural and necessary result of science and civilization.

---

a *Cic. de Off*. 1. 11. and 23. *Grotius*, b. 1. ch. 1. *Burlamaqui*, part 4. c. 1. sec. 4. *Vattel*, b. 4. c. 1.
b *Bacon's Works*, vol. 3. p. 40.
c *Leviathan*. part 1. c. 13.

The right of self-defence is part of the law of our nature, and it is the indispensable duty of civil society to protect its members in the enjoyment of their rights, both of person and property. This is the fundamental principle of the social compact. An injury either done or threatened, to the perfect rights of the nation, or of any of its members, and susceptible of no other redress, is a just cause of war. The injury may consist, not only in the direct violation of personal or political rights, but in wrongfully withholding what is due, or in the refusal of a reasonable reparation for injuries committed, or of adequate explanation or security in respect to manifest and impending danger.[a] Grotius condemns the doctrine, that war may be undertaken to weaken the power of a neighbour, under the apprehension that its further increase may render him dangerous. This would be contrary to justice, unless we were morally certain, not only of a capacity, but of an actual intention to injure us. We ought rather to meet the anticipated danger by a diligent cultivation, and prudent management of our own resources. We ought to conciliate the respect and good will of other nations, and secure their assistance in case of need, by the benevolence and the justice of our conduct. War is not to be resorted to without absolute necessity, nor unless peace would be more dangerous, and more miserable, than war itself. An injury to an individual member of a state, is a just cause of war, if redress be refused, but a nation is not bound to go to war on so slight a foundation; for it may of itself grant indemnity to the injured party, and if this cannot be done, yet the good of the whole is to be preferred to the welfare of a part.[b] Every milder method of redress is to be tried, before the nation makes an appeal to arms; and this is the sage and moral precept of the writers on natural law.

---

a *Grotius*, b. 2. c. 1. and 22. *Rutherforth*, b. 2. c. 9. *Vattel*, b. 3. c. 3. sec. 26.

b *Grotius*, b. 2. c. 22—25. *Rutherforth*, b. 2. c. 9.

If the question of right between two powers be in any degree dubious, they ought to forbear proceeding to extremities; and a nation would be condemned by the impartial voice of mankind, if it voluntarily went to war upon a claim of which it doubted the legality. But, on political subjects, we cannot expect, and are not to look, for the same rigorous demonstration, as in the physical sciences. Policy is a science of calculations and combinations, arising out of times, places, and circumstances, and it cannot be reduced to absolute simplicity and certainty. We must act according to the dictates of a well informed judgment, resting upon a diligent and careful examination of facts, and every pacific mode of redress is to be tried faithfully and perseveringly, before the nation resorts to arms.

If one nation be bound by treaty to afford assistance, in a case of war between its ally and a third power, the assistance is to be given whenever the *casus fœderis* occurs; but a question will sometimes arise, whether the government which is to afford the aid, is to judge for itself of the justice of the war on the part of the ally, and to make the right to assistance depend upon its own judgment. Grotius is of opinion,[a] that treaties of that kind do not oblige us to participate in a war, which appears to be manifestly unjust on the part of the ally; and it is said to be a tacit condition annexed to every treaty made in time of peace, and stipulating to afford succours in time of war, that the stipulation is only to apply to a just war. To give assistance in an unjust war, on the ground of the treaty, would be contracting an obligation to do injustice, and no such contract is valid.[b] But to set up a pretext of this kind, to avoid a positive engagement, is extremely hazardous, and it cannot be done, except in a very clear case, without exposing the nation to the imputation of a breach of public faith. In doubtful cases, the

---

[a] B. 2. ch. 25.
[b] *Vattel*, b. 2. c. 12. sec. 168.—b. 3. c. 6. sec. 86, 87.

presumption ought rather to be in favour of our ally, and of the justice of his war.

The doctrine that one nation is not bound to assist another, under any circumstances, in a war clearly unjust, is similar to the principle in the feudal law, to be met with in the *Book of Feuds*, compiled from the usages of the Lombards, and forming part of the common law of Europe, during the prevalence of the feudal system. A vassal refusing to assist his liege lord in a just war, forfeited his feud. If the justice of the war was even doubtful, or not known affirmatively to be unjust, the vassal was bound to assist; but, if the war appeared to him to be manifestly unjust, he was under no obligation to help his lord to carry it on offensively.[a]

A nation which has agreed to render assistance to another, is not obliged to furnish it when the case is hopeless, or when giving the succours would expose the state itself to imminent danger. Such extreme cases are tacit exceptions to the obligation of the treaty; but the danger must not be slight, remote, or contingent, for this would be to seek a frivolous cause to violate a solemn engagement.[b] In the case of a defensive alliance, the condition of the contract does not call for the assistance, unless the ally be engaged in a *defensive* war, for in a defensive alliance, the nation engages only to defend its ally, in case he be attacked, and even then we are to inquire whether he be not justly attacked.[c] The defensive alliance applies only to the case of a war first commenced, in point of fact, against the ally, and the power that first declares, or actually begins the war, makes what is deemed, in the conventional law of nations, an *offensive* war. The treaty of alliance between France and the United States, in 1778, was declared, by the second article, to be a defensive alliance, and that declaration gave a character to the whole instrument, and consequently the

---

[a] *Feud.* lib. 2. tit. 28. sec. 1.   [b] *Vattel*, b. 3. c. 6. sec. 93.
[c] *Vattel*, b. 3. c. 6. sec. 79.

guaranty, on the part of the United States, of the French possessions in America, could only apply to future defensive wars on the part of France. Upon that ground, the government of this country in 1793, did not consider themselves bound to depart from their neutrality, and to take part with France in the war in which she was then engaged.ᵃ The war of 1793 was first actually declared and commenced by France, against all the allied powers of Europe, and the nature of the guaranty required us to look only to that fact.

In the ancient republics of Greece and Italy, the right of declaring war resided with the people, who retained, in their collective capacity, the exercise of a large portion of the sovereign power. Among the ancient Germans it belonged also to the popular assemblies,ᵇ and the power was afterwards continued in the same channel, and actually resided in the Saxon Wittenagemote.ᶜ But in the monarchies of Europe, which arose upon the ruins of the feudal system, this important prerogative was generally assumed by the king, as appertaining to the duties of the executive department of government. Many publicists, however,ᵈ consider the power as a part of the sovereign authority of the state, of which the legislative department is an essential branch. There are, however, several exceptions to the generality of this position; for in the limited monarchies of England, France, and Holland, the king alone declares war, and yet the power, to apply an observation of Vattel to the case, is but a slender prerogative of the crown, if the parliaments or legislative bodies of those kingdoms will act independently, since the king cannot raise the money requisite to carry on the war without their consent. The wild

---

a See *Pacificus*, written, in 1793, by Mr. Hamilton, then Secretary of the Treasury, and the *Instructions from the Secretary of State to the American Ministers to France, July 15th*, 1797.
b *Tacit. de M. G.* c. 11.
c *Millar's View of the English Government*, b. 1. c. 7
d *Puff*. b. 8. c. 6. sec. 10. *Vattel*, b. 3. c. 1. sec. 4.

and destructive wars of Charles XII. led the states in Sweden to reserve to themselves the right of declaring war; and in the form of government adopted in Sweden in 1772,[a] the right to make war was continued in the same legislative body. This was the provision in those ephemeral constitutions which appeared in Poland and France the latter part of the last century; and as evidence of the force of public opinion on this subject, it may be observed, that in the constitution proposed by Bonaparte, on his reascension of the throne of France in 1815, the right to levy men and money for war, was to rest entirely upon a law, to be proposed to the House of Representatives of the people, and assented to by them. In this country, the power of declaring war, as well as of raising the supplies, is wisely confided to the legislature of the Union, and the presumption is, that nothing short of a strong case deeply affecting our essential rights, and which cannot receive a pacific adjustment, after all reasonable efforts shall have been exhausted, will ever prevail upon Congress to declare war.

It has been usual to precede hostilities by a public declaration communicated to the enemy. It was the custom of the ancient Greeks and Romans, to publish a declaration of the injuries they had received, and to send a herald to the enemy's borders to demand satisfaction, before they actually engaged in war; and invasions, without notice, were not looked upon as lawful.[b] War was declared with religious preparation and solemnity. According to Ulpian,[c] they alone were reputed enemies against whom the Roman people had publicly declared war. During the middle ages, a previous declaration of war was held to be requisite by the laws of honour, chivalry, and religion. Lewis IX. refused to attack the Sultan of Egypt until he made a previous de-

---

[a] Art. 48.
[b] *Potter's Antiquities of Greece*, b. 3. c. 7. *Livy*, b. 1. c. 32. *Cic. de Off.* b. 1. c. 11.
[c] *Dig.* 49. 15. 24.

claration to him by a herald at arms, and one of his successors sent a herald with great formality to the Governor of the Low Countries, when he declared war against that power in 1635.[a] But, in modern times, the practice of a solemn declaration made to the enemy, has fallen into disuse, and the nation contents itself with making a public declaration of war within its own territory, and to its own people. The jurists are, however, divided in opinion, in respect to the necessity or justice of some previous declaration to the enemy in the case of offensive war. Grotius[b] considers a previous demand of satisfaction, and a declaration, as requisite to a solemn and lawful war; and Puffendorf[c] holds acts of hostility, which have not been preceded by a formal declaration of war, to be no better than acts of piracy and robbery. Emerigon[d] is of the same opinion; and he considered the hostilities exercised by England in the year 1755, prior to any declaration of war, to have been in contempt of the law of nations, and condemned by all Europe. Vattel strongly recommends[e] a previous declaration of war, as being required by justice and humanity; and, he says, that the fecial law of the Romans gave such moderation and religious solemnity to a preparation of war, and bore such marks of wisdom and justice, that it laid the solid foundation of their future greatness.

Bynkershoeck has devoted an entire chapter to this question,[f] and he maintains, that a declaration of war is not requisite by the law of nations, and that though it may very properly be made, it cannot be required as a matter of right. The practice rests entirely on manners and magnanimity, and it was borrowed from the ancient Romans. All

---

a 1 *Emerigon, Traite des Ass.* p. 561.
b B. 1. c. 3. sec. 4.
c B. 8. c. 6. sec. 9.
d *Traite des Ass.* tom. 1. p. 563.
e B. 3. c. 4. sec. 51.
f *Quæst. J. Pub.* b. 1. c. 2.

that he contends for is, that a demand of what we conceive to be due should be previously made. We are not bound to accompany that demand with threats of hostility, or to follow it with a public declaration of war; and he cites many instances to show, that within the two last centuries, wars have been frequently commenced without a previous declaration. Since the time of Bynkershoeck, it has become settled by the practice of Europe, that war may lawfully exist by a declaration which is unilateral only, or without a declaration on either side. It may begin with mutual hostilities.[a] Since the peace of Versailles in 1763, formal declarations of war of any kind seem to have been discontinued, and all the necessary and legitimate consequences of war flow at once from a state of public hostilities, duly recognised, and explicitly announced, by a domestic manifesto or state paper. In the war between England and France in 1778, the first public act on the part of the English government, was recalling its minister, and that single act was considered by France as a breach of the peace between the two countries. There was no other declaration of war, though each government afterwards published a manifesto in vindication of its claims and conduct. The same thing may be said of the war which broke out in 1793, and again in 1803; and, indeed, in the war of 1756, though a solemn and formal declaration of war, in the ancient style, was made in June 1756, vigorous hostilities had been carried on between England and France for a year preceding. In the war declared by the United States against England in 1812, hostilities were immediately commenced on our part, as soon as the act of Congress was passed, without waiting to communicate to the English government any notice of our intentions.

But, though a solemn declaration, or previous notice to

---

[a] Sir *Wm.* Scott, 1 *Dodson's Adm. Rep.* 247.

Though an alien may purchase land, or take it by devise, yet he is exposed to the danger of being devested of the fee, and of having his lands forfeited to the state, upon an inquest of office found; and if he dies before any such proceeding be had, we have seen that the inheritance cannot descend, but escheats of course. If the alien should undertake to sell to a citizen, yet the prerogative right of forfeiture is not barred by the alienation, and it must be taken to be subject to the right of the government to seize the land. His conveyance is good as against himself, and he may, by a fine, bar persons in reversion and remainder, but the title is still voidable by the sovereign.[a] In Virginia, this prerogative right of seizing lands *bona fide* sold by an alien to a citizen, is abolished by statute;[b] and so it was, to a limited degree, in this state, by an act in 1826.[c] An alien may take a lease for years of a house, for the benefit of trade. According to Lord Coke,[d] none but an alien merchant can lease land at all, and he is restricted to a house, and if he dies before the termination of the lease, the remainder of the term is forfeited to the king, for the law gave him the privilege for habitation only, as necessary to trade, and not for the benefit of his representatives. The force of this rigorous doctrine of the common law is undoubtedly suspended with us, in respect to the subjects of those nations with whom we have commercial treaties; and it is now justly doubted,[e] whether the common law be really so inhospitable, for it is inconsistent with the established maxims of sound policy, and the social intercourse of nations. Foreigners are admitted to the rights of citizenship with us on liberal terms, and as the law requires five,

---

a 4 *Leon.* 84. *Sheppard's Touchstone*, by *Preston.* 56. 232. 7. *Wheaton*, 545.

b. *Griffith's Law Register*, tit. Virginia.

c *Laws of N. Y.* sess. 49. ch. 297. sec. 3.

d Co. Litt. 2. b.

e Harg. Co. Litt. n. 9. to b. 1.

and only five years residence, to entitle them *and their families* to the benefits of naturalization, it would seem to imply a right, in the mean time, to the necessary use of real property; and if it were otherwise, the means would be interdicted which are requisite to render the five years residence secure and comfortable.

Aliens are under the like disabilities as to uses and trusts arising out of real estates. An alien can be seized to the use of another, but the use cannot be executed as against the state, and will be defeated on office found. Nor can an alien be a *cestui que trust* but under the like disability, and the sovereign may, in chancery, compel the execution of the trust.[b]

Aliens are capable of acquiring, holding, and transmitting moveable property, in like manner, as our own citizens, and they can bring suits for the recovery and protection of that property.[c] They may even take a mortgage upon real estate by way of security for a debt, and this I apprehend they may do without any statute permission, for it has been the English law from the early ages.[d] It was so held lately in the Supreme Court of the United States,[e] and that the alien creditor was entitled to come into a court of equity to have the mortgage foreclosed, and the lands sold for the payment of his debt. The question whether the alien in such a case could become a valid purchaser of the mortgaged premises sold at auction at his instance, is left untouched; and as such a privilege is not necessary for his security, and would

---

a *Gilbert on Uses*, by Sugden, 10. 367. 445. *Preston on Conveyancing*, vol. ii. p. 247.

b Attorney General v. Sands, 3 *Ch. Rep.* 20. *Com. Dig.* tit. Alien, c. 3. *Gilbert on Uses*, by *Sugden*, 86. 404.

c 7 Co. 7 . *Dy.* 2. b.

d *Year Book*, 11 *Edw.* III. cited in the marginal note to 1 *Dy.* 2. b.

e Hughes v. Edwards, 9 *Wheaton*, 489.

be in contravention of the general policy of the common law, the better opinion would seem to be, that he could not, in that way, without special provision by statute, become the permanent and absolute owner of the fee.

Even alien enemies, resident in the country, may sue and be sued as in time of peace, for protection to their persons and property is due, and implied from the permission to them to remain, without being ordered out of the country by the President of the United States. The lawful residence does, *pro hac vice,* relieve the alien from the character of an enemy, and entitles his person and property to protection.[a] The effect of war upon the rights of aliens we need not here discuss, as it has been already considered in a former part of this course of lectures, when treating of the law of nations.[b]

During the residence of aliens amongst us, they owe a local allegiance, and are equally bound with natives to obey all general laws for the maintenance of peace, and the preservation of order, and which do not relate specially to our own citizens. This is a principle of justice and of public safety universally adopted; and if they are guilty of any illegal act, or involved in disputes with our citizens, or with each other, they are amenable to the ordinary tribunals of the country.[c] They and their sons are liable to be enrolled in the militia of this state, provided they are seised of any real estate within this state.[d] This is a reasonable duty required of them in consideration of the special benefit which is conferred. It is in the nature of a charge upon their property, and the personal service can be omitted under the penalty of a moderate pecuniary assessment.

---

[a] Wells v. Williams, 1 *Lord Raym.* 282. Daubigny v. Davallon, 2 *Anst.* 462. Clark v. Morey, 10 *Johns. Rep.* 69. Russel v. Skipwith, 6 *Binney,* 241.

[b] See vol. i. p. 53. to 62. 158.

[c] *Vattel,* b. 2. c. 8. s. 101, 102, 108.

[d] *Militia Act, Laws of N. Y.* sess. 46. ch. 244. sec. 8.

If aliens come here, with an intention to make this country their permanent residence, they will have many inducements to become citizens, since they are unable as aliens, to have a stable freehold interest in land, or to hold any civil office, or vote at elections, or take any active share in the administration of the government. There is a convenient and easy mode provided, by which the disabilities of alienism may be removed, and the qualifications of natural born citizens obtained. The terms upon which any alien, being a free white person, can be naturalized, are prescribed by the acts of Congress of the 14th of April, 1802, ch. 28.; the 3d of March, 1813, ch. 184.; and 22d of March, 1816, ch. 32. It is required, that he declare, on oath, before a state court, being a court of record with a seal and clerk, and having common law jurisdiction, or before a circuit or district court of the United States, three years, at least, before his admission, his intention to become a citizen, and to renounce his allegiance to his own sovereign. At the time of his admission, his country must be at peace with the United States, and he must, before one of these courts, take an oath to support the constitution of the United States, and likewise, on oath, renounce and abjure his native allegiance. He must, at the time of his admission, satisfy the court, that he has resided five years, at least, within the United States, and one year, at least, within the state where the court is held; and if he shall have arrived after the peace of 1815, his residence must have been continued for five years next preceding his admission, without being at any time during the five years out of the territory of the United States. The evidence of the time of his arrival within the United States, is to consist of the registry of his arrival made upon his report, or the report of his parent or guardian, before a court of the United States; and the certificate of that report and registry, and of his declared intention to become a citizen, must be produced to the court admitting him; and he must satisfy the court, that during that time, he has behaved as a man of good moral character, attached to the principles of the constitution of the United States, and well disposed to the good order and happiness of the same. He must, at the same time, renounce any title, or order of nobility, if any he hath. The act further provides, that the children of persons duly naturalized, being minors at that time, shall, if dwelling in the United States, be deemed citizens. It is further provided,*a* that if any alien shall die after his report and declaration, and before actual admission as a citizen, his widow and children shall be deemed citizens.

A person thus duly naturalized, becomes entitled to all the privileges and immunities of natural born subjects, except that a residence of seven years is requisite to enable him to hold a seat in congress, and no person, except a natural born citizen, is eligible to the office of governor of this state, or president of the United States.

The laws of Congress on the subject of naturalization, have been subject to great variations. In 1790, only two years' previous residence was required. In 1795, the period was enlarged to five years; and in 1798, to 14 years; and in 1802, it was reduced back to five years, where it still remains. This period of probation has probably been deemed as liberal as was consistent with a due regard to our peace and safety. A moderate previous residence becomes material, to enable aliens to acquire the knowledge and habits proper to make wholesome citizens, who can combine the spirit of freedom with a love of the laws. Strangers, on their first arrival, and before they have had time to acquire property, and form connexions and attachments, are not to be presumed to be acquainted with our political institutions, or to feel pride or zeal in their stability and success.*b*

---

a Act of Congress, March 26th, 1804, ch. 47.

b During the elevation and splendour of the Athenian power, the privilege of a citizen of Athens was deemed a very distinguished favour. It could only be obtained by the consent and decree of two successive assemblies of the people, and was granted to none but to men of the highest rank and reputation, or who had performed some signal service to the republic. 1 *Potter's Greek Antiquities*, 44, 45. 150. In the time of Demetrius Phalereus, there were resident in Attica, 10,000 freemen, being

If an alien dies before he has taken any steps under the act of naturalization, his personal estate goes according to his will, or if he died intestate, then according to the law of distribution of the place of his domicil, at the time of his death.*a* The stationary place of residence of the party at his death, determines the rule of distribution,*b* and this is a rule of public right, as well as of natural justice. *Mobilia personam sequuntur, immobilia situm.c* The unjust and inhospitable rule of the most polished states of antiquity, prevailed in many parts of Europe, down to the middle of the last century; and Vattel expressed his astonishment that there should have remained any vestiges of so barbarous a usage in an age so enlightened. The law, which claimed, for the benefit of the state, the effects of deceased foreigners, who left no heirs, who were natives, existed in France as late

---

foreigners, or of foreign extraction, or freed slaves, who had not the rights of Athenian citizens. 1 *Mitf. Hist.* 354, 355. And yet it is said, that foreigners could not dispose of their goods by will, but they were appropriated, at their death, for the public use. 2 *Potter*, 344. In Rome, foreigners could not make a will, and the effects of a foreigner, at his death, went to the public, or to his patron, under the *jus applicationis. Cic. de Orat.* 139. *Dig.* 49. 15. 52. *Ibid.* lib. 35, *ad legem fulcidiam, Præ. Dict. du Dig.* tit. *Etrangers.* The Romans were noted for their peculiar jealousy of the *jus civitatis,* or rights of a Roman citizen. It was, at first, limited to the *Pomœria* of Rome, and then gradually extended to the bounds of *Latium.* In the time of Augustus, as we are informed by Suetonius, *De Aug.* sect. 40. the same anxiety was discovered to keep the Roman people pure and untainted of foreign blood; and he gave the freedom of the city with a sparing hand. But when Caracalla, for the purpose of a more extended taxation, levelled all distinctions, and communicated the freedom of the city to the whole Roman world, the national spirit was lost among the people, and the pride of their country was no longer felt, nor its honour observed. 1 *Gibb. Hist.* 268.

a 1 *Binney*, 336. 3 *Johns. Ch. Rep.* 210. 1 *Mason's Rep.* 408.
b Pipon v. Pipon. *Amb.* 25. Burn v. Cole. *Amb.* 415.
c Hub. *Prælec.* tom. i. 278. tom. ii. 542. *De conflictu legum,* sect. 15. *Vattel,* b. 2. c, 8. sect. 110, 111.

as the commencement of their revolution.[a] This rule of the French law, was founded not only on the Roman law, but it was attempted to be justified by the narrow and absurd policy of preventing the wealth of the kingdom from passing into the hands of subjects of other countries.[b] It was abolished by the constitution of the first constituent assembly, in 1791, and foreigners were admitted upon the most liberal terms, and declared capable of acquiring and disposing of property equally with natural born citizens. The treaty of commerce between the United States and France, in 1778, provided against the evil effects of this law, by declaring that the inhabitants of the United States were to be exempted from the *droit d'aubaine,* and might dispose by will of their property, real and personal, (*biens meubles et immeubles,*) and if they died intestate, it was to descend to their heirs, whether residing in France, or elsewhere, and the like privilege was conferred upon Frenchmen dying in this country. The treaties of France with other powers, usually contained the same relaxation of her ancient rule ; and though the treaty of 1778 was abolished in 1798, yet, in the renewed treaty of 1801, the same provision was inserted, and under it American citizens in France, and French subjects in the United States, could acquire, hold, and transmit, real as well as personal property, equally as if they were natives, and without the necessity of an act of naturalization, or special permission. This last treaty expired in 1809, and the rights of Frenchmen arising thereafter, were left, like those of other aliens, to be governed by the general law of the land.

The Napoleon code did not pursue the liberal policy of the French constituent assembly of 1791, and it seems to have revived the harsh doctrine of the *Droit D'Aubaine,* under the single exception, that aliens should be entitled to enjoy in France the same civil rights secured to Frenchmen *by treaty* in the country to which the alien belongs.

---

a 1 *Domat,* 26. sect. 11.   *b Ibid.* 555. sect. 13.
c Code Napoleon, No. 11. 726. 912.

It is not sufficient to create the exemption in favour of the alien, that civil rights are granted to Frenchmen by the local laws of the foreign country, unless that concession be founded upon treaty.[a] The law at present in France is, that a stranger cannot, except by special favour, dispose of his property by will; and when he dies, the sovereign succeeds by right of inheritance to his estate.[b]

British subjects, under the treaty of 1794, between the United States and Great Britain, were confirmed in the titles which they then held to lands in this country, so far as the question of alienism existed; and they were declared competent to sell, devise, and transmit the same, in like manner as if they were natives; and that neither they, nor their heirs or assigns, should, as to those lands, be regarded as aliens. The treaty applied to the title, whatever it might be; but it referred only to titles existing at the time of the treaty, and not to titles subsequently acquired.[c] It was, therefore, a provision of a temporary character, and by the lapse of time it is rapidly becoming unimportant and obsolete.

The legislature of this state, and probably of many other states, are in the practice of annually granting to particular aliens, by name, the privilege of holding real property. In 1825,[d] they passed a general and permanent statute, enabling aliens to take and hold lands in fee, and to sell, mortgage, and devise, but not demise or lease the same, equally, as if they were native citizens, provided the party had previously taken an oath that he was a resident in the United

---

[a] *M. Toullier*, in his *Droit Civil Francais*, tom. 1. n. 265. cites for that rule a decree of the Court of Cassation in 1806; and he says, that this article in the Napoleon code was taken from one in the new Prussian code.

[b] *Repertoire de Juris. par Merlin*, tit. *Aubaine*, and tit. *Etranger*, ch. 1. No. 6.

[c] 1 *Wheaton*, 300. 4 *Ibid*. 463. 7 *Ibid*. 535. 9 *Ibid*. 496. 12 *Mass. Rep.* 143.

[d] *Laws of N. Y. sess.* 48. ch. 307.

States, and intended always to reside therein, and to become a citizen thereof as soon as he could be naturalized, and that he had taken the incipient measures required by law for that purpose. There are similar statute provisions in favour of aliens in South Carolina, Indiana, Illinois and Missouri; and in Louisiana, Pennsylvania and Ohio, the disability of aliens to take, hold, and transmit real property, seems to be entirely removed.[a] In North Carolina and Vermont, there is even a provision inserted in their constitutions, that every person of good character, who comes into the state, and settles, and takes an oath of allegiance to the same, may thereupon purchase, and by other just means, acquire, hold, and transfer land, and after one year's residence, become entitled to most of the privileges of a natural born subject. These civil privileges, conferred upon aliens, by state authority, are dictated by a just and liberal policy; but they must be taken to be strictly local; and until a foreigner is duly naturalized, according to the act of Congress, he is not entitled in any other state to any other privileges than those which the laws of that state allow to aliens. No other state is bound to admit, nor would the United States admit, any alien to any privileges, to which he is not entitled by treaty, or the laws of nations, or the laws of the United States, or of the state in which he dwells. The article in the constitution of the United States,[b] declaring that citizens of each state were entitled to all the privileges and immunities of citizens in the several states, applies only to natural born or duly naturalized citizens, and if they remove from one state to another, they are entitled to the privileges that persons of the same description are entitled to in the state to which the removal is made, and to none other. If, therefore, for instance, free persons of colour are not entitled to vote in Carolina; free persons of colour emigrating there from a north-

---

a Griffith's Law Reg. passim. 1 *Const. Rep.* S. C. 412. *Christy's Dig.* tit. *alien.*
b Art. 4. sect. 2.

ern state, would not be entitled to vote. The laws of each state ought, and must, govern within its jurisdiction; and the laws and usages of one state cannot be permitted to prescribe qualifications for citizens, to be claimed and exercised in other states, in contravention to their local policy.*a*

The act of Congress confines the description of aliens capable of naturalization to "free white persons." I presume that this excludes the inhabitants of Africa, and their descendants; and it may become a question, to what extent persons of mixed blood, as mulattoes, are excluded, and what shades and degrees of mixture of colour disqualify an alien from application for the benefits of the act of naturalization. Perhaps there might be difficulties also as to the copper-coloured natives of America, or the yellow or tawny races of Asiatics, though I should doubt whether any of them were "white persons" within the purview of the law. It is the declared law of this state,*b* that Indians are not citizens, but distinct tribes, living under the protection of the government, and, consequently, they never can be made citizens under the act of Congress.

Before the adoption of the present constitution of the United States, the power of naturalization resided in the several states; and the constitution of this state, as it was originally passed,*c* required all persons born out of the United States, and naturalized by our legislature, to take an oath abjuring all foreign allegiance and subjection, in all matters, *ecclesiastical* as well as civil. This was intended, and so it operated, to exclude from the benefits of naturali-

---

a It is a curious fact in ancient Grecian history, that the Greek states indulged such a narrow and excessive jealousy of each other, that intermarriage was forbidden, and none were allowed to possess lands within the territory of another state. When the Olynthian republic introduced a more liberal and beneficial policy in this respect, it was considered as a portentous innovation. *Mitford's Hist.* vol. v. p. 9.

b Goodwell v. Jackson, 20 *Johns. Rep.* 693.

c Art. 42.

zation Roman Catholics who acknowledged the spiritual supremacy of the pope, and it was the result of former fears and prejudices (still alive and active at the commencement of our revolution) respecting the religion of the Romish church, which European history had taught us to believe was incompatible with perfect national independence, or the freedom and good order of civil society. So extremely strong, and so astonishingly fierce and unrelenting, was public prejudice on this subject, in the early part of our colonial history, that we find it declared by law in the beginning of the last century,[a] that every Jesuit and popish priest who should continue in the colony after a given day, should be condemned to perpetual imprisonment; and if he broke prison and escaped, and was retaken, he should be put to death. That law, said Mr. Smith, the historian of the colony as late as the year 1756,[b] was worthy of perpetual duration!

---

[a] *Colony Laws*, vol. i. p. 38. *Livingston* & *Smith's* ed.
[b] *Smith's History of N. Y.* p. 111.

LECTURE XXVI.

OF THE LAW CONCERNING MARRIAGE.

THE primary and most important of the domestic relations, is that of husband and wife. It has its foundation in nature, and is the only lawful relation by which Providence has permitted the continuance of the human race. In every age it has had a propitious influence on the moral improvement and happiness of mankind. It is one of the chief foundations of social order. We may justly place to the credit of the institution of marriage, a great share of the blessings which flow from refinement of manners, the education of children, the sense of justice, and the cultivation of the liberal arts.*a* In the examination of this interesting contract, I shall, in the first place, consider how a marriage may be lawfully made, and, secondly, how it may be lawfully dissolved; and, lastly, I shall take a view of the rights and duties which belong to that relation.

(1.) All persons who have not the regular use of the understanding, sufficient to deal with discretion in the common affairs of life, as idiots and lunatics, (except in their

---

a The great philosophical poet of antiquity, who was, however, most absurd in much of his philosophical theory, but eminently beautiful, tender, and sublime in his poetry, supposes the civilization of mankind to have been the result of marriage and family establishments.

> *Castaque privatæ veneris connubia læta*
> *Cognita sunt, prolemque ex se videre creatam:*
> *Tum genus humanum primum mollescere cœpit.*
> Lucret. de Rer. Nat. lib. 5.

lucid intervals,) are incapable of agreeing to any contract, and of course to that of marriage. But though marriage with an idiot or lunatic, be absolutely void, and no sentence of avoidance be absolutely necessary;[a] yet, as well for the sake of the good order of society, as for the peace of mind of all persons concerned, it is expedient that the nullity of the marriage should be ascertained and declared by the decree of a court of competent jurisdiction. The existence and extent of mental disease, and how far it may be sufficient, by the darkness and disorder which it brings upon the human faculties, to make void the marriage contract, may sometimes be a perplexing question, extremely distressing to the injured party, and fatal to the peace and happiness of families. Whether the relation of husband and wife lawfully exists, never should be left uncertain. Suits to annul a marriage, by reason of idiocy or lunacy, have consequently been often instituted and sustained in the spiritual courts in England.[b] The proper tribunal for the investigation of this question, when it is brought up directly, and for the mere purpose of testing the validity of the contract, will depend upon the local institutions of every state. In those states, which have no tribunals distinct from the supreme courts of common law jurisdiction, for the exercise of equity powers, whatever jurisdiction is exercised over the matrimonial contract, must be in the common law courts. In this state, it has been adjudged to belong to the Court of Chancery, which possesses, exclusively, all the powers of the ecclesiastical courts in England, which can be lawfully exercised over the question under our constitution and laws.[c]

A marriage procured by force or fraud, is also void *ab initio*, and may be treated as null by every court, in which its validity may be incidentally drawn in question. The basis

---

[a] 2 *Phillimore's Rep.* 19. 69.

[b] Ash's case, *Prec. in Ch.* 203. 1 *Eq. Ca. Abr.* 278. pl. 6. *Ex parte* Turing, 1 *Ves. & Bea.* 140. Turner v. Myers, 1 *Haggard*, 414.

[c] Wightman v. Wightman, 4 *Johns. Ch. Rep.* 343.

of the marriage contract, is consent and the ingredient of fraud or duress, is as fatal in this, as in any other contract, for the free assent of the mind to the contract is wanting.[a] The common law allowed divorces *a vinculo, causa metus, causa impotentiæ*, and those were cases of a fraudulent contract. It is equally proper in this case, as in those of idiocy or lunacy, that the fraud or violence should be judicially investigated, in a suit instituted for the very purpose of annulling the marriage; and such a jurisdiction in the case, belongs to the ecclesiastical courts in England, and to the Court of Chancery in this state, and was lately sustained in a case of gross fraud.[b] It is said that error will, in some cases, destroy a marriage, and render the contract void, as if one person be substituted for another. This, however, would be a case of palpable fraud, going to the substance of the contract; and it would be difficult to state a case, in which error simply, and without any other ingredient, as to the parties, or one of them, in respect to the other, would vacate the contract. It is well understood, that error, and even disingenuous representations in respect to the qualities of one of the contracting parties, as his condition, rank, fortune, manners, and character, would be insufficient. The law makes no provision for the relief of a blind credulity, however it may have been produced.[c]

(2.) No persons are capable of binding themselves in marriage, until they have arrived at the age of consent, which, by the common law of the land, is fixed at fourteen in males, and twelve in females. The law supposes that the parties at that age, have sufficient discretion for such a

---

[a] *Voet ad Pand.* lib. 24. 2. 15. *Toullier's Droit Civil Francais*, tom. 1. No. 501. 504. 506. 512. *Reeve's Domestic Relations* 201. 207. *Pothier's Traite du Contrat de Mariage*, No. 307, 308. 2 *Haggard*, 104. 246.

[b] Ferlat v. Gojon, 1 *Hopkins*, 478.

[c] *Toullier*, ibid. No. 515 521. *Pothier*, ibid. No. 310. 314. 1 *Phillimore*, 137. 2 *Haggard*, 248. 1 *Day's Rep.* 111. Benton v. Benton.

contract, and they can then bind themselves irrevocably, and cannot afterwards be permitted to plead even their egregious indiscretion, however distressing the result of it may be. Marriage, before that age, is voidable at the election of either party, on arriving at the age of consent, if either of the parties be under that age when the contract is made.[a] But this rule of reciprocity, however true in its application to actual marriages, does not apply to other contracts made by a competent party with an infant, nor even to a promise of marriage *per verba de futuro* with an infant, under the age of discretion. The person of full age is absolutely bound, and the contract is only voidable at the election of the infant. This point was ruled by the K. B. in *Holt* v. *Ward Clarencieux*,[b] after the question had been argued by civilians, to see what light might be thrown upon it from the civil and canon law. Though this be the rule of the English law, the civilians and canonists are not agreed upon the question; and Swinburne was of opinion, that the contract in that case was not binding upon the one party more than upon the other.[c]

The age of consent, by the English law, was no doubt borrowed from the Roman law, which established the same periods of twelve and fourteen, as the competent age of consent to render the marriage contract binding. Nature has not fixed any precise period, and municipal laws must operate by fixed and reasonable rules. The same rule was adopted in France, before their revolution;[d] but by the Napoleon code,[e] the age of consent was raised to eighteen in males, and fifteen in females, though a dispensation from the rule may be granted for good cause.

(3.) No person can marry while the former husband or wife is living. Such second marriage is, by the common law,

---

[a] *Co. Litt.* 33. a. 79. b.
[b] 2 *Str.* 937.
[c] *Harg. Co. Litt.* lib. 2. n. 45.
[d] 1 *Domat,* 24.
[e] No. 144.

absolutely null and void;" and it is probably a statute offence in most, if not in all of the states in the Union. In this state, it is made a felony in all but certain excepted cases. Those cases are, when the husband or wife, as the case may be, of the party who remarries, remains continually without the United States for five years together, or when one of the married parties shall have absented from the other by the space of five years together, and the one not knowing the other to be living within that time; or the persons, who at the time of such marriage, are divorced by the sentence of a competent court, or whose former marriage has been duly declared void, or was made within the age of consent.[b] This statute was a transcript of the statute of 1 Jas. I. c. 11., with a reduction of the time of absence, from seven to five years; and though the penal consequences of a second marriage do not apply in those excepted cases, yet if the former husband or wife be living, though the fact be unknown, and there be no divorce *a vinculo* duly pronounced, or the first marriage has not been duly annulled, the second marriage is absolutely void, and the party remarrying incurs the guilt of an unlawful connection. If there be no statute regulation in the case, the principle of the common law, and not only of England, but generally of the Christian world, is, that no length of time, or absence, and nothing but death, or the decree of a court, confessedly competent to the case, can dissolve the marriage tie.[c]

The statute of this state is susceptible of the same construction as that given to the statute of James, and therefore, if one of the married parties shall have continually remained abroad for five years, and be living, even within the knowledge of the party here, or the parties were at the time only under a divorce *a mensa et thoro*, yet the second

---

a Cro. Eliz. 858. 1 *Salk.* 121.
b Laws N. Y. 11th sess. ch. 24.
c 1 *Roll. Abr.* 340. pl. 2. 357. pl. 40. 360. F. Williamson v. Parisien, 1 *Johns. Ch. Rep.* 389. Fenton v. Reed, 4 *Johns. Rep.* 52.

marriage, though void in law, would not be within the penalties of the act. It is still a divorce, and the act does not distinguish between the two species of divorce.*a* The crime of bigamy, or of polygamy, as it ought more properly to be termed,*b* has been made a capital offence in some, and punished very severely in other parts of Europe;*c* but the new civil code of France,*d* only renders such second marriage unlawful, without annexing any penalty for the offence.

The direct and serious prohibition of polygamy contained in our law, is founded on the precepts of christianity, and the laws of our social nature, and it is supported by the sense and practice of the civilized nations of Europe.*e* Though the Athenians, at one time, permitted polygamy, yet, generally, it was not tolerated in ancient Greece, but was regarded as the practice of barbarians.*f* It was also forbidden by the Romans throughout the whole period of their history, and the prohibition is inserted in the Institutes of Justinian.*g* Polygamy may be regarded as exclusively the feature of Asiatic manners, and of half-civilized life, and to be incompatible with civilization, refinement, and domestic felicity.

(4.) In most countries of Europe in which the canon

---

a 4 *Blacks. Com.* 163, 164. This point was raised and discussed in Porter's case, *Cro. Car.* 461, and while the court admitted the second marriage to be unlawful and void, yet they did not decide whether the statute penalty would attach upon such a case of bigamy.

b Harg. Co. Litt. lib. 2. n. 48.

c Barrington on the Statutes, p. 401.

d No. 147.

e Paley's Moral Philosophy, b. 3. c. 6.

f 2 *Potter's Greek Antiq.* 264. *Taylor's Elem Civil Law,* 340—344.

g Cic. de Orat.. 1. 40. *Suet. Jul.* 52. *Inst.* 1. 10. b. *ad fin. Taylor, ibid.* 314—347. The more ancient laws of Rome, prohibiting divorces, were extremely praised by *Dionysius of Halycarnassus,* lib. 2.

laws has had authority or influence, marriages are prohibited between near relations by blood or marriage. Prohibitions similar to the canonical disabilities in the English ecclesiastical law, were contained in the Jewish laws, from which the canon law was, in this respect, deduced; and they existed also in the laws and usages of the Greeks and Romans, subject to considerable alternations of opinion, and with various modifications and extent.[a] These regulations, as far at least as they prohibit marriages among near relations, by blood or marriage, (for the canon and common law made no distinction on this point between connexions by consanguinity and affinity,[b]) are evidently founded in the law of nature; and incestuous marriages have generally (but with some strange exceptions at Athens[c]) been regarded with abhorrence by the soundest writers and the most polished states of antiquity. Under the influence of christianity, a purer taste, and stricter doctrine, has been inculcated; and an incestuous connexion between an uncle and niece, has been recently adjudged by a great master of public and municipal law, to be a nuisance extremely offensive to the laws and manners of society, and tending to endless confusion, and the pollution of the sanctity of private life.[d]

It is very difficult to ascertain exactly the point at which the laws of nature have ceased to discountenance the union. It is very clearly established, that marriages between relations by blood in the lineal, or ascending and descending lines, are unnatural and unlawful, and they lead to a confusion of rights and duties. On this point, the civil, the ca-

---

[a] 1 *Potter's Greek Antiq.* 107. 2 *Ibid.* 267, 268, 269. *Tacit. Ann.* 12. sec. 4, 5, 6, 7.

[b] *Co. Litt.* 235. a. *Gibson's Cod.* 412. 1 *Phillimore's Rep.* 201. 355.

[c] *Mitford's Hist. of Greece*, vol. vii. p. 374.

[d] Burgess v. Burgess, 1 *Haggard*, 386. Such a connexion was held in equal abomination by Justinian's code. *Code*, 5. 0. 2.

non, and the common law, are in perfect harmony. In the very learned opinion which Ch. J. Vaughan delivered on this subject in *Harrison* v. *Burwell,*[a] upon consultation with all the judges of England, he considered that such marriages were against the law of nature, and contrary to a moral prohibition binding upon all mankind. But when we go to collaterals, it is not easy to fix the forbidden degrees by clear and established principles.[b]

In several of the United States, marriages within the levitical degrees are made void by statute; but in this state we have no statute defining the forbidden degrees, and in England, the prohibition to marry within the levitical degrees rests on the canon law, which, in that respect, received the sanction of several statutes passed in the reign of Hen. VIII. It was considered, in the case of *Wightman* v. *Wightman,*[c] that marriages between brothers and sisters in the collateral line, were equally, with those between persons in the lineal line of consanguinity, unlawful and void, as being plainly repugnant to the first principles of society, and the moral sense of the civilized world. It would be difficult to carry the prohibition farther without legislative sanction; and it was observed, in the case last referred to, that in this state, independent of any positive institution, the courts would not probably be authorized to interfere with marriages in the collateral line beyond the first degree, especially as the levitical degrees were not considered to be binding as a mere rule of municipal obe-

---

[a] *Vaughan's Rep.* 206. 2 *Vent.* 9. S. C.

[b] Doctor Taylor, in his *Elements of the civil law,* p. 314—389. has gone deeply into the Greek and Roman learning as to the extent of the prohibition of marriage between near relations, and he says, the fourth degree of collateral consanguinity is the proper point to stop at; that the marriage of first cousins is lawful, and the civil law properly established the fourth as the first degree that could match with decency.

[c] 4 *Johns. Ch. Rep.* 343.

dience. The Napoleon code*a* has adopted precisely the same extent of prohibition, as forming the impassable line between lawful and incestous marriages; and though the prohibition goes deeper into the collateral line, yet the government reserved to itself the power to dispense, at its pleasure, with such further prohibitions. It is evident, that the compilers of that code considered the marriage between collaterals in the first degree of consanguinity, to be founded on a prohibition which was of absolute, uniform, and universal obligation, because, as to the prohibition between brothers and sisters, the sovereign had no dispensing power. In England, the question was considered by the Court of Delegates in the case of *Butler* v. *Gastrill*,*b* and though the court did not agree to admit marriages between brothers and sisters to be against the law of nature, as marriages were so considered, between parties connected in the lineal line; yet they admitted them to be against the law of God, and against good morals and policy. It is not consistent with my purpose to pursue this inquiry more minutely. The books abound with curious discussions on the limitations which ought to be prescribed; and in the English cases, in particular, to which I have referred, the courts bestowed immense labour, and displayed profound learning, in their investigations on the subject.*c*

(5.) The consent of parents, or guardians, to the mar-

---

a No. 161, 162.

b Gilbert's Eq. Rep. 156.

c Whether it be proper or lawful, in a religious or moral sense, for a man to marry his disceased wife's sister, has been discussed by American writers. Mr. N. Webster, in his *Essays*, published at Boston in 1790, No. 26. held the affirmative; and it is made lawful by statute in Connecticut. Dr. Livingston, in his *Dissertations*, published at New-Brunswick in 1816, and confined exclusively to that point, maintained the negative side of the question. It is not my object to meddle with that question; but such a marriage is clearly not incestuous or invalid by our municipal law.

riage of minors, is not requisite. In this state, we have no statute provision in the case, and marriages are left to the freedom of the common law, and, consequently, with as few checks in the formation of the marriage contract, as in any part of the civilized world. The matrimonial law of Scotland, and of Ireland, is similar to our own,[a] and so was the English law prior to the statute of 26 Geo. II. c. 33. That statute, among other things, declared all marriages under licenses, when either of the parties were under the age of twenty-one years, if celebrated without publication of banns, or without the consent of the father, or unmarried mother, or guardian, to be absolutely null and void. The English statute pursued the policy of the civil law, and of the law of the present day in many parts of Europe, in holding clandestine marriages to be a grievous evil, so far as they might affect the happiness of families, and the control of property.[b] Though the Roman law greatly favoured marriages by the famous *jus trium liberorum*, allowing certain special privileges to the parent of three or more children; yet it held the consent of the father to be indispensable to the validity of the marriage of children, of whatever age, except where that consent could not be given, as in cases of captivity, or defect of understanding.[c] Parental restraints upon marriage existed likewise in ancient Greece,[d] and they exist to a

---

[a] *Erskine's Inst.* vol. i. 89—91. *M'Douall's Inst.* vol. i. 112. 2 *Addam's Rep.* 375. 1 *Ibid* 64.

[b] The rigour of the act of Geo. II. was somewhat softened by the new marriage act of 3 Geo. IV. c. 75., and the provisions rendering void all marriages solemnized by license, by minors, without consent, was repealed, and marriages had by previous publication of banns were rendered valid, though there had been false names used in the publication of the banns. 1 *Addam's Rep.* 29. 94. 479.

[c] *Inst.* 1. 10. Pr. Taylor's *Elements of the Civil Law*, 310—313.

[d] Potter's *Greek Antiq.* vol. ii. 270, 271.

very great extent in Germany,^a Holland,^b and France.^c The marriage of minors, under these European regulations, is absolutely void, if had without the consent of the father, or mother, if the survivor; and minority in France extends to the age of twenty-five in males, and twenty-one in females, and even after that period the parental and family check continues in a mitigated degree.

(6.) No peculiar ceremonies are requisite by the common law to the valid celebration of the marriage. The consent of the parties is all that is required; and as marriage is said to be a contract *jure gentium*, that consent is all that is required by natural or public law. The Roman lawyers strongly inculcated the doctrine, that the very foundation and essence of the contract consisted in consent freely given, by parties competent to contract. *Nihil proderit signasse tabulas, si mentem matrimonii non fuisse constabit. Nuptias non concubitus, sed consensus facit.* This is the language equally of the common and canon law, and of common reason.

If the contract be made *per verba de præsenti*, or if made *per verba de futuro*, and be followed by consummation, it amounts to a valid marriage, and which the parties (being competent as to age and consent) cannot dissolve, and it is equally binding as if made *in facie ecclesiæ*. There is no recognition of any ecclesiastical authority in forming the connexion, and it is considered entirely in the light of a civil contract. This is the doctrine of the common law, and also of the canon law, which governed marriages in England prior to the marriage act of 26 Geo. II.; and the canon law is also the general law throughout Europe as to

---

a *Heinec. Elem. Jur. Ger.* lib. 1. s. 138.
b *Van Leeuwen's Com. on the Roman Dutch Law*, p. 73.
c *Pothier, Traite du Contrat de Mar.* No. 321—342. *Code Napoleon*, No. 148—160. *Toullier, Droit Civil Franc.* tom, 1. 453—468.
d *Grotius*, b. 2. c. 5. s. 10. *Bracton*, lib. 1. ch. 5. sec. 7.

marriages except where it has been altered by the local municipal law. The only doubt entertained by the common law was, whether cohabitation was also necessary to give validity to the contract.*a* It is not necessary that a clergyman should be present to give validity to the marriage, though it is, dobtless, a very becoming practice, and suitable to the solemnity of the occasion. The consent of the parties may be declared before a magistrate, or simply before witnesses, or subsequently confessed or acknowledged, or the marriage may even be inferred from continual cohabitation, and reputation as husband and wife, except in cases of civil actions for adultery, or in public prosecutions for bigamy.*b*

By the Scots law, a previous publication of the intention of the parties is required, though a clandestine marriage without such public notice is still valid in law, and only subjects the parties to certain penalties.*c* It has been the usual practice with nations, to precribe certain forms and ceremonies, and generally of a religious nature, as being requisite to accompany the celebration of the marriage solemnity.*d* In the Roman Catholic church, marriage was elevated to the dignity of a sacrament, and was clothed with formalities, and made a complicated institution. But in France, under the revolutionary constitution of 1791, marriage was declared to be regarded in law as a mere civil contract. The same principle was adopted in the code Napoleon; and now, says

---

a 6 *Mod.* 155. 2 *Salk* 437. S. C. Dalrymple v. Dalrymple, 2 *Haggard.* 54. La Tour v. Teesdale, 8 *Taunton*, 830. Fenton v. Reed, 4 *Johns Rep.* 52.

b 1 *Salk.* 119. 4 *Burr.* 2057. *Doug* 171. The King v. Stockland, *Burr. Sett. Cases.* 509. Cunninghams v. Cunninghams, 2 *Dow.* 482. M'Adam v. Walker, 1 *Dow*, 148. Fenton v. Reed, 4 *Johns. Rep.* 52.

c 1 *Ersk. Inst.* 91. 93. *M'Douall's Inst.* vol. i. 112.

d *Seldon's Uxor Ebraica*, b. 2. c. 1. 2 *Potter's Greek Antiq.* 279. 283. Dr. *Taylor's Elem.* 275. 278.

Toullier,[a] the law separates the civil contract entirely from the sacrament of marriage, and does not attend to the laws of the church and the nuptial benediction, which bind only the conscience of the faithful. The statute of 26 Geo. II. required all marriages in England, without special license to the contrary, to be celebrated in a parish church, or public chapel, and rendered the place indispensable to the validity of them. In most cases, the observance of the positive municipal regulations, was made necessary to the validity of the marriage; but the painful consequences of such a doctrine, have recommended a less severe discipline, in respect to the parties themselves and their issue. The statute of 3 Geo. IV. relaxed the rigour of the former statute, in some particulars, as in the case of the marriage of minors by license, without parental consent, or without due publication of banns, for the severity of that statute frequently led to cases of the most alarming nature, such as the annulling of marriages after the parties had lived happily for a great many years, and reared children. In the states of Maine and Massachusetts, it is requisite, by statute, to a valid marriage, that it be made in the presence and with the assent of a magistrate, or a stated or ordained minister of the gospel; and though a marriage without publication of banns, and without the consent of the parents or guardians, will expose the officer to a penalty for breach of the statute, yet a marriage so had, would nevertheless be lawful and binding, provided there was the presence and assent of a magistrate or minister.[b] The statute law of Connecticut, requires the marriage to be celebrated by a clergyman or magistrate, and requires the previous publication of the intention of marriage, and the consent of parents, and it inflicts a penalty on those who disobey the regulation; but it is the opinion of the learned

---

[a] *Droit Civil Francais*, tom. 1. No. 494.
[b] Milford v. Worcester, 7 *Mass. Rep.* 48. Ligonia v. Buxton, 2 *Greenleaf*, 102.

author of the Treatise on the Domestic Relations,[a] that the marriage, if made according to the common law, without observing any of those statute regulations, would still be a valid marriage. This I should infer, from the case of *Wyckoff* v. *Boggs*,[b] to be the rule in New-Jersey, where the marriage contract is under similar legislative regulations. It is the doctrine judicially declared in New-Hampshire and Kentucky, and the marriage is held valid as to the parties, though it be not solemnized in form, according to the requisitions of their statute law. There are probably statute provisions of a similar import in other states of the Union ; and wherever they do not exist and specially apply, the contract is, every where in this country, (except in Louisiana,) under the government of the English common law.

(7.) It has been a point much discussed in the English courts, whether a clandestine marriage in Scotland, of English parties, who resided in England, and resorted to Scotland, with an intent to evade the operation of the English marriage act, could be received and considered in England, as valid. Though we may not, in this country, have at present any great concern with that question, the principle is nevertheless extremely important in the study of the general jurisprudence, applicable to the marriage contract.

As the law of marriage is a part of the *jus gentium*, the general rule undoubtedly is, that a marriage valid by the law of the place where it is made, is valid every where. An exception to this rule is stated by Huberus,[d] who maintains, that if two persons, in order to evade the law of Holland, which requires the consent of the guardian or curator, should go to Friezeland, or elsewhere, where no such consent is necessary, and there marry, and return to Holland, the courts of Holland would not be bound by the law of nations

---

[a] *Reeve's Domestic Relations*, p. 196. 200. 290.
[b] 2 *Halsted*, 138.
[c] 2 *N. Hamp. Rep.* 268. 3 *Marshall*, 370.
[d] *De Conflictu Legum*, sec. 8.

to hold the marriage valid, because it would be an act done *ad eversionem juris nostri*. In opposition to this opinion, we have the decision of the Court of Delegates in England in 1768, in *Compton* v. *Bearcroft*,^a where the parties, being English subjects, and one of them a minor, ran away, without the consent of the guardian, to avoid the English law, and married in Scotland. In a suit in the Spiritual Court, to annul the marriage, it was decided, that the marriage was valid. This decision of the Spiritual Court has been since frequently and gravely questioned. Lord Mansfield, a few years before that decision of the delegates, intimated, pretty strongly,^b his opinion in favour of the doctrine in Huberus, though he admitted the case remained undecided in England. The settled law is now understood to be, that which was decided in the Spiritual Court. It was assumed and declared by Sir George Hay, in 1776, in *Harford* v. *Morris*,^c to be the established law. The principle is, that, in respect to marriage, the *lex loci contractus* prevails over the *lex domicilii*, as being the safer rule, and one dictated by just and enlightened views of international jurisprudence. This rule was shown by the foreign authorities referred to by Sir Edward Simpson in 1752, in the case of *Scrimshire* v. *Scrimshire*,^d to be the law and practice in all civilized countries by common consent and general adoption. It is a part of the *jus gentium* of Christian Europe, and infinite mischief and confusion would ensue with respect to legitimacy, succession, and other rights, if the validity of the marriage contract was not to be tested by the laws of the country where it was made. This doctrine of the English ecclesiastical courts, was recognised by the Supreme Court of Massachusetts, in *Medway* v. *Needham*;^e and though the parties in that case

---

a Buller's N. P. 114. 2. *Haggard*, 443, 444. S. C.
b Robinson v. Bland, 2 *Burr.* 1077.
c 2 *Haggard*, 428—433.
d 2 *Haggard*, 412—416.
e 16 *Mass. Rep.* 157.

left the state on purpose to evade its statute law, and to marry in opposition to it, and being married returned again, it was held, that the marriage must be deemed valid, if it be valid according to the laws of the place where it was contracted, notwithstanding the parties went into the other state with an intention to evade the laws of their own. It was admitted, that the doctrine was repugnant to the general principles of law relating to other contracts; but it was adopted in the case of marriage, on grounds of policy, with a view to prevent the public mischief and the disastrous consequences which would result from holding such marriages void. It was hinted, however, that this comity giving effect to the *lex loci*, might not be applied to gross cases, such as incestuous marriages, which were repugnant to the morals and policy of all civilized nations. This comity has been carried so far[a] as to admit the legitimacy of the issue of a person who had been divorced *a vinculo* for adultery, and who was declared incompetent to re-marry, and who had gone to a neighbouring state where it was lawful for him to re-marry, and there married.[b]

---

[a] West ambridge v. Lexington, 1 *Pickering*, 506.

[b] By the French civil code, No. 63.; publication of banns is to precede marriage; and by the article No. 170. if a Frenchman marries in a foreign country, the same regulation is still to be observed; and yet, according to Toullier, *Droit Civil Francais*, tom. 1. No. 578. and note *ib.* the omission to comply with the prescribed publication does not render the marriage void, whether celebrated at home or abroad. But if the marriage by a Frenchman abroad, be within the age of consent fixed by the French code, though beyond the age of consent fixed by our law, it would seem, that the marriage would not be regarded in France as valid, though valid by the law of the place where it was celebrated. The French code, No. 170., requires the observance by Frenchmen of the ordinances of that code, though the marriage be abroad, for personal laws follow Frenchman wherever they go. Toullier, *Droit Francais*, tom. 1. Nos. 118. and 576.

LECTURE XXVII.

OF THE LAW CONCERNING DIVORCE.

When a marriage is duly made, it becomes of perpetual obligation, and cannot be renounced at the pleasure of either or both of the parties. It continues, until dissolved by the death of one of the parties, or by divorce.

By the ecclesiastical law, a marriage may be dissolved, and declared void *ab initio*, for canonical causes of impediment, existing previous to the marriage. Divorces *a vinculo matrimonii*, said Lord Coke,[a] are *causa præcontractus, causa metus, causa impotentiæ seu frigiditatis, causa affinitatis, causa consanguinitatis*. We have seen how far a marriage may be adjudged void, as being procured by fear or fraud, or contracted within the forbidden degrees. The courts in Massachusetts are authorised by statute to grant divorces *causa impotentiæ ;* and in Connecticut, imbecility has been adjudged sufficient to dissolve a marriage, on the ground of fraud.[b] The canonical disabilities, such as consanguinity, and affinity, and corporeal infirmity, existing prior to the marriage, render it voidable only, and such marriages are valid for all civil purposes, unless sentence of nullity be declared in the lifetime of the parties ; and it cannot be declared void for those causes after the death of either party. But the civil disabilities, such as a prior marriage, want of age, or idiocy, make the contract void *ab initio*, and the union meretricious.[c] In this state, it has been recently adjudg-

---

[a] Co. Litt. 235. a.
[b] 1 Day's Rep. 111. Benton v. Benton. *Dane's Abr. of American Law*, ch. xlvi. art. 9. sec. 14.
[c] Elliott v. Gurr, 2 Phillimore, 16.

ed,[a] that corporeal impotence is not, under our existing laws, a cause of divorce, and that the English law of divorce on that point has never been adopted. The new French code is silent on this point; and Toullier[b] condemns a decree of divorce *causa impotentiæ*, which was pronounced in France in 1808, as contrary to the spirit of the code, and leading to scandalous inquiry.

During the period of our colonial government, for more than one hundred years preceding the revolution, no divorce took place in the colony of New-York; and for many years after we became an independent state, there was not any lawful mode of dissolving a marriage in the lifetime of the parties, but by a special act of the legislature. This strictness was productive of public inconvenience, and often forced the parties, in cases which rendered a separation fit and necessary, to some other state, to avail themselves of a more easy and certain remedy. At length, the legislature, in 1787, authorized the Court of Chancery to pronounce divorces *a vinculo*, in the single case of adultery, upon a bill filed by the party aggrieved. As the law now stands, a bill for a divorce for adultery, can be sustained in two cases only: (1.) If the married parties are inhabitants of this state, at the time of the commission of the adultery: (2.) If the marriage took place in this state, and the party injured be an actual resident at the time of the adultery committed, and at the time of filing the bill.[c] If the defendant answers the bill, and denies the charge, a feigned issue is to be awarded, under the direction of the Chancellor, to try the truth of the charge before a jury, in a court of law. Upon the trial of the issue, the fact must be sufficiently proved by testimony, independent of the confession of the party; for, to guard against all kind of improper influence, collusion, and fraud, it is the general policy of the law on this subject, not to proceed

---

a Burtis v. Burtis, 1 *Hopkins*, 557.
b *Droit Civil Francais*, tom. 1. No. 525.
c *Laws of N. Y.* act of 13th April, 1813. ch. 102.

solely upon the ground of the confession of the party to a dissolution of the marriage contract. The rule that the confession of the party was not sufficient, unless supported by other proof, was derived from the canon law, and arose from the jealousy that the confession might be extorted, or made collusively, in order to furnish means to effect a divorce.*a*

If the defendant suffers the bill to be taken *pro confesso*, or admits the charge, it would be equally dangerous to act upon that admission of the bill, and the statute therefore directs that the case be referred to a master in chancery, to take proof of the adultery, and to report the same, with his opinion thereon. If the report of the master, or the verdict of the jury, as the case may be, shall satisfy the Chancellor of the truth of the charge of adultery, he is then to decree a dissolution of the marriage; but this dissolution is not to affect the legitimacy of the children; and the defendant, by way of punishment for the guilt, is disabled from re-marrying during the life of the other party.*b*

The statute further provides, that if the wife be the complainant, the court is to make a suitable allowance in sound discretion out of the defendant's property, for the maintenance of her and her children, and to compel the defendant to give reasonable security to abide the decree, by the sequestration of his estate. The Chancellor is also to give to the wife, being the injured party, the absolute enjoyment of any real estate belonging to her, or of any personal property derived by title through her, or acquired by her industry. If, on the other hand, the husband be the complainant, then he is entitled to retain the same interest in his wife's real estate, which he would have had, if the marriage had continued; and he is also entitled to her personal estate and choses in action which she pos-

---

a Burns' Eccl. Law, tit. Marriage, sect. 11. *Traité de l'Adultere*, par. *Fournel*, p. 160. Baxter v. Baxter, 1 *Mass. Rep.* 346. Betts v. Betts, 1 *Johns. Ch. Rep.* 197.

b Laws of N. Y. act of 13th April, 1813, ch. 102.

sessed at the time of the divorce, equally as if the marriage had continued; and the wife loses her title to dower, and to a distributive share in the husband's personal estate.

These are all the statute provisions in this state on the subject of a divorce *a vinculo matrimonii;* and it has been decided, that if the marriage was solemnized out of the state, it must distinctly and certainly appear upon the bill, that both parties were inhabitants of the state at the time of the commission of the adultery, and this was held necessary to give the court jurisdiction.[a] It must also appear, if the parties were married within the state, that the complainant was an actual resident at the time of the offence, and of bringing the suit; and this means, that the party's domicil was here, or that he had fixed his residence *animo manendi.*[b] It has also been adjudged, that though the fact of adultery be made out, it does not follow, as a matter of course, that a divorce is to be awarded, for the remedy by divorce is purely a civil and private prosecution, under the control, and at the volition of the party aggrieved, and he may bar himself of the remedy by his own act. Neither party can obtain a divorce for adultery, if the other party recriminates, and can prove a correspondent infidelity. The *delictum,* in that case, must be of the same kind, and not an offence of a different character. The *compensatio criminis* is the standard canon law of England in all cases of divorce, and the same principle, it is to be presumed, prevails in these United States.[c] So, if the husband, subsequently to the adultery, cohabits with his wife, after just grounds of belief in her guilt, it is, in judgment of law, a remission of the offence, and a bar to the divorce. This is a general principle every where pervading this branch of jurisprud-

---

[a] Mix v Mix, 1 *Johns. Ch. Rep.* 204.
[b] Williamson v Parisien. 1 *Johns. Ch. Rep.* 389.
[c] Oughton's ordo Judiciorum. vol. i. tit. 214. Forster v. Forster, 1 *Haggard.* 144. Proctor v. Proctor, 2 *Haggard,* 292. Chambers v. Chambers, 1 *Haggard,* 439.

LECTURE V.

OF THE RIGHTS OF BELLIGERENT NATIONS IN RELATION TO EACH OTHER.

The end of war is to procure by force the justice which cannot otherwise be obtained; and the law of nations allows the means requisite to the end. The persons and property of the enemy may be attacked, and captured, or destroyed, when necessary to procure reparation or security. There is no limitation to the career of violence and destruction, if we follow the earlier writers on this subject, who have paid too much deference to the violent maxims and practices of the ancients, and the usages of the Gothic ages. They have considered a state of war as a dissolution of all moral ties, and a license for every kind of disorder and intemperate fierceness. An enemy was regarded as a criminal and an outlaw, who had forfeited all his rights, and whose life, liberty, and property, lay at the mercy of the conqueror. Every thing done against an enemy was held to be lawful. He might be destroyed, though unarmed and defenceless. Fraud might be employed as well as force, and force without any regard to the means.[a] But these barbarous rights of war have been questioned, and checked, in the progress of civilization. Public opinion, as it becomes enlightened and refined, condemns all cruelty, and all wanton destruction of life and property, as equally useless and injurious;

---

[a] *Grotius*, b. 3. c. 4. and 5. *Puff.* lib. 2. c. 16. sec. 6. *Bynk. Q. J. Pub.* b. 1. c. 1, 2, 3. *Burlamaq.* part 4. c. 5.

and it controls the violence of war by the energy and severity of its reproaches.

Grotius, even in opposition to many of his own authorities, and under a due sense of the obligations of religion and humanity, placed bounds to the ravages of war, and mentioned that many things were not fit and commendable, though they might be strictly lawful; and that the law of nature forbade what the law of nations (meaning thereby the practice of nations) tolerated. He held, that the law of nations prohibited the use of poisoned arms, or the employment of assassins, or violence to women, or to the dead, or making slaves of prisoners;[a] and the moderation which he inculcated, had a visible influence upon the sentiments and manners of Europe. Under the sanction of his great authority, men began to entertain more enlarged views of national policy, and to consider a mild and temperate exercise of the rights of war, to be dictated by an enlightened self-interest, as well as by the precepts of Christianity. And, notwithstanding some subsequent writers, as Bynkershoeck and Wolfius, restored war to all its horrors, by allowing the use of poison, and other illicit arms, yet such rules became abhorrent to the cultivated reason, and growing humanity, of the Christian nations. Montesquieu insisted,[b] that the laws of war gave no other power over a captive than to keep him safely, and that all unnecessary rigour was condemned by the reason and conscience of mankind. Rutherforth[c] has spoken to the same effect, and Martens[d] enumerates several modes of war, and species of arms, as being now held unlawful by the laws of war. Vattel[e] has entered largely into the subject, and he argues with great strength of reason and eloquence, against all unnecessary cruelty, all base revenge, and all mean and

---

a B. 3. c. 4, 5. 7. *c* *Inst.* b. 2. c. 9.
b B. 15. c. 2. *d* *Summary*, b. 8. c. 3. sec. 3.
e B. 3. c. 8.

perfidious warfare, and he recommends his benevolent doctrines by the precepts of exalted ethics and sound policy, and by illustrations drawn from some of the most pathetic and illustrious examples.

There is a marked difference in the rights of war carried on by land, and at sea. The object of a maritime war is the destruction of the enemy's commerce and navigation, in order to weaken or destroy the foundations of his naval power. The capture or destruction of private property is essential to that end, and it is allowed in maritime wars by the law and practice of nations. But there are great limitations imposed upon the operations of war by land, though depredations upon private property, and despoiling and plundering the enemy's territory, is still too prevalent a practice, especially when the war is assisted by irregulars. Such conduct has been condemned in all ages by the wise and virtuous, and it is usually severely punished by those commanders of disciplined troops who have studied war as a science, and are animated by a sense of duty, or the love of fame. We may infer the opinion of Xenophon on this subject, (and he was a warrior as well as a philosopher,) when he states, in the *Cyropædia*,[a] that Cyrus of Persia gave orders to his army, when marching upon the enemy's borders, not to disturb the cultivators of the soil; and there have been such ordinances in modern times for the protection of innocent and pacific pursuits.[b] Vattel condemns very strongly the spoliations of a country without palpable necessity; and he speaks with a just indignation of the burning of the Palatinate by Turenne, under the cruel instruc-

---

a Lib. 5.

b 1 *Emerigon des Ass.* 129, 130. 457. refers to ordinances of France and Holland, in favour of protection to fishermen; and to the like effect was the order of the British government in 1810, for abstaining from hostilities against the inhabitants of the Feroe islands, and Iceland.

tions of Louvois, the war minister of Louis XIV.ᵃ The general usage now is not to touch private property upon land, without making compensation, unless in special cases dictated by the necessary operations of war, or when captured in places carried by storm, and which repelled all the overtures for a capitulation. Contributions are sometimes levied upon a conquered country, in lieu of a confiscation of property, and as some indemnity for the expenses of maintaining order, and affording protection.ᵇ If the conqueror goes beyond these limits wantonly, or when it is not clearly indispensable to the just purposes of war, and seizes private property of pacific persons for the sake of gain, and destroys private dwellings, or public edifices, devoted to civil purposes only; or makes war upon monuments of art, and models of taste, he violates the modern usages of war, and is sure to meet with indignant resentment, and to be held up to the general scorn and detestation of the world.ᶜ

Cruelty to prisoners, and barbarous destruction of private property, will provoke the enemy to severe retaliation upon the innocent. Retaliation is said by Rutherforthᵈ not to be a justifiable cause for putting innocent prisoners, or hostages, to death; for no individual is chargeable, by the law of nations, with the guilt of a personal crime, merely because the community, of which he is a member, is guilty. He is only responsible as a member of the state, in his property, for reparation in damages for the acts of others; and it is on this principle, that, by the law of nations, private property may be taken and appropriated in war. Retaliation, to be just, ought to be confined to the guilty individuals, who may have committed some enormous violation of public law. On this subject of retaliation, Professor Martens

---

a *Vattel*, b. 3. c. 9. sec. 167.
b *Vattel*, b. 2. c. 8. sec. 147.—c. 9. sec. 165.
c *Vattel*, b. 3. c. 9. sec. 168.
d *Inst.* b. 2. c. 9.

is not so strict.[a] While he admits that the life of an innocent man cannot be taken, unless in extraordinary cases, yet he declares that cases will sometimes occur, when the established usages of war are violated, and there are no other means, except the influence of retaliation, of restraining the enemy from further excesses. Vattel speaks of retaliation as a sad extremity, and it is frequently threatened without being put in execution, and, probably, without the intention to do it, and in hopes that fear will operate to restrain the enemy. Instances of resolutions to retaliate on innocent prisoners of war, occurred in this country during the revolutionary war, as well as during the war of 1812; but there was no instance in which retaliation, beyond the measure of severe confinement, took place in respect to prisoners of war.[b]

Although a state of war puts all the subjects of the one nation in a state of hostility with those of the other, yet by the customary law of Europe, every individual is not allowed to fall upon the enemy. If subjects confine themselves to simple defence, they are to be considered as acting under the presumed order of the state, and are entitled to be treated by the adversary as lawful enemies, and the captures which they make in such a case, are allowed to be lawful prize. But they cannot engage in offensive hostilities, without the express permission of their sovereign; and if they have not a regular commission, as evidence of that consent, they run the hazard of being treated by the enemy as lawless banditti, not entitled to the protection of the mitigated rules of modern war.[c]

It was the received opinion in ancient Rome, in the times

---

[a] B. 8. c. 1. sec. 3. note.

[b] *Journals of Congress*, vol. 2. p. 245. vol. 7. p. 9. and 147. vol. 8. p. 10. *British Orders in Canada of 27th October, and December 12th, 1813, and President's Message to Congress of December 7th, 1813, and of October 28th, 1814.*

[c] Bynk. Q. J. P. ch. 20. Vattel, b. 3. c. 15. sec. 226. *Journals of Congress*, vol. 7. 187. Martens, b. 8. c. 3. sec. 2.

of Cato and Cicero,[a] that one who was not regularly enrolled as a soldier, could not lawfully kill an enemy. But the law of Solon, by which individuals were permitted to form associations for plunder, was afterwards introduced into the Roman law, and has been transmitted to us as part of their system.[b] During the lawless confusion of the feudal ages, the right of making reprisals was claimed, and exercised, without a public commission. It was not until the fifteenth century that commissions were held necessary, and began to be issued to private subjects in time of war, and that subjects were forbidden to fit out vessels to cruise against enemies without license, and there were ordinances in Germany, France and England, to that effect.[c] It is now the practice for maritime states to make use of the voluntary aid of individuals against their enemies, as auxiliary to the public force; and Bynkershoeck says, that the Dutch formerly employed no vessels of war but such as were owned by private persons, and to whom the government allowed a proportion of the captured property, as well as indemnity from the public treasury. Vessels are now fitted out and equipped by private adventurers, at their own expense, to cruise against the commerce of the enemy. They are duly commissioned, and it is said not to be lawful to cruise without a regular commission.[d] Sir Matthew Hale held it to be depredation in a subject to attack the enemy's vessels, except in his own defence, without a commission.[e] The subject has been repeatedly discussed in the Supreme Court of the United States,[f] and the doctrine of the law of nations is

---

a *De Off.* b. 1. c. 11.
b *Dig.* 47. 22. 4. *Bynk. Q. J. P.* b. 1. c. 18.
c *Code des Prizes*, tom. 1. p. 1. *Martens on Privateers*, p. 18. *Robinson's Collectanea Maritima*, p. 21.
d *Bynk. ub. sup. Martens*, b. 8. c. 3. sec. 2.
e *Harg. Law T.* 245, 246, 247.
f Brown v. United States, 8 *Cranch*, 132—135. The Nereide, 9 *Cranch*, 449. The Dos Hermanos, 2 *Wheaton*, 76. and 10 *Wheaton*. 306. The Amiable Isabella, 6 *Wheaton*, 1.

considered to be, that private citizens cannot acquire a title to hostile property, unless seized under a commission, but they may still lawfully seize hostile property in their own defence. If they depredate upon the enemy without a commission, they act upon their peril, and are liable to be punished by their own sovereign, but the enemy are not warranted to consider them as criminals, and as respects the enemy, they violate no rights by capture.

Such hostilities, without a commission, are, however, contrary to usage, and exceedingly irregular and dangerous, and they would probably expose the party to the unchecked severity of the enemy, but they are not acts of piracy. Vattel, indeed, says,^a that private ships of war, without a regular commission, are not entitled to be treated like captures made in a formal war. The observation is rather loose, and the weight of authority undoubtedly is, that non-commissioned vessels of a belligerent nation, may at all times capture hostile ships, without being deemed, by the law of nations, pirates. They are lawful combatants, but they have no interest in the prizes they may take, and the property will remain subject to condemnation in favour of the government of the captor, as *droits of the admiralty*. It said, however, that, in the United States, the property is not strictly and technically condemned upon that principle, but *jure reipublicæ;* and it is the settled law of the United States, that all captures made by non-commissioned captors, are made for the government.[b]

In order to encourage privateering, it is usual to allow the owners of private armed vessels to appropriate to themselves the property, or a large portion of the property they may capture; and to afford them, and the crews, other facilities and rewards for honourable and successful efforts.

---

a B. 3. c. 15. sec. 226.
b Com. Dig. tit. Admiralty, E. 3. 2 *Wood. Lec.* 432. 1 *Dodson's Adm.* 397. The Georgiana. 1 *Gall. Rep.* 545. The brig Joseph. The Dos Hermanos. 10 *Wheaton.* 306.

This depends upon the municipal regulations of each particular power, and as a necessary precaution against abuse, the owners of privateers are required, by the ordinances of the commercial states, to give adequate security that they will conduct the cruise according to the laws and usages of war, and the instructions of the government, and that they will regard the rights of neutrals, and bring their prizes in for adjudication. These checks are essential to the character and safety of maritime nations.*a* Privateering, under all the restrictions which have been adopted, is very liable to abuse. The object is not fame or chivalric warfare, but plunder and profit. The discipline of the crews is not apt to be of the highest order, and privateers are often guilty of enormous excesses, and become the scourge of neutral commerce.*b* They are sometimes manned and officered by foreigners, having no permanent connexion with the country, or interest in its cause. This was a complaint made by the United States, in 1819, in relation to irregularities and acts of atrocity, committed by private armed vessels, sailing under the flag of Buenos Ayres.*c* Under the best regulations, the business tends strongly to blunt the sense of private right, and to nourish a lawless and fierce spirit of rapacity. Efforts have been made, from time to time, to abolish the practice. In the treaty of amity and commerce between Prussia and the United States, in 1785, it was stipulated

---

a Bynk. Q. J. P. c. 19. *Journals of Congress,* 1776, vol. 2. 102. 114. *Acts of Congress of* 26*th June,* 1812, ch. 107. and *April* 20*th,* 1818, ch. 83. sec. 10. President's instructions to private armed vessels, 2 *Wheaton,* app. p. 80. Danish instructions of 10th March, 1810, *Hall's L. J.* vol. 4. 263. and app. to 5 *Wheaton,* 91. *Vattel,* b. 3. c. 15. sec. 229. *Martens' Summ.* 289, 290. note. Ord. of Buenos Ayres, May, 1817, in app. to 4 *Wheaton,* 28. Digest of the code of British instructions, app. to 5 *Wheaton,* 129.

b Reports of the Secretary of State, March 2*d,* 1794, and *June* 21*st,* 1797.

c Mr. Adams' Letter of 1*st January,* 1819, *to Mr. De Forest, and his Official Report of* 28*th January,* 1819.

that, in case of war, neither party should grant commissions to any private armed vessel to attack the commerce of the other. But the spirit and policy of maritime warfare, will not permit such generous provisions to prevail. That provision was not renewed with the renewal of the treaty. A similar attempt to put an end to the practice was made in the agreement between Sweden and Holland, in 1675, but the agreement was not performed. The French legislature, soon after the breaking out of the war with Austria, in 1792, passed a decree for the total suppression of privateering, but that was a very transitory act, and it was soon swept away in the tempest of the revolution. The efforts to stop the practice have been very feeble and fruitless, notwithstanding that enlightened and enlarged considerations of national policy have shown it to be for the general benefit of mankind, to surrender the licentious practice, and to obstruct as little as possible, the freedom and security of commercial intercourse among the nations."

It has been a question, whether the owners and officers of private armed vessels were liable, in damages, for illegal conduct, beyond the amount of the security given. Bynkershoeck[b] has discussed this point quite at large, and he concludes that the owner, master, and sureties, are jointly and severally liable, *in solido*, for the damages incurred; and that the master and owners are liable to the whole extent of the injury, though it may exceed the value of the privateer and her equipment, and the sureties are bound only to the amount of the sums for which they became bound. This rule is liable to the modifications of municipal regulations, and though the French law of prize was formerly the same as the rule laid down by Bynkershoeck, yet the new commercial code of France,[c] exempts the owners of private

---

a 1 Emerigon des Ass. 129—132. 457. Mably's Droit Public, ch. 12. sec. 1. Edinburgh Review, vol. 8. p. 13—15. North American Review, N. S. vol. 2. p. 166.

b Q. J. Pub. b. 1. ch. 19.

c Code de Commerce, art. 217.

armed vessels, in time of war, from responsibility for trespasses at sea, beyond the amount of the security they may have given, unless they were accomplices in the tort. The English statute of 7 Geo. II. c. 15. is to the same effect, in respect to embezzlements in the merchants' service. It limits the responsibility to the amount of the vessel and freight, but it does not apply to privateers in time of war; and where there is no positive local law on the subject, (and there is none with us,) the general principle is, that the liability is commensurate with the injury. This was the rule, as declared by the Supreme Court of the United States, in *Del Col* v. *Arnold*,[a] and though that case has since been shaken as to other points,[b] it has not been disturbed as to the point before us. We may, therefore, consider it to be a settled rule of law and equity, that the measure of damages is the value of the property unlawfully injured or destroyed, and that each individual owner is responsible for the entire damages, and not rateably *pro tanto*.[c]

Vattel admits,[d] that an individual may, with a safe conscience, serve his country by fitting out privateers; but he holds it to be inexcusable and base, to take a commission from a foreign prince, to prey upon the subjects of a state in amity with his native country. The laws of the United States have made ample provision on this subject, and they may be considered as in affirmance of the law of nations, and as prescribing specific punishment for acts which were before unlawful.[e] An act of Congress prohibits citizens to accept, within the jurisdiction of the United States, a commission, or for any person, not transiently within the United States, to consent to be retained or enlisted, to serve a fo-

---

a 3 *Dallas*, 333.
b 1 *Wheaton*, 259.
c 5 *Rob.* 291. The Karasan. 2 *Wheaton*, 327. The Anna Maria.
d B. 3. c. 15. sec. 229.
e Talbot v. Janson, 3 *Dallas*, 133. Brig Alerta v. Blas Moran, 9 *Cranch*, 359.

reign state in war, against a government in amity with us. It likewise prohibits American citizens from being concerned, without the limits of the United States, in fitting out, or otherwise assisting, any private vessel of war, to cruise against the subjects of friendly powers.[a] Similar prohibitions are contained in the laws of other countries;[b] and the French ordinance of the marine of 1681, treated such acts as piratical. The better opinion is, that a cruiser, furnished with commissions from two different powers, is liable to be treated as a pirate; for though the two powers may be allies, yet one of them may be in amity with a state with whom the other is at war.[c] In the treaty of 1825, between the United States and the republic of Colombia, it is declared, that no citizen, of either nation, shall accept a commission or letter of marque, to assist an enemy in hostilities against the other, under pain of being treated as a pirate.

The right to all captures vests primarily in the sovereign, and no individual can have any interest in a prize, whether made by a public or private armed vessel, but what he receives under the grant of the state. This is a general principle of public jurisprudence, *bello parta cedunt reipublicæ*, and the distribution of the proceeds of prizes, depends upon the regulations of each state, and unless the local laws have otherwise provided, the prizes vest in the sovereign.[d] But the general practice under the laws and ordinances of the belligerent governments is, to distribute the proceeds of captured property, when duly passed upon, and condemned as prize, (and whether captured by public or private com-

---

[a] *Act of Congress of 20th of April,* 1818, c. 83.
[b] See the *Austrian Ordinance of Neutrality of August 7th,* 1803, art. 2, 3.
[c] *Valin's Com.* tom. 2. 235, 6. *Bynkershoeck,* c. 17. and note by *Duponceau* to his Translation, p. 129. *Sir L. Jenkins' Works,* 714.
[d] *Grotius,* b. 3. c. 6. *Vattel,* b. 3. c. 9. sec. 164. The Elsebe, 5 *Rob.* 173.

missioned vessels,) among the captors, as a reward for bravery, and a stimulus to exertion.

When a prize is taken at sea, it must be brought, with due care, into some convenient port, for adjudication by a competent court; though, strictly speaking, as between the belligerent parties, the title passes, and is vested when the capture is complete, and that was formerly held to be complete and perfect when the battle was over, and the *spes recuperandi* was gone. *Voet,* in his Commentaries upon the Pandects,*a* and the authors he refers to, maintain with great strength, as Lord Mansfield observed in *Goss* v. *Withers*,*b* that occupation of itself transferred the title to the captor, *per solam occupationem dominium prædæ hostibus acquiri.* The question never arises but between the original owner and a neutral purchasing from the captor, and between the original owner and a recaptor. If a captured ship escapes from the captor, or is retaken, or if the owner ransoms her, his property is thereby revested. But if neither of these events happens, the question as to the change of title is open to dispute, and many arbitrary lines have been drawn, partly from policy, to prevent too easy dispositions of the property to neutrals, and partly from equity, to extend the *jus postliminii* in favour of the owner. Grotius,*c* and many other writers, and some marine ordinances, as those of Lewis XIV. and of Congress during the American war, made twenty hours quiet possession by the enemy, the test of title by capture. Bynkershoeck*d* says, that such a rule is repugnant to the laws and customs of Holland, and he insists, that a firm possession, at any time, vests the property in the captor, and that ships and goods brought *infra præsidia,* do most clearly change the property. But by the modern usage of nations, neither the twenty-four hours possession, nor the bringing the prize *infra præsidia,* is sufficient to change the

---

a Tom. 2. p. 1155.
b 2 Burr. 683.
c B. 8. c. 6.
d Q. J. Pub. b. 1. c. 4. and c. 5.

property in the case of a maritime capture. A judicial inquiry must pass upon the case, and the present enlightened practice of the commercial nations, has subjected all such captures to the scrutiny of judicial tribunals, as the only sure way to furnish due proof that the seizure was lawful. The property is not changed in favour of a vendee or recaptor, so as to bar the original owner, until a regular sentence of condemnation has been pronounced by some court of competent jurisdiction, belonging to the sovereign of the captor; and the purchaser must be able to show documentary evidence of that fact, to support his title. This salutary rule, and one so necessary to check irregular conduct, and individual outrage, has been long established in the English admiralty,[a] and it is now every where recognised as the law and practice of nations.[b]

The condemnation must be pronounced by a prize court of the government of the captor, sitting either in the country of the captor or of his ally. The prize court of an ally cannot condemn. Prize or no prize is a question belonging exclusively to the courts of the country of the captor. The reason of this rule is said to be,[c] that the sovereign of the captors has a right to inspect their behaviour, for he is answerable to other states for the acts of the captor. The prize court of the captor may sit in the territory of the ally, but it is not lawful for such a court to act in a neutral territory. Neutral ports are not intended to be auxiliary to the operations of the power at war, and the law of nations has clearly ordained, that a prize court of a belligerent captor cannot exercise jurisdiction in a neutral country. This prohibition rests not merely on the unfitness and danger of

---

a *Carth.* 423.   10 *Mod.* 79.   12 *Mod.* 143.   2 *Burr.* 694.   3 *Rob.* 97. *in notis.*

b Flad Owen, 1 *Rob.* 117. Henrick and Maria, 4 *Rob.* 43. *Vattel*, b. 3. c. 14. sec. 216.   *Heineccii Opera*, edit. Geneva, 1744, tom. 2. 310. 360.   5 *Rob.* 294.   *Doug.* 591.   8 *Cranch*, 226.   4 *Wheaton*, 298.   6 *Taunton*, 25.   2 *Dallas*, 1, 2. 4.

c *Rutherforth's Institutes*, b. 2. c. 9.

making neutral ports the theatre of hostile proceedings, but it stands on the ground of the usage of nations.[a]

It was for some time supposed that a prize court, though sitting in the country of its own sovereign, or of his ally, had no jurisdiction over prizes lying in a neutral port, because the court wanted that possession which was deemed essential to the exercise of a jurisdiction in a proceeding *in rem*. The principle was admitted to be correct by Sir William Scott, in the case of the *Henrick & Maria*,[b] and he acted upon it in a prior case.[c] But he considered that the English admiralty had gone too far, in supporting condemnations, in England, of prizes abroad in a neutral port, to permit him to recall the vicious practice of the court to the acknowledged principle; and the English rule is now definitively settled, agreeably to the old usage, and the practice of other nations. The Supreme Court of the United States has followed the English rule, and it has held valid the condemnations, by a belligerent court, of prizes carried into a neutral port, and remaining there. This was deemed the most convenient practice for neutrals, as well as for the parties at war, and though the prize was in fact within a neutral jurisdiction, it was still to be deemed under the control, or *sub potestate*, of the captor.[d]

Sometimes circumstances will not permit property captured at sea to be sent into port; and the captor, in such cases, may either destroy it, or permit the original owner to ransom it. It was formerly the general custom to redeem property from the hands of the enemy by ransom, and the

---

a Glass v. The sloop Betsey, 3 *Dallas*, 6. Flad Owen, 1 *Rob.* 114. Havelock v. Rockwood, 8 *Term*, 268. Oddy v. Bovill, 2 *East*, 475. *Answer to the Prussian Memorial*, 1753. The L'Invincible, 1 *Wheat*. 238. The Estrella, 4 *Wheaton*, 298.

b 4 *Rob.* 43.

c Note to the case of the Herstelder, 1 *Rob. Adm. Rep.*

d 6 *Rob.* 138. Note to the case of the schooner Sophie. Smart v. Wolf, 3 *Term*, 323. Bynk. by *Duponceau*, p. 38. note. Hudson v. Guestier, 4 *Cranch*, 293. Williams v. Armroyd, 7 *Cranch*, 423.

contract is undoubtedly valid, when municipal regulations do not intervene. It is now but little known in the commercial law of England, for several statutes in the reign of Geo. III. absolutely prohibited to British subjects the privilege of ransom of property captured at sea, unless in a case of extreme necessity, to be judged of by the court of admiralty.[a] A ransom bill, when not locally prohibited, is a war contract, protected by good faith and the law of nations, and notwithstanding that the contract is considered in England as tending to relax the energy of war, and deprive cruisers of the chance of recapture, it is, in many views, highly reasonable and humane. Other maritime nations regard ransoms as binding, and to be classed among the few legitimate *commercia bella*. They have never been prohibited in this country; and the act of Congress of August 2d, 1813, interdicting the use of British licenses or passes, did not apply to the contract of ransom.[b]

The effect of a ransom is equivalent to a safe conduct granted by the authority of the state to which the captor belongs, and it binds the commanders of other cruisers to respect the safe conduct thus given, and under the implied obligation of the treaty of alliance, it binds equally the cruisers of the allies of the captor's country.[c] From the very nature of the connexion between allies, their compacts with the common enemy must bind each other, when they tend to accomplish the objects of the alliance. If they did not, the ally would reap all the fruits of the compact, without being subject to the terms and conditions of it; and the enemy with whom the agreement was made, would be exposed, in regard to the ally, to all the disadvantages of it, without participating in the stipulated benefits. Such an

---

[a] 1 *Chitty on Comm. Law*, 423.

[b] 2 *Azuni on Maritime Law*, ch. 4. art. 6. 1 *Emerigon*, ch. 12. sec. 21. 2 *Valin*, art. 66. p. 149. *Le Guidon*, ch. 6. art. 2. *Grotius*. b. 3. c. 19. 15 *Johnson*, 6. Goodrich v. Gordon.

[c] 2 *Dallas*, 15. Miller v. The Resolution.

inequality of obligation is contrary to every principle of reason and justice.[a]

The safe conduct implied in a ransom bill, requires that the vessel should be found within the course prescribed, and within the time limited by the contract, unless forced out of her course by stress of weather, or unavoidable necessity.[b] If the vessel ransomed perishes by a peril of the sea, before arrival in port, the ransom is, nevertheless, due, for the captor has not insured the prize against the perils of the sea, but only against recapture by cruisers of his own nation, or of the allies of his country. If there should be a stipulation in the ransom contract, that the ransom should not be due if the vessel was lost by sea perils, the provision ought to be limited to total losses by shipwreck, and not to mere stranding, which might lead to frauds, in order to save the cargo at the expense of the ship.[c]

If the vessel should be recaptured out of the route prescribed by the contract for her return, or after the time allowed for her return, and be adjudged lawful prize, it has been made a question whether the debtors of the ransom are discharged from their contract. Valin[d] says, that, according to the constant practice, the debtors are discharged in such case, and the price of the ransom is deducted from the proceeds of the prize, and given to the first captor, and the residue goes to the second taker. So, if the captor himself should afterwards be taken by an enemy's cruiser, together with his ransom bill, the ransom becomes part of the lawful conquest of the enemy, and the debtors of the ransom are, consequently, discharged.[e]

In the case of *Ricard* v. *Bettenham*,[f] an English vessel

---

a 2 *Dallas*, 15. Pothier, *Traite du Droit de Propriete*, No. 134.
b Pothier, ibid. No. 134, 135.
c Pothier, ibid. No. 138.
d *Ord. des Prises*, art. 19.
e Pothier, *Traite de Propriete*, No. 139, 140.
f 3 *Burr.* 1734.

was captured by a French privateer in the war of 1756, and ransomed, and a hostage given as a security for the payment of the ransom bill. The hostage died while in possession of the French, and it was made a question in the K. B. in a suit brought upon the ransom bill after the peace, whether the death of the hostage discharged the contract, and whether the alien could sue on the ransom bill in the English courts. It was shown, that such a contract was valid among the other nations of Europe, and that the owner of the bill was entitled to sue upon it, and that it was not discharged by the death of the hostage, who was taken as a mere collateral security, and the plaintiff was, accordingly, allowed to recover. But, it has been since decided, and it is now understood to be the law, that, during war, and while the character of alien enemy continues, no suit will lie in the British courts, by the enemy, in proper person, on a ransom bill, notwithstanding it is a contract arising *jure belli*.[a] The remedy to enforce payment of the ransom bill for the benefit of the enemy captor, is by an action by the imprisoned hostage, in the courts of his own country, for the recovery of his freedom. This severe technical objection would seem to be peculiar to the British courts, for it was shown, in the case of *Ricard* v. *Bettenham*, to be the practice in France and Holland, to sustain such actions by the owner of the ransom contract. Lord Mansfield considered the contract as worthy to be sustained by sound morality and good policy, and as governed by the law of nations, and the eternal rules of justice.[b] The practice in France,[c] when a French vessel has been ransomed, and a hostage given to the enemy, is for the officers of the admiralty to seize the vessel and her cargo, on her return to port, in order to compel the owners to pay the ransom debt, and relieve the hostage.

---

[a] Anthon v. Fisher, *Doug.* 649. note. 1 *Rob.* 169. The Hoop.
[b] Cornu v. Blackburne, *Doug.* 641.
[c] *Pothier de Propriete*, No. 144.

and this is a course dictated by a prompt and liberal sense of justice.

The recapture of the ransom bill, according to Valin,[a] puts an end to the claim of the captor. He may be deprived of the entire benefit of his prize, as well as of the ransom bill, either by recapture or rescue, and the questions arising on them lead to the consideration of postliminy and salvage. Upon recapture from pirates, the property is to be restored to the owner, on the allowance of a reasonable compensation to the retaker, in the nature of salvage; for it is a principle of the law of nations, that a capture by pirates does not, like a capture by an enemy in solemn war, change the title, or devest the original owner of his right to the property, and it does not require the doctrine of postliminy to restore it.[b] In France, property may be reclaimed by the owner within a year and a day;[c] but in some other countries (and Grotius mentions Spain and Venice) the rule formerly was, that the whole property recaptured from pirates went to the retaker, and this rule was founded on the consideration of the desperate nature of the recovery.

The *jus postliminii* was a fiction of the Roman law, by which persons or things taken by the enemy, were restored to their former state, upon coming again under the power of the nation to which they formerly belonged. *Postliminium fingit eum qui captus est, in civitate semper fuisse.*[d] It is a right recognised by the law of nations, and contributes essentially to mitigate the calamities of war. When, therefore, property taken by the enemy is either recaptured or rescued from him, by the fellow subjects or allies of the original owner, it does not become the property of the recaptor or rescuer, as if it had been a new prize, but it is restored to the original owner, by right of postliminy, upon

---

[a] Tom. 2. liv. 3. tit. 9. art. 19.
[b] *Grotius*, b. 3. c. 9. sec. 16, 17.   *Bynk*. Q. J. P. c. 15. and 17.
[c] *Valin Com.* tom. 2. 261.
[d] *Inst.* 1. 12. 5.

certain terms. Moveables are not entitled, by the strict rules of the law of nations, to the full benefit of postliminy, unless retaken from the enemy promptly after the capture, for then the original owner neither finds a difficulty in recognising his effects, not is presumed to have relinquished them. Real property is easily identified, and, therefore, more completely within the right of postliminy; and the reason for a stricter limitation of it in respect to personal property, arises from the transitory nature of it, and the difficulty of identifying it, and the consequent presumption that the original owner had abandoned the hope of recovery.[a] This right does not take effect in neutral countries, because the neutral nation is bound to consider the war on each side as equally just, so far as relates to its effects, and to look upon every acquisition made by either party, as a lawful acquisition. If one party was allowed, in a neutral territory, to enjoy the right of claiming goods taken by the other, it would be a departure from the duty of neutrality. The right of postliminy takes place, therefore, only within the territories of the nation of the captor, or of his ally.[b] If a prize be brought into a neutral port by the captors, it does not return to the former owner by the law of postliminy, because neutrals are bound to take notice of the military right which possession gives, and which is the only evidence of right acquired by military force, as contradistinguished from civil rights and titles. They are bound to take the fact for the law. With respect to persons, the right of postliminy takes place even in a neutral country, so that if a captor brings his prisoners into a neutral port, he may, perhaps, confine them on board his ship, as being, by fiction of law, part of the territory of his sovereign, but he has no control over them on shore.[c]

---

[a] *Vattel,* b. 3. c. 14. sec. 209.
[b] *Vattel, ibid.* sec. 207, 208.
[c] *Vattel,* b. 3. c. 7. sec. 132. *Bynk.* by *Duponceau,* p. 116, 117. notes. *Austrian Ord. of Neutrality, August 7th,* 1803, art. 19.

In respect to real property, the acquisition by the conqueror is not fully consummated until confirmed by the treaty of peace, or by the entire submission or destruction of the state to which it belonged. If it be recovered by the original sovereign, it returns to the former proprietor, notwithstanding it may, in the mean time, have been transferred by purchase. The purchaser is understood to have taken the property at the hazard of a recovery or reconquest before the end of the war. But if the real property, as a town or portion of the territory, for instance, be ceded to the conqueror by the treaty of peace, the right of postliminy is gone for ever, and a previous alienation by the conqueror would be valid.^a

In a land war, moveable property, after it has been in complete possession of the enemy for twenty-four hours, becomes absolutely his, without any right of postliminy in favour of the original owner; and much more ought this species of property to be protected from the operation of the rule of postliminy, when it has not only passed into the complete possession of the enemy, but been *bona fide* transferred to a neutral. By the ancient and strict doctrine of the law of nations, captures at sea fell under the same rule as other moveable property, taken on land, and goods so taken were not recoverable by the original owner from the rescuer or retaker. But the municipal regulations of most states, have softened the rigour of the law of nations on this point, by an equitable extension of the right of postliminy, as against any recaption by their own subjects. The ordinances of several of the continental powers confined the right of restoration, on recaption, to cases where the property had not been in possession of the enemy above twenty-four hours. This was the rule of the French ordinance of 1681,^b but now the right is every where understood to continue until sentence of condemnation, and no longer.

---

a *Vattel*, b. 3. c. 14. sec. 212. *Martens*, b. 8. c. 3. sec. 11, 12.
b Liv. 3. tit. 9. *Des Prizes*, art. 8.

It is also a rule on this subject, that if a treaty of peace makes no particular provisions relative to captured property, it remains in the same condition in which the treaty finds it, and it is tacitly conceded to the possessor. The right of postliminy no longer exists, after the conclusion of the peace. It is a right which belongs exclusively to a state of war,[a] and, therefore, a transfer to a neutral, before the peace, even without a judicial sentence of condemnation, is valid, if there has been no recovery or recaption before the peace. The intervention of peace cures all defects of title, and vests a lawful possession in the neutral, equally as the title of the enemy captor himself is quieted by the intervention of peace.[b] The title, in the hands of such a neutral, could not be defeated in favour of the original owner, even by his subsequently becoming an enemy. It would only be liable, with his other property, to be seized as prize of war.[c]

Every power is obliged to conform to these rules of the law of nations relative to postliminy, where the interests of neutrals are concerned. But in cases arising between her own subjects, or between them and those of her allies, the principle may undergo such modifications as policy dictates. Thus, by several English statutes, the maritime right of postliminy, as among English subjects, subsists to the end of the war; and, therefore, ships or goods, captured at sea by an enemy, and retaken at any period during the war, and whether before or after sentence of condemnation, are to be restored to the original proprietor, on securing to the recaptors certain rates of salvage, as a compensation or reward for the service they have performed.[d] The maritime law of England gives the benefit of this liberal rule of restitution, with respect to the recaptured property of her own subjects, to her allies, unless it appears that they act on a

---

a *Vattel*, b. 3. c. 14. sec. 216.
b Schooner Sophie, 6 *Rob.* 138.
c The Purissima Conception, 6 *Rob.* 45.
d 1 *Chitty on Comm. Law*, 435.

less liberal principle, and then it treats them according to their own measure of justice.* The allotment of salvage, on recapture or rescue, is a question not of municipal law merely, except as to the particular rates of it. It is a question of the *jus gentium*, when the subjects of allies or neutral states claim the benefit of the recaption. The restitution is a matter not of strict right, after the property has been vested in the enemy, but one of favour and relaxation; and the belligerent recaptor has a right to annex a reasonable condition to his liberality.* Neutral property, retaken from the enemy, is usually restored, without the payment of any salvage, unless, from the nature of the case, or the usages of the enemy, there was a probability that the property would have been condemned, if carried into the enemy's ports, and, in that case, a reasonable salvage ought to be allowed, for a benefit has been conferred.*

The United States, by the act of Congress of 3d March, 1800, directed restoration of captured property, at sea, to the foreign and friendly owner, on the payment of reasonable salvage; but the act was not to apply where the property had been condemned as prize by a competent court, before recapture; nor where the foreign government would not restore the goods or vessels of the citizens of the United States, under the like circumstances. The statute continued the *jus postliminii*, until the property was devested by a sentence of condemnation, and no longer; and this was the rule adopted in the English courts, before the extension of the right of postliminy by statutes, in the two last reigns.*

---

a The Santa Cruz, 1 *Rob.* 49.
b The Two Friends, 1 *Rob.* 271. *Marshall on Ins.* 474. *Doug.* 648.
c The War Onskan, 2 *Rob.* 299. The Carlotta, 5 *Rob.* 54.
d 2 *Burr.* 691. 1209. The L'Actif, 1 *Edw. Adm.* 186.

LECTURE VI.

OF THE GENERAL RIGHTS AND DUTIES OF NEUTRAL NATIONS.

The rights and duties which belong to a state of neutrality form a very interesting title in the code of international law. They ought to be objects of particular study in this country, inasmuch as it is our true policy to cherish a spirit of peace, and to keep ourselves free from those political connexions which would tend to draw us into the vortex of European contests. A nation that maintains a firm and scrupulously impartial neutrality, and commands the respect of all other nations by its prudence, justice, and good faith, has the best chance to preserve unimpaired the blessings of its commerce, the freedom of its institutions, and the prosperity of its resources. Belligerent nations are interested in the support of the just rights of neutrals, for the intercourse which is kept up by means of their commerce contributes greatly to mitigate the evils of war. The public law of Europe has established the principle, that, in time of war, countries not parties to the war, nor interposing in it, shall not be materially affected by its action; but they shall be permitted to carry on their accustomed trade, under the few necessary restrictions which we shall hereafter consider.

It belongs not to a common friend to judge between the belligerent parties, or to determine the question of right between them.[a] The neutral is not to favour one of them to the detriment of the other; and it is an essential charac-

---

[a] *Bynk.* l. 1. c. 9. *Burlamaqui,* vol. 2. part 4. c. 5. sec. 16, 17.

ter of neutrality, to furnish no aids to one party, which the neutral is not equally ready to furnish to the other. A nation which would be admitted to the privileges of neutrality, must perform the duties it enjoins. Even a loan of money to one of the belligerent parties, is considered to be a violation of neutrality.^a A fraudulent neutrality is no neutrality. But the neutral duty does not extend so far as to prohibit the fulfilment of antecedent engagements, which may be kept consistently with an exact neutrality, unless they go so far as to require the neutral nation to become an associate in the war.^b If a nation be under a previous stipulation, made in time of peace, to furnish a given number of ships or troops to one of the parties at war, the contract may be complied with, and the state of peace preserved. In 1788, Denmark furnished ships and troops to Russia, in her war with Sweden, in consequence of a previous treaty prescribing the amount, and this was declared by Denmark to be an act consistent with a spirit of amity and commercial intercourse with Sweden. It was answered by the latter, in her counter declaration, that though she could not reconcile the practice with the law of nations, yet she embraced the Danish declaration, and confined her hostility, so far as Denmark was concerned, to the Danish auxiliaries furnished to Russia.^c But if a neutral power be under contract to furnish succours to one party, he is said not to be bound if his ally was the aggressor; and in this solitary instance the neutral may examine into the merits of the war, so far as to see whether the *casus fœderis* exists.^d An inquiry of this kind, instituted by the party to the contract, for the purpose of determining on its binding obligation, holds out strong

---

a *Mr. Pickering's Letter to Messrs. Pinckney, Marshall, and Gerry, 2d of March,* 1798.

b *Vattel,* b. 3. c. 7. sec. 104, 105. *Mr. Jefferson's Letter to Mr. Pinckney, September 7th,* 1793.

c *New A. Reg.* for 1788, tit. Public Papers, p. 99.

d *Bynk. Q. J. P.* b. 1. c. 9. *Vattel,* b. 2. c. 12. sec. 168.

temptations to abuse; and, in the language of Mr. Jenkinson,[a] "when the execution of guaranties depends on questions like these, it will never be difficult for an ally, who hath a mind to break his engagements, to find an evasion to escape."

A neutral has a right to pursue his ordinary commerce, and he may become the carrier of the enemy's goods, without being subject to any confiscation of the ship, or of the neutral articles on board; though not without the risk of having the voyage interrupted by the seizure of the hostile property. As the neutral has a right to carry the property of enemies in his own vessel, so, on the other hand, his own property is inviolable, though it be found in the vessels of enemies. But the general inviolability of the neutral character goes further than merely the protection of neutral property. It protects the property of the belligerents when within the neutral jurisdiction. It is not lawful to make neutral territory the scene of hostility, or to attack an enemy while within it; and if the enemy be attacked, or any capture made under neutral protection, the neutral is bound to redress the injury, and effect restitution.[b] The books are full of cases recognising this principle of neutrality. In the year 1793, the British ship Grange was captured in Delaware bay by a French frigate, and, upon due complaint, the American government caused the British ship to be promptly restored.[c] So, in the case of the *Anna*,[d] the sanctity of neutral territory was fully asserted and vindicated, and restoration made of property captured by a British cruiser near the mouth of the Mississippi, and within the jurisdiction of the United States. It is a violation of

---

a Discourse on the Conduct of the Government of Great Britain in respect to neutral nations, 1757.

b *Grotius*, b. 3. c. 4. sec. 8. n. 2. *Bynk.* b. 1. c. 8. *Vattel*, b. 3. c. 7. sec. 132. *Burlamaqui*, vol. 2. part 4. c. 5. sec. 19.

c Mr. Jefferson's Letter to M. Ternant, of 15th May, 1793.

d 5 *Rob.* 373.

neutral territory, for a belligerent ship to take her station within it, in order to carry on hostile expeditions from thence, or to send her boats to capture vessels being beyond it. No use of neutral territory, for the purposes of war, can be permitted. This is the doctrine of the government of the United States.[a] It was declared judicially in England in the case of the *Twee Gebroeders*;[b] and though it was not understood that the prohibition extended to remote objects and uses, such as procuring provisions and other innocent articles, which the law of nations tolerated, yet it was explicitly declared, that no proximate acts of war were in any manner to be allowed to originate on neutral ground; and for a ship to station herself within the neutral line, and send out her boats on hostile enterprises, was an act of hostility much too immediate to be permitted. No act of hostility is to be commenced on neutral ground. No measure is to be taken that will lead to immediate violence. The neutral is to carry himself with perfect equality between both belligerents, giving neither the one nor the other any advantage; and if the respect due to neutral territory be violated by one party, without being promptly punished by just animadversion, it would soon provoke a similar treatment from the other party, and the neutral ground would become the theatre of war.

If a belligerent cruiser inoffensively passes over a portion of water lying within neutral jurisdiction, that is not usually considered such a violation of the territory as to affect and invalidate an ulterior capture made beyond it. The passage of ships over territorial portions of the sea, is a thing less guarded than the passage of armies on land, because less inconvenient, and permission to pass over them is not usually required or asked. To vitiate a subsequent capture, the

---

a Mr. Randolph's Circular to the Governors of the several states, April 16th, 1795.
b 3 Rob. 162.

passage must at least have been expressly refused, or the permission to pass obtained under false pretences.^a

The right of refusal of a pass over neutral territory to the troops of a belligerent power, depends more upon the inconvenience falling on the neutral state, than on any injustice committed to the third party, who is to be affected by the permission or refusal. It is no ground of complaint against the intermediate neutral state, if it grants a passage to belligerent troops, though inconvenience may thereby ensue to the adverse belligerent. It is a matter resting in the sound discretion of the neutral power, who may grant or withhold the permission, without any breach of neutrality.[b]

Bynkershoeck[c] makes one exception to the general inviolability of neutral territory, and supposes that if an enemy be attacked on hostile ground, or in the open sea, and flee within the jurisdiction of a neutral state, the victor may pursue him *dum fervet opus*, and seize his prize within the neutral state. He rests his opinion entirely on the authority and practice of the Dutch, and admits that he had never seen the distinction taken by the publicists, or in the practice of nations. It appears, however, that Casaregis, and several other foreign jurists mentioned by Azuni,[d] held a similar doctrine. But d'Abreu, Valin, Emerigon, Vattel, Azuni, and others, maintain the sounder doctrine, that when the flying enemy has entered neutral territory, he is placed immediately under the protection of the neutral power. The same broad principle that would tolerate a forcible entrance upon neutral ground or waters, in pursuit of the foe, would lead the pursuer into the heart of a commercial port. There is no exception to the rule, that every voluntary entrance into neutral territory, with hostile purposes, is abso-

---

[a] The Twee Gebroeders, 3 *Rob.* 336.
[b] *Grotius,* b. 2. c. 2. sec. 13. *Vattel,* b. 3. c. 7. sec. 119. 123. 127. Sir Wm. Scott, 3 *Rob.* 353.
[c] *Q. J. P.* b. 1. ch. 8.
[d] *Maritime Law,* vol. 2. 223. edit. N. Y.

lutely unlawful.[a] The neutral border must not be used as a shelter for making preparations to renew the attack; and though the neutral is not obliged to refuse a passage and safety to the pursued party, he ought to cause him to depart as soon as possible, and not to lie by and watch his opportunity for further contest. This would be making the neutral country directly auxiliary to the war, and to the comfort and support of one party. In the case of the *Anna*,[b] Sir William Scott was inclined to agree with Bynkershoeck to this extent: that if a vessel refused to submit to visitation and search, and fled within neutral territory, to places which were uninhabited, like the little mud islands before the mouth of the Mississippi, and the cruiser, without injury or annoyance to any person, should quietly take possession of his prey, he would not stretch the point so far, on that account only, as to hold the capture illegal. But, in this, as well as in every other case of the like kind, there is, *in stricto jure*, a violation of neutral jurisdiction, and the neutral power would have a right to insist on a restoration of the property. It was observed by the same high authority, in another case, depending on a claim of territory,[c] "that when the fact is established, it overrules every other consideration. The capture is done away; the property must be restored, notwithstanding that it may actually belong to the enemy."

A neutral has no right to inquire into the validity of a capture, except in cases in which the rights of neutral jurisdiction were violated; and, in such cases, the neutral power will restore the property, if found in the hands of the offender, and within its jurisdiction, regardless of any sentence of condemnation by a court of the belligerent captor.[d] It

---

[a] *Vattel*, b. 3. c. 7. sec. 133. 1 *Emerig. Traite des Ass.* 449. *Azuni*, vol. 2. 223.

[b] 5 *Rob.* 385.

[c] The Vrow Anna Catharina, 5 *Rob.* 15.

[d] The Arrogante Barcelones, 7 *Wheaton*, 496. *The Austrian Ordinance of Neutrality, August* 7, 1803, art. 18.

Lecture VI.] OF THE LAW OF NATIONS. 113

belongs solely to the neutral government to raise the objection to a capture and title, founded on the violation of neutral rights. The adverse belligerent has no right to complain, when the prize is duly libelled before a competent court.[a] If any complaint is to be made on the part of the captured, it must be by his government to the neutral government, for a fraudulent, or unworthy, or unnecessary submission to a violation of its territory, and such submission will naturally provoke retaliation. In the case of prizes brought within a neutral port, the neutral sovereign exercises jurisdiction so far as to restore the property of its own subjects, illegally captured; and this is done, says Valin,[b] by way of compensation for the asylum granted to the captor and his prize. It has been held, in this country, that foreign ships, offending against our laws, within our jurisdiction, may be pursued and seized upon the ocean, and rightfully brought into our ports for adjudication.[c]

The government of the United States was warranted by the law and practice of nations, in the declarations made in 1793, of the rules of neutrality, which it particularly recognised as necessary to be observed by the belligerent powers, in their intercourse with this country.[d] These rules were, that the original arming or equipping of vessels in our ports, by any of the powers at war, for military service, was unlawful; and no such vessel was entitled to an asylum in our ports. The equipment by them of government vessels of war, in matters which, if done to other vessels, would be applicable equally to commerce or war, was lawful. The equipment by them of vessels fitted for merchandise and war, and applicable to either, was lawful; but if it were of a nature solely applicable to war, it was un-

---

a 3 *Rob.* 162. note, case of the Etrusco.
b *Com.* tom. 2. 274.
c 11 *Wheaton*, 42.
d *Vattel*, b. 3. sec. 104. *Wolfius*, sec. 1174. *Austrian Ordinance of Neutrality*, August 7, 1803.

lawful. And if the armed vessel of one nation should depart from our jurisdiction, no armed vessel, being within the same, and belonging to an adverse belligerent power, should depart until twenty-four hours after the former, without being deemed to have violated the law of nations.^a Congress have repeatedly, by statute, made suitable provision for the support and due observance of similar rules of neutrality, and given sanction to the principle of them, as being founded in the universal law of nations. It is declared to be a misdemeanor for any person, within the jurisdiction of the United States, to increase or augment the force of any armed vessel, belonging to one foreign power at war with another power, with whom we are at peace; or to set on foot or prepare any military expedition, against the territory of any foreign nation with whom we were at peace; or to hire or enlist troops or seamen, for foreign military or naval service; or to be concerned in fitting out any vessel, to cruise or commit hostilities in foreign service, against a nation at peace with us; and the vessel, in this latter case, is made subject to forfeiture. The President of the United States is also authorized to employ force to compel any foreign vessel to depart, which, by the law of nations, or by treaty, ought not to remain within the United States, and to employ the public force generally, in enforcing the observance of the duties of neutrality prescribed by law.^b In the case of the *Santissima Trinidad*,^c it was decided, that captures made by a vessel so illegally fitted out, whether a public or private armed ship, were torts, and that the original owner was entitled to restitution, if the property was brought within our jurisdiction; but that an illegal outfit did

---

a *Instructions to the Collectors of the Customs, August 4th*, 1793. Mr. *Jefferson's Letters to M. Genet, of 5th and 17th June*, 1793. His *Letter to Mr. Morris, of 16th August*, 1793. Mr. *Pickering's Letter to Mr. Pinckney, Jan. 16th, 1797. His Letter to M. Adet, Jan. 20th, 1796.*

b *Acts of Congress of 5th June, 1794, and 20th April, 1818, ch. 88.*
c 7 *Wheaton*, 283.

not affect a capture made after the cruise to which the outfit had been applied had terminated. The offence was deposited with the voyage, and the *delictum* ended with the termination of the cruise.

Though a belligerent vessel may not enter within neutral jurisdiction, for hostile purposes, she may, consistently with a state of neutrality, until prohibited by the neutral power, bring her prize into a neutral port, and sell it.[a] The neutral power is, however, at liberty to refuse this privilege, provided the refusal be made, as the privilege ought to be granted, to both parties, or to neither. The United States, while a neutral power, frequently asserted the right to prohibit, at discretion, the sale, within their ports, of prizes brought in by the belligerents, and the sale of French prizes was allowed as an indulgence merely, until it interfered with the treaty with England of 1794, in respect to prizes made by privateers.[b] In the opinion of some jurists, it is more consistent with a state of neutrality, and the dictates of true policy, to refuse this favour; for it must be very inconvenient to permit the privateers of contending nations to assemble, together with their prizes, in a neutral port. The edict of the States General of 1656, forbid foreign cruisers to sell their prizes in their neutral ports, or to cause them to be unladen; and the French ordinance of the marine of 1681, contained the same prohibition, and that such vessels should not continue in port longer than twenty-four hours, unless detained by stress of weather.[c] The admission into neutral ports of the public ships of the belligerent parties, without prizes, is considered to be a favour, required on the

---

[a] *Bynk.* b. 1. c. 15. *Vattel*, b. 3. c. 7. sec. 132. *Martens*, b. 8. c. 6. sec. 6.

[b] *Instructions to the American Ministers to France, July* 15*th,* 1797. *Mr. Pickering's Letters to M. Adet, May* 24*th, and November* 15*th,* 1796. *His Letter to Mr. Pinckney, January* 16*th.* 1797.

[c] *Valin's Com.* tom. 2. 272.

principle of hospitality among friendly powers, and it has been uniformly conceded on the part of the United States.[a]

But neutral ships do not afford protection to enemy's property, and it may be seized if found on board of a neutral vessel, beyond the limits of the neutral jurisdiction. This is a clear and well settled principle of the law of nations.[b] It was formerly a question, whether the neutral ship conveying enemy's property, was not liable to confiscation for that cause. This was the old law of France, in cases in which the master of the vessel knowingly took on board enemy's property; but Bynkershoeck truly observes, that the master's knowledge is immaterial in this case, and that the rule in the Roman law, making the vessel liable for the fraudulent act of the master, was a mere fiscal regulation, and did not apply; and for the neutral to carry enemy's goods is not unlawful, like smuggling, and does not affect the neutral ship. If there be nothing unfair in the conduct of the neutral master, he will even be entitled to his reasonable demurrage, and his freight for the carriage of the goods, though he has not carried them to the place of destination. They are said to be seized and condemned, not *ex delicto*, but only *ex re*. The capture of them by the enemy, is a delivery to the person, who, by the rights of war, was substituted for the owner.[c] Bynkershoeck[d] thinks the master is not entitled to freight, because the goods were not carried to the port of destination, though he admits that the Dutch lawyers, and the *consolato*, give freight. But the allowance of freight in that case has been the uniform practice of the English admiralty for near two centuries past, except when

---

[a] Mr. Jefferson's Letter to Mr. Hammond, Sept. 9th, 1793. Instructions to the American Commissioners to France, July 15th, 1797.

[b] Grotius, l. 3. c. 6. sec. 6. Heinecc. de Nav. ob. vect. c. 2. sec. 9. Bynk. Q. J. Pub. c. 14. Vattel, b. 3. c. 7. sec. 115. Answer in 1753 to the Prussian Memorial. Consulat de la Mer, par Boucher, tom. 2. c. 276. sec. 1004.

[c] Vattel, b. 3. c. 7. sec. 115.

[d] C. 14.

there was some circumstance of *mala fides*, or a departure from a strictly proper neutral conduct.ᵃ The freight is paid, not *pro rata*, but *in toto*, because capture is considered as delivery, and the captor pays the whole freight, because he represents his enemy, by possessing himself of the enemy's goods *jure belli*, and he interrupts the actual delivery to the consignee.ᵇ

The right to take enemy's property on board a neutral ship, has been much contested by particular nations, whose interests it strongly opposed. This was the case with the Dutch in the war of 1756, and Mr. Jenkinson (afterwards Earl of Liverpool) published, in 1757, a discourse very full and satisfactory, on the ground of authority and usage, in favour of the legality of the right, when no treaty intervened to control it. The rule has been steadily maintained by Great Britain. In France it has been fluctuating. The ordinance of the marine of 1681, asserted the ancient and severe rule, that the neutral ship, having on board enemy's property, was subject to confiscation. The same rule was enforced by the arrets of 1692 and 1704, and relaxed by those of 1744 and 1778.ᶜ In 1780, the Empress of Russia proclaimed the principles of the Baltic code of neutrality, and declared she would maintain them by force of arms. One of the articles of that code was, that " all effects belonging to the subjects of the belligerent powers, should be looked upon as free on board of neutral ships, except only such goods as were contraband." The principal powers of Europe, as Sweden, Denmark, Prussia, Germany, Holland, France, Spain, Portugal, and Naples, and also these United States, acceded to the Russian principles of neutrality.ᵈ But the want of the consent of a power of such decided mari-

---

a *Jenkinson's Discourse in* 1757, p. 13. The *Atlas*, 3 *Rob.* 304. note. *Answer to the Prussian Memorial*, 1753.

b The *Copenhagen*, 1 *Rob.* 289.

c *Valin's Com.* l. 3. tit. 9. *des Prizes*, art. 7.

d *N. A. Reg.* for 1780, tit. Public Papers, p. 113—120. *Martens' Summary*, 327. edit. Phil. *Journals of Congress*, vol. 7. p. 68. 185.

time superiority as that of Great Britain, was an insuperable obstacle to the success of the Baltic conventional law of neutrality; and it was soon abandoned, as not being sanctioned by the existing law of nations, in every case in which the doctrines of that code did not rest upon positive compact. During the whole course of the wars growing out of the French revolution, the government of the United States admitted the English rule to be valid, as the true and settled doctrine of international law; and that enemy's property was liable to seizure on board of neutral ships, and to be confiscated as prize of war.[a] It has, however, been very usual in commercial treaties, to stipulate, that free ships should make free goods, contraband of war always excepted; but such stipulations are to be considered as resting on conventional law merely, and as exceptions to the operation of the general rule, which every nation not a party to the stipulation, is at perfect liberty to exact or surrender. The Ottoman Porte was the first power to abandon the ancient rule, and she stipulated, in her treaty with France in 1604, that free ships should make free goods, and she afterwards consented to the same provision in her treaty with Holland in 1612; and, according to Azuni,[b] Turkey has, at all times, on international questions, given an example of moderation to the more civilized powers of Europe.

The effort made by the Baltic powers in 1801, to recall and enforce the doctrines of the armed neutrality in 1780, was met, and promptly overpowered, and the confederacy dissolved, by the naval power of England. Russia gave up the point, and, by her convention with England of the 17th of June, 1801, expressly agreed, that enemy's property was not to be protected on board of neutral ships. The rule

---

[a] Mr. *Jefferson's Letter to M. Genet, July 24th,* 1793. Mr. *Pickering's Letter to Mr. Pinckney, January 16th,* 1797. *Letter of Messrs. Pinckney, Marshall, and Gerry, to the French government, January* 27*th,* 1798.

[b] *Maritime Law of Europe,* vol. 2. 163.

has since been very generally acquiesced in; and it was expressly recognised in the Austrian ordinance of neutrality, published at Vienna the 7th of August, 1803. Its reason and authority have been ably vindicated by English statesmen and jurists, and particularly by Mr. Ward, in his treatise *of the relative rights and duties of belligerent and neutral powers in maritime affairs*, published in 1801, and which exhausted all the law and learning applicable to the question.

It is also a principle of the law of nations relative to neutral rights, that the effects of neutrals, found on board of enemy's vessels, shall be free; and it is a right as fully and firmly settled as the other, though, like that, it is often changed by positive agreement.[a] The principle is to be met with in the *Consolato del Mare*, and the property of the neutral is to be restored without any compensation for detention, and the other necessary inconveniences incident to the capture. The former ordinances of France of 1543, 1584, and 1681, declared such goods to be lawful prize; and Valin[b] justifies the ordinances, on the ground, that the neutral, by putting his property on board of an enemy's vessel, favours the enemy's commerce, and agrees to abide the fate of the vessel. But it is fully and satisfactorily shown, by the whole current of modern authority, that the neutral has a perfect right to avail himself of the vessel of his friend, to transport his property; and Bynkershoeck has devoted an entire chapter to the vindication of the justice and equity of the right.[c]

---

a Grotius, b. 3. c. 6. and 16. *Bynk.* c. 13. *Vattel*, b. 3. c. 7. sec. 116. *Answer to the Prussian Memorial*, 1753. Mr. *Jefferson's Letter to M. Genet, July 24th*, 1793. Mr. *Pickering's Letter to Mr. Pinckney, January 16th*, 1797.

b Com: b. 3. tit. 9. *des Prizes*, art. 7.

a Consulat de la Mer, par Boucher, tom. 2. c. 276. sec. 1012, 1013. *Heineccius, de Nav. ob. vect.* c. 2. sec. 9. *Opera*, tom. 2. part 1. p. 349—355. *Vattel*, b. 3. c. 7. sec. 116. *Bynk*. c. 13.

The two distinct propositions, that enemy's goods found on board a neutral ship, may lawfully be seized as prize of war, and that the goods of a neutral found on board of an enemy's vessel, were to be restored, have been explicitly incorporated into the jurisprudence of the United States, and declared by the Supreme Court[a] to be founded in the law of nations. The rule, as it was observed by the Court, rested on the simple and intelligible principle, that war gave a full right to capture the goods of an enemy, but gave no right to capture the goods of a friend. The neutral flag constituted no protection to enemy's property, and the belligerent flag communicated no hostile character to neutral property. The character of the property depended upon the fact of ownership, and not upon the character of the vehicle in which it is found. After vindicating the simplicity and justice of the original rule of the law of nations, against the speculations of modern theorists, and the *ultima ratio* of the armed neutrality, which attempted to effect by force a revolution in the law of nations; the Court stated, that nations have changed this simple and natural principle of public law, by conventions between themselves, in whole or in part, as they believed it to be for their interest, but that the one proposition, that free ships should make free goods, did not necessarily imply the converse proposition, that enemy's ships should make enemy's goods. If a treaty established the one proposition, and was silent as to the other, the other stood precisely as if there had been no stipulation, and upon the ancient rule. The stipulation that neutral bottoms should make neutral goods, was a concession made by the belligerent to the neutral, and it gave to the neutral flag a capacity not given to it by the law of nations. On the other hand, the stipulation subjecting neutral property found in the vessel of an enemy to condemnation as prize of war, was a concession made by the neutral to the

---

[a] The Nereide, 9 *Cranch,* 388.

belligerent, and took from the neutral a privilege he possessed under the law of nations; but neither reason nor practice rendered the two concessions so indissoluble, that the one could not exist without the other. It rested entirely in the discretion of the contracting parties, whether either or both should be granted. The two propositions are distinct and independent of each other, and they have frequently been kept distinct by treaties, which stipulated for the one, and not for the other.

The government of the United States, in their recent negotiations with the republics in South America, have pressed very earnestly for the introduction and establishment of the principle of the Baltic code of 1780, that the friendly flag should cover the cargo; and this principle is incorporated into the treaty between the United States and Colombia, in 1825. The introduction of those new republics into the great community of civilized nations, has justly been deemed a very favourable opportunity to inculcate and establish, under their sanction, more enlarged and liberal doctrines on the subject of national rights. It has been the desire of our government to obtain the recognition of the fundamental principles, consecrated by the treaty with Prussia in 1785, relative to the perfect equality and reciprocity of commercial rights between nations; the abolition of private war upon the ocean; and the enlargement of the privileges of neutral commerce. The rule of public law, that the property of an enemy is liable to capture in the vessel of a friend, is now declared, on the part of our government, to have no foundation in natural right; and that the usage rests entirely on force. Though the high seas are a general jurisdiction, common to all, yet each nation has a special jurisdiction over its own vessels, and all the maritime nations of modern Europe, have, at times, acceded to the principle, that the property of an enemy should be protected in the vessel of a friend. No neutral nation, it is said, is bound to submit to the usage; and the neutral may have yielded, at one time, to the usage, without sacrificing the right to vindicate by force, the security of the neutral flag at another. The neutral right to cover enemy's property is conceded to be subject to this qualification: that a belligerent nation may justly refuse to neutrals the benefit of this principle, unless admitted also *by their enemy*, for the protection of her property, by the same neutral flag.[a]

But, whatever may be the utility or reasonableness of the neutral claim, under such a qualification, I should apprehend the belligerent right to be no longer an open question; and that the authority and usage on which that right rests in Europe, and the long, explicit, and authoritative admission of it by this country, have concluded us from making it a subject of controversy; and that we are bound, in truth and justice, to submit to its regular exercise, in every case, and with every belligerent power who does not freely renounce it.

It has been a matter of discussion, whether the captor of the enemy's vessel be entitled to freight from the owner of the neutral goods found on board, and restored. Under certain circumstances, the captor has been considered to be entitled to freight, even though the goods were carried to the claimant's own country, and restored; and he clearly is entitled to freight, if he performs the voyage, and carries the goods to the port of original destination. In no other case is freight due to the captor, and the doctrine of *pro rata* freight is entirely rejected, because it would involve a prize court in a labyrinth of minute inquiries and considerations, in the endeavour to ascertain, in every case, the balance of advantage or disadvantage, which an interruption and loss of the original voyage, by capture, might have produced to the owner of the goods.[b]

In the case of the *Nereide*, the Supreme Court of the United States carried the principle of immunity of neutral

---

[a] *Letter of Mr. Adams, Secretary of State, to Mr. Anderson*, 27th May, 1823. *President's Message to the Senate of 26th December*, 1825, and *to the House of Representatives, March 15th, 1826*.

[b] Bynk. Q. P. J. b. 1. ch. 13. The Fortuna, 4 Rob. 278. The Diana, 5 Rob. 67. Vrow Anna Catharina, 6 Rob. 269.

property on board an enemy's vessel, to the extent of allowing it to be laden on board an *armed* belligerent cruiser; and it was held, that the goods did not lose their neutral character, not even in consequence of resistance made by the armed vessel, provided the neutral did not aid in such armament or resistance, notwithstanding he had chartered the whole vessel, and was on board at the time of the resistance. The act of arming was the act of the belligerent party, and the neutral goods did not contribute to the armament, further than the freight, which would be paid if the vessel was unarmed, and neither the goods nor the neutral owner were chargeable for the hostile acts of the belligerent vessel, if the neutral took no part in the resistance. A contemporary decision of an opposite character, on the same point, was made by the English High Court of Admiralty in the case of the *Fanny*;" and it was there observed, that a neutral subject was at liberty to put his goods on board the merchant vessel of a belligerent; but if he placed them on board an armed belligerent ship, he showed an intention to resist visitation and search, by means of the association, and, so far as he does this, he was presumed to adhere to the enemy, and to withdraw himself from his protection of neutrality. If a neutral chooses to take the protection of a hostile force, instead of his own neutral character, he must take (it was observed) the inconvenience with the convenience, and his property would, upon just and sound principles, be liable to condemnation along with the belligerent vessel.

The question decided in the case of the *Nereide* is a very important one in prize law, and of infinite importance in its practical results; and it is to be regretted, that the decisions of two courts of the highest character, on such a point, should have been in direct contradiction to each other. The same point afterwards arose, and was again argued, and the former decision repeated, in the case of the *Atalanta*.[b] It

---

a 1 *Dodson*, 443.   *b* 3 *Wheaton*, 409.

was observed in this latter case, that the rule with us was correct in principle, and the most liberal and honourable to the jurisprudence of this country. The question may, therefore, be considered here as at rest, and as having received the most authoritative decision that can be rendered by any judicial tribunal on this side of the Atlantic.

LECTURE VII.

OF RESTRICTIONS UPON NEUTRAL TRADE.

The principal restriction which the law of nations imposes on the trade of neutrals, is the prohibition to furnish the belligerent parties with warlike stores, and other articles which are directly auxiliary to warlike purposes. Such goods are denominated contraband of war, but in the attempt to define them the authorities vary, or are deficient in precision, and the subject has long been a fruitful source of dispute between neutral and belligerent nations.

In the time of Grotius, some persons contended for the rigour of war, and others for the freedom of commerce. As neutral nations are willing to seize the opportunity which war presents, of becoming carriers for the belligerent powers, it is natural that they should desire to diminish the list of contraband as much as possible. Grotius distinguishes[a] between things which are useful only in war, as arms and ammunition, and things which serve merely for pleasure, and things which are of a mixed nature, and useful both in peace and war. He agrees with other writers in prohibiting neutrals from carrying articles of the first kind to the enemy, as well as in permitting the second kind to be carried. As to articles of the third class, which are of indiscriminate use in peace and war, as money, provisions, ships, and naval stores, he says that they are sometimes lawful articles of neutral commerce, and sometimes not; and the question will depend upon circumstances existing

---

[a] B. 3. c. 1. sec. 5.

at the time. They would be contraband if carried to a besieged town, camp, or port. In a naval war, it is admitted, that ships, and materials for ships, become contraband, and horses and saddles may be included.*a* Vattel speaks with some want of precision, and only says, in general terms,*b* that commodities particularly used in war, are contraband, such as arms, military and naval stores, timber, horses, and even provisions, in certain junctures, when there are hopes of reducing the enemy by famine. Loccenius,*c* and some other authorities referred to by Valin, consider provisions as generally contraband; but Valin and Pothier insist that they are not so, either by the law of France, or the common law of nations, unless carried to besieged or blockaded places.*d* The marine ordinance of Lewis XIV.*e* included horses, and their equipage, transported for military service, within the list of contraband, because they were necessary to war equipments, and this is, doubtless, the general rule. They are included in the restricted list of contraband articles mentioned in the treaty between the United States and Colombia in 1825. Valin says, that naval stores have been regarded as contraband from the beginning of the last century, and the English prize law is very explicit on this point. Naval stores, and materials for ship building, and even corn, grain, and victuals of all sorts, going to the dominions of the enemy, were declared contraband by an ordinance of Charles I. in 1626.*f* Sailcloth is now held to be universally contraband, even on a destination to ports of mere mercantile naval equipment;*g* and in the case of the *Maria*,*h* it was held, that

---

a Rutherforth's Inst. b. 2. c. 9.
b B. 3. c. 7. sec. 112.
c De Jure Maritimo, lib. 1. c. 4. n. 9.
d Valin's Com. tom. 2. p. 264. *Pothier, de Propriete*, No. 104.
e Des Prises, art. 11.
f Robinson's Collec. Mar. p. 63.
g The Neptunus, 3 *Rob.* 108.
h 1 *Rob.* 287. Phil. edit.

tar, pitch, and hemp, and whatever other materials went to the construction and equipment of vessels of war, were contraband by the modern law of nations, though, formerly, when the hostilities of Europe were less naval than at the present day, they were of a disputable nature. The executive government of this country has frequently conceded, that the materials for the building, equipment, and armament of ships of war, as timber and naval stores, were contraband.*a* But it does not seem, that ship timber is, *in se*, in all cases, to be considered a contraband article, though destined to an enemy's port. In the case of the Austrian vessel *Il Volante*, captured by the French privateer *L'Etoile de Bonaparte*, and which was carrying ship timber to Messina, an enemy's port, it was held, by the Council of Prizes at Paris, in 1807, upon the opinion of the Advocate General, M. Collet Descotils, that the ship timber in that case was not contraband of war, it being ship timber of an ordinary character, and not exclusively applicable to the building of ships of war.*b*

Questions of contraband were much discussed during the continuance of our neutral character, in the furious war between England and France, commencing in 1793, and we professed to be governed by the modern usage of nations on this point.*c* The national convention of France, on the 9th of May, 1793, decreed, that neutral vessels, laden with provisions, destined to an enemy's port, should be arrested, and carried into France; and one of the earliest acts of England in that war,*d* was to detain all neutral vessels going to France, and laden with corn, meal, or

---

a Mr. Randolph's Letter to M. Adet, July 6th, 1795. Mr. Pickering's Letter to Mr. Pinckney, January 16th, 1797. Letter of Messrs. Pinckney, Marshall, and Gerry, to the French Minister, January 27th, 1798.

b Repertoire universel et raisonne de Jurisprudence, par M. Merlin, tom. 9. tit. Prise Maritime, sec. 3. art. 3.

c President's Proclamation of Neutrality, April 22d, 1793.

d Instructions of 8th of June, 1793.

flour. It was insisted, on the part of England,^a that, by the law of nations, all provisions were to be considered as contraband, in the case where the depriving the enemy of those supplies was one of the means employed to reduce him to reasonable terms of peace; and that the actual situation of France was such, as to lead to that mode of distressing her, inasmuch as she had armed almost the whole labouring class of her people, for the purpose of commencing and supporting hostilities against all the governments of Europe. This claim on the part of England, was promptly and perseveringly resisted by the United States; and they contended, that corn, flour, and meal, being the produce of the soil, and labour of the country, were not contraband of war, unless carried to a place actually invested.^b The treaty of commerce with England, in 1794, in the list of contraband, stated, that whatever materials served directly to the building and equipment of vessels, with the exception of unwrought iron, and fir planks, should be considered contraband, and liable to confiscation; but the treaty left the question of provisions open and unsettled, and neither power was understood to have relinquished the construction of the law of nations, which it had assumed. The treaty admitted, that provisions were not generally contraband, but might become so, according to the existing law of nations, in certain cases, and those cases were not defined. It was only stipulated, by way of relaxation of the penalty of the law, that whenever provisions were contraband, the captors, or their government, should pay to the owner the full value of the articles, together with the freight, and a reasonable profit. Our government has repeatedly admitted, that as far as that treaty enumerated contraband arti-

---

a Mr. Hammond's Letter to Mr. Jefferson, September 12th, 1793, and his Letter to Mr. Randolph, 11th of April, 1794.
b Mr. Jefferson's Letter to Mr. Pinckney, September 7th, 1793, and Mr. Randolph's Letter to Mr. Hammond, May 1st, 1794.

cles, it was declaratory of the law of nations, and that the treaty conceded nothing on the subject of contraband.[a]

The doctrine of the English admiralty, on the subject of provisions being considered contraband, was laid down very fully and clearly, in the case of the *Jonge Margaretha*.[b] It was there observed, that the catalogue of contraband had varied very much, and, sometimes, in such a manner as to make it difficult to assign the reasons of the variations, owing to particular circumstances, the history of which had not accompanied the history of the decisions. In 1673, certain articles of provision, as corn, wine, and oil, were deemed contraband, according to the judgment of a person of great knowledge and experience in the practice of the admiralty; and, in much later times, many other sorts of provisions have been condemned as contraband. In 1747 and 1748, butter, and salted fish, and rice, were condemned as contraband; and those cases show that articles of human food have been considered as contraband, when it was probable they were intended for naval or military use. The modern established rule is, that provisions are not generally contraband, but may become so, under circumstances arising out of the particular situation of the war, or the condition of the parties engaged in it. Among the circumstances which tend to preserve provisions from being liable to be treated as contraband, one is, that they are of the growth of the country which produces them. Another circumstance to which some indulgence is shown by the practice of nations, is, when the articles are in their native and unmanufactured state. Thus, iron is treated with indulgence, though anchors, and other instruments fabricated out of it, are directly contraband. Hemp is more favourably considered than cordage;

---

[a] Mr. Pickering's *Letter to Mr. Monroe, September* 12th, 1795. *His Letter to Mr. Pinckney, January* 16th, 1797. *Instructions from the Secretary of State to the American Ministers to France, July* 15th, 1797.

[b] 1 *Rob.* 159. edit. Phil.

and wheat is not considered as so noxious a commodity, when going to an enemy's country, as any of the final preparations of it for human use. The most important distinction is, whether the articles were intended for the ordinary use of life, or even for mercantile ships' use, or whether they were going with a highly probable destination to military use. The nature and quality of the port to which the articles are going, is not an irrational test. If the port be a general commercial one, it is presumed the articles are going for civil use, though occasionally a ship of war may be constructed in that port. But if the great predominant character of that port, like Brest, in France, or Portsmouth, in England, be that of a port of naval military equipment, it will be intended that the articles were going for military use, although it is possible that the articles might have been applied to civil consumption. As it is impossible to ascertain the final use of an article *ancipitis usus*, it is not an injurious rule, which deduces the final use from the immediate destination; and the presumption of a hostile use, founded on its destination to a military port, is very much inflamed, if, at the time when the articles were going, a considerable armament was notoriously preparing, to which a supply of those articles would be eminently useful.

These doctrines of the English prize law were essentially the same with that adopted by the American Congress in 1775, for they declared, that all vessels, to whomsoever belonging, carrying provisions, or other necessaries, to the British army or navy, within the colonies, should be liable to seizure and confiscation.[a] They were likewise fully adopted by the Supreme Court of the United States, when we came to know and feel the value of belligerent rights, by becoming a party to a maritime war. In the case of the *Commercen*,[b] a neutral vessel, captured by one of our cruisers, in the act of carrying provisions for the use of the British armies in Spain, the court held, that provisions, being

---

[a] *Journals of Congress*, vol. 1. 241.   [b] 1 *Wheaton*, 382.

neutral property, but the growth of the enemy's country, and destined for the supply of the enemy's military or naval force, were contraband. The court observed, that, by the modern law of nations, provisions were not generally contraband, but that they might become so on account of the particular situation of the war, or on account of their destination. If destined for the ordinary use of life, in the enemy's country, they were not contraband; but it was otherwise if destined for the army or navy of the enemy, or for his ports of military or naval equipment. And if the provisions were the growth of the enemy's country, and destined for the enemy's use, they were to be treated as contraband, and liable to forfeiture, even though the army or navy were in a neutral port, for it would be a direct interposition in the war.

This case followed the decisions of Sir William Scott, and carried the doctrine of contraband, as applied to provisions, to as great an extent. It held the voyage of the Swedish neutral so illegal, as to deserve the infliction of the penalty of loss of freight.

It is the *usus bellici* which determines an article to be contraband; and as articles come into use as implements of war, which were before innocent, there is truth in the remark, that as the means of war vary and shift from time to time, the law of nations shifts with them; not, indeed, by the change of principles, but by a change in the application of them to new cases, and in order to meet the varying uses of war. When goods are once clearly shown to be contraband, confiscation to the captor is the natural consequence. This is the practice in all cases, as to the article itself, excepting provisions; and as to them, when they become contraband, the ancient and strict right of forfeiture is softened down to a right of pre-emption, on reasonable terms.[a] But, generally, to stop contraband goods, would, as Vattel observes,[b] prove an ineffectual relief, especially at sea. The penalty of confiscation is applied, in order that

---

[a] Case of the Haabet, 2 *Rob.* 182.   [b] B. 3. c. 7. sec. 113.

the fear of loss might operate as a check on the avidity for gain, and deter the neutral merchant from supplying the enemy with contraband articles. The ancient practice was, to seize the contraband goods, and keep them, on paying the value. But the modern practice of confiscation is far more agreeable to the mutual duties of nations, and more adapted to the preservation of their rights. It is a general understanding, grounded on true principles, that the powers at war may seize and confiscate all contraband goods, without any complaint on the part of the neutral merchant, and without any imputation of a breach of neutrality in the neutral sovereign himself.*a* It was contended, on the part of the French nation, in 1796, that neutral governments were bound to restrain their subjects from selling or exporting articles, contraband of war, to the belligerent powers. But it was successfully shown, on the part of the United States, that neutrals may lawfully sell, at home, to a belligerent purchaser, or carry, themselves, to the belligerent powers, contraband articles, subject to the right of seizure *in transitu.*b This right has since been explicitly declared by the judicial authorities of this country.*c* The right of the neutral to transport, and of the hostile power to seize, are conflicting rights, and neither party can charge the other with a criminal act.

Contraband articles are said to be of an infectious nature, and they contaminate the whole cargo belonging to the same owners. The innocence of any particular article is not usually admitted, to exempt it from the general confiscation. By the ancient law of Europe, the ship, also, was liable to condemnation; and such a penalty was deemed

---

a *Vattel*, b. 3. c. 7. sec. 113.

b *M. Adet's Letter to Mr. Pickering, March 11th, 1796. Mr. Pickering's Letters to M. Adet, January 20th, and May 25th, 1796. Circular Letter of the Secretary of the Navy to the Collectors, August 4th,* 1793.

c Richardson v. Marine Ins. Company, 6 *Mass. Rep.* 113. The Santissima Trinidad, 7 *Wheaton,* 283.

just, and supported by the general analogies of law, for the owner of the ship had engaged it in an unlawful commerce, and contraband goods are seized and condemned *ex delicto*. But the modern practice of the courts of admiralty, since the age of Grotius, is milder; and the fact of carrying contraband articles is attended only with the loss of freight and expenses, unless the ship belongs to the owner of the contraband articles, or the carrying of them has been connected with malignant and aggravating circumstances; and among those circumstances, a false destination and false papers are considered as the most heinous. In those cases, and in all cases of fraud in the owner of the ship, or of his agent, the penalty is carried beyond the refusal of freight and expenses, and is extended to the confiscation of the ship, and the innocent parts of the cargo.[a] This is now the established doctrine; but it is sometimes varied by treaty, in like manner as all the settled principles and usages of nations are subject to conventional modification.[b]

A neutral may also forfeit the immunities of his national character by violations of blockade; and, among the rights of belligerents, there is none more clear and incontrovertible, or more just and necessary in the application, than that which gives rise to the law of blockade. Bynkershoeck[c] says, it is founded on the principles of natural reason, as well as on the usage of nations; and Grotius[d] considers the carrying of supplies to a besieged town, or a blockaded port, as

---

[a] *Bynk*. Q. J. *Pub*. b. 1. ch. 12 and 14. *Heinec. de Nav. ob. Vect. Merc. vetit. Com*. ch. 2. sec. 6. *Opera*, tom. 2. 348. The Staadt Embden. 1 *Rob*. 23. The Jonge Tobias, 1 *Rob*. 277. The Franklin, 3 *Rob*. 217. The Neutralitat, 3 *Rob*. 295. The Edward, 4 *Rob*. 68. The Ranger, 6 *Rob*. 125.

[b] In the treaty between the United States and the Republic of Colombia, it is provided, that contraband articles shall not affect the rest of the cargo, or the vessel, for it is declared that they shall be left free to the owner.

[c] Q. J. P. b. 1. c. 4. sec. 11.

[d] B. 3. c. 1. sec. 5.

an offence exceedingly aggravated and injurious. They both agree, that the neutral may be dealt with severely; and Vattel says, he may be treated as an enemy.[a] The law of blockade is, however, so harsh and severe in its operation, that, in order to apply it, the fact of the actual blockade must be established by clear and unequivocal evidence; and the neutral must have had due previous notice of its existence; and the squadron allotted for the purposes of its execution, must be fully competent to cut off all communication with the interdicted place or port; and the neutral must have been guilty of some act of violation, either by going in, or attempting to enter, or by coming out with a cargo laden after the commencement of the blockade. The failure of either of the points requisite to establish the existence of a legal blockade, amounts to an entire defeasance of the measure, even though the notification of the blockade had issued from the authority of the government itself.[b]

A blockade must be existing in point of fact, and, in order to constitute that existence, there must be a power present to enforce it. All decrees and orders declaring extensive coasts, and whole countries, in a state of blockade, without the presence of an adequate naval force to support it, are manifestly illegal and void, and have no sanction in public law. The ancient authorities all referred to a strict and actual siege or blockade. The language of Grotius[c] is *oppidum obsessum vel Portus clausus*, and the investing power must be able to apply its force to every point of the blockaded place, so as to render it dangerous to attempt to enter, and there is no blockade of that part where its power cannot be brought to bear.[d] The definition of a blockade

---

a B. 3. c. 7. sec. 117.
b The Betsey, 1 *Rob.* 78. 1 *Chitty on Commercial Law*, 450.
c B. 3. c. 1. sec. 5.
c The Mercurius, 1 *Rob.* 67. The Betsey, 1 *Rob.* 78. The Stert, 4 *Rob.* 65. *Letter of the Secretary of the Navy to Commodore Preble, February 4th,* 1804.

given by the convention of the Baltic powers in 1780, and again in 1801, and by the ordinance of Congress in 1781, required that there should be actually a number of vessels stationed near enough to the port to make the entry apparently dangerous. The government of the United States have uniformly insisted, that the blockade should be effective by the presence of a competent force, stationed, and present, at or near the entrance of the port; and they have protested with great energy against the application of the right of seizure and confiscation to ineffectual or fictitious blockades.[a]

The occasional absence of the blockading squadron, produced by accident, as in the case of a storm, and when the station is resumed with due diligence, does not suspend the blockade, provided the suspension, and the reason of it, be known; and the law considers an attempt to take advantage of such an accidental removal, as an attempt to break the blockade, and as a mere fraud.[b] The American government seemed disposed to admit the continuance of the blockade in such a case;[c] and the language of the judicial authorities in this state, has been in favour of the solidity and justness of the English doctrine of blockade on this point.[d] But if the blockade be raised by the enemy, or by applying the naval force, or part of it, though only for a time, to other objects, or by the mere remissness of the cruisers, the commerce of neutrals to the place ought to be free. The presence of a sufficient force is the natural cri-

---

[a] Mr. King's Letter to Lord Grenville, May 23d, 1799. Mr. Marshall's Letter to Mr. King, September 20th, 1799. Mr. Madison's Letter to Mr. Pinckney, October 25th, 1801. Letter of the Secretary of the Navy to Commodore Preble, February 4th, 1804. Mr. Pinckney's Letter to Lord Wellesley, January 14th, 1811.

[b] The Frederick Molke, 1 *Rob.* 72. The Columbia, 1 *Rob.* 130. The Juffrow Maria Schroeder, 3 *Rob.* 155. The Hoffnung, 6 *Rob.* 116, 7.

[c] Mr. Marshall's Letter to Mr. King, September 20th, 1799.

[d] Radcliff, J. 2 *Johnson's Cases*, 187. Radcliff v. U. Ins. Co. 7 *Johnson's Rep.* 38.

terion by which the neutral is enabled to ascertain the existence of the blockade. He looks only to the matter of fact, and if the blockading squadron is removed when he arrives before the port, and he is ignorant of the cause of the removal, or if he be not ignorant, and the cause be not an accidental one, but voluntary, or produced by an enemy, he may enter, without being answerable for a breach of the blockade. When a blockade is raised voluntarily, or by a superior force, it puts an end to it absolutely; and if it be resumed, neutrals must be charged with notice *de novo*, and without reference to the former state of things, before they can be involved in the guilt of a violation of the blockade.[a]

The object of a blockade is not merely to prevent the importation of supplies, but to prevent export as well as import, and to cut off all communication of commerce with the blockaded port. The act of egress is as culpable as the act of ingress, if it be done fraudulently; and a ship coming out of a blockaded port is, in the first instance, liable to seizure, and to obtain a release, the party must give satisfactory proof of the innocence of his intention.[b] But, according to modern usage, a blockade does not rightfully extend to a neutral vessel found in port when the blockade was instituted, nor prevent her coming out with the cargo, *bona fide* purchased, and laden on board before the commencement of the blockade.[c] The modern practice does not require that the place should be invested by land as well as by sea, in order to constitute a legal blockade; and if a place be blockaded by sea only, it is no violation of

---

[a] Williams v. Smith, 2 *Caines*, 1. *Letter of the Secretary of State to Mr. King, September 20th,* 1799. The Hoffnung, 6 *Rob.* 112.

[b] *Bynk. Q. J. P.* b. 1. ch. 4. The Frederick Molke, 1 *Rob.* 72. The Neptunus, 1 *Rob.* 144. The Vrow Judith, 1 *Rob.* 126.

[c] The Betsey, 1 *Rob.* 78. The Vrow Judith, 1 *Rob.* 126. The Comet, 1 *Edw.* 32. Olivera v. Union Ins. Com. 3 *Wheaton*, 183.

belligerent rights for the neutral to carry on commerce with it by inland communications.ª

It is absolutely necessary that the neutral should have had due notice of the blockade, in order to affect him with the penal consequences of a violation of it. This information may be communicated to him in two ways: either actually, by a formal notice from the blockading power; or constructively, by notice to his government, or by the notoriety of the fact. It is immaterial in what way the neutral comes to the knowledge of the blockade. If the blockade actually exists, and he has knowledge of it, he is bound not to violate it. A notice to a foreign government, is a notice to all the individuals of that nation, and they are not permitted to aver ignorance of it, because it is the duty of the neutral government to communicate the notice to their people.ᵇ In the case of a blockade without regular notice, notice in fact is generally requisite; and there is this difference between a blockade regularly notified, and one without such notice: that, in the former case, the act of sailing for the blockaded place, with an intent to evade it, or to enter contingently, amounts, from the very commencement of the voyage, to a breach of the blockade, for the port is to be considered as closed up, until the blockade be formally revoked, or actually raised; whereas, in the latter case of a blockade *de facto*, the ignorance of the party as to its continuance, may be received as an excuse for sailing to the blockaded place, on a doubtful and provisional destination.ᶜ The question of notice is a question of evidence, to be determined by the facts applicable to the case. The notoriety of a blockade is of itself sufficient notice of it to vessels lying within the blockaded port. In the case of the *Adelaide*,ᵈ it was the doctrine of the English admiralty,

---

a The Ocean, 3 *Rob.* 297. The Stert, *ibid.* 299. note. *Letter of the Secretary of State to Mr. King, Sept. 20th, 1799.*

b The Neptunus, 2 *Rob.* 110. The Adelaide, 2 *Rob.* 111. note.

c The Columbia, 1 *Rob.* 130. The Neptunus, 2 *Rob.* 110.

d 2 *Rob.* 111. *in notis.*

that a notification given to one state, must be presumed, after a reasonable time, to have reached the subjects of neighbouring states, and it affects them with the knowledge of the fact, on just grounds of evidence. And after the blockade is once established, and due notice received, either actually or constructively, the neutral is not permitted to go to the very station of the blockading force, under pretence of inquiring whether the blockade had terminated, because this would lead to fraudulent attempts to evade it, and would amount, in practice, to a universal license to attempt to enter, and, on being prevented, to claim the liberty of going elsewhere. Some relaxation was very reasonably given to this rule, in its application to distant voyages from America; and ships sailing for Europe before knowledge of the blockade reached them, were entitled to notice, even at the blockaded port. If they sailed after notice, they might sail on a contingent destination for the blockaded port, with the purpose of calling for information at some European port, and be allowed the benefit of such a contingent destination, to be rendered definite by the information. But in no case is the information as to the existence of the blockade, to be sought at the mouth of the port.[a]

A neutral cannot be permitted to place himself in the vicinity of the blockaded port, if his situation be so near that he may, with impunity, break the blockade whenever he pleases, and slip in without obstruction. If that were to be permitted, it would be impossible that any blockade could be maintained. It is a presumption, almost *de jure*, that the neutral, if found on the interdicted waters, goes there with an intention to break the blockade; and it would require very clear and satisfactory evidence to repel the presumption of a criminal intent.[b]

---

[a] The Spes and Irene, 5 *Rob.* 76.
[b] The Neutralitat, 6 *Rob.* 30. The Charlotte Christine, *ibid.* 101. The Gute Erwartung, *ibid.* 182. Bynk. Q. J. Pub. b. 1. c. 11. The Arthur, 1 *Edw. Rep.* 202. Radcliff v. U. Ins. Co. 7 *Johnson's Rep.* 47. Fitzsimmons v. Newport Ins. Co. 4 *Cranch*, 185.

The judicial decisions in England, and in this country, have given great precision to the law of blockade, by the application of it to particular cases, and by the extent, and clearness, and equity of their illustrations. They are distinguished, likewise, for general coincidence and harmony in their principles. All the cases admit, that the neutral must be chargeable with knowledge, either actual or constructive, of the existence of the blockade, and with an intent, and with some attempt, to break it, before he is to suffer the penalty of a violation of it. The evidence of that intent, and of the overt act, will greatly vary, according to circumstances; and the conclusion to be drawn from those circumstances will depend, in some degree, upon the character and judgment of the prize courts; but the true principles which ought to govern, have rarely been a matter of dispute. The fact of clearing out or sailing for a blockaded port, is, in itself, innocent, unless it be accompanied with knowledge of the blockade. Such a vessel, not possessed of such previous knowledge, is to be first warned of the fact, and a subsequent attempt to enter constitutes the breach. This was the provision in the treaty with England in 1794, and it has been declared in other cases, and is considered to be a correct exposition of the law of nations.[a]

It has been a question in the courts in this country, whether they ought to admit the law of the English prize courts, that sailing for a blockaded port, knowing it to be blockaded, was, in itself, an attempt, and an act sufficient to charge the party with a breach of the blockade, without reference to the distance between the port of departure and the port invested, or to the extent of the voyage performed when the vessel was arrested.[b] But in *Yeaton* v. *Fry*,[c] the Supreme

---

[a] Fitzsimmons v. Newport Ins. Co. 4 *Cranch*, 185. *British Instructions to their fleets on the West India station, 5th of January, 1804. Letter of the Secretary of the Navy to Commodore Preble, February 4th, 1804.*

[b] Fitzsimmons v. Newport Ins. Co. 4 *Cranch*, 185. Voss & Graves v. U. Ins. Co. 2 *Johnson's Cases*, 180. 469.

[c] 5 *Cranch*, 335.

Court of the United States coincided essentially with the doctrine of the English prize courts, for they held, that sailing from Tobago for Curracoa, knowing the latter to be blockaded, was a breach of the blockade; and, according to the opinion of Mr. Justice Story, in the case of the *Nereide*,[a] the act of sailing with an intent to break a blockade, is a sufficient breach to authorize confiscation. The offence continues, although, at the moment of capture, the vessel be, by stress of weather, driven in a direction from the port, for the hostile intention still remains unchanged. The distance, or proximity of the two ports, would certainly have an effect upon the equity of the application of the rule. A Dutch ordinance, in 1630, declared, that vessels bound to the blockaded ports of Flanders, were liable to confiscation, though found at a distance from them, unless they had voluntarily altered the voyage before coming in sight of the port, and Bynkershoeck contends for the reasonableness of the order.[b] What that distance must be is not defined; and if the ports be not very wide apart, the act of sailing for the blockaded port may reasonably be deemed evidence of a breach of it, and an overt act of fraud upon the belligerent rights. But a relaxation of the rule has been required and granted in the case of distant voyages, such as those across the Atlantic, and the vessel is allowed to sail on a contingent destination, subject to the duty of subsequent inquiry at suitable places.[c] The ordinance of Congress of 1781, seems to have conceded this point to the extent of the English rule, for it made it lawful to take and condemn all vessels, of all nations, " destined to any such port," without saying any thing of notice or proximity.[d]

The consequence of a breach of blockade is the confis-

---

a 9 *Cranch*, 440. 446.
b Q. J. P. b. 1. c. 11. 3 *Rob.* 326. *in notis*.
c 5 *Rob.* 76. 6 *Cranch*, 29.
d *Journals of Congress*, vol. 7. p. 186.

cation of the ship, and the cargo is always, *prima facie*, implicated in the guilt of the owner, or master of the ship, and it lays with them to remove the presumption, that the vessel was going in for the benefit of the cargo, and with the direction of the owner.ᵃ The old doctrine was much more severe, and often inflicted, not merely a forfeiture of the property taken, but imprisonment, and other personal punishment;ᵇ but the modern, and milder usage, has confined the penalty to the confiscation of the ship and goods. If a ship has contracted guilt by a breach of blockade, the offence is not discharged until the end of the voyage. The penalty never travels on with the vessel further than to the end of the return voyage, and if she is taken in any part of that voyage, she is taken *in delicto*. This is deemed reasonable, because no other opportunity is afforded to the belligerent force to vindicate the law.ᶜ The penalty for a breach of blockade is also held to be remitted, if the blockade has been raised before the capture. The *delictum* is completely done away when the blockade ceases.ᵈ

There are other acts of illegal assistance afforded to a belligerent, besides supplying him with contraband goods, and relieving his distress under a blockade. Among these acts, the conveyance of hostile despatches is the most injurious, and deemed to be of the most hostile and noxious character. The carrying of two or three cargoes of stores, is necessarily an assistance of a limited nature; but in the transmission of despatches may be conveyed the entire plan of a campaign, and it may lead to a defeat of all the projects of the other belligerent in that theatre of the war. The appropriate remedy for this offence is the confiscation of the ship,

---

a 1 *Rob.* 67. The Mercurius. *Ibid.* 180. The Columbia. 3 *Rob.* 173. The Neptunus. 4 *Rob.* 95. The Alexander. 1 *Edw.* 39. The Exchange.

b Bynk. Q. J. P. b. 1. c. 11.

c 2 *Rob.* 128. The Welvaart Van Pillaw. 3 *Rob.* 147. The Juffrow Maria Schroeder.

d 6 *Rob.* 387. The Lisette.

and, in doing so, the courts make no innovation on the ancient law, but they only apply established principles to new combinations of circumstances. There would be no penalty in the mere confiscation of the despatches. The proper and efficient remedy is the confiscation of the vehicle employed to carry them; and if any privity subsists between the owners of the cargo and the master, they are involved by implication in his delinquency. If the cargo be the property of the proprietor of the ship, then, by the general rule, *ob continentiam delicti*, his other property shares the same fate, and especially if there was an active interposition in the service of the enemy, concerted and continued in fraud.[a]

A distinction has been made between carrying despatches of the enemy between different parts of his dominions, and carrying despatches of an ambassador from a neutral country to his own sovereign. The effect of the former despatches is presumed to be hostile; but the neutral country has a right to preserve its relations with the enemy, and it does not necessarily follow that the communications are of a hostile nature. Ambassadors resident in a neutral country, are favourite objects of the protection of the law of nations, and their object is to preserve the relations of amity between the governments, and the presumption is that the neutral state preserves its integrity, and is not concerned in any hostile design.[b]

In order to enforce the rights of belligerent nations against the delinquencies of neutrals, and to ascertain the real as well as assumed character of all vessels on the high seas, the law of nations arms them with the practical power of visitation and search. The duty of self preservation gives to belligerent nations this right. It is founded upon necessity, and is strictly and exclusively a war right, and does not exist in time of peace. All writers upon the law of nations, and the highest authorities, acknowledge the right as resting on sound principles of public jurisprudence, and upon the

---

[a] The Atalanta, 6 *Rob.* 440. [b] The Caroline, 6 *Rob.* 461.

institutes and practice of all great maritime powers.^a And if, upon making the search, the vessel be found employed in contraband trade, or in carrying enemy's property, or troops, or despatches, she is liable to be taken and brought in for adjudication before a prize court.

Neutral nations have frequently been disposed to question and resist the exercise of this right. This was particularly the case with the Baltic confederacy, during the American war, and with the convention of the Baltic powers in 1801. The right of search was denied, and the flag of the state was declared to be a substitute for all documentary and other proof, and to exclude all right of search. Those powers armed for the purpose of defending their neutral pretensions; and England did not hesitate to consider it as an attempt to introduce, by force, a new code of maritime law, inconsistent with her belligerent rights, and hostile to her interests, and one which would go to extinguish the right of maritime capture. The attempt was speedily frustrated and abandoned, and the right of search has, since that time, been considered incontrovertible.

The whole doctrine was very ably discussed in the English High Court of Admiralty, in the case of the *Maria*;[b] and it was adjudged, that the right was incontestable, and that a neutral sovereign could not, by the interposition of force, vary that right. Two powers may agree among themselves, that the presence of one of their armed ships along with their merchant ships, shall be mutually understood to imply that nothing is to be found, in that convoy of merchant ships, inconsistent with amity or neutrality. But no belligerent power can legally be compelled, by mere force, to accept of such a pledge; and every belligerent power who is no party to the agreement, has a right to insist on the only security known to the law of nations on this subject, independent of

---

a Vattel, b. 3. c. 7. sec. 114. The Maria, 1 *Rob.* 287. 2 *Dodson's Adm. Rep.* 245. 11 *Wheaton*, 42.
b 1 *Rob.* 287.

any special covenant, and that is the right of personal visitation and search, to be exercised by those who have an interest in making it. The penalty for the violent contravention of this right, is the confiscation of the property so withheld from visitation; and the infliction of this penalty is conformable to the settled practice of nations, as well as to the principles of the municipal jurisprudence of most countries in Europe. There may be cases in which a neutral ship may be authorized, by the natural right of self-preservation, to defend himself against extreme violence threatened by a cruiser, grossly abusing his commission; but, except in extreme cases, a merchant vessel has no right to say for itself, and an armed vessel has no right to say for it, that it will not submit to visitation or search, or to be carried into a proximate court for judicial inquiry. Upon these principles, a fleet of Swedish merchant ships, sailing under convoy of a Swedish ship of war, and under instructions from the Swedish government, to resist, by force, the right of search claimed by British lawfully commissioned cruisers, was condemned. The resistance of the convoying ship was a resistance of the whole convoy, and justly subjected the whole to confiscation.[a]

The doctrine of the English admiralty on the right of visitation and search, and on the limitation of the right, has been recognised in its fullest extent by the courts of justice in this country.[b] The very act of sailing under the protection of a belligerent, or neutral convoy, for the purpose of resisting search, is a violation of neutrality. The Danish government asserted the same principle in its correspondence with the government of the United States, and in the royal instructions of the 10th of March, 1810;[c] and none

---

[a] The Maria, 1 *Rob.* 287. The Elsebe, 4 *Rob.* 408.

[b] The Nereide, 9 *Cranch*, 427. 438. 443. 445. 453. The Marianna Flora, 11 *Wheaton*, 42.

[c] 4 Hall's L. Journal, 263. *Letters of Count Rosenkrantz to Mr. Erving, 28th and 30th of June, and 9th of July,* 1811.

of the powers of Europe have called in question the justice of the doctrine.[a] Confiscation is applied by way of penalty for resistance of search to all vessels, without any discrimination as to the national character of the vessel or cargo, and without separating the fate of the cargo from that of the ship.

This right of search is confined to private merchant vessels, and does not apply to public ships of war. Their immunity from the exercise of any jurisdiction but that of the sovereign power to which they belong, is uniformly asserted, claimed, and conceded. A contrary doctrine is not to be found in any jurist or writer on the law of nations, or admitted in any treaty, and every act to the contrary has been promptly met and condemned.[b]

The exercise of the right of visitation and search must be conducted with due care, and regard to the rights and safety of the vessel.[c] If the neutral has acted with candour and good faith, and the inquiry has been wrongfully pursued, the belligerent cruiser is responsible to the neutral in costs and damages, to be assessed by the prize court which sustains the judicial examination. The mere exercise of the right of search involves the cruiser in no trespass, for it is strictly lawful. But if he proceeds to capture the vessel as prize, and sends her in for adjudication, and there was no probable cause, he is responsible. It is not the search, but the subsequent capture, which is treated in such a case as a tortious act.[d] If the capture be justifiable, the subsequent

---

[a] The Austrian ordinance of neutrality of August 7th, 1803, enjoined it upon all their vessels to submit to visitation on the high seas, and not to make any difficulty as to the production of the documentary proofs of property.

[b] *Thurloe's State Papers*, vol. 2. p. 503. *Mr. Canning's Letter to Mr. Monroe, August 3d*, 1807. *Edinburgh Review for October*, 1807, art. 1.

[c] The Anna Maria, 2 *Wheaton*, 327.

[d] 2 *Mason*, 439.

detention for adjudication is never punished with damages; and in all cases of marine torts, courts of admiralty exercise a large discretion in giving or withholding damages.*a*

A rescue effected by the crew, after capture, and when the captors are in actual possession, is unlawful, and considered to be a resistance within the application of the penalty of confiscation, for it is a delivery by force from force.*b* And where the penalty attaches at all, it attaches as completely to the cargo as to the ship, for the master acted as agent of the owner of the cargo, and his resistance was a fraudulent attempt to withdraw it from the rights of war.*c*

A neutral is bound not only to submit to search, but to have his vessel duly furnished with the genuine documents requisite to support her neutral character.*d* The most material of these documents are, the register, passport, sea letter, muster roll, log book, charter party, invoice, and bill of lading. The want of some of these papers is strong presumptive evidence against the ship's neutrality; yet the want of any one of them is not absolutely conclusive.*e* *Si aliquid ex solemnibus deficiat, cum equitas poscit, subveniendum est.* The concealment of papers material for the preservation of the neutral character, justifies a capture, and carrying into port for adjudication, though it does not absolutely require a condemnation. It is good ground to refuse costs and damages on restitution, or to refuse further proof to relieve the obscurity of the case, where the cause laboured under heavy doubts, and there was *prima facie* ground for condemnation independent of the concealment.*f* The

---

a 11 *Wheaton*, 54—56.

b The Despatch, 8 *Rob.* 295. Brown v. Union Ins. Co. 5 *Day's Rep.* 1.

c The Catharina Elizabeth, 5 *Rob.* 232.

d *Answer to the Prussian Memorial*, 1753.

e *Danish Instructions*, 10th March, 1810. 8 *Term*, 434. 4 *Taunton*, 367.

f Livingston & Gilchrist v. Mar. Ins. Co. 7 *Cranch*, 544.

spoliation of papers is a still more aggravated and inflamed circumstance of suspicion. That fact may exclude further proof, and be sufficient to infer guilt; but it does not in England, as it does by the maritime law of other countries, create an absolute presumption *juris et de jure;* and yet, a case that escapes with such a brand upon it, is saved so as by fire.[a] The Supreme Court of the United States has followed the less rigorous English rule, and held that the spoliation of papers was not, of itself, sufficient ground for condemnation, and that it was a circumstance open for explanation, for it may have arisen from accident, necessity, or superior force.[b] If the explanation be not prompt and frank, or be weak and futile; if the cause labours under heavy suspicions, or there be a vehement presumption of bad faith, or gross prevarication, it is good cause for the denial of further proof; and the condemnation ensues from defects in the evidence, which the party is not permitted to supply. The observation of Lord Mansfield, in *Bernardi* v. *Motteaux,*[c] was to the same effect. By the maritime law of all countries, he said, throwing papers overboard was considered as a strong presumption of enemy's property; but, in all his experience, he had never known a condemnation on that circumstance only.

---

a The Hunter, 1 *Dodson,* 480.
b The Pizarro, 2 *Wheaton,* 227.
c *Doug.* 581.

LECTURE VIII.

OF TRUCES, PASSPORTS, AND TREATIES OF PEACE.

Having considered the rights and duties appertaining to a state of war, I proceed to examine the law of nations relative to negotiations, conventions, and treaties, which either partially interrupt the war, or terminate in peace.

(1.) A truce, or suspension of arms, does not terminate the war, but it is one of the *commercia belli* which suspends its operations. These conventions rest upon the obligation of good faith, and as they lead to pacific negotiations, and are necessary to control hostilities, and promote the cause of humanity, they are sacredly observed by civilized nations.

A particular truce is only a partial cessation of hostilities, as between a town and an army besieging it. But a general truce applies to the operations of the war; and if it be for a long or indefinite period of time, it amounts to a temporary peace, which leaves the state of the contending parties, and the questions between them, remaining in the same situation as it found them. A partial truce may be made by a subordinate commander, and it is a power necessarily implied in the nature of his trust; but it is requisite to a general truce, or suspension of hostilities throughout the nation, or for a great length of time, that it be made by the sovereign of the country, or by his special authority.[a] The general principle on the subject is, that if a commander makes a compact

---

[a] *Vattel*, b. 3. c. 16. sec. 233—288. *Grotius*. b. 3. c. 21.

with the enemy, and it be of such a nature that the power to make it could be reasonably implied from the nature of the trust, it would be valid and binding, though he abused his trust. The obligation he is under not to abuse his trust, regards his own state, and not the enemy.[a]

A truce binds the contracting parties from the time it is concluded, but it does not bind the individuals of the nation so as to render them personally responsible for a breach of it, until they have had actual or constructive notice of it. Though an individual may not be held to make pecuniary compensation for a capture made, or destruction of property, after the suspension of hostilities, and before notice of it had reached him, yet the sovereign of the country is bound to cause restoration to be made of all prizes made after the date of a general truce. To prevent the danger and damage that might arise from acts committed in ignorance of the truce, it is common and proper to fix a prospective period for the cessation of hostilities, with a due reference to the distance and situation of places.[b]

A truce only temporarily stays hostilities; and each party to it may, within his own territories, do whatever he would have a right to do in time of peace. He may continue active preparations for war, by repairing fortifications, levying and disciplining troops, and collecting provisions, and articles of war. He may do whatever, under all the circumstances, would be deemed compatible with good faith, and the spirit of the agreement; but he is justly restrained from doing what would be directly injurious to the enemy, and could not safely be done in the midst of hostilities. Thus, in the case of a truce between the governor of a fortified town, and the army besieging it, neither party is at liberty to continue works, constructed either for attack or defence, and which could not safely be done if hostilities had

---

[a] *Rutherforth*, b. 2. c. 9. *Vattel*, b. 3. c. 16. sec. 261. *Grotius*, b. 3. c. 22. sec. 4.
[b] *Vattel*, b. 3. c. 15. sec. 239. 244.

continued; for this would be to make a mischievous and fraudulent use of the cessation of arms. So, it would be a fraud upon the rights of the besieging army, and an abuse of the armistice, for the garrison to avail themselves of the truce to introduce provision and succours into the town, in a way, or through passages, which the besieging army would have been competent to prevent.[a] The meaning of every such compact is, that all things should remain as they were in the places contested, and of which the possession was disputed, at the moment of the conclusion of the truce.[b]

At the expiration of the truce, hostilities may recommence without any fresh declaration of war; but if it be for an indefinite time, justice and good faith would require due notice of an intention to terminate it.[c]

Grotius and Vattel,[d] as well as other writers on national law, have agitated the question, whether a truce for a given period, as, for instance, from the first of January to the first of February, will include or exclude the first day of each of those months. Grotius says, that the day from whence a truce is to be computed, is not one of the days of the truce, but that it will include the whole of the first day of February, as being the day of its termination. Vattel, on the other hand, is of opinion, that the day of the commencement of the truce would be included, and as the time ought to be taken largely and liberally, for the sake of humanity, the last day mentioned would also be included. Every ambiguity of this kind ought always to be prevented, by positive and precise stipulations, as from such a day to such a day, both inclusive.

(2.) A passport, or safe conduct, is a privilege granted in war, and exempting the party from the effects of its operation, during the time, and to the extent prescribed in the

---

a *Vattel*, b. 3. c. 16. sec. 247, 248.
b *Ibid.* sec. 250.
c *Ibid.* b. 3. c. 16. sec. 260.
d *Grotius*, b. 3. c. 21. sec. 4. *Vattel*, b. 3. c. 16. sec. 244.

permission. It flows from the sovereign authority; but the power of granting a passport may be delegated by the sovereign to persons in subordinate command, and they are invested with that power either by an express commission, or by the nature of their trust.[a] The general of an army, from the very nature of his power, can grant safe conducts; but the permission is not transferable by the person named in the passport, for it may be that the government had special reasons for granting the privilege to the very individual named, and it is to be presumed to be personal. If the safe conduct be granted, not for persons, but for effects, those effects may be removed by others besides the owner, provided no person be selected as the agent, against whom there may exist a personal objection sufficient to render him an object of suspicion or danger within the territories of the power granting the permission.

He who promises security, by a passport, is morally bound to afford it against any of his subjects or forces, and to make good any damage the party might sustain by a violation of the passport. The privilege being so far a dispensation from the legal effects of war, it is always to be taken strictly, and must be confined to the purpose, and place, and time for which it was granted. A safe conduct generally includes the necessary baggage and servants of the person to whom it is granted; and to save doubt and difficulty, it is usual to enumerate, with precision, every particular branch and extent of the indulgence. If a safe conduct be given for a stated term of time, the person in whose favour it was granted, must leave the enemy's country before the time expires, unless detained by sickness, or some unavoidable circumstance, and then he remains under the same protection. The case is different with an enemy who comes into the country of his adversary during a truce. He, at his own peril, takes advantage of a general liberty, allowed by the suspension of hostilities, and at the expiration of the truce.

---

[a] *Vattel.* b. 3. c. 17.

the war may freely take its course, without being impeded by any claims of such a party for protection.*

It is stated that a safe conduct may even be revoked by him who granted it, for some good reason; for it is a general principle in the law of nations, that every privilege may be revoked, when it becomes detrimental to the state. If it be a gratuitous privilege, it may be revoked purely and simply; but if it be a purchased privilege, the party interested in it is entitled to indemnity against all injurious consequences, and every party affected by the revocation is to be allowed time and liberty to depart in safety.*

The effect of a license given by the enemy, to the subjects of the adverse party, to carry on a specified trade, has already been considered, in respect to the light in which it is viewed by the government of the citizens accepting it. A very different effect is given to these licenses by the government which grants them, and they are regarded and respected as lawful relaxations or suspensions of the rules of war. It is the assumption of a state of peace to the extent of the license, and the act rests in the discretion of the sovereign authority of the state, which alone is competent to decide how far considerations of commercial and political expediency may, in particular cases, control the ordinary consequences of war. In the country which grants them, licenses to carry on a pacific commerce are *stricti juris*, as being exceptions to a general rule; though they are not to be construed with pedantic accuracy, nor will every small deviation be held to vitiate the fair effect of them.* An excess in the quantity of goods permitted to be imported, might not be considered as noxious to any extent; but a variation in the quality or substance of the goods might be more significant. Whenever any part of the trade assumed under the license, is denuded of any authority under it, such part is subject to condemnation.

---

a Vattel, b. 3. c. 17. sec. 273, 274.   *b Vattel*, b. 3. c. 17. sec. 276.
c The Cosmopolite, 4 *Rob.* 8.

Another material circumstance in all licenses, is the limitation of time in which they are to be carried into effect, for what is proper at one time, may be very unfit and mischievous at another time. Where a license was limited to be in force until the 29th of September, and the ship did not sail from the foreign port until the 4th of October, yet as the goods were laden on board by the 12th of September, and there was an entire *bona fides* on the part of the person holding the license, this was held to be legal.[a] But where a license was to bring away a cargo from Bourdeaux, and the party thought proper to change the license, and accommodate it to another port in France, it was held to be a case not protected by the license; and the English admiralty, in the case of the *Twee Gebroeders*,[b] held, that the license was vitiated, and the vessel and cargo were condemned. It has also been held, that the license must be limited to the use of the precise persons for whose benefit it was obtained. The great principle in these cases is, that subjects are not to trade with the enemy without the special permission of the government; and a material object of the control which the government exercises over such a trade, is, that it may judge of the particular persons who are fit to be intrusted with an exemption from the ordinary restrictions of a state of war.[c]

(3.) The object of war is peace, and it is the duty of every belligerent power to make war fulfil its end with the least possible mischief, and to accelerate, by all fair and reasonable means, a just and honourable peace. The same power which has the right to declare and carry on war, would seem naturally to be the proper power to make and conclude a treaty of peace; but the disposition of this power will depend upon the local constitution of every nation; and it sometimes happens, that the power of making

---

a 15 *East*, 52. 3 *Campb. N. P.* 83.
b 1 *Edw.* 95.
c The Jonge Johannes, 4 *Rob.* 263.

peace is committed to a body of men who have not the power to make war. In Sweden, after the death of Charles XII. the king could declare war without the consent of the national Diet, but he made peace in conjunction with the Senate.[a] So, by the constitution of the United States, the President, by and with the advice and consent of two thirds of the Senate, may make peace, but it is reserved to Congress to declare war. This provision in our constitution is well adapted (as will be shown more fully hereafter) to unite in the negotiation and conclusion of treaties, the advantage of talents, experience, stability, and a comprehensive knowledge of national interests, with the requisite secrecy and despatch.

Treaties of peace, when made by the competent power, are obligatory upon the whole nation. If the treaty requires the payment of money to carry it into effect, and the money cannot be raised but by an act of the legislature, the treaty is morally obligatory upon the legislature to pass the law, and to refuse it would be a breach of public faith. The department of the government that is intrusted by the constitution with the treaty making power, is competent to bind the national faith in its discretion; for the power to make treaties of peace must be coextensive with all the exigencies of the nation, and necessarily involves in it that portion of the national sovereignty which has the exclusive direction of all diplomatic negotiations and contracts with foreign powers. All treaties made by that power become of absolute efficacy, because they are the supreme law of the land.

There can be no doubt that the power competent to bind the nation by treaty, may alienate the public domain and property by treaty. If a nation has conferred upon its executive department, without reserve, the right of treating and contracting with other states, it is considered as having invested it with all the power necessary to make a valid contract. That department is the organ of the nation, and

---

[a] *Vattel.* b. 4. c. 2. sec. 10.

the alienations by it are valid, because they are done by the reputed will of the nation. The fundamental laws of a state may withhold from the executive department the power of alienating what belongs to the state, but if there be no express provision of that kind, the inference is, that it has confided to the department charged with the power of making treaties, a discretion commensurate with all the great interests, and wants, and necessities of the nation. A power to make treaties of peace necessarily implies a power to decide the terms on which they shall be made, and foreign states could not deal safely with the government upon any other presumption. The power that is intrusted generally and largely with authority to make valid treaties of peace, can, of course, bind the nation by alienation of part of its territory, and this is equally the case whether that territory be already in the occupation of the enemy, or remains in the possession of the nation, and whether the property be public or private.[a] In the case of the schooner *Peggy*,[b] the Supreme Court of the United States admitted, that individual rights acquired by war, and vested rights of the citizens, might be sacrificed by treaty for national purposes. So, in the case of *Ware* v. *Hylton*,[c] it was said to be a clear principle of national law, that private rights might be sacrificed by treaty to secure the public safety, though the government would be bound to make compensation and indemnity to the individuals whose rights had thus been surrendered. The power to alienate, and the duty to make compensation, are both laid down by Grotius[d] in equally explicit terms.

A treaty of peace is valid and binding on the nation, if made with the present ruling power of the nation, or the

---

a *Vattel*, b. 1. c. 21. sec. 262.—b. 4. c. 2. sec. 11, 12.
b 1 *Cranch*, 108.
c 3 *Dallas*, 199.
d B. 3. c. 20. sec. 7.

government *de facto*. Other nations have no right to interfere with the domestic affairs of any particular nation, or to examine and judge of the title of the party in possession of the supreme authority. They are to look only to the fact of possession.ᵃ And it is an acknowledged rule of international law, that the principal party in whose name the war is made, cannot justly make peace without including those defensive allies in the pacification who have afforded assistance, though they may not have acted as principals; for it would be faithless and cruel for the principal in the war to leave his weaker ally to the full force of the enemy's resentment. The ally is, however, to be no farther a party to the stipulations and obligations of the treaty, than he has been willing to consent. All that the principal can require, is, that his ally be considered as restored to a state of peace. Every alliance in which all the parties are principals in the war, obliges the allies to treat in concert, though each one makes a separate treaty of peace for himself.ᵇ

The effect of a treaty of peace is to put an end to the war, and to abolish the subject of it. Peace relates to the war which it terminates. It is an agreement to waive all discussion concerning the respective rights of the parties, and to bury in oblivion all the original causes of the war. It forbids the revival of the same war, by taking arms for the cause which at first kindled it, though it is no objection to any subsequent pretensions to the same thing, on other foundations.ᶜ After peace, the revival of grievances arising before the war is not to be encouraged, for treaties of peace are intended to put an end to such complaints; and if grievances then existing are not brought forward at the time when peace is concluded, it is to be presumed that it is not intended to bring them forward at any future time.ᵈ Peace leaves the contracting parties without any right of committing hostility for the very cause which kin-

---

a *Vattel*, b. 4. c. 2. sec. 14.
b *Ibid.* b. 4. c. 2. sec. 16.
c *Vattel*, b. 4. c. 2. sec. 19.
d 1 *Dodson's Adm. Rep.* 396.

dled the war, or for what has passed in the course of it. It is, therefore, no longer permitted to take up arms again for the same cause.^a But this will not preclude the right to complain and resist, if the same grievances which kindled the war be renewed and repeated, for that would furnish a new injury and a new cause of war equally just with the former war. If an abstract right be in question between the parties, the right, for instance, to impress at sea one's own subjects, from the merchant vessels of the other, and the parties make peace without taking any notice of the question, it follows, of course, that all past grievances, damages, and injury, arising under such claim, are thrown into oblivion, by the amnesty which every treaty implies; but the claim itself is not thereby settled, either one way or the other. It remains open for future discussion, because the treaty wanted an express concession or renunciation of the claim itself.[b]

A treaty of peace leaves every thing in the state in which it finds it, if there be no express stipulation on the subject. If nothing be said in a treaty of peace about the conquered country or places, they remain with the possessor, and his title cannot afterwards be called in question. During war, the conqueror has only a usufructuary right to the territory he has subdued, and the latent right and title of the former sovereign continues, until a treaty of peace, by its silence, or by its express stipulation, shall have extinguished his title for ever.[c]

The peace does not affect rights which had no relation to the war. Debts existing prior to the war, and injuries committed prior to the war, but which made no part of the reasons for undertaking it, remain entire, and the remedies are revived.[d] There are certain cases in which even debts

---

a *Vattel*, b. 4. c. 2. sec. 19.

b *Ibid*. b. 4. c. 2. sec. 19, 20.

c 1 *Dodson*, 452. *Vattel*, b. 4. c. 2. sec. 21. *Grotius*, lib. 3. c. 6. sec. 4, 5. *Mably's Droit de l'Europe*, tom. 1. c. 2. p. 144.

d *Grotius*, b. 3. c. 20. sec. 16. 18.

contracted, or injuries committed, between two subjects of the belligerent powers, during the war, are the ground of a valid claim. This would be the case if the debt between them was contracted, or the injury was committed, in a neutral country.[a]

A treaty of peace binds the contracting parties from the moment of its conclusion. But, like a truce, it cannot affect the subjects of the nation with guilt, by reason of acts of hostility subsequent to the date of the treaty, provided they were committed before the treaty was known. All that can be required in such cases is, that the government make immediate restitution of things captured after the cessation of hostilities; and to guard against inconvenience from the want of due knowledge of the treaty, it is usual to fix the periods at which hostilities are to cease at different places, and for the restitution of property taken afterwards.[b]

But though individuals are not deemed criminal for continuing hostilities after the date of the peace, so long as they are ignorant of it, a more difficult question to determine is, whether they are responsible, *civiliter*, in such cases. Grotius[c] says, they are not liable to answer in damages, but it is the duty of the government to restore what has been captured and not destroyed. In the case of the American ship *Mentor*,[d] which was taken and destroyed, off Delaware bay, by British ships of war, in 1783, after the cessation of hostilities, but before that fact had come to the knowledge of either of the parties, the point was much discussed; and it was held, that the injured party could not pass over the person from whom the alleged injury had been received, and fix it on the commander of the English squadron on that station, who was totally ignorant of the whole transaction, and at the distance of thirty leagues from the place where it passed.

---

a *Vattel*, b. 4. c. 2. sec. 22.
b *Ibid.* b. 4. c. 3. sec. 24, 25. 2 *Dallas*, 40. *Azuni*, vol. 2. 227.
c B. 3. c. 21. sec. 5.
d 1 *Rob.* 151.

There was no instance in the annals of the prize courts, of such a remote and consequential responsibility, in such a case. The actual wrong-doer is the person to answer in judgment, and to him the responsibility (if any) is attached. He may have other persons responsible over to him, but the injured party could look only to him. The better opinion was, that though such an act be done through ignorance of the cessation of hostilities, yet mere ignorance of that fact would not protect the officer from civil responsibility in a prize court; and that, if he acted through ignorance, his own government must protect him and save him harmless. When a place or country is exempted from hostility by articles of peace, it is the duty of the government to use due diligence to give its subjects notice of the fact, and the government ought, in justice, to indemnify its subjects, who act in ignorance of the peace. And yet it would seem, from that case, that the American owner was denied redress in the British admiralty, not only against the admiral of the fleet on that station, but against the immediate author of the injury. Sir William Scott denied the relief against the admiral; and ten years before that time, relief had equally been denied by his predecessor, against the person who did the injury. If that decision was erroneous, an appeal ought to have been prosecuted. We have then the decision of the English High Court of Admiralty, denying any relief in such a case, and an opinion of Sir William Scott, many years afterwards, that the original wrong-doer was liable. The opinions cannot otherwise be reconciled, than upon the ground that the prize courts have a large and equitable discretion, in allowing or withholding relief, according to the special circumstances of the individual case; and that there is no fixed or inflexible general rule on the subject.

If a time be fixed by the treaty for hostilities to cease in a given place, and a capture be previously made, but with knowledge of the peace, it has been a question among the writers on public law, whether the captured property should be restored. The better, and the more reasonable opinion, is, that the capture would be null, though made before the day limited, provided the captor was previously informed of the peace; for, as Emerigon observes, since constructive knowledge of the peace, after the time limited in the different parts of the world, renders the capture void, much more ought actual knowledge of the peace to produce that effect.[b]

---

[a] Valin, *Traite des Prises*, ch. 4. sec. 4. and 5. *Emerigon, Traite des Ass.* c. 12. sec. 19. Azuni on Maritime Law, edit. N. Y. vol. 2. p. 231.

[b] This point was very extensively discussed in the French prize courts, in the case of the capture of the British ship *Swineherd*, by the French privateer *Bellona*, and what was sufficient knowledge of the fact of the peace, to annul the capture, was the great question. It appeared that the *Bellona* sailed from the isle of France the 27th of November, 1801, before news had arrived at the island of the signing of the preliminaries of peace between France and England, and which had been signed on the 1st of October preceding. The capture was made on the 24th of February, 1802, within the period of five months from the date of the treaty; and, by the 11th article of the treaty, it was provided, that captures made in any part of the world, after five months from the ratification of the treaty, should be null and void. The capture was made in a place where a shorter period than five months did not apply. The proclamation of the King of Great Britain of the 12th of October, 1801, announced the fact of the signature of the preliminary articles of peace; and it stated the substance of the 11th article, and ordered all hostilities to cease in the different places, from and after the respective periods mentioned in that article; and this proclamation was published in the Calcutta Gazette, and made known by the production of that paper, to the French cruiser, at several times, by distinct vessels, some days previous to the capture. This evidence of the peace was also communicated to the captain of the French vessel as soon as the capture took place, and yet, notwithstanding this notice, the English ship was taken possession of, and carried into the isle of France, and libelled, and condemned, as lawful prize of war. The sentence of condemnation was affirmed in 1803, on appeal to the Council of Prizes at Paris, and M. *Merlin* has reported at large the elaborate argument and opinion of M. Collet Descotils, the Imperial Advocate General in the Council of Prizes, in favour of the captors. The

Another question arose subsequent to the treaty of Ghent of 1814, in one of the British vice-admiralty courts, on the validity of a recapture by a British ship of war, of a British vessel captured by an American privateer. The capture made by the American cruiser was valid, being made before the period fixed for the cessation of hostilities, and in ignorance of the fact; but the prize had not been carried into port and condemned, and while at sea she was recaptured by the British cruiser after the period fixed for the cessation of hostilities, but without knowledge of the peace. It was decided, that the possession of the vessel by the American privateer was a lawful possession, and that the British cruiser could not, after the peace, lawfully use force to divest this lawful possession. The restoration of peace put an end, from the time limited, to all force, and then the general principle applied, that things acquired in war remain, as to title and possession, precisely as they stood when the peace took place. The *uti possidetis* is the basis of every treaty of peace, unless it be otherwise agreed. Peace gives a final and perfect title to captures without condemnation, and as it forbids all force, it destroys all hopes of recovery as much as if the vessel was carried *infra præsidia*, and condemned.^a A similar doctrine was held in the case of

---

ground he took, and upon which the Council of Prizes proceeded, was, that the king's proclamation, unaccompanied by any French attestation, was not that sufficient and indubitable evidence to the French cruiser, of the fact of the peace, upon which he ought to have acted, and that the period of the five months had not elapsed, within which it was lawful, in the Indian seas, to continue hostilities. The learned and venerable author of that immense work, the *Repertory of Jurisprudence*, says, on introducing the case, that he shall be silent on the question, and contents himself with giving the discussions, and particularly the opinion of the Advocate General, and the reasons of the Council of Prizes. See *Repertoire universel et raisonne de Jurisprudence*, par M. le Comte Merlin, tom 9. tit. *Prise Maritime*, sec. 5.

a *Case of the Legal Tender*, Halifax, April, 1815, cited *Wheaton's Dig.* 302.

the schooner *Sophie*,[a] and the treaty of peace had the effect of quieting all titles of possession arising from the war, and of putting an end to the claim of all former proprietors, to things of which possession was acquired by right of war.

If nothing be said to the contrary, things stipulated to be restored are to be returned in the condition they were taken; but this does not relate to alterations which have been the natural consequence of time, and of the operations of war. A fortress or a town is to be restored in that condition it was when taken, as far as it shall still be in the condition when the peace is made.[b] There is no obligation to repair, as well as restore, a dismantled fortress, or a ravaged territory. The peace extinguishes all claim for damages done in war, or arising from the operations of war. Things are to be restored in the condition the peace found them; and to dismantle a fortification, or to waste a country, after the conclusion of the peace, and previous to the surrender, would be an act of perfidy.[c]

Treaties of every kind, when made by the competent authority, are as obligatory upon nations, as private contracts are binding upon individuals; and they are to receive a fair and liberal interpretation, and to be kept with the most scrupulous good faith. Their meaning is to be ascertained by the same rules of construction and course of reasoning which we apply to the interpretation of private contracts.[d] If a treaty should in fact be violated by one of the contracting parties, either by proceedings incompatible with the particular nature of the treaty, or by an intentional breach of any of its articles, it rests alone with the injured party to pronounce it broken. The treaty, in such a case, is not

---

a 6 *Rob.* 138.
b *Vattel*, b. 4. c. 3. sec 31. 34.
c *Ibid.* b. 4. c. 3. sec. 32.
d *Ibid.* b. 2. c. 17. Eyre, Ch. J. in 1 *Bos. & Pull.* 438, 459. Opinion of Sir James Marriot, cited in 1 *Chitty on Commercial Law.* 44.

absolutely void, but voidable, at the election of the injured party.ᵃ If he chooses not to come to a rupture, the treaty remains obligatory. He may waive or remit the infraction committed, or he may demand a just satisfaction.

There is a very material and important distinction made by the writers on public law, between a new war for some new cause, and a breach of a treaty of peace. In the former case, the rights acquired by the treaty subsist, notwithstanding the new war; but, in the latter case, they are annulled by the breach of the treaty of peace, on which they are founded. A new war may interrupt the exercise of the rights acquired by the former treaty, and, like other rights, they may be wrested from the party by the force of arms. But then they become newly acquired rights, and partake of the operation and result of the new war. To re-commence a war, by breach of the articles of a treaty of peace, is deemed much more odious than to provoke a war by some new demand and aggression, for the latter is simply injustice, but, in the former case, the party is guilty both of perfidy and injustice.ᵇ The violation of any one article of a treaty, is a violation of the whole treaty; for all the articles are dependent on each other, and one is to be deemed a condition of the other, and a violation of any single article overthrows the whole treaty, if the injured party elects so to consider it. This may, however, be prevented by an express provision, that if one article be broken, the others shall, nevertheless, continue in full force.ᶜ We have a strong instance in our own history of the annihilation of treaties by the act of the injured party. In 1798, the Congress of the United Statesᵈ declared that the treaties with France were no

---

a *Grotius*, b. 2. c. 15. sec. 15.—b. 3. c. 20. sec. 35—38. *Burlamaqui*, p. 355. part 4. c. 14. sec. 8. *Vattel*, b. 4. c. 4. sec. 54.

b *Grotius*, b. 3. c. 20. sec. 27, 28. *Vattel*, b. 4. c. 4. sec. 42.

c *Grotius*, b. 3. c. 19. sec. 14. *Vattel*, b. 4. c. 4. sec. 47, 48.—b. 2. c. 13. sec. 202.

d Act of July 7th, 1798.

longer obligatory on the United States, as they had been repeatedly violated on the part of the French government, and all just claims for reparation refused.

As a general rule, the obligations of treaties are dissipated by hostility. But if a treaty contains any stipulations which contemplate a state of future war, and make provision for such an exigency, they preserve their force and obligation when the rupture takes place. All those duties of which the exercise is not necessarily suspended by the war, subsist in their full force. The obligation of keeping faith is so far from ceasing in time of war, that its efficacy becomes increased, from the increased necessity of it. What would become of prisoners of war, and the terms of capitulation of garrisons and towns, if the word of an enemy was not to be relied on? The faith of promises and treaties which have reference to a state of war, is to be held as sacred in war as in peace, and among enemies as among friends. All the writers on public law admit this position, and they have never failed to recommend the duty and the observance of good faith, by the most powerful motives, and the most pathetic and eloquent appeals which could be addressed to the reason and to the moral sense of nations.[a] The 10th article of the treaty between the United States and Great Britain, in 1794, may be mentioned as an instance of a stipulation made for war. It provided, that debts due from individuals of the one nation to those of the other, and the shares or moneys which they might have in the public funds, or in public or private banks, should never, in any event of war, be sequestered or confiscated. There can be no doubt that the obligation of that article was not impaired by the war of 1812, but remained throughout that war, and continues to this day, binding upon the two nations, and will continue so until they mutually agree to rescind the article; for it is a principle of universal jurisprudence, that a compact cannot be rescinded by one party only, if the other party does not

---

[a] *Vattel.* b. 3. c. 10. sec. 174. *Grotius,* b. 3. c. 25.

consent to rescind it, and does no act to destroy it. In the case of *The Society for Propagating the Gospel* v. *New-Haven*,[a] the Supreme Court of the United States would not admit the doctrine that treaties became extinguised *ipso facto* by war, unless revived by an express or implied renewal on the return of peace. Such a doctrine is not universally true. Where treaties contemplate a permanent arrangement of national rights, or which, by their terms, are meant to provide for the event of an intervening war, it would be against every principle of just interpretation to hold them extinguished by the event of war. They revive at peace, unless waived, or new and repugnant stipulations be made.

With respect to the cession of places or territories by a treaty of peace, though the treaty operates from the making of it, it is a principle of public law, that the national character of the place agreed to be surrendered by treaty, continues as it was under the character of the ceding country, until it be actually transferred. Full sovereignty cannot be held to have passed by the mere words of the treaty, without actual delivery. To complete the right of property, the right to the thing, and the possession of the thing, must be united. This is a necessary principle in the law of property in all systems of jurisprudence. There must be both the *jus in rem*, and the *jus in re*, according to the distinction of the civilians, and which Barbeyrac[b] says they borrowed from the canon law. This general law of property applies to the right of territory no less than to other rights. The practice of nations has been conformable to this principle, and the conventional law of nations is full of instances of this kind, and several of them were stated by Sir Wm. Scott in the opinion which he gave in the case of the *Fama*.[c]

---

a 8 *Wheaton*, 494.
b *Puff. par Barbeyrac*, liv. 4. c. 9. sec. 8. n. 2.
c 5 *Rob.* 106.

The release of a territory from the dominion and sovereignty of the country, if that cession be the result of coercion or conquest, does not impose any obligation upon the government to indemnify those who may suffer a loss of property by the cession. The annals of our own state furnish a strong illustration of this position. The territory composing the state of Vermont belonged to this state, and it separated from it, and erected itself into an independent state, without the consent, and against the will, of the government of this state. The latter continued for many years to object to the separation, and to discover the strongest disposition to reclaim by force the allegiance of the inhabitants of that state. But they were unable to do it; and it was the case of a revolution effected by force, analogous to that which was then in action between this country and Great Britain. And when this state found itself under the necessity of acknowledging the independence of Vermont, a question arose before our legislature, whether they were bound in duty to make compensation to individual citizens whose property would be sacrificed by the event, because their titles to land lying within the jurisdiction of Vermont, and derived from New-York, would be disregarded by the government of that state. The claimants were heard at the bar of the House of Assembly, by counsel, in 1787, and it was contended on their behalf, that the state was bound, upon the principles of the social compact, to protect and defend the rights and property of all its members, and that, whenever it became necessary, upon grounds of public expediency and policy, to withdraw the protection of government from the property of any of its citizens, without actually making the utmost efforts to reclaim the jurisdiction of the country, the state was bound to make compensation for the loss. In answer to this argument, it was stated, that the independence of Vermont was an act of force beyond the power of this state to control, and equivalent to a conquest of that territory, and the state had not the competent ability to recover, by force of arms, their sovereignty over it, and it would have been folly and ruin to have attempted it. All pacific means had been tried without success, and as the state was compelled to yield to a case of necessity, it had discharged its duty, and it was not required, upon any of the doctrines of public law, or principles of political or moral obligation, to indemnify the sufferers. The cases in which compensation had been made for losses consequent upon revolutions in government, were peculiar and gratuitous, and rested entirely on benevolence, and were given from motives of policy, or as a reward for extraordinary acts of loyalty and exertion. No government can be supposed to be able, consistently with the welfare of the whole community, and it is, therefore, not required, to assume the burthen of losses produced by conquest, or the violent dismemberment of the state. It would be incompatible with the fundamental principles of the social compact.

This was the doctrine which prevailed in the legislature of this state; and when the act of July 14th, 1789, was passed, authorizing commissioners to declare the consent of the state to the independence of Vermont, it was expressly declared, that the act was not to be construed to give any person claiming lands in Vermont, under title from this state, any right to any compensation whatsoever from New-York.

LECTURE IX.

OF OFFENCES AGAINST THE LAW OF NATIONS.

The violation of a treaty of peace, or other national compact, is a violation of the law of nations, for it is a breach of public faith.[a] Nor is it to be understood that the law of nations is a code of mere elementary speculation, without any efficient sanction. It has a real and propitious influence on the fortunes of the human race. It is a code of present, active, durable, and binding obligation. As its great fundamental principles are founded in the maxims of eternal truth, in the immutable law of moral obligation, and in the suggestions of an enlightened public interest, they maintain a steady influence, notwithstanding the occasional violence by which that influence may be disturbed. The law of nations is placed, in the first place, under the protection of public opinion. It is enforced by the censures of the press, and by the moral influence of those great masters of public law, who are consulted by all nations as oracles of wisdom ; and who have attained, by the mere force of written reason, the majestic character, and almost the authority of universal lawgivers, controlling by their writings the conduct of rulers, and laying down precepts for the government of mankind. No nation can violate public law, without being subjected to the penal consequences of reproach and disgrace, and without incurring the hazard of punishment, to be inflicted in open and solemn war by the injured

---

[a] *Vattel*, b. 2. c. 15. sec. 221. *Resolution of Congress of November 23d*, 1781.

party. The law of nations is likewise enforced by the sanctions of municipal law, and the offences which fall more immediately under its cognizance, and which are the most obvious, the most extensive, and most injurious in their effects, are the violations of safe conduct, infringements of the rights of ambassadors, and piracy. To these we may add the slave trade, which may now be considered, not, indeed, as a piratical trade, absolutely unlawful by the law of nations, but as a trade condemned by the general principles of justice and humanity, openly professed and declared by the powers of Europe.

(1.) A safe conduct or passport contains a pledge of the public faith, that it shall be duly respected, and the observance of this duty is essential to the character of the government which grants it. The statute law of the United States has provided, in furtherance of the general sanction of public law, that if any person shall violate any safe conduct or passport, granted under the authority of the United States, he shall, on conviction, be imprisoned not exceeding three years, and fined at the discretion of the Court.[a]

(2.) The same punishment is inflicted upon those persons who infringe the law of nations, by offering violence to the persons of ambassadors, and other public ministers, or by being concerned in prosecuting or arresting them.[b] This is an offence highly injurious to a free and liberal communication between different governments, and mischievous in its consequences to the dignity and well being of the nation. It tends to provoke the resentment of the sovereign whom the ambassador represents, and to bring upon the state the calamities of war. The English parliament, under an impression of the danger to the community from violation of the rights of embassy, and urged by the spur of a particular occasion, carried the provisions of the statute of 7 Ann, c. 12. to a dangerous extent. That statute prostrated all the

---

[a] Act of Congress, April 30th, 1790, sec. 27.
[b] Ibid. sec. 25, 26.

safeguards to life, liberty, and property, which the wisdom of the English common law had established. It declared, that any person convicted of suing out or executing civil process, upon an ambassador, or his domestic servants, by the oath of the party, or of one witness, before the Lord Chancellor, and the two Chief Justices, or any two of them, might have such penalties and corporal punishment inflicted upon him, as the judges should think fit. The preamble to the statute contains a special and inflamed recital of the breach of the law of nations which produced it, by the arrest of the Russian minister in the streets of London.

The Congress of the United States, during the time of the American war, discovered great solicitude to maintain inviolate the obligations of the law of nations, and to have infractions of it punished in the only way that was then lawful, by the exercise of the authority of the legislatures of the several states. They recommended to the states to provide expeditious, exemplary, and adequate punishment, for the violation of safe conducts or passports, granted under the authority of Congress, to the subjects of a foreign power in time of war; and for the commission of acts of hostility against persons in amity or league with the United States; and for the infractions of treaties and conventions to which the United States were a party; and for infractions of the immunities of ambassadors, and other public ministers.[a]

(3.) Piracy is robbery, or a forcible depredation on the high seas, without lawful authority, and done *animo furandi*. It is the same offence at sea with robbery on land; and all the writers on the law of nations, and on the maritime law of Europe, agree in this definition of piracy.[b] Pirates have been regarded by all civilized nations as the enemies of the human race, and the most atrocious violators of the univer-

---

[a] *Journals of Congress*, vol. 7. 181.

[b] The United States v. Smith. 5 *Wheaton*, 153 and note, ibid. 163.

sal law of society.^a They are every where pursued and punished with death; and the severity with which the law has animadverted upon this crime, arises from its enormity and danger, the cruelty that accompanies it, the necessity of checking it, the difficulty of detection, and the facility with which robberies may be committed upon pacific traders, in the solitude of the ocean. Every nation has a right to attack and exterminate them without any declaration of war; for though pirates may form a loose and temporary association among themselves, and re-establish in some degree those laws of justice which they have violated with the rest of the world, yet they are not considered as a national body, or entitled to the laws of war as one of the community of nations. They acquire no rights by conquest; and the law of nations, and the municipal law of every country, authorize the true owner to reclaim his property taken by pirates, wherever it can be found; and they do not recognise any title to be derived from an act of piracy. The principle, that *a piratis et latronibus capta dominium non mutant*, is the received opinion of ancient civilians, and modern writers on general jurisprudence; and the same doctrine was maintained in the English courts of common law prior to the great modern improvements made in the science of the law of nations.^b

By the constitution of the United States, Congress were authorized to define and punish piracies and felonies committed on the high seas, and offences against the law of nations. In pursuance of this authority, it was declared by the act of Congress of April 30th, 1790, sec. 8. that murder or robbery committed on the high seas, or in any river, haven, or bay, out of the jurisdiction of any particular state, or any other offence, which, if committed within the

---

a *Cic. in Verrem*, lib. 5. 3 *Inst.* 113.

b *Bynk. Q. J. Pub.* b. 1. c. 17. *Rutherforth*, b. 2. c. 9. *Azuni*, vol. 2. p. 351. 361, 362. edit. N. Y. *Cro. E.* 685. *Anon.* 2 *Woodd. Lec.* 429.

body of a county, would, by the laws of the United States, be punishable with death, should be adjudged to be piracy and felony, and punishable with death. It was further declared, that if any captain or mariner should piratically and feloniously run away with any vessel, or any goods or merchandise to the value of fifty dollars; or should yield up any such vessel voluntarily to pirates; or if any seaman should forcibly endeavour to hinder his commander from defending the ship or goods committed to his trust, or should make a revolt in the ship; every such offender should be adjudged a pirate and felon, and be punishable with death. Accessaries to such piracies before the fact, are punishable in like manner; but accessaries after the fact are only punishable with fine and imprisonment. And, by the act of March 3d, 1819, sec. 5. (and which act was made perpetual by the act of 15th of May, 1820, sec. 2.) Congress declared, that if any person on the high seas should commit the crime of *piracy, as defined by the law of nations*, he should, on conviction, suffer death. It was again declared, by the act of Congress of 15th of May, 1820, sec. 3. that if any person upon the high seas, or in any open roadstead, or bay, or river, where the sea ebbs and flows, commits the crime of robbery in and upon any vessel, or the lading thereof, or the crew, he should be adjudged a pirate. So, if any person concerned in any particular enterprise, or belonging to any particular crew, should land, and commit robbery on shore, such an offender should also be adjudged a pirate. The statute, in this respect, seems to be only declaratory of the law of nations; for, upon the doctrine of the case of *Lindo v. Rodney*,[a] such plunder and robbery ashore, by the crew, and with the aid of vessels, is a marine case, and of admiralty jurisdiction.

Under these legislative provisions, it has been made a question, whether it was sufficient to refer to the law of nations for a definition of piracy, without giving the crime a

---

[a] *Doug.* 613.

precise definition in terms. The point was settled in the case of the *United States* v. *Smith*;[a] and it was there held not to be necessary to give by statute a more logical enumeration in detail of all the facts constituting the offence, and that Congress might as well define it by using a term of a known and determinate meaning, as by expressly mentioning all the particulars included in that term. The crime of piracy was defined by the law of nations with reasonable certainty, and it does not depend upon the particular provisions of any municipal code for its definition and punishment. Robbery on the high seas is, therefore, piracy by the act of Congress, as well as by the law of nations.

There can be no doubt of the right of Congress to pass laws punishing pirates, though they may be foreigners, and may have committed no particular offence against the United States. It is of no importance for the purpose of giving jurisdiction on *whom* or *where* a piratical offence has been committed. A pirate, who is one by the law of nations, may be tried and punished in any country where he may be found, for he is reputed to be out of the protection of all laws and privileges.[b] The statute of any government may declare an offence committed on board its own vessels to be piracy, and such an offence will be punishable exclusively by the nation which passes the statute. But piracy, under the law of nations, is an offence against all nations, and punishable by all. In the case of the *United States* v. *Palmer*,[c] it was held, that the act of Congress of 1790 was intended to punish offences against the United States, and not offences against the human race; and that the crime of robbery, committed by a person who was not a citizen of the United States, on the high seas, on board of a ship belonging exclusively to subjects of a foreign state, was not piracy under the act, and was not punishable in the courts of the United States. The offence, in such a case, must, there-

---

[a] 5 *Wheaton*, 153. [b] *Bynk. Q. J. Pub.* ch. 17.
[c] 3 *Wheaton*, 610.

fore, be left to be punished by the nation under whose flag the vessel sailed, and within whose particular jurisdiction all on board the vessel were. This decision was according to the law and practice of nations, for it is a clear and settled principle, that the jurisdiction of every nation extends to its own citizens, on board of its own public and private vessels at sea.[a] The case applied only to the fact of robbery committed at sea, on board of a foreign vessel, at the time belonging exclusively to subjects of a foreign state; and it was not intended to decide, that the same offence, committed on board of a vessel not belonging to the subjects of any foreign power, was not piracy. The same court, afterwards, in the case of the *United States* v. *Klintock*,[b] admitted, that murder or robbery, committed on the high seas, by persons on board of a vessel not at the time belonging to the subjects of any foreign power, but in possession of a crew acting in defiance of all law, and acknowledging obedience to no government or flag whatsoever, fell within the purview of the act of Congress, and was punishable in the courts of the United States. Persons of that description were pirates, and proper objects for the penal code of all nations. The act of Congress did not apply to offences committed against the particular sovereignty of a foreign power; or to murder or robbery committed in a vessel belonging at the time, in fact as well as in right, to the subject of a foreign state, and, in virtue of such property, subject at the time to his control. But it applied to offences committed against all nations, by persons who, by common consent, were equally amenable to the laws of all nations.

It was further held, in the case of the *United States* v. *Pirates*,[c] and in the case of the *United States* v. *Holmes*,[d] in

---

[a] *Rutherforth's Ins.* b. 2. ch. 9. Mr. *Jefferson's Letter to M. Genet,* 17th June, 1793.

[b] 5 *Wheaton,* 144.

[c] *Ibid,* 184.

[d] *Ibid.* 412.

pursuance of the same principle, that the moment a vessel assumed a piratical character, and was taken from her officers, and proceeded on a piratical cruise, she lost all claim to national character, and the crew, whether citizens or foreigners, were equally punishable, under the act of Congress, for acts of piracy; and it would be immaterial what was the national character of the vessel before she assumed a piratical character. Piracy is an offence within the criminal jurisdiction of all nations. It is against all, and punished by all; and the plea of *autrefois acquit*, resting on a prosecution instituted in the courts of any civilized state, would be a good plea in any other civilized state. As the act of Congress of 1790, declares every offence committed at sea to be piracy, which would be punishable with death if committed on land, it may be considered as enlarging the definition of piracy, so as not only to include every offence which is piracy by the law of nations, and the act of Congress of 1819, but other offences which were not piracy until made so by statute.

An alien, under the sanction of a national commission, cannot commit piracy while he pursues his authority. His acts may be hostile, and his nation responsible for them. They may amount to a lawful cause of war, but they are never to be regarded as piracy. The Barbary powers, notwithstanding some doubts which formerly existed, are now, and have for a century past, been regarded as lawful powers, and not pirates. They have all the *insignia* of regular independent governments, and are competent to maintain the European relations of peace and war. Cicero, and, after him, Grotius, define a regular enemy to be a power which hath the elements or constituents of a nation, such as a government, a code of laws, a national treasury, the consent and agreement of the citizens, and which pays a regard to treaties of peace and alliance;[a] and all these things,

---

a *Cic. Philip.* 4. c. 6.   *Grotius,* b. 3. c. 3. sec. 1.

says Bynkershoeck,[a] are to be found among the states of Barbary. In some respects, their laws of war have retained the barbarity of the middle ages, for they levy tribute or contributions on all such Christian powers as are not able to protect their commerce by force; and they also make slaves of their prisoners, and require a heavy ransom for their redemption. But this, Bynkershoeck insists, is conformable to the strict laws of war; and the nations of Europe who carried on war with the Barbary states, such as Spain, Naples, Holland, &c. have heretofore exercised the same rule of ancient warfare, upon the principle of retaliation. When Lord Exmouth, in 1816, attacked Algiers, and compelled the Dey to terms of peace, he compelled him also to stipulate, that in the event of future wars with any European power, no Christian prisoners of war should be consigned to slavery, but they should be treated with all humanity as prisoners of war, until regularly exchanged according to the European practice, and at the termination of hostilities the prisoners should be restored without ransom. By that treaty of peace, upwards of 1000 prisoners belonging to Italy, Spain, Portugal, Holland, and Greece, were released from galling slavery, and in which part of them had subsisted for thirty-five years. This stipulation in favour of general humanity, deserves some portion of that exalted eulogy bestowed by Montesquieu[b] on the treaty made by Gelon, King of Syracuse, with the Carthagenians. It would have been still more worthy of a comparison, if it had not left colour for the construction, that the renunciation of the practice of condemning Christian prisoners of war to slavery, was to be confined to the " event of future wars with any European power ;" and if a great Christian power on this side of the Atlantic, whose presence and whose trade is constantly seen and felt in the Mediterranean, had not seemed to have been entirely forgotten.

---

a *Q. J. Pub.* b. 1. c. 17.   b *Esprit des Loix,* b. 10. c. 5.

But, notwithstanding Bynkershoeck had insisted, near a century ago, that captures by the Barbary powers worked a change of property by the laws of war, in like manner as captures made by regular powers, yet, in a case in the English admiralty so late as 1801,[a] it was contended, that the capture and sale of an English ship by Algerines, was an invalid and unlawful conversion of the property, on the ground of being a piratical seizure. It was, however, decided, that the African states had long acquired the character of established governments, and that though their notions of justice differ from those entertained by the Christian powers, their public acts could not be called in question; and a derivative title, founded on an Algerine capture, and matured by a confiscation *in their way*, was good against the original owner. In the time of Richard I. when the laws of Oleron were compiled, all infidels were, by that code,[b] regarded as pirates, and their property liable to seizure wherever found. It was a notion, at that time, that such persons could not have any fellowship or communion with Christians.

In a case which occurred in 1675, Sir Leoline Jenkins held, that the commander of a privateer regularly commissioned, was liable to be treated as a pirate, if he exceeded the bounds of his commission. Bynkershoeck justly opposes this dangerous opinion;[c] and the true rule undoubtedly is, that the vessel must have lost its national and assumed a piratical character, before jurisdiction over it, to that extent, could be exercised.

If a natural born subject was to take prizes belonging to his native country, in pursuance of a foreign commission, he would, on general principles, be protected by his commission from the charge of piracy. But to prevent the mischief of such conduct, the United States have followed the provisions of the English statute of 11 and 12 Wm. III. c. 7.

---

a The Helena, 4 *Rob.* 3.   b Sec. 45.
c *Quæst. J. P.* b. 1. c. 17.

and have, by the act of Congress of April 30th, 1790, sec. 9. declared, that if any citizen should commit any act of hostility against the United States, or any citizen thereof, upon the high seas, under colour of any commission from any foreign prince or state, or on pretence of authority from any person, such offender shall be adjudged to be a pirate, felon, and robber, and, on being thereof convicted, shall suffer death. The act of congress not only authorizes a capture, but a condemnation in the courts of the United States, for all piratical aggressions by foreign vessels; and whatever may be the responsibility incurred by the nation to foreign powers, in executing such laws, there can be no doubt that courts of justice are bound to obey and administer them. All such hostile and criminal aggressions on the high seas, under the flag of any power, render property taken *in delicto* subject to confiscation by the law of nations.[a]

(4.) The African slave trade is an offence against the municipal laws of most nations in Europe, and it is declared to be piracy by the statute laws of England and the United States. Whether it is to be considered as an offence against the law of nations, independent of compact, has been a grave question, much litigated in the courts charged with the administration of public law; and it will be useful to take a short view of the progress and present state of the sense and practice of nations on this subject.

Personal slavery, arising out of forcible captivity, has existed in every age of the world, and among the most refined and civilized people. The possession of persons so acquired, has been invested with the character of property. The slave trade was a regular branch of commerce among the ancients; and a great object of Athenian traffic with the Greek settlements on the Euxine, was procuring slaves from the barbarians for the Greek market.[b] In modern times, treaties have been framed, and national monopolies sought, to facilitate and extend commerce in this species of property.

---

[a] *Story. J.* 11 *Wheaton.* 39—41.   [b] *Mitford's Hist.* vol. 4. 236.

It has been interwoven into the municipal institutions of all the European colonies in America, and with the approbation and sanction of the parent states. It forms to this day the foundation of large masses of property in the southern parts of these United States. But, for half a century past, the African slave trade began to awaken a spirit of remorse and sympathy in the breasts of men, and a conviction that the traffic was repugnant to the principles of Christian duty, and the maxims of justice and humanity.

Montesquieu, who has disclosed so many admirable truths, and so much profound reflection, in his Spirit of Laws, not only condemned all slavery as useless and unjust, but he animadverted upon the African slave trade by the most pungent reproaches. It was impossible, he observed, that we could admit the negroes to be human beings, because, if we were once to admit them to be men, we should soon come to believe that we ourselves were not Christians. Why has it not, says he, entered into the heads of the European princes, who make so many useless conventions, to make one general stipulation in favour of humanity.[a] We shall see presently that this suggestion was, in some degree, carried into practice by a modern European congress.

The constitution of the United States laid the foundation of a series of provisions, to put a final stop to the progress of this great moral pestilence, by admitting a power in Congress to prohibit the importation of slaves, *after* the expiration of the year 1807. The constitution evidently looked forward to the year 1808 as the commencement of an epoch in the history of human improvement. Prior to that time, Congress did all on this subject that it was within their competence to do. By the acts of March 22d, 1794, and May 10th, 1800, the citizens of the United States, and residents within them, were prohibited from engaging in the transportation of slaves from the United States to any foreign place or country, or from one foreign country or place to

---

[a] *L'Esprit des Loix,* liv. 15. ch. 5.

another. These provisions prohibited our citizens from all concern in the slave trade, with the exception of direct importation into the United States; and the most prompt and early steps were taken, within the limits of the constitution, to interdict that part of the traffic also. By the act of 2d March, 1807, it was prohibited, under severe penalties, to import slaves into the United States, after the 1st January, 1808; and, on the 20th April, 1818, the penalties and punishments were increased, and the prohibition extended not only to importation, but generally against any citizen of the United States being concerned in the slave trade. It has been decided,[a] that these statute prohibitions extend as well to the carrying slaves on freight, as to cases where they were the property of American citizens, and to carrying them from one port to another of the same foreign empire, as well as from one foreign country to another. The object was to prevent, on the part of our citizens, all concern whatever in such a trade.

The act of March 3d, 1819, went a step further, and authorized national armed vessels to be sent to the coast of Africa, to stop the slave trade, so far as citizens or residents of the United States were engaged in that trade; and their vessels and effects were made liable to seizure and confiscation. The act of 15th May, 1820, went still further, and declared, that if any citizen of the United States, being of the crew of any foreign vessel engaged in the slave trade, or any person whatever, being of the crew of any vessel armed in whole or in part, or navigated for or on behalf of any citizen of the United States, should land on any foreign shore, and seize any negro or mulatto, with intent to make him a slave, or should decoy, or forcibly bring, or receive such negro on board such vessel, with like intent, such citizen or person should be adjudged a pirate, and, on conviction, should suffer death.

It is to be observed, that the statute operates only where

---

[a] The Merino. 9 *Wheaton*, 391.

our municipal jurisdiction might be applied consistently with the general theory of public law, to the persons of our citizens, or to foreigners on board of American vessels. Declaring the crime piracy, does not make it so, within the purview of the law of nations, if it were not so without the statute; and the legislature intended to legislate only where they had a right to legislate, over their own citizens and vessels. The question, notwithstanding these expressions in the statute, still remained to be discussed and settled, whether the African slave trade could be adjudged piracy, or any other crime within the contemplation of the code of international law. It has been attempted, by negotiation between this country and Great Britain, to agree that both nations should consider the slave trade piratical; but the convention for that purpose between the two nations has not, as yet, been ratified, though the British nation have carried their statute denunciation of the trade as far as the law of the United States.

The first British statute that declared the slave trade unlawful, was in March, 1807.[a] This was a great triumph of British justice. It was called for by the sense of the British nation, which had become deeply convinced of the impolicy and injustice of the slave trade; and by the subsequent statute of 51 Geo. III. the trade was declared to be contrary to the principles of justice, humanity, and sound policy; and lastly, by the act of Parliament of 31st March, 1824, the trade is declared to be piracy. England is thus, equally with the United States, honestly and zealously engaged in promoting the universal abolition of the trade, and in holding out to the world their sense of its extreme criminality. Almost every maritime nation in Europe has also deliberately and solemnly, either by legislative acts, or by treaties and other formal engagements, acknowledged the injustice and inhumanity of the trade, and pledged itself to promote its abolition. By the treaty of Paris of the 30th

---

a Stat. 47 Geo. III.

May, 1814, between Great Britain and France, Lewis XVIII. agreed that the traffic was repugnant to the principles of natural justice, and he engaged to unite his efforts at the ensuing congress, to induce all the powers of christendom to decree the abolition of the trade, and that it should cease definitively, on the part of the French government, in the course of five years. The ministers of the principal European powers who met at the congress at Vienna, on the 8th February, 1815, solemnly declared, in the face of Europe and the world, that the African slave trade had been regarded by just and enlightened men, in all ages, as repugnant to the principles of humanity and of universal morality, and that the public voice in all civilized countries demanded that it should be suppressed; and that the universal abolition of it was conformable to the spirit of the age, and the generous principles of the allied powers. In March, 1815, the Emperor Napoleon decreed that the slave trade should be abolished; but this effort of ephemeral power was afterwards held to be null and void, as being the act of an usurper; and in July following, Lewis XVIII. gave directions that this odious and wicked traffic should from that present time cease. The first French decree, however, that was made public, abolishing the trade, was of the date of the 8th January, 1817, and that was only a partial and modified decree. In December, 1817, the Spanish government prohibited the purchase of slaves on any part of the coast of Africa, after the 31st May, 1820; and in January, 1818, the Portuguese government made the like prohibition as to the purchase of slaves on any part of the coast of Africa north of the equator. In 1821, there was not a flag of any European state which could legally cover this traffic, to the north of the equator; and yet, in 1825, the importation of slaves covertly continued, if it was not openly countenanced, from the Rio de la Plata to the Amazon, and through the whole American archipelago.[a]

---

[a] *Report of a Committee of the House of Representatives of the United States, February* 16th, 1825.

The case of the *Amedie*[a] was the earliest decision in the English courts on the great question touching the legality of the slave trade, on general principles of international law. That was the case of an American vessel, employed in carrying slaves from the coast of Africa to a Spanish colony. She was captured by an English cruiser, and the vessel and cargo were condemned to the captors, in a vice-admiralty court in the West Indies, and, on appeal to the Court of Appeals in England, the judgment was affirmed. Sir Wm. Grant, who pronounced the opinion of the court, observed, that the slave trade being abolished by both England and the United States, the court was authorized to assert, that the trade, abstractedly speaking, could not have a legitimate existence, and was, *prima facie*, illegal, upon principles of universal law. The claimant, to entitle him to restitution, must show affirmatively a right of property under the municipal laws of his own country; for, if it be unprotected by his own municipal law, he can have no right of property in human beings carried as his slaves, for such a claim is contrary to the principles of justice and humanity. The *Fortuna*[b] was condemned on the authority of the *Amedie*, and the same principle was again affirmed. But, in the subsequent case of the *Diana*,[c] the doctrine was not carried so far as to hold the trade itself to be piracy, or a crime against the law of nations. A Swedish vessel was taken by a British cruiser on the coast of Africa, engaged in carrying slaves from Africa to a Swedish island in the West Indies, and she was restored to the owner, on the ground that Sweden had not then prohibited the trade, and had tolerated it in practice. England had abolished the trade as unjust and criminal, but she claimed no right of enforcing that prohibition against the subjects of those states which had not adopted the same opinion; and England did not mean to set herself up as the legislator, and *custos morum*, for the whole world,

---

[a] 1 *Acton's Rep.* 240.   [b] 1 *Dodson*, 81.   [c] 1 *Dodson*, 95.

or presume to interfere with the commercial regulations of other states. The principle of the case of the *Amedie* was, that where the municipal law of the country to which the parties belonged had prohibited the trade, English tribunals would hold it to be illegal, upon general principles of justice and humanity, but they would respect the property of persons engaged in it, under the sanction of the laws of their own country.

The doctrine of these cases is, that the slave trade is, abstractedly speaking, immoral and unjust, and it is illegal, when declared so by treaty, or municipal law; but that it is not piratical or illegal by the common law of nations, because, if it were so, every claim founded on the trade would at once be rejected every where, and in every court, on that ground alone.

The whole subject underwent further, and a most full, elaborate, and profound discussion, in the case of the *Le Louis*.[a] A French vessel, owned and documented as a French vessel, was captured by a British armed force on the coast of Africa, after resistance made to a demand to visit and search. She was carried into Sierra Leone, and condemned by a court of vice-admiralty, for being concerned in the slave trade contrary to the French law. On appeal to the British High Court of Admiralty, the question respecting the legality of the capture and condemnation, was argued, and it was judicially decided, that the right of visitation and search, on the high seas, did not exist in time of peace. If it belonged to one nation, it equally belonged to all, and would lead to gigantic mischief, and universal war. Other nations had refused to accede to the English proposal of a reciprocal right of search in the African seas, and it would require an express convention to give the right of search in time of peace. The slave trade, though unjust and condemned by the statute law of England, was not pi-

---

[a] 2 *Dodson*, 210.

racy, nor was it a crime by the universal law of nations. To make it piracy, or such a crime, it must have been so considered and treated in practice by all civilized states, or made so by virtue of a general convention. On the contrary, it had been carried on by all nations, even by Great Britain herself, until within a few years, and was then carried on by Spain and Portugal, and not absolutely prohibited by France. It was, therefore, not a criminal traffic by the law of nations; and every nation, independent of treaty, retained a legal right to carry it on. No one nation had a right to force the way to the liberation of Africa, by trampling on the independence of other states; or to procure an eminent good by means that were unlawful; or to press forward to a great principle, by breaking through other great principles that stood in the way. The condemnation of the French vessel at Sierra Leone was, therefore, reversed, and the penalties imposed by the French law, (if any there were,) were left to be enforced, not in an English, but in a French court.

The same subject was brought into discussion in the K. B. in 1820, in *Madrazo* v. *Willes*.[a] The Court held, that the British statutes against the slave trade, were only applicable to British subjects, and only rendered the slave trade unlawful when carried on by them. The British parliament could not prevent the subjects of other states from carrying on the trade out of the limits of the British dominions. If a ship be acting contrary to the general law of nations, she is thereby subject to condemnation; but it is impossible to say that the slave trade was contrary to the general law of nations. It was, until lately, carried on by all the nations of Europe; and a practice so sanctioned can only be rendered illegal, on the principles of international law, by the consent of all the powers. Many states had so consented, but others had not, and the cases had gone no further than

---

[a] 3 *Barnewall & Alderson*, 353.

to establish the rule, that ships belonging to countries that had prohibited the trade, were liable to capture and condemnation, if found engaged in it.

The final decision of the question, in this country, has been the same as in the case of the *Le Louis.* In the case of the *La Jeune Eugenie,*[a] it was decided in the Circuit Court of the United States, in Massachusetts, after a masterly discussion, that the slave trade was prohibited by universal law. But, subsequently, in the case of the *Antelope,*[b] the Supreme Court of the United States declared that the slave trade had been sanctioned, in modern times, by the laws of all nations who possessed distant colonies; and a trade could not be considered as contrary to the law of nations, which had been authorized and protected by the usages and laws of all commercial nations. It was not piracy, except so far as it was made so by the treaties or statutes of the nation to which the party belonged. It might still be lawfully carried on by the subjects of those nations who have not prohibited it by municipal acts or treaties.

---

[a] 2 *Mason,* 409. [b] 10 *Wheaton,* 66.

PART II.

OF THE GOVERNMENT AND CONSTITUTIONAL JURISPRUDENCE OF THE UNITED STATES.

LECTURE X.

OF THE HISTORY OF THE AMERICAN UNION.

The government of the United States was erected by the free voice and the joint will of the people of America, for their common defence and general welfare. Its powers apply to those great interests which relate to this country in its national capacity, and which depend for their stability and protection on the consolidation of the Union. It is clothed with the principal attributes of political sovereignty, and it is justly deemed the guardian of our best rights, the source of our highest civil and political duties, and the sure means of national greatness. The constitution and jurisprudence of the United States deserve the most accurate examination; and an historical view of the rise and progress of the Union, and of the establishment of the present constitution, as the necessary fruit of it, will tend to show the genius and value of the government, and prepare the mind of the student for an investigation of its powers.

The association of the American people into one body politic, took place while they were colonies of the British empire, and owed allegiance to the British crown. That the union of this country was essential to its safety, its prosperity, and its greatness, had been generally known, and frequently avowed, long before the late revolution, or the claims of the British parliament which produced it. The people of the New-England colonies were very early in the habit of confederating together for their common defence. As their origin and their interests were the same, and their manners, their religion, their laws, and their civil institutions exceedingly similar, they were naturally led to a very intimate connexion, and were governed by the same wants and wishes, the same sympathies and spirit. The colonies of Massachusetts, Plymouth, Connecticut, and New-Haven, as early as 1643, under the impression of danger from the surrounding tribes of Indians, entered into a league offensive and defensive, which they declared should be firm and perpetual, and be distinguished by the name of the United Colonies of New-England. By their articles of confederation, each colony was to have exclusive jurisdiction within its own territory; and in every war, offensive and defensive, each of the confederates was to furnish its quota of men and money, in a ratio to its population; and a congress of two commissioners, delegated from each colony, was to be held annually, with power to deliberate and decide on all points of common concern; and every determination, in which three fourths in number of the assembly concurred, was to be binding upon the whole confederacy.[a]

This association may be considered as the foundation of a series of efforts for a more extensive and more perfect union of the colonies. It contained some provident and jealous provisions, calculated to give security and stability to the whole. It provided that no two colonies were to join in jurisdiction, without the consent of all; and it required the like unanimous consent to admit any other colo-

---

[a] *Hazard's State Papers*, 496. 588. 590. *Hutchinson's History of Massachusetts*, vol. 1. 124. 126. *Robertson's Posthumous History of America*, b. 10. p. 191, 192.

ny into the confederacy; and if any one member violated any article of it, or any way injured another colony, the commissioners of the other colonies were to take cognizance of the matter, and determine upon it. Though in this transaction the New-England colonies acted in fact as independent sovereignties, and free from the control of any superior power, yet the civil war in which England was then involved, occupied the whole attention of the mother country, and this first step towards a future independence was suffered to pass without much notice, and without any animadversion. The confederacy subsisted, with some alterations, for upwards of forty years, and for part of that time with the countenance of the government in England. It was not dissolved until the year 1686, when the charters of the New-England colonies were in effect vacated by a commission from King James II.

The people of this country, after the dissolution of this earliest league, continued to afford other instructive precedents of association for their safety. A congress of governors and commissioners from other colonies, as well as from New-England, was occasionally held, to make arrangements for the more effectual protection of our interior frontier, and we have an instance of one of these assemblies at Albany, in 1722.[a] But a much more interesting congress was held there in the year 1754, and it consisted of commissioners from New-Hampshire, Massachusetts, Rhode-Island, Connecticut, New-York, Pennsylvania, and Maryland, and it was called at the instance of the lords commissioners for trade and the plantations, to take into consideration the best means of defending America, in case of a war with France, which was then impending. The object of the English administration in calling this convention, was merely in reference to treaties of friendship with the Indian tribes; but the colonies had more enlarged views; and the commissioners which met in congress, and who enrolled among their

---

[a] *Smith's History of New-York*, p. 171.

number some of the most distinguished names in our colonial history, asserted and promulgated several invaluable truths, the proper reception of which, in the minds of their countrymen, prepared the way for their future independence and our present greatness. Two of the colonies expressly instructed their delegates to enter into articles of union and confederation with the other colonies, for their general security in peace as well as in war. The convention unanimously resolved, that a union of the colonies was absolutely necessary for their preservation. They rejected all proposals for a division of the colonies into separate confederacies, and proposed a plan of federal government, consisting of a general council of delegates, to be triennially chosen by the provincial assemblies, and a president general, to be appointed by the crown. In this council was vested, subject to the immediate negative of the president, and the eventual negative of the king in council, the rights of war and peace, in respect to the Indian nations; and the confederacy was to embrace all the then existing colonies, from New-Hampshire to Georgia. The council were to have authority to make laws for the government of new settlements, upon territories to be purchased from the Indians, and to raise troops and build forts, and even to equip vessels of force, to guard the coast and protect trade, as well on the ocean as upon the lakes and rivers. They were likewise to make laws, and lay and levy general duties, imposts, and taxes, for those necessary purposes.[a] But the times were not yet ripe, nor the minds of men sufficiently enlarged, for such a comprehensive proposition; and this bold project of a continental union had the singular fate of being rejected, not only on the part of the crown, but by every provincial assembly. It was probably supposed, on the one hand, that the operation of the union would teach the colonies the se-

---

[a] *Minot's History of Massachusetts*, vol. 1. ch. 9. *Franklin's Works*, p. 85. London ed. 1779. *Belknap's New-Hampshire*, vol. 2. 285.

cret of their own strength, and the proper means to give it activity and direction; while, on the other part, the colonies were jealous of the preponderating influence of the royal prerogative. We were destined to remain, for some years longer, separate, and, in a considerable degree, alien commonwealths, emulous of each other in obedience to the parent state, and in devotion to her interests; but jealous of each other's prosperity, and divided by policy, institutions, prejudice and manners. So strong was the force of these considerations, and so exasperated were the people of the colonies in their disputes with each other, concerning boundaries and charter claims, that Doctor Franklin (who was one of the commissioners to the congress that formed the plan of union in 1754) observed, in the year 1761, that a union of the colonies was absolutely impossible, or at least without being forced by the most grievous tyranny and oppression.[a]

The great value of a federate union of the colonies had, however, sunk deep into the minds of men. The subject was familiar to our colonial ancestors. They had been in the habit, especially in seasons of danger and difficulty, of forming associations, more or less extensive. The necessity of union had been felt, its advantages perceived, its principles explained, the way to it pointed out, and the people of this country were led, by the force of irresistible motives, to resort to the same means of defence and security, when they considered that their liberties were in danger, not from the vexatious and irregular warfare of the Indian tribes, but from the formidable claims and still more formidable power of the parent state. When the first unfriendly attempt upon our chartered privileges was made, in the year 1765, a congress of delegates from nine colonies was assembled at New-York, at the recommendation of Massachusetts, and they digested a bill of rights, in which the sole power of taxation was declared to reside in their own colo-

---

[a] *Franklin's Works,* p. 152. 192.

nial legislatures.[a] This was preparatory to a more extensive and general association of the colonies, which took place in September, 1774, and laid the foundations of our independence and permanent glory. The more serious claims of the British parliament, and the impending oppressions of the British crown at this last critical period, induced the twelve colonies, which were spread over this vast continent from Nova Scotia to Georgia, to an interchange of opinions and views, and to unite in sending delegates to Philadelphia, " with authority and direction to meet and consult together for the common welfare." In pursuance of their authority, this first continental congress, whose names and proceedings are still familiar to the present age, and will live in the gratitude of a distant posterity, took into consideration the afflicted state of their country; asserted, by a number of declaratory resolutions, what they deemed to be the unalienable rights of English freemen; pointed out to their constituents, the system of violence which was preparing against those rights; and bound them by the most sacred of all ties, the ties of honour and of their country, to renounce commerce with Great Britain, as being the most salutary means to avert the one, and to secure the blessings of the other. These resolutions received prompt and universal obedience; and the Union being thus auspiciously formed, it was continued by a succession of delegates in congress; and through every period of the war, and through every revolution of our government, this union has been revered and cherished as the guardian of our peace, and the only solid foundation of national independence.

In May, 1775, a congress again assembled at Philadelphia, and was clothed with ample discretionary powers. The delegates were instructed to " concert, agree upon, direct, order, and prosecute," such measures as they should deem

---

[a] 2 Belknap's N. H. 326.

most fit and proper, to obtain redress of American grievances, or, in more general terms, they were to take care of the liberties of the country.[a] Soon after their meeting, Georgia acceded to, and completed the confederacy of the thirteen colonies. Hostilities had already commenced in the province of Massachusetts, and the claim of the British parliament to an unconditional and unlimited sovereignty over the colonies, was to be asserted by an appeal to arms. The continental congress, charged with the protection of the rights and interests of the United Colonies, and intrusted with the power, and sustained by the zeal and confidence of their constituents, prepared for resistance. They published a declaration of the causes and necessity of taking up arms, and proceeded immediately to levy and organize an army, to prescribe rules for the government of their land and naval forces, to contract debts, and emit a paper currency upon the faith of the Union, and gradually assuming all the powers of sovereignty, they, at last, on the 4th day of July, 1776, took a separate and equal station among the nations of the earth, by declaring the United Colonies to be free and independent states.

This memorable declaration, in imitation of that published by the United Netherlands on a similar occasion, recapitulated the oppressions of the British king, asserted it to be the natural right of every people to withdraw from tyranny, and with the dignity and the fortitude of conscious rectitude, it contained a solemn appeal to mankind in vindication of the necessity of the measure. By this declaration, made in the name, and by the authority of the people, the colonies were absolved from all allegiance to the British crown, and all political connexion between them and Great Britain was totally dissolved. The principle of self-preservation, and the right of every community to freedom and happiness, gave a sanction to this separation. When the government established over any people becomes in-

---

[a] *Journals of Congress*, vol. 1. p. 74.

competent to fulfil its purpose, or destructive to the essential ends for which it was instituted, it is the right of that people, founded on the law of nature and the reason of mankind, and supported by the soundest authority and some very illustrious precedents, to throw off such government, and provide new guards for their future security. This right is the more apparent, and the duty of exercising it becomes the more clear and unequivocal, in the case of colonies which are situated at a great distance from the mother country, and which cannot be governed by it without vexatious and continually increasing inconvenience; and when they have arrived at maturity in strength and resources, or, in the language of Montesquieu, which he applied to our very case, " when they have grown great nations in the forests they were sent to inhabit." If, in addition to these intrinsic causes, gradually and powerfully tending to a separation, the parent state should think fit, in the arrogance of power and superiority, to deny to her colonies the equal blessings of her own free government, and should put forth a claim to an unlimited control, in her own discretion, over all their rights, and the whole administration of their affairs, the consequence would then be almost inevitable, that the colonists would rise, and repel the claim; and more certainly would this be the case, if they were a spirited and intelligent race of men, true to themselves, and just to their posterity.

The general opinion in favour of the importance and value of the Union, appears evident in all the proceedings of congress; and as early as the declaration of independence, it was thought expedient, for its security and duration, to define with precision, and by a formal instrument, the nature of our compact, the powers of Congress, and the residuary sovereignty of the states. On the 11th of June, 1776, Congress undertook to digest and prepare articles of confederation. But the business was attended with much embarrassment and delay, and notwithstanding these states were then surrounded with the same eminent dangers, and were contending for the same illustrious prize, it was not until the

15th of November, 1777, that Congress could so far unite the discordant interests and prejudices of thirteen distinct communities, as to agree to the articles of confederation. And when those articles were submitted to the state legislatures for their perusal and ratification, they were declared to be the result of impending necessity, and of a disposition for conciliation, and that they were agreed to, not for their intrinsic excellence, but as the best system which could be adapted to the circumstances of all, and, at the same time, afford any tolerable prospect of general assent.[a]

These celebrated articles met with still greater obstacles in their progress through the states. Most of the legislatures ratified them with a promptitude which showed their sense of the necessity of the confederacy, and of the indulgence of a liberal spirit of accommodation. But Delaware did not accede to them until the year 1779, and Maryland explicitly rejected them.[b] She instructed her delegates to withhold their assent to the articles, until there was an amendment, or additional agreement, to appropriate the new lands in the western parts of the Union, as a common fund to defray the expenses of the war.[c] These lands were claimed by the states within whose asserted limits and jurisdiction they were situated, and several of them, from a deep sense of the importance of the Union, agreed to an unconditional ratification of the articles, or, in other words, to a separate confederacy between the states so ratifying the same, though Maryland, or other states, should withhold their approbation and sanction.[d] The legislature of New-York, by their acts of 23d of October, 1779, and 19th of February, 1780, even consented to a release of the unsettled lands in the western part of the state, for the use and benefit of such of the United States as should become members of the federal alliance; and to resign the jurisdiction, as well as the right

---

[a] *Journals of Cong.* vol. 3.
[b] *Ibid.* vol. 7.
[c] *Journals of Cong.* vol. 5. p. 208.
[d] *Ibid.* vol. 5.

of pre-emption, over her waste and uncultivated territory. The refusal of Maryland, so long persisted in, gave encouragement to the enemy, and injured the common cause, and damped the hopes of the friends of America at home and abroad. These considerations at last induced that state to make a generous sacrifice of her pretensions, and on the first of March, 1781, and which was upwards of three years from their first promulgation, the articles of confederation received the unanimous approbation of the United States.

The difficulties which impeded the framing and adopting the articles of confederation, even during the pressure of a common calamity, and which nothing at last but a sense of common danger could surmount, form a striking example of the mighty force of local interests and discordant passions, and they teach a monitory lesson of moderation to political councils.

Notwithstanding the articles of confederation conferred upon Congress (though in a very imperfect manner, and under a most unskilful organization,) the chief rights of political supremacy, the *jura summi imperii*, yet they were, in fact, but a digest, and even a limitation, in the shape of a written compact, of those undefined and discretionary sovereign powers, which were delegated by the colonies to Congress in 1775, and which had been freely exercised, and implicitly obeyed. A remarkable instance of the exercise of this original, dormant, and vast discretion, appears on the Journals of Congress the latter end of the year 1776. The progress of the British arms had, at that period, excited the most alarming apprehensions for our safety, and Congress transferred to the commander in chief, for the term of six months, complete dictatorial power over the liberty and property of the citizens of the United States, in like manner as the Roman senate, in the critical times of the republic, was wont to have recourse to a dictator, *ne quid respublica detrimenti capiat*.[a] Such loose undeterminate authority

---

[a] *Journals of Congress*, vol. 2. p. 475.

as the Union originally possessed, was absolutely incompatible with any regular notions of liberty. Though it was exercised in the instance we have referred to, and in other strong cases, with the best intentions, and under the impulse of an irresistible necessity, yet such an irregular sovereignty never could be durable. It would either dwindle into insignificance, or degenerate into a despotism.

The powers of congress, as enumerated in the articles of confederation, would perhaps have been competent for all the essential purposes of the union, had they been duly distributed among the departments of a well-balanced government, and been carried down, through the medium of a federal judicial and executive power, to the individual citizens of the union. The exclusive cognizance of our foreign relations, the rights of war and peace, and the right to make unlimited requisitions of men and money, were confided to congress, and the exercise of them was binding upon the states. But, in imitation of all the former confederacies of independent states, either in ancient Greece or in modern Europe, the articles of confederation carried the decrees of the federal council to the states in their sovereign or collective capacity. This was the great fundamental defect in the confederation of 1781; it led to its eventual overthrow; and it has proved pernicious or destructive to all other federal governments which adopted the principle. Disobedience to the laws of the union must either be submitted to by the government to its own disgrace, or those laws must be enforced by arms. The mild influence of the civil magistrate, however strongly it may be felt and obeyed by private individuals, will not be heeded by an organized community, conscious of its strength, and swayed by its passions. The history of the federal governments of Greece, Germany, Switzerland, and Holland, afford melancholy examples of destructive civil war springing from the disobedience of the separate members. I will mention only a *single instance* to this effect, taken from the generally uninteresting annals of the Swiss cantons. By one of the articles of the Helvetic alliance, the cantons were bound to submit any difference which might arise between them to arbitrators. In the year 1440, a dispute arose between Zuric on the one side, and the cantons of Schweitz and Glaris on the other, respecting some territorial claims. Zuric refused to submit to a decision against her, and the contending parties took to arms. All Switzerland were of course armed against Zuric, the refractory member. She sought protection from her ancient enemy the House of Austria, and the controversy was not terminated in favour of the federal decree, until after six years of furious and destructive war.[a]

Had there been sufficient energy in the government of the United States, under the articles of confederation, to have enforced the constitutional requisitions, it might have proved fatal to public liberty; for congress, as then constituted, was a most unfit and unsafe depository of political power, since all the authority of the nation, in one complicated mass of jurisdiction, was vested in a single body of men. It was, indeed, exceedingly fortunate, as the event has subsequently shown, that the state legislatures even refused to confer upon congress the right to levy and collect a general impost, notwithstanding the refusal appeared to be extremely disastrous at the time, and was deeply regretted by the intelligent friends of the union. Had such a power been granted, the effort to amend the confederation would probably not have been made, and the people of this country might have been languishing, to this day, the miserable victims of a feeble and incompetent union.

There was no provision in the articles of confederation, enabling congress to add a sanction to its laws. In this respect, they were more defective than some of the other federal governments which are to be met with in history. The Amphyctionic Council in Greece had authority to fine and punish their refractory states. Lacedemon and Phocis were both prosecuted before the Council of the Amphyc-

---

[a] *Hist. de la Confed. Helv. par Watteville*, liv. 5. *Planta's Hist. of Switzerland*, vol. 1. last ch.

tions, (which was a council of the representatives of twelve nations of Greece,) and all the Greek states were required by proclamation to enforce the decree. The Germanic Diet, as it formerly existed, could put its members under the ban of the empire, by which their property was confiscated; and it was aided in enforcing obedience to its laws by a federal judiciary, and an executive head. Congress, under the old confederation, like the States General under the Dutch confederacy, were restricted from any constructive assumption of power, however essential it might have been deemed to the complete enjoyment and exercise of that which was given. No express grant conveyed any implied power; and it is easy to perceive that a strict and rigorous adherence to the letter of the grant, without permission to give it a liberal and equitable interpretation, in furtherance of the beneficent ends of the government, must, in many cases, frustrate entirely the purposes of the power. A government too restricted for the due performance of its high trusts, will either become insignificant, or be driven to usurpation. We have examples of this in the government of the United Netherlands, before it was swept away by the violence of the French revolution. While that government moved within its constitutional limits, it was more absolutely nerveless than any other government which ever existed. The States General could neither make war or peace, or contract alliances, or raise money, without the consent of every province; nor the provincial states conclude those points without the consent of every city having a voice in their assemblies. The consequence was, that the federal head was frequently induced, by imperious necessity, to assume power unwarranted by the fundamental charter of the union, and to dispense with the requisite unanimity. This was done in the years 1648, 1657, and 1661, as well as in another strong instance given by Sir William Temple, and of which he was the author.[a]

---

[a] *Temple's Works*, vol. 1. 115. 128. 387.

The former confederation of this country was defective also, in not giving complete authority to congress to interfere in contests between the several states, and to protect each state from internal violence and rebellion. In many respects, our confederation was superior to those of Germany, Holland, or Switzerland, and particularly in the absolute prohibition to the several states, from any interference or concern in foreign or domestic alliances, or from the maintenance of land or naval forces in time of peace. But in the leading features which I have suggested, and in others of inferior importance, it was a most unskilful fabric, and totally incompetent to fulfil the ends for which it was erected. Almost as soon as it was ratified, the states began to fail in a prompt and faithful obedience to its laws. As danger receded, instances of neglect became more frequent, and by the time of the peace of 1783, the disease of the government had displayed itself with alarming rapidity. The delinquencies of one state became a pretext or apology for those of another. The idea of supplying the pecuniary exigencies of the nation, from requisitions on the states, was soon found to be altogether delusive. The national engagements seemed to have been entirely abandoned. Even the contributions for the ordinary expenses of the government, fell almost entirely upon the two states which had the most domestic resources. Attempts were very early made by congress, and in remonstrances the most manly and persuasive, to obtain from the several states the right of levying, for a limited time, a general impost, for the exclusive purpose of providing for the discharge of the national debt. It was found impracticable to unite the states in any provision for the national safety and honour. Interfering regulations of trade, and interfering claims of territory, were dissolving the friendly attachments, and the sense of common interest, which had cemented and sustained the Union during the arduous struggles of the revolution. Symptoms of distress, and marks of humiliation, were rapidly accumulating. It was with difficulty that the attention of the states could be sufficiently exerted to induce them to keep up a sufficient representation in congress to form a quorum for business. The finances of the nation were annihilated. The whole army of the United States was reduced, in 1784, to 80 persons, and the states were urged to provide some of the militia to garrison the western posts. In short, to use the language of the authors of the *Federalist*, " each state, yielding to the voice of immediate interest or convenience, successively withdrew its support from the confederation, till the frail and tottering edifice was ready to fall upon our heads, and to crush us beneath its ruins."

Most of the federal constitutions in the world have degenerated or perished in the same way, and by the same means. They are to be classed among the most defective political institutions which have been erected by mankind for their security. The great and incurable defect of all former federal governments, such as the Amphictyonic, the Achæan, and Lycian confederacies in ancient Greece; and the Germanic, the Helvetic, the Hanseatic, and the Dutch republics, in modern history, is, that they were sovereignties over sovereigns, and legislations, not for private individuals, but for communities in their political capacity. The only coercion for disobedience was physical force, instead of the decree and the pacific arm of the civil magistrate. The inevitable consequence in every case in which a member chose to be disobedient, was either a civil war, or an annihilation of national authority.

The first effort to relieve the people of this country from a state of national degradation and ruin, came from Virginia, in a proposition for a convention of delegates to regulate our commerce with foreign nations. The proposal was well received by the other states, and several of them sent delegates to a convention which met at Annapolis, in September, 1786. This small assembly, being only a partial representation of the states, and being deeply sensible of the radical defects of the system of the existing federal government, thought it inexpedient to attempt a partial, and probably only a temporary and delusive alleviation of our national calamities. They concurred, therefore, in a strong application to congress for a general convention, to take into consideration the situation of the United States, and to devise such further provisions as should be proper to render the federal government not a mere phantom, as heretofore, but a real government, adequate to the exigencies of the union. Congress perceived the wisdom, and felt the patriotism of the suggestion, and recommended a convention of delegates from the several states, to revise, amend and alter the articles of confederation. All the states, except Rhode-Island, acceded to the proposal, and appointed delegates, who assembled in a general convention at Philadelphia in May, 1787.

This was a crisis most solemn and eventful, in respect to our future fortune and prosperity. All the fruits of the revolution, and perhaps the final destiny of republican government, were staked on the experiment which was then to be made to reform the system of our national compact. Happily for this country, and probably as auspiciously for the general liberties of mankind, the convention combined a very rare union of the best talents, experience, information, patriotism, probity and character which the country afforded; and it commanded that universal public confidence which such qualifications were calculated to inspire. After several months of tranquil deliberation, the convention agreed with unprecedented unanimity on the plan of government which now forms the constitution of the United States. This plan was directed to be submitted to a convention of delegates, to be chosen by the people at large in each state, for their assent and ratification. This was laying the foundations of the fabric of our national polity, where alone they ought to be laid, on the broad consent of the people. The constitution underwent a severe scrutiny and long discussion, not only in public prints and private circles, but solemnly and publicly, by the many illustrious statesmen who composed these local conventions. Near a year elapsed before it received the ratification of a requisite number of the states to give it a political existence. New-Hampshire was the ninth state which adopted the constitution, and thereby, according to one of its articles, it was to become the government of the states so ratifying the same. Her example was immediately followed by the powerful states of Virginia and New-York, and on the 4th of March, 1789, the government was duly organized and put in operation. North-Carolina and Rhode-Island withheld some time longer their assent. Their scruples were, however, gradually overcome, and in June, 1790, the constitution had received the unanimous ratification of all the members of the original confederacy.

The peaceable adoption of this government, under all the circumstances which attended it, presented the case of an effort of deliberation, combined with a spirit of amity and of mutual concession which was without example. It must be a source of just pride and of the most grateful recollection to every American, who reflects seriously on the difficulty of the experiment, the manner in which it was conducted, the felicity of its issue, and the fate of similar trials in other nations of the earth.

LECTURE XI.

OF CONGRESS.

The power of making laws is the supreme power in a state, and the department in which it resides will naturally have such a preponderance in the political system, and act with such mighty force upon the public mind, that the line of separation between that and the other branches of the government ought to be marked very distinctly, and with the most careful precision.

The constitution of the United States has effected this purpose with great felicity of execution, and in a way well calculated to preserve the equal balance of the government, and the harmony of its operations. It has not only made a general delegation of the legislative power to one branch of the government, of the executive to another, and of the judicial to the third, but it has specially defined the general powers and duties of each of those departments. This was essential to peace and safety in a government clothed only with specific powers for national purposes, and erected in the midst of numerous state governments retaining the exclusive control of their local concerns. It will be the object of this lecture to review the legislative department, and I shall consider this great title in our national polity under the following heads: (1.) The constituent parts of congress, and the mode of their appointment; (2.) Their joint and separate powers and privileges; (3.) Their method of enacting laws, with the qualified negative of the President.

(1.) By the constitution,[a] all the legislative powers there-

---

[a] Art. 1. sec. 1.

in granted, are vested in a congress, consisting of a senate and house of representatives.

The division of the legislature into two separate and independent branches, is founded in such obvious principles of good policy, and is so strongly recommended by the unequivocal language of experience, that it has obtained the general approbation of the people of this country. The great object of this separation of the legislature into two houses, acting separately, and with co-ordinate powers, is to destroy the evil effects of sudden and strong excitement, and of precipitate measures springing from passion, caprice, prejudice, personal influence, and party intrigue, and which have been found, by sad experience, to exercise a potent and dangerous sway in single assemblies. A hasty decision is not so likely to arrive to the solemnities of a law, when it is to be arrested in its course, and made to undergo the deliberation, and probably the jealous and critical revision, of another and a rival body of men, sitting in a different place, and under better advantages to avoid the prepossessions and correct the errors of the other branch. The legislatures of Pennsylvania and Georgia consisted originally of a single house. The instability and passion which marked their proceedings were very visible at the time, and the subject of much public animadversion; and in the subsequent reform of their constitutions, the people were so sensible of this defect, and of the inconvenience they had suffered from it, that in both states a senate was introduced. No portion of the political history of mankind is more full of instructive lessons on this subject, or contains more striking proof of the faction, instability, and misery of states, under the dominion of a single unchecked assembly, than that of the Italian republics of the middle ages; and which arose in great numbers, and with dazzling but transient splendour, in the interval between the fall of the Western and the Eastern empire of the Romans. They were all alike ill constituted, with a single unbalanced assembly.

They were all alike miserable, and all ended in similar disgrace.[a]

Many speculative writers and theoretical politicians, about the time of the commencement of the French revolution, were struck with the simplicity of a legislature with a single assembly, and concluded that more than one house was useless and expensive. This led the elder President Adams to write and publish his great work, entitled, "A Defence of the Constitutions of Government of the United States," in which he vindicates, with much learning and ability, the value and necessity of the division of the legislature into two branches, and of the distribution of the different powers of the government into distinct departments. He reviewed the history, and examined the construction of all mixed and free governments which had ever existed, from the earliest records of time, in order to deduce with more certainty and force his great practical truth, that single assemblies, without check or balance, or a government with all authority collected into one centre, according to the notion of M. Turgot, were visionary, violent, intriguing, corrupt and tyrannical dominations of majorities over minorities, and uniformly and rapidly terminating their career in a profligate despotism.

This visionary notion of a single house of the legislature was carried into the constitution which the French national assembly adopted in 1791. The very nature of things, said the intemperate and crude politicians of that assembly, was adverse to every division of the legislative body; and that, as the nation which was represented was one, so the representative body ought to be one also. The will of the nation was indivisible, and so ought to be the voice which pronounced it. If there were two chambers, with a *veto* upon the acts of each other, in some cases they would be reduced to perfect inaction. By such reasoning, the national assembly of France, consisting of upwards of one thousand mem-

---

[a] *Adams' Defence of the American Constitutions*, vol. 3. 502.

bers, after a short and tumultuous debate, almost unanimously voted to reject the proposition of an upper house.[a] The same false and vicious principle continued for some time longer to prevail with the theorists of that country; and a single house was likewise established in the plan of government published by the French convention in 1793. The instability and violent measures of that convention, which continued for some years to fill all Europe with astonishment and horror, tended to display in a most forcible and affecting light, the miseries of a single unchecked body of men, clothed with all the legislative powers of the state. It is very possible that the French nation might have been hurried into the excesses of a revolution even under a better organization of their government; but if the proposition of M. Lally Tolendal to constitute a senate, or upper house, to be composed of members chosen for life, had prevailed, the constitution would have had much more stability, and afforded infinitely greater probability of preserving the nation in order and tranquillity. Their own sufferings taught the French people to listen to that oracle of wisdom, the experience of other countries and ages, and which for some years they had utterly disregarded, amidst the hurry and the violence of those passions by which they were inflamed. No people, said M. Boissy d'Angles in 1795, can testify to the world with more truth and sincerity than Frenchmen can do, the dangers inherent in a single legislative assembly, and the point to which factions may mislead an assembly without reins or counterpoise. We accordingly find that in the next constitution, which arose in 1797, there was a division of the legislature, and a council of ancients was introduced to give stability and moderation to the government; and this idea of two houses was never afterwards abandoned.

The senate of the United States is composed[b] of two senators from each state, chosen by the legislature thereof

---

[a] N. A. Reg. for 1791. Hist. p. 49. [b] Art. 1. sec. 3.

for six years, and each senator has one vote. The senate at present consists of forty-eight members, representing the twenty-four states of the union. In this part of the constitution, we readily perceive the features of the old confederation. Each state has its equal voice and equal weight in the senate, without any regard to disparity of population, wealth or dimensions. This arrangement must have been the result of that spirit of amity and mutual concession, which was rendered indispensable by the peculiarity of our political condition. It is grounded on the idea of sovereignty in the states; and every independent community, as we have already seen,*a* is equal by the law of nations, and has a perfect right to dictate its own terms before it enters into a social compact. On the principle of consolidation of the states, this organization would have been inadmissible, for in that case each state would have been merged in one single and entire government. At the time the articles of confederation were preparing, it was attempted to allow the states an influence and power in congress in a ratio to their numbers and wealth, but the idea of separate and independent states was at that day so strongly cherished, that the proposition met with no success.*b*

The election of the senate by the state legislatures, is also a recognition of their separate and independent existence, and renders them absolutely essential to the operation of the national government. There were difficulties some years ago as to the true construction of the constitution in the choice of senators. They were to be *chosen by the legislatures*, and the legislature was to prescribe the times, places and manner of holding elections for senators, and congress are authorized to make and alter such regulations, except as to the place.*c* As the legislature may prescribe the *manner*, it has been considered and settled in this state, that the legislature may prescribe that they shall be chosen

---

a Lecture 2. p. 21 *b* *Journals of Congress.* vol. 9. 416.
c Art. 1. sec. 4.

by joint vote or ballot of the two houses, in case the two houses cannot separately concur in a choice, and then the weight of the senate is dissipated and lost in the more numerous vote of the assembly. This construction has become too convenient, and has been too long settled by the recognition of senators so elected, to be now disturbed; though I should think, if the question was a new one, that when the constitution directed that the senators should be chosen *by the legislature*, it meant not the members of the legislature *per capita*, but the legislature in the true technical sense, being the two houses acting in their separate and organized capacities, with the ordinary constitutional right of negative on each other's proceedings. This was a contemporary exposition of the clause in question, and was particularly maintained in the well known letters of the *Federal Farmer*,[a] who surveyed the constitution with a jealous and scrutinizing eye.

The small number, and long duration of the Senate, were intended to render them a safeguard against the influence of those paroxysms of heat and passion, which are apt to prevail occasionally in the most enlightened communities, and to enter into the deliberation of popular assemblies. In this point of view, a firm and independent senate is justly regarded as an anchor of safety amidst the storms of political faction; and for the want of such a stable body, the republics of Athens and Florence were overturned by the fury of commotions, which the senates of Sparta and Rome might have been able to withstand. The characteristical qualities of the senate, in the intendment of the constitution, are wisdom and stability. The legal presumption is, that the senate will entertain more enlarged views of public policy, will feel a higher and juster sense of national character, and a greater regard for stability in the administration of the government. These qualities, it is true, may, in most cases, be equally found in the other branch of the legislature, but

---

a Letter 12.

the constitutional structure of the house is not equally calculated to produce them; for, as the house of representatives comes more immediately from the people, and the members hold their seats for a much shorter time, they are presumed to partake, with a quicker sensibility, of the prevailing temper and irritable disposition of the times, and to be in much more danger of adopting measures with precipitation, and of changing them with levity. A mutable legislation is attended with a formidable train of mischiefs to the community. It weakens the force, and increases the intricacy of the laws, hurts credit, lessens the value of property, and it is an infirmity very incident to republican establishments, and has been a constant source of anxiety and concern to their most enlightened admirers.[a] A disposition to multiply, and to change laws, upon the spur of the occasion, and to be making constant and restless experiments with the statute code, seems to be the natural disease of popular assemblies. In order, therefore, to counteract such a dangerous propensity, and to maintain a due portion of confidence in the government, and to insure its safety and character at home and abroad, it is requisite that another body of men, coming likewise from the people, and equally responsible for their conduct, but resting on a more permanent basis, and constituted with stronger inducements to moderation in debate, and to tenacity of purpose, should be placed as a check upon the intemperance of the more popular department.

The senate have been, from the first formation of the government, divided into three classes; and the rotation of the classes was originally determined by lot, and the seats of one class are vacated at the expiration of every second year, and one third of the senate are chosen every second year.[b] This provision was borrowed from a similar one in some of the state constitutions, of which Virginia gave the first example; and it is admirably calculated, on the one hand, to in-

---

[a] *Federalist*, vol. 2. No. 62. [b] Art. 1. sec. 3.

fuse into the senate biennially, renewed public confidence and vigour; and, on the other, to retain a large portion of experienced members, duly initiated into the general principles of national policy, and the forms and course of business in the house.

The superior weight and delicacy of the trust confided to the senate, and which will be shown more fully hereafter, is a reason why the constitution[a] requires that a senator should be thirty years of age, and nine years a citizen of the United States, and, at the time of his election, an inhabitant of the state for which he is chosen. The same age was also requisite for a Roman senator, though, in their executive offices, no qualification of age was required. *Ne ætas quidem distinguebatur quin prima juventa consulatum ac dictaturas inirent.*[b] It has also been deemed fit and proper, in a country which was colonized originally from several parts of Europe, and has been disposed to adopt the most liberal policy towards the rest of mankind, that a period of citizenship sufficient to create an attachment to our government, and a knowledge of its principles, should render an emigrant eligible to office. The English policy is not quite so enlarged. No alien born can become a member of parliament. This disability was imposed by the act of settlement of 12 Wm. III c. 2. and no bill of naturalization can be received in either house of parliament, without such disabling clause in it.

The house of representatives is composed of members chosen every second year by the people of the several states, who are qualified electors of the most numerous branch of the legislature of the state to which they belong. No person can be a representative until he hath attained the age of twenty-five years, and hath been seven years a citizen of the United States, and is, at the time of his election, an inhabitant of the state in which he is chosen.[c]

---

a Art. 1. sec. 3.   b *Tac. Ann.* lib. 11. 22.
c Art. 1. sec. 2.

The general qualifications of electors of the assembly, or most numerous branch of the legislature in the several state governments, are, that they be of the age of twenty-one years and upwards, and free resident citizens of the state in which they vote, and have paid taxes, and in some of the states they are required to possess property, and to be white, as well as free citizens. The description is almost every where so large, as to include all persons who are of competent discretion, and are interested in the welfare of the government, and liable to bear any of its duties or burdens. The house of representatives may, therefore, very fairly be said to represent the whole body of the American people. Several of the state constitutions have prescribed the same, or higher qualifications, as to property in the elected, than in the electors, and some of them have required a religious test. But the constitution of the United States requires no evidence of property in the representative, nor any declaration of religious belief. He is only required to be a citizen of the competent age, and free from any undue bias or dependence, by not holding any office under the United States.[a]

The term for which a representative is to serve ought not to be so short as to prevent him from obtaining a comprehensive acquaintance with the business to which he is deputed; nor so long as to make him forget the transitory nature of his seat, and his state of dependence on the approbation of his constituents. It ought also to be considered as a fact deeply interesting to the character and utility of representative republics, that very frequent elections have a tendency to render the office less important than it ought to be deemed, and the people inattentive in the exercise of their right; whilst, on the other hand, long intervals between the elections are apt to make them produce too much excitement, and consequently to render the periods of their return a time of too much competition and conflict for the

---

a Art. 1. sec. 6.

public tranquillity. The constitution has certainly not deviated in this respect to the latter extreme, in the establishment of biennial elections. It has probably selected a medium, which, considering the situation and extent of our country, combines as many advantages and avoids as many inconveniences as any other term which might have been inserted.

The representatives are directed to be apportioned among the states, according to numbers, which is determined by adding to the whole number of free persons, exclusive of Indians not taxed, three fifths of all other persons.[a] The number of representatives cannot exceed one for every thirty thousand, but each state is entitled to have at least one representative. By the act of 7th March, 1822, the representatives were apportioned among the several states according to the fourth census, and to a ratio of one representative for every forty thousand persons in each state, making in the whole two hundred and thirteen members, the number of which the present house of representatives is composed, besides delegates from three of the territories belonging to the United States, and which have a right to debate, but not to vote.

The rule of apportionment established by the constitution, is exposed to the objection, that three fifths of the slaves in the southern states are computed in establishing the apportionment of the representation. But this article was the result of necessity, and grew out of the fact of the existence of domestic slavery in a portion of our country. The evil has been of too long standing, and is too extensive and too deeply rooted to be speedily eradicated, or even to be discussed without great judgment and discretion. But the same rule which apportions the representatives, extends to direct taxes; and the slaves in the southern states, while they give those states an increased number of representatives, contribute, on the other hand, when that mode of

---

[a] Art. 1. sec. 2.

taxation is resorted to, equally to increase the measure of their contributions.[a]

The number of the house of representatives would seem to be quite large enough on its present computation, and unless the ratio be hereafter enlarged beyond one to every forty thousand persons, the house will be in danger of increasing too rapidly, and it will probably become, in time, much too unwieldy a body for convenience of debate and joint consultation. A due acquaintance with the local interests of every part of the union ought to be carried into the house, and a sufficient number collected for all the purposes of information, discussion, and diffusive sympathy with the wants and wishes of the people. When these objects are obtained, any further increase neither promotes deliberation, nor increases the public safety. All numerous bodies of men, although selected with the greatest care, are too much swayed by passion, and too impatient of protracted deliberation.

The United States, in their improvements upon the exercise of the right of representation, may certainly claim pre-eminence over all other governments, ancient and modern. Our elections are held at stated seasons established by law. The people vote by ballot in small districts, and public officers preside over the elections, receive the votes, and maintain order and fairness. Though the competition between candidates is generally active, and the zeal of rival parties sufficiently excited, the elections are every where conducted with tranquillity. The legislature of each state prescribes the times, places, and manner of holding elections, subject, however, to the interference and control of congress, which is permitted them for the sake of their own preservation, and which it is to be presumed they will never be disposed to exercise, except when any state shall neglect or refuse to make adequate provision for the purpose. The privilege of voting, as we have already seen, is conferred

---

[a] *Federalist*, vol. 2. No. 54.

upon all persons who are of sufficient competency by their age, and of sufficient ability to take care of themselves. The ancient Greeks and Romans had not only very imperect notions of the value of representation, but the number and power of their popular assemblies were so great, and they were so liable to disorder, as to render it a very provident measure with them to be guarded in diffusing the privileges of free citizens. Not a tenth part of the people of Athens were admitted to the privilege of voting in the assemblies of the people; and indeed nine tenths of the inhabitants throughout all Greece were slaves.*a* In Sparta, the number of votes was fixed at ten thousand. In Rome this privilege was for many ages confined to the *Pomœria* of the city, and it continued to be so confined, and to be tolerable in its operation,*b* until the memorable focial war extended it to all the inhabitants of Italy. As no test of property or character was required, and as the people assembled within the walls of Rome in immense masses, and

---

a Mitford's Greece, vol. 1. 354. 357.

b The Roman mode of passing laws, and voting in their *comitia*, was orderly, and under great checks, during the best periods of the government. When a law was proposed and discussed, and the religious rites duly performed, and no intercession made, the people proceeded to vote, and every citizen was ordered to repair to his century. The method of voting was originally *viva voce*, but afterwards by ballot by the *leges tabellariæ*, which applied equally to the election of magistrates, to public trials, and to making and repealing laws. The people were made to pass in order over some narrow planks, called *pontes*, into the *septa* or inclosures, where certain officers delivered to every voter two tablets, one for and one against the proposition, and each person threw into a chest which of them he pleased, and they were pointed off, and the greatest number of points either way determined the sense of the century, and the greatest number of centuries passed for the voice of the whole people, who either passed or rejected the law. See *Heineccius' Antiquit. Rom. Jur.* lib. 1. tit. 2. sec. 3—11. *Opera*, tom. 4. where the ancient learning on the subject is collected; and see *Hooke's Rom. Hist.* b. 1. c. 7. sec. 4. note.

not merely to vote, but to make laws, this great innovation produced the utmost anarchy and corruption, and has justly been regarded as precipitating the fall of that commonwealth.^a

The English nation, in common with the other feudal governments of Europe, very anciently enjoyed the blessings of popular representation, and the knights, citizens and burgesses were intended to represent the farmers, merchants and manufacturers, being the several orders and classes of people of which the nation was composed.^b But the mutations of time, and commerce, and manufacturing establishments, in depopulating ancient boroughs, and in establishing new cities, have insensibly changed the structure of the house of commons, and rendered it, in theory at least, a very inadequate and imperfect organ of the will of the nation. Archdeacon Paley observed, forty years ago,^c that about one half of the commons were elected by the people, and the other half came in by purchase, or by the nomination of single proprietors of great estates. So extremely unequal is the popular vote at elections in England, that less than seven thousand voters return nearly one half of the house of commons. But, notwithstanding the great imperfection of the constitution of the English house of commons, if it were to be tested by the arithmetical accuracy of our own political standards, it has, nevertheless, in all periods of English history, felt strongly the vigour of the popular principle. While on the continent of Europe the degeneracy of the feudal system, the influence of the papal hierarchy, the political maxims of the imperial or civil law, and the force of standing armies, extinguished the bold and irregular freedom of the Gothic governments, and abolished

---

a Montesquieu's Esprit des Loix, tom. 1. l. 2. c. 2.—*Grand. et Decad. des Rom.* ch. 9.

b 1 *Black. Com.* 174. *Millar on the English Constitution.* b. 2. c. 6. sec. 1.

c Moral Philosophy, p. 369.

the representation of the people, the English house of commons continued to be the asylum of European liberty; and it maintained its station against all the violence of the Plantagenet line of princes, the haughty race of the Tudors, and the unceasing spirit of despotism in the house of Stuart. And when we take into consideration the admirable plan of their judicial polity, and those two distinguished guardians of civil liberty, trial by jury, and the freedom of the press, it is no longer a matter of astonishment, that the nation in full possession of those inestimable blessings, should enjoy greater security of person and property, than ever was enjoyed in Athens or Sparta, Carthage or Rome, or in any of the commonwealths of Italy, during the period of the middle ages.

I proceed next to consider the privileges and powers of the two Houses of Congress, both aggregately and separately.

Each house is made the sole judge of the election, return, and qualifications of its members.[a] The same power is vested in the British house of commons, and in the legislatures of the several states; and there is no other body known to the constitution to which such a power might safely be trusted. It is requisite to preserve a pure and genuine representation, and to control the evils of irregular, corrupt, and tumultuous elections; and as each house acts in these cases in a judicial character, its decisions, like the decisions of any other court of justice, ought to be regulated by known principles of law, and strictly adhered to, for the sake of uniformity and certainty. A majority of each house constitutes a quorum to do business, but a smaller number may adjourn from day to day, and compel the attendance of absent members, in such manner, and under such penalties, as each house may provide. Each house, likewise, determines the rules of its proceedings, and can punish its members for disorderly behaviour; and

---

[a] Art. 1. sec. 5.

with the concurrence of two thirds, expel a member. Each house is likewise bound to keep a journal of its proceedings, and from time to time publish such parts as do not require secrecy, and to enter the yeas and nays on the journal, on any question, when desired by one fifth of the members present.[a] The members of both houses are likewise privileged from arrest during their attendance on congress, and in going to and returning from the same, except in cases of treason, felony, and breach of the peace.[b] These privileges of the two houses are obviously necessary for their preservation and character; and what is still more important to the freedom of deliberation, no member can be questioned out of the house for any speech or debate therein.[c]

There is no power expressly given to either house of congress to punish for contempts, except when committed by their own members; but in the case of *Anderson*, who was committed by order of the house of representatives, for a contempt of the house, and taken into custody by the Serjeant at Arms, an action of trespass was brought against the officer, and the question on the power of the house to commit for a contempt, was carried by writ of error to the supreme court of the United States.[d] The court decided, that the house had that power, and that it was an implied power, and of vital importance to the safety, character, and dignity of the house. The necessity of its existence and exercise, was founded on the principle of self-preservation; and the power to punish extends no further than imprisonment, and that will continue no longer than the duration of the power that imprisons. The imprisonment will terminate with the adjournment or dissolution of congress.

The house of representatives has the exclusive right of originating all bills for raising revenue, and this is the only

---

a Art. 1. sec. 5.   b Art. 1. sec. 6.   c Art. 1. sec. 6.
d *Anderson* v. *Dun*. 6 *Wheaton*. 204.

privilege that house enjoys in its legislative character, which is not shared equally by the other, and even these bills are amendable by the senate in its discretion.*a* The two houses are an entire and perfect check upon each other, in all business appertaining to legislation; and one of them cannot even adjourn, during the session of congress, for more than three days, without the consent of the other, nor to any other place than that in which the two houses shall be sitting.

The powers of congress extend generally to all subjects of a national nature. Many of those powers will hereafter become the subject of particular observation and criticism. At present, it will be sufficient to observe, generally, that congress are authorized to provide for the common defence and general welfare, and for that purpose, among other express grants, they are authorized to lay and collect taxes, duties, imposts, and excises;—to borrow money on the credit of the United States;—to regulate commerce with foreign nations, and among the several states, and with the Indian tribes;—to declare war, and define and punish offences against the law of nations;—to raise, maintain, and govern armies, and a navy;—to organize, arm, and discipline the militia;—and to give full efficacy to all the powers contained in the constitution. Some of these powers, as the levying of taxes, duties, and excises, are concurrent with similar powers in the several states; but in most cases, these powers are exclusive, because the concurrent exercise of them by the states separately, would disturb the general harmony and peace, and because they would be apt to be repugnant to each other in practice, and lead to dangerous collisions. The powers which are conferred upon congress, and the prohibitions which are imposed upon the states, would seem, upon a fair and just construction of them, to be indispensable to secure to this country the inestimable blessings of union. The articles of con-

---

a Art. 1. sec. 7.   *b* Art. 1. sec. 8.

federation digested during the American war, intended to confer upon congress powers nearly equal to those with which they are now invested; but that compact gave them none of the means requisite to carry those powers into effect. And if the sentiment which has uniformly pervaded the minds of the people of this country be a just one, that the consolidated union of these states is indispensable to our national prosperity and happiness—and if we do not wish to be once more guilty of the great absurdity of proposing an end, and denying the means to attain it—then we must conclude, that the powers conferred upon congress are not disproportionate to the magnitude of the trust confided to the union, and which the union alone is competent to fulfil.

The rules of proceeding in each house are substantially the same, and though they are essential to the transaction of business with order and safety, they are too minute to be treated at length in an elementary survey of the constitutional polity and general jurisprudence of the United States. The house of representatives choose their own speaker, but the Vice-President of the United States is *ex officio* president of the senate, and gives the casting vote when they are equally divided. The proceedings and discussions in the two houses are public. This affords the community early and authentic information of the progress, reason, and policy of measures pending before congress, and it is likewise a powerful stimulus to industry, to research, and to the cultivation of talent and eloquence in debate. Though these advantages may be acquired at the expense of much useless and protracted discussion, yet the balance of utility is greatly in favour of open deliberation; and it is certain, from the general opposition to the experiment that was made and continued for some years by the senate of the United States, of sitting with closed doors, that such a practice, by any legislative body in this country, would not be endured.

The ordinary mode of passing laws is briefly as follows:[a] One day's notice of a motion for leave to bring in a bill in cases of a general nature, is required. Every bill must have three readings previous to its being passed, and these readings must be on different days, and no bill can be committed or amended until it has been twice read. Such little checks in the forms of doing business, are prudently intended to guard against surprise or imposition. In the house of representatives, bills, after being twice read, are committed to a committee of the whole house, when the speaker leaves the chair, and takes a part in the debate as an ordinary member, and a chairman is appointed to preside in his stead. When a bill has passed one house, it is transmitted to the other, and goes through a similar form; though, in the senate, there is less formality, and bills are often committed to a select committee chosen by ballot. If a bill be altered or amended in the house to which it is transmitted, it is then returned to the house in which it originated, and if the two houses cannot agree, they appoint committees to confer together on the subject. When a bill is engrossed, and has passed the sanction of both houses, it is transmitted to the President of the United States for his approbation: If he approves of the bill he signs it. If he does not, it is returned, with his objections, to the house in which it originated, and that house enters the objections at large on their journals, and proceeds to reconsider the bill. If, after such reconsideration, two thirds of that house should agree to pass the bill, it is sent, together with the objections, to the other house, by which it is likewise reconsidered, and

---

[a] See *the standing rules and orders of the house of representatives*, printed in 1795 by Francis Childs. Legislation was a science cultivated with so much care and refinement among the ancient Romans, that they had laws to instruct them how to make laws. The *Lex Licinia*, and *Lex Ebutia*, the *Lex Cæcilia*, and *Lex Didia*, provided checks, that the law should not unintentionally contain any particular personal privileges, or weaken the force of former laws, or be crowded with multifarious matter. *Gravina, De Ortu et Progressu Juris Civilis*, lib. 1. ch. 29.

if approved by two thirds of that house it becomes a law. But, in all such cases, the votes of both houses are determined by yeas and nays, and the names of the persons voting for and against the bill are entered on the journals. If any bill shall not be returned by the president within ten days (Sundays excepted) after it shall have been presented to him, the same becomes a law equally as if he had signed it, unless congress, by adjournment, in the mean time, prevents its return, and then it does not become a law."

The practice in congress, and especially in the second or last session of each congress, of retaining most of their bills until within the last ten days, is attended with the disadvantage of shortening the time allowed to the president for perusal and reflection upon them, and of placing within the power of the president, the absolute negative of every bill presented within the last ten days preceding the 4th of March; and this he can effect merely by retaining them, without being obliged to assign any reason whatever, for he is entitled to ten days to deliberate. Most of the bills that are presented to the president in the second session of every congress, were, a few years ago, presented to him within the last ten days, and generally within the last two days; but the rules of congress have latterly checked the evils and danger of such an accumulation of business on the last days of the session.

This qualified negative of the president upon the formation of laws, is, theoretically at least, some additional security against the passage of improper laws, through prejudice or want of due reflection; but it was principally intended to give to the president a constitutional weapon to defend the executive department, as well as the just balance of the constitution, against the usurpations of the legislative power. To enact laws is a transcendent power; and if the body that possesses it be a full and equal representation of the people, there is danger of its pressing with destructive

---

a Art. 1. sec. 7.

weight upon all the other parts of the machinery of the government. It has, therefore, been thought necessary, by the most skilful and the most experienced artists in the science of civil polity, that strong barriers should be erected for the protection and security of the other necessary powers of the government. Nothing has been deemed more fit and expedient for that purpose, than the provision that the head of the executive department should be so constituted as to secure a requisite share of independence, and that he should have a negative upon the passing of laws, and that the judiciary power, resting on a still more permanent basis, should have the right of determining upon the validity of laws by the standard of the constitution. A qualified negative answers all the salutary purposes of an absolute one, for it is not to be presumed that two thirds of both houses of congress, on reconsideration, with the reasoning of the president in opposition to the bill spread at large upon their journals, will ever concur in any unconstitutional measure. In the English constitution, the king has an absolute negative; but it has not been necessary to exercise it since the time of William III. The influence of the crown has been exerted in a more gentle manner, to destroy any obnoxious measure in its progress through the two houses of parliament. Charles I. stood for a long time upon the strict and forbidding rights of his prerogative; but he was compelled, by the spirit and clamour of the nation, to give his assent to bills which cut down that prerogative, and placed the powers of government in the hands of the parliament. The peremptory *veto* of the Roman tribunes, who were placed at the door of the senate, would not be reconcileable with the spirit of deliberation and independence which distinguishes the councils of modern times. The French constitution of 1791, a laboured and costly fabric, on which the philosophers and statesmen of France exhausted all their ingenuity, and which was prostrated in the dust in the course of one year from its existence, gave to the king a negative upon the acts of the legislature, with some very feeble limitations. Every bill was to be presented to the king, who might refuse his assent; but if the two following legislatures should successively present the same bill in the same terms, it was then to become a law. The constitutional negative given to the President of the United States, appears to be more wisely digested than any of the examples which have been mentioned.

LECTURE XII.

OF JUDICIAL CONSTRUCTIONS OF THE POWERS OF CONGRESS.

I proceed to consider the cases in which the powers of congress have been made the subject of judicial investigation.

(1.) Congress have declared by law, that the United States were entitled to priority of payment over private creditors, in cases of insolvency, and in the distribution of the estates of deceased debtors. The act of congress of 31st July, 1789, sec. 21. confined the priority to custom house bonds. The act of 4th August, 1790, ch. 35. sec. 45. limited the priority in the same manner. The act of 2d May, 1792, placed the surety in a custom house bond, who paid the debt, on the same footing, in respect to priority, as the United States; and it confined the cases of insolvency mentioned in the former law, to those of a voluntary assignment, and of attachments against absconding, concealed, or absent debtors. The act of 3d March, 1797, ch. 74. sec. 5. went further, and gave the United States a preference in all cases whatsoever, whoever might be the debtor, or however he might be indebted, in case the debtor became insolvent, or the assets in the hands of his representatives, after his death, were insufficient to pay his debts. This priority was declared to extend to cases in which the debtor had made a voluntary assignment of his property, or in which his effects had been attached as an absconding or absent debtor, or in which an act of legal bankruptcy had been committed. The act of March 2d, 1799. ch. 128. sec. 65, provided, that in all cases of insolvency, or where any estate in the hands of executors or administrators should be insufficient, debts due to the United States, on bonds taken under the collection act, should have preference.

These were the legislative provisions giving preference to debts due to the United States; and in *Fisher* v. *Blight*,[a] the authority of congress to pass such laws was drawn in question. The point discussed in that case was, whether the United States, as holders of a protested bill of exchange, negotiated in the ordinary course of trade, were to be preferred to the general creditors, when the debtor becomes bankrupt. The Supreme Court decided, that the acts of congress, giving that general priority to the United States. were constitutional. It was a power founded on the authority to make all laws which should be necessary and proper to carry into effect the powers vested by the constitution in the government of the United States. Where the end was within the lawful powers of the government, congress possessed the choice of the means, and were empowered to use any means which were in fact conducive to the exercise of the powers granted. The government is to pay the debts of the union, and must be authorized to use the means most eligible to effect that object. It has a right to make remittances by bills or otherwise, and to take those precautions which will render the transaction safe. If this claim of priority interferes with the right of the state sovereignties, respecting the dignity of debts, and defeats the measures which they have a right to adopt to secure themselves, it is a necessary consequence of the supremacy of the laws of the union on all subjects to which the legislative power of congress extends.

The principle is here settled, that the United States are entitled to secure to themselves the exclusive privilege of being preferred as creditors to private citizens, and even to the state authorities, in all cases of the insolvency or bank-

---

[a] 2 *Cranch*, 358.

ruptcy of their debtor. But the court observed, that no lien was created by the statutes giving the preference. No *bona fide* transfer of property in the ordinary course of business was overreached. It was only a priority of payment, which, under different modifications, was a regulation in common use, and a *bona fide* alienation of property, before the right of priority attached, was admitted to be good.

The next case that brought into discussion this question of priority, was that of the *United States* v. *Hooe*.[a] It was there held, that the priority to which the United States were entitled, did not partake of the character of a lien on the property of public debtors. The United States have no lien on the real estate of their debtor until suit brought. If the priority existed from the time the debt was contracted, and the debtor should continue to transact business with the world, the inconvenience would be immense. The priority only applied to cases where the debtor had become actually and notoriously insolvent, and being unable to pay his debts, had made a voluntary assignment of all his property, or having absconded or absented himself, his property had been attached by process of law. A *bona fide* conveyance of part of the property of the debtor, not for the fraudulent purpose of evading the law, but to secure a fair creditor, is not a case within the act of congress giving priority. In this case of the *United States* v. *Hooe*, a collector of the revenue had mortgaged part of his property to his surety in his official bond, to indemnify him from his responsibility as surety, and to secure him from his existing and future endorsements for the mortgagor at bank; and the mortgage was held valid against the claim of the United States, although the collector was, in point of fact, unable to pay all his debts at the time the mortgage was given, and although the mortgagee knew when he took the mortgage, that the mortgagor was largely indebted to the United States.

---

a 3 *Cranch*, 73.

Afterwards, in *Harrison* v. *Sterry*,^a it was held, that in the distribution of a bankrupt's effects, the United States were entitled to their preference, although the debt was contracted by a foreigner in a foreign country, and the United States had proved their debt under a commission of bankruptcy. Though the law of the place where the contract is made, be, generally speaking, the law of the contract, yet the right of priority forms no part of the contract. The insolvency which was to entitle the United States to a preference, was declared, in *Prince* v. *Bartlett*,^b to mean a legal and known insolvency, manifested by some notorious act of the debtor pursuant to law. This was giving to the world some reasonable and definite test by which to ascertain the existence of the latent and dangerous preference given by law to the United States. In this last case, the effects of an insolvent debtor, duly attached in June, were considered not to be liable to the claim of the United States on a custom house bond given prior to the attachment, and put in suit in August following. The private creditor had acquired a lien by his attachment, which could not be devested by process on the part of the United States subsequently issued. But the decision in *Thelusson* v. *Smith*,^c established the principle, that the preference in favour of the United States, whenever it existed, cut out a prior judgment creditor, for the law made no exception in favour of such a creditor. It was considered, that the word insolvency in the acts of congress of 1790, 1797, and 1799, meant a legal insolvency, and that a mere state of insolvency, or inability in a debtor to pay all his debts, gave no right of preference to the United States, unless it was accompanied by a voluntary assignment of all the property for the benefit of creditors, or some legal act of insolvency. The United States, in all such cases, are to be first satisfied out of the debtor's estate; but if, before the right of preference has accrued, he

---

a 5 *Cranch*, 289.   *b* 3 *Cranch*, 431.
c 2 *Wheaton*, 396.

has made a *bona fide* conveyance of his estate to a third person, or has mortgaged the same to secure a debt, or if the property has been seized under an execution, the property is devested from the debtor, and cannot be made liable to the United States. The act of congress defeats the ordinary preference of a judgment lien, in favour of the preference of the United States, in the cases specified in the 65th section of the act of 1799.

The United States have, accordingly, a preference as creditors to the extent above declared, in four cases, viz. (1.) In the case of the death of the debtor without sufficient assets; (2) bankruptcy or legal insolvency manifested by some act pursuant to law; (3) a voluntary assignment by the insolvent of all his property to pay his debts; (4) in the case of an absent, concealed, or absconding debtor, whose effects are attached by process of law. The priority was intended to operate only where, by law, or by the act of the debtor, his property was sequestered for the use of his creditors, and it is proper that this prerogative right of the United States should be strictly construed, and precisely defined, for it is in derogation of the general rights of creditors.[a]

2. The next question which called forth a construction from every part of the government, as to the implied powers of congress, was, whether congress had power to incorporate a bank. In the year 1791, the secretary of the treasury had recommended the institution of a national bank, as being of primary importance to the prosperous administration of the finances, and of the greatest utility in the operations connected with the support of public credit. But the bill for establishing a bank was opposed in the house of representatives, as not authorized by the constitution. It was contended, that the government of the United States was limited to the exercise of the enumerated powers, and that the power to incorporate a bank was not one of

---

[a] Watkins v. Otis, 2 *Pickering*, 102.

them, and if vested in the government, it must be an implied power; and it was contended, that the power given to congress to pass all laws necessary and proper to execute the specified powers, must be limited to means necessary to the end, and incident to the nature of the specified powers. On the other hand, it was urged in favour of the bill, that incidental, as well as express powers, necessarily belonged to every government, and that when a power was delegated to effect particular objects, all the known and usual means of effecting them passed as incidental to them; and it was insisted, that a bank was a known and usual instrument, by which several of the enumerated powers of government were exercised. After the bill had passed the two houses of congress, the question touching its constitutionality was agitated with equal ability and ardour in the executive cabinet. The secretary of state, and the attorney general, conceived that congress had transcended their powers, but the secretary of the treasury maintained the opposite opinion. Their respective opinions were founded on a train of reasoning denoting great investigation of all the leading and fundamental principles of the constitution, and they were submitted to the consideration of the President of the United States. It was argued against the constitutionality of the act, that the power to incorporate a bank was not among the enumerated powers, and to take a single step beyond the boundaries specially drawn around the powers of congress, would be to take possession of an undefined and undefinable field of power; that though congress were authorized to make all laws necessary and proper for carrying into execution the enumerated powers, they were confined to those means which were necessary, and not merely convenient. It meant those means without which the grant of the power would be nugatory, and that if such a latitude of construction was allowed as to give to congress any implied power on the ground of convenience, it would swallow up all the list of enumerated powers, and reduce the whole to one phrase. On the other hand, it was contended, that every power vested in a government was, in its nature, sovereign, and gave a right to employ all the means fairly applicable to the attainment of the end of the power, and not specially precluded by specified exceptions, nor contrary to the essential ends of political society; that though the government of the United States was one of limited and specified powers, it was sovereign with regard to its proper objects, and to its declared purposes and trusts; that it was incident to sovereign power to erect corporations, and, consequently, it was incident to the United States to erect one in relation to the objects entrusted to its management; that implied powers are as completely delegated as those which are expressed, and the power of erecting a corporation may as well be implied as any other instrument or means of carrying into execution any of the specified powers; that the exercise of the power in that case had a natural relation to the lawful ends of the government, and it was incident to the sovereign power to regulate and to employ all the means which apply with the best advantage to that regulation; that the word *necessary* in the constitution, ought not to be confined to those means, without which the grant of power would be nugatory, and it often means no more than needful, requisite, useful, or conducive to, and that was the true sense in which the word was used in the constitution. The relation between the measure and the end, was the criterion of constitutionality, and not whether there was a greater or less necessity or utility. The infinite variety, extent, and complexity, of national exigencies, necessarily required great latitude of discretion in the selection and application of means; and the authority intrusted to government ought, and must be exercised, on principles of liberal construction.

President Washington gave these arguments of his cabinet a deliberate and profound contemplation, and it terminated in a conviction, that the incorporation of a bank was a measure authorized by the constitution, and the bill passed into a law.

This same question came before the supreme court of the United States in 1819. in the case of *M'Culloch* v. *The*

State of Maryland,[a] in reference to the new bank of the United States, which was incorporated in 1816, and upon which the legislature of Maryland had imposed a tax. Notwithstanding the question arising on the construction of the powers of congress had been settled so far as an act of congress could settle it, in 1791, and again in 1816, it was thought worthy of a renewed discussion in that case. The Chief Justice, in delivering the opinion of the court, observed, that the question could scarcely be considered as an open one, after the principle had been so early introduced and recognised by many successive legislatures, and had been acted upon by the judicial department as a law of undoubted obligation. He admitted that it belonged to the supreme court alone, to make a final decision in the case, and that the question involved a consideration of the constitution in its most interesting and vital parts.

It was admitted, that the government of the United States was one of enumerated powers, and that it could exercise only the powers granted to it; but though limited in its powers, it was supreme within its sphere of action. It was the government of the people of the United States, and emanated from them. Its powers were delegated by all, and it represented all, and acted for all. In respect to those subjects on which it can act, it must necessarily bind its component parts; and this was the express language of the constitution, when it declared that the constitution, and the laws made in pursuance thereof, were the supreme law of the land, and required all the officers of the state governments to take an oath of fidelity to it. There was nothing in the constitution which excluded incidental or implied powers. The articles of the confederation gave nothing to the United States but what was expressly granted; but the new constitution dropped the word *expressly*, and left the question, whether a particular power was granted, to depend on a fair construction of the whole instrument. No consti-

---

[a] 4 *Wheaton,* 316.

tution can contain an accurate detail of all the subdivisions of its powers, and of all the means by which they might be carried into execution. It would render it too prolix. Its nature requires that only the great outlines should be marked, and its important objects designated, and all the minor ingredients left to be deduced from the nature of those objects. The sword and the purse, all the external relations, and no inconsiderable portion of the industry of the nation, were intrusted to the general government; and a government intrusted with such ample powers, on the due execution of which the happiness and prosperity of the nation vitally depended, must also be intrusted with ample means for their execution. Unless the words imperiously require it, we ought not to adopt a construction which would impute to the framers of the constitution, when granting great powers for the public good, the intention of impeding their exercise, by withholding a choice of means.

The powers given to the government imply the ordinary means of execution; and the government, in all sound reason and fair interpretation, must have the choice of the means which it deems the most convenient and appropriate to the execution of the power. The power of creating a corporation, though appertaining to sovereignty, was not a great, substantive and independent power, but merely a means by which other objects were accomplished; in like manner, as no seminary of learning is instituted in order to be incorporated, but the corporate charter is conferred to subserve the purposes of education. The power of creating a corporation is never used for its own sake, but for the purpose of effecting something else. It is nothing but ordinary means to attain some public and useful end. The constitution has not left the right of congress to employ the necessary means for the execution of its powers to general reasoning. It is expressly authorized to employ such means; and *necessary* means, in the sense of the constitution, does not import an absolute physical necessity, so strong that one thing cannot exist without the other. It means any means calculated to produce the end. The word necessary admits of all degrees of comparison. A thing may be necessary, or very necessary, or absolutely and indispensably necessary. The word is used in various senses, and in its construction, the subject, the context, the intention, are all to be taken into view. The powers of the government were given for the welfare of the nation. They were intended to endure for ages to come, and to be adapted to the various crises of human affairs. To prescribe the specific means by which government should in all future time execute its power, and to confine the choice of means to such narrow limits as should not leave it in the power of congress to adopt any which might be appropriate and conducive to the end, would have been most unwise and pernicious, because it would be an attempt to provide by immutable rules for exigencies, which, if foreseen at all, must have been seen dimly, and would deprive the legislature of the capacity to avail itself of experience, or to exercise its reason, and accommodate its legislation to circumstances.

If the end be legitimate and within the scope of the constitution, all means which are appropriate, and plainly adapted to this end, and which are not prohibited, are lawful; and a corporation was a means not less usual, nor of higher dignity, nor more requiring a particular specification, than other means. A national bank was a convenient, a useful and essential instrument in the prosecution of the fiscal operations of the government. It was clearly an appropriate measure; and while the Supreme Court declared it to be within its power and its duty to maintain that an act of congress exceeding its power was not the law of the land, yet if a law was not prohibited by the constitution, and was really calculated to effect an object intrusted to the government, the court did not pretend to the power to inquire into the degree of its necessity. That would be passing the line which circumscribes the judicial department, and be treading on legislative ground.

The court, therefore, decided, that the law creating the Bank of the United States, was one made in pursuance of the constitution; and that the branches of the national bank, proceeding from the same stock, and being conducive to the complete accomplishment of the object, were equally constitutional.

The Supreme Court were afterwards led in some degree to review this decision, in the case of *Osborn* v. *The United States Bank*,[a] and they there admitted, that congress could not create a corporation for its own sake, or for private purposes. The whole opinion of the court, in the case of *M'Culloch* v. *The State of Maryland*, was founded on, and sustained by, the idea, that the bank was an instrument which was necessary and proper for carrying into effect the powers vested in the government. It was created for national purposes only, though it was undoubtedly capable of transacting private as well as public business; and while it was the great instrument by which the fiscal operations of the government were effected, it was also trading with individuals for its own advantage. The bank, on any rational calculation, could not effect its object, unless it was endowed with the faculty of lending and dealing in money. This faculty was necessary to render the bank competent to the purposes of government, and, therefore, it was constitutionally and rightfully engrafted on the institution.

(3.) The construction of the powers of congress relative to taxation, was brought before the Supreme Court in 1796, in the case of *Hylton* v. *The United States*.[b] By the act of 5th June, 1794, congress laid a duty upon carriages for the conveyance of persons, and the question was, whether this was a direct tax within the meaning of the constitution. If it was not a direct tax, it was admitted to be rightly laid, under that part of the constitution which declares that all duties, imposts and excises, shall be uniform throughout the United States; but if it was a direct tax, it was not constitutionally laid, for it must then be laid according to the census, under that part of the constitution which declares that direct taxes shall be apportioned among the several states,

---

[a] 9 *Wheaton*, 859, 860.   [b] 3 *Dallas*, 171.

according to numbers. The Circuit Court in Virginia was divided in opinion on the question, but on appeal to the Supreme Court, it was decided, that the tax on carriages was not a direct tax, within the letter or meaning of the constitution, and was therefore constitutionally laid.

The question was deemed of very great importance, and was elaborately argued. It was held, that a general power was given to congress to lay and collect taxes of every kind or nature, without any restraint. They had plenary power over every species of taxable property except exports. But there were two rules prescribed for their government, the rule of uniformity, and the rule of apportionment. Three kinds of taxes, viz. duties, imposts, and excises, were to be laid by the first rule; and capitation, and other direct taxes, by the second rule. If there were any other species of taxes, as the court seemed to suppose there might be, that were not direct, and not included within the words duties, imposts, or excises, they were to be laid by the rule of uniformity or not, as congress should think proper and reasonable.

The constitution contemplated no taxes as direct taxes, but such as congress could lay in proportion to the census, and the rule of apportionment could not reasonably apply to a tax on carriages, nor could the tax on carriages be laid by that rule without very great inequality and injustice. If two states, equal in census, were each to pay 80,000 dollars, by a tax on carriages of eight dollars on every carriage, and in one state there were 100 carriages, and in the other 1,000, the owner of carriages in one state would pay ten times the tax of owners in the other. While A., in the one state, would pay for his carriage eight dollars, B., in the other state, would pay for his carriage 80 dollars. In this way, it was shown by the court, that the notion that a tax on carriages was a direct tax within the purview of the constitution, and to be apportioned according to the census, would lead to the grossest abuse and oppression. This argument was conclusive against the construction set up, and the tax on carriages was considered as included within the power to lay duties, and the better opinion seemed to be, that the direct taxes contemplated by the constitution, were only two, viz. a capitation or poll tax, and a tax on land. The court concluded, that a tax on carriages was an indirect tax on expense or consumption, and, therefore, properly laid pursuant to the rule of uniformity.

In *Loughborough* v. *Blake*,[a] the power of taxation was again brought under judicial discussion. The question was immediately of a local nature, and it was whether congress had the right to impose a direct tax upon the unrepresented District of Columbia; but there were principles involved in the decision, which had an extensive and important relation to the whole United States.

It was declared, that the power to tax extended equally to all places over which the government extended. It extended as well to the District of Columbia, and to the territories which were not represented in congress, as to the rest of the United States. Though duties were to be uniform, and taxes were to be apportioned according to numbers, the power was coextensive with the empire. The inhabitants of the territories of Michigan, and of Florida and Arkansas, for instance, as well as the District of Columbia, though without any representation in congress, were subject to the full operation of the power of taxation, equally as the people of New-York or Massachusetts. But the court held, that congress are not bound, though they may, in their discretion, extend a direct tax to the territories as well as to the states. A direct tax, if laid at all, must be laid on every state conformably to the census, and, therefore, congress has no power to exempt any state from its due share of the burthen. But it is understood that congress are under no necessity of extending a tax to the unrepresented District of Columbia, and to the territories; though, if they be taxed, then the constitution gives the rule of assessment. This

---

a 5 *Wheaton*, 317.

construction must be admitted to be most convenient, for the expense of assessing and collecting a tax in a territory, as the North West Territory, for instance, might exceed the amount of the tax. Here is an anomalous case in our government, in which representation and taxation are not inseparable, though the principle that the power of taxation could not rightfully exist without representation, was a fundamental ground of our revolution. The court did not consider a departure from a general principle, in this case, to be very material or important, because the case was that of territories which were in a state of infancy, advancing to manhood, and looking forward to complete equality as soon as that state of manhood should be attained. It was the case also of the District of Columbia, which had voluntarily relinquished the right of representation, and adopted the whole body of congress for its legitimate government.

(4.) Congress have the exclusive right of pre-emption to all Indian lands lying within the territories of the United States. This was so decided in the case of *Johnson* v. *M'Intosh*.[a] Upon the doctrine of the court in that case, and in that of *Fletcher* v. *Peck*,[b] the United States own the soil, as well as the jurisdiction, of the immense tracts of wild and unpatented lands, included within their territories, and of all the productive funds which these lands may hereafter create. The title is in the United States, by the treaty of peace with Great Britain, and by subsequent cessions from France and Spain; and the Indians have only a right of occupancy, and the United States possess the legal title subject to that occupancy, and with an absolute and exclusive right to extinguish the Indian title of occupancy either by conquest or purchase. The title of the European nations, and which passed to the United States, to this immense territorial empire, was founded on discovery and conquest; and, by the European customary law of nations, prior discovery gave this title to the soil, subject to the possessory

---

a 8 *Wheaton*, 548. b 6 *Cranch*, 142, 143.

right of the natives, and which occupancy was all the right that European conquerors and discoverers, and which the United States, as succeeding to their title, would admit to reside in the native Indians. The principle is, that the Indians are to be considered merely as occupants, to be protected while in peace in the possession of their lands, but to be deemed incapable of transferring the absolute title to any other than the sovereign of the country. The constitution gave to congress the power to dispose of, and to make all needful rules and regulations respecting the territory, or other property belonging to the United States, and to admit new states into the union. Since the constitution was formed, the value and efficacy of this power have been magnified to an incalculable extent, by the purchase of Louisiana and Florida; and under the doctrine contained in the case I have referred to, congress have a large and magnificent portion of territory under their absolute control and disposal. This immense property has become national and productive stock, and congress, in the administration of this stock, have erected temporary governments under the provisions of the ordinance of the congress under the confederation; and they have appointed the officers to each territory, and allowed delegates in congress to be chosen by the inhabitants every second year, and with a right to debate, but not to vote, in the house of representatives.*a*

(5.) By the constitution of the United States, congress were, by general laws, to prescribe the manner in which the public acts, records, and judicial proceedings of every state, should be proved, and the effect thereof in every other state. In pursuance of this power, congress, by the act of May 26, 1790, provided the mode by which records and judicial proceedings should be authenticated, and then declared, that they should have such faith and credit given to them in every court within the United States, as they had

---

a Acts of 7th of August, 1789. *January* 14*th,* 1805. *March 3d.* 1817. *February* 16*th.* 1819. *April* 24*th.* 1820.

by law or usage in the courts of the state from whence the records were taken. Under this act it was decided, in the case of *Mills* v. *Duryee*,[a] that if a judgment, duly authenticated, had, in the state court from whence it was taken, the faith and credit of the highest nature, viz. record evidence, it must have the same faith and credit in every other court. It was declaring the effect of the record, to declare the faith and credit that were to be given to it. The constitution intended something more than to make the judgments of state courts *prima facie* evidence only. It contemplated a power in congress to give a conclusive effect to such judgments. A judgment is, therefore, conclusive in every other state, if a court of the particular state where it was rendered would hold it conclusive. *Nil debet* is not a good plea in a suit on a judgment in another state, because not a good plea in such state. *Nul tiel record* is the proper plea in such a case. This same decision was followed in *Hampton* v. *M'Connel*,[b] and the doctrine contained in it may now be considered as the settled law of the land. It is not, however, to be understood, that *nul tiel record* is, in all cases, the necessary plea; but any special plea may be pleaded which would be good to avoid the judgment in the state where it was pronounced.[c] And in *Mayhew* v. *Thatcher*,[d] the court would seem to imply, that a judgment in one state, founded on an attachment *in rem*, would not be conclusive evidence of the debt in other states, if the defendant had not personal notice of the suit, so as to have enabled him to defend it.

(6.) Congress have authority to provide for calling forth the militia to execute the laws of the union, suppress insurrections, and repel invasions; and to provide for organizing, arming, and disciplining the militia, and for governing such part of them as may be employed in the service of the United States; reserving to the states re-

---

a 7 *Cranch*, 481.
b 3 *Wheaton*, 234.
c Shumway v. Stillman, 4 *Cowen*, 292.
d 6 *Wheaton*, 129.

spectively, the appointment of the officers, and the authority of training the militia, according to the discipline prescribed by congress. The president of the United States is to be the commander of the militia when called into actual service. The act of 28th of February, 1795, authorized the president, in case of invasion, or of imminent danger of it, to call forth such number of the militia most convenient to the scene of action as he might judge necessary. The militia so called out are made subject to the rules of war, and the law imposes a fine upon every delinquent, to be adjudged by a court martial composed of militia officers only. These militia court martials are to be held and conducted in the manner prescribed by the articles of war, and the act of 18th of April, 1814, prescribes the manner of holding them.

During the last war, the authority of the president of the United States over the militia, became a subject of doubt and difficulty, and of a collision of opinion between the general government and the governments of some of the states. It was the opinion of the government of Connecticut, that the militia could not be called out, upon the requisition of the general government, except in a case declared, and founded upon the existence of one of the specified exigencies; that when called out, they could not be taken from under the command of the officers duly appointed by the states, or placed under the immediate command of an officer of the army of the United States. Nor could the United States lawfully detach a portion of the privates from the body of the company to which they belonged, and which was organized with proper officers. This would, in the opinion of the government of Connecticut, impair, and eventually destroy, the state militia. When the militia are duly called into the service of the United States, they must be called as militia furnished with proper officers by the state.

Similar difficulties arose between the government of the United States and that of the state of Massachusetts, on the power of the national government over the militia. Both those states refused to furnish detachments of militia for the maritime frontier, on an exposition of the constitution, which they deemed sound and just.

In Connecticut, the claim of the governor to judge whether the exigency existed, authorizing a call of the militia of that state, or any portion of it, into the service of the union, and the claim on the part of that state to retain the command of the militia, when duly ordered out, as against any subordinate officer of the army of the United States, were submitted to and received the strong and decided sanction not only of the governor and council of that state, but of the legislature itself.[a] In Massachusetts, the governor consulted the judges of the supreme judicial court, as to the true construction of the constitution on these very interesting points. The judges of the supreme court, who were consulted, were of opinion, that it belonged to the governors of the several states to determine when any of the exigencies contemplated by the constitution of the United States existed, so as to require them to place the militia, or any part of it, in the service of the union, and under the command of the president. It was observed, that the constitution of the United States did not give that right, by any express terms, to the president or congress, and that the power to determine when the exigency existed, was not prohibited to the states, and that it was, therefore, as of course, reserved to the states. A different construction would place all the militia in effect at the will of congress, and produce a military consolidation of these states. The act of 28th February, 1795, vested in the president the power of calling forth the militia when any one of the exigencies existed, and if to that be superadded the power of determining when the *casus fœderis* occurred, the militia would in fact be under the president's control.

As to the question how the militia were to be commanded, when duly called out, the judges were of opinion, that the president alone, of all the officers acting under the United

---

[a] See *Documents, August,* 1812.

States, was authorized to command them, and that he must command them as they were organized, under officers appointed by the states. The militia could not be placed under the command of any officer not of the militia, except that officer be the president of the United States. But the judges did not determine how the militia were to be commanded, in case of the absence of the president, and of a union of militia with troops of the United States; and whether they were to act under their separate officers, but in concert as allied forces; or whether the officer present who was highest in rank, be he of the militia or of the federal troops, was to command the whole, was a difficult and perplexing question, which the judges did not undertake to decide.[a]

The president of the United States declared that these constructions of the constitutional powers of the general government over the militia were novel and unfortunate, and he was evidently and decidedly of a different opinion. He observed, in his message to congress on the 4th November, 1812, that if the authority of the United States to call into service and to command the militia, could be thus frustrated, we were not one nation for the purpose most of all requiring it. These embarrassing questions, and the high authority by which each side of the argument is supported, have remained to this day unsettled by the proper and final decision of the tribunal that is competent to put them to rest. The case of *Houston* v. *Moore*,[b] is the only one in which the national command of the militia seems to have been at all a subject of judicial discussion, and that case does not touch the points at issue between the United States and the states of Massachusetts and Connecticut, though the opinion of one of the judges[c] went far towards destroying the claims advanced on the part of those states. I do not wish to interfere in this place with vexed and undecided questions. My object, in the course of these elementary

---

a 8 *Mass. Rep.* 554.   b 5 *Wheaton*, 1.   c *Johnson*, J.

lectures, is to confine myself to a comprehensive and just survey of the principles of our government as they have been discussed, or as they have been practically explained and settled by competent authority. It may, however, be truly observed, that since the year 1812, when those questions were raised, many great and deeply interesting questions arising on the powers of the union, have been investigated and decided, and the progress of opinion, and the course of those decisions, have been in favour of a pretty liberal and enlarged construction of the constitution of the United States. The principles of the government, as now understood, would be much more favourable than they were in 1812, to the claim of the President of the United States, to judge exclusively and authoritatively *when* the militia were to be called out into the service of the union.

The case of *Houston* v. *Moore*[a] settled some important questions arising upon the national authority over the militia. The acts of congress already referred to, and the act of 8th March, 1792, for establishing a uniform militia, were considered as covering the whole ground of congressional legislation over the subject. The manner in which the militia were to be organized, armed, disciplined and governed, was fully prescribed; provision was made for drafting, detaching and calling forth the state quotas, when requested by the president. His orders were to be given to the chief executive magistrate, or to any militia officer he might think proper. Neglect or refusal to obey his orders was declared to be a public offence, and subjected the offender to trial and punishment, to be adjudged by a court martial, and the mode of proceeding was perspicuously detailed.

The question before the Supreme Court of the United States was, whether it was competent for a court martial, deriving its jurisdiction under state authority, to try and punish militia men drafted, detached and called forth by the president into the service of the United States, and who had re-

---

[a] 5 *Wheaton*, 1.

fused or neglected to obey the call. The court decided, that the militia, when called into the service of the United States, were not to be considered as being in that service, or in the character of national militia, until they were mustered at the place of rendezvous, and that until then, the state retained a right, concurrent with the government of the United States, to punish their delinquency. But after the militia had been called forth, and had entered into the service of the United States, their character changed from state to national militia, and the authority of the general government over such detachments was exclusive. Actual service was considered by congress as the criterion of national militia, and the place of rendezvous was the *terminus a quo* the service, the pay, and subjection to the articles of war were to commence. And if the militia, when called into the service of the United States, refuse to obey the order, they remain within the military jurisdiction of the state, and it is competent for the state to provide for trying and punishing them by a state court martial, to the extent and in the manner prescribed by the act of congress. The act of Pennsylvania of 1814, provided for punishing, by a state court martial, delinquent militia men, who were called into the service of the United States, and neglected or refused to serve; and they were to be punished by the infliction of the penalties prescribed by the act of congress, and such an act was held not to be repugnant to the constitution and laws of the United States. It was the lawful exercise of concurrent power, and could be concurrently exercised by the national and state courts martial, as it was authorized by the laws of the state, and not prohibited by those of the United States. It would remain to be so exercised, until congress should vest the power exclusively elsewhere, or until the states should divest their courts martial of such a jurisdiction. This was the decision, in the first instance, of the supreme court of Pennsylvania;*

---

a 3 *Serg. and Rawle.* 169.

and it was affirmed, on appeal, by the majority of the Supreme Court of the United States.

(7.) The authority of congress to appropriate public moneys for internal improvements, has been much discussed on public occasions, and between the legislative and executive branches of the government; but the point has never been brought under judicial consideration.

It has been contended, that under the power to establish post offices and post roads, and to raise moneys to provide for the general welfare, and as incident thereto, congress have the power to set apart funds for internal improvements in the states, with their assent, by means of roads and canals. Such a power has been exercised to a certain extent. It has been the constant practice to allow to the new states a certain proportion of the proceeds arising from the sale of public lands, to be laid out in the construction of roads and canals within those states, or leading thereto. In 1806, congress authorized a road to be opened from Nashville, in Tennessee, to Natchez; and, in 1809, they authorized the canal of Carondelet, leading from lake Ponchartraine, to be extended to the river Mississippi. The Cumberland road was constructed under the act of March 29th, 1806, and this road had been made under a covenant with the state of Ohio, by the act of April 30, 1802, that a portion of the proceeds of lands lying within that state, should be applied to the opening of roads leading to that state, with the consent of the states through which the road might pass. But the expenditures on that road have exceeded the proceeds of sales of public lands in Ohio, above one million of dollars, and, in 1817, the President of the United States objected to a bill, on the ground that the constitution did not extend to making roads and canals, and improving water-courses through the different states; nor could the assent of those states confer the power. Afterwards, in 1822, the president objected to a bill appropriating money for repairing Cumberland road, and establishing gates and tolls on it.

On these, and other occasions, there has been a great

and decided difference of opinion between congress and the president on this constitutional question. President Jefferson, in his message of December 2d, 1806, and President Madison, in his message of December 3d, 1816, equally denied any such power in congress. On the other hand, it appears, that congress claim the power to lay out, construct, and improve, post roads, with the assent of the states through which they pass. They also claim the power to open, construct, and improve, military roads on the like terms, and the right to cut canals through the several states, with their assent, for promoting and securing internal commerce, and for the more safe and economical transportation of military stores in time of war; and leaving, in all these cases, the jurisdictional right over the soil in the respective states.

In the inaugural address of President Adams, on the 4th of March, 1825, he alluded to this question, and his opinion seemed to be in favour of the constitutional right, and of the policy and wisdom of the liberal application of the national resources to the internal improvement of the country. He intimated, that speculative scruples on this subject would probably be solved by the practical blessings resulting from the application of the power, and the extent and limitations of the general government, in relation to this important interest, settled and acknowledged to the satisfaction of all. This declaration may be considered as withdrawing the influence of the official authority of the president, from the side on which it has hitherto pressed, and adding it to the support of the preponderating opinion, in favour of the competency of the power claimed by congress.

LECTURE XIII.

OF THE PRESIDENT.

The title of the present lecture may conveniently be examined in the following order: 1. The unity of this department. 2. The qualifications required by the constitution for the office of president. 3. The mode of his appointment. 4. His duration. 5. His support. 6. His powers.

(1.) By the constitution, it is ordained, that the executive power shall be vested in a president.[a]

The object of this department is the execution of the law; and good policy dictates that it should be organized in the mode best calculated to attain that end with precision and fidelity. Consultation is necessary in the making of laws. The defect or grievance they are intended to remove, must be distinctly perceived, and the operation of the remedy upon the interests, the morals, and the opinion of the community, profoundly considered. A comprehensive knowledge of the great interests of the nation, in all their complicated relations and practical details, seems to be required in sound legislation; and it shows the necessity of a free, full, and perfect representation of the people, in the body intrusted with the legislative power. But when laws are duly made and promulgated, they only remain to be executed. No discretion is submitted to the executive officer. It is not for him to deliberate and decide upon the wisdom or expediency of the law. What has been once declared to be law, under all the cautious forms of deliberation prescribed by the constitution, ought to receive prompt and irresistible obedience. The characteristical qualities re-

---

[a] Art. 2. sec. 1.

quired in the executive department, are promptitude, decision, and force; and these qualities are most likely to exist when the executive authority is limited to a single person, moving by the unity of a single will. Division, indecision, and delay, are exceedingly unfavourable to that steady and vigorous administration of the law, which is necessary to secure tranquillity at home, and command the confidence of foreign nations. Every government, ancient and modern, which has been constituted on different principles, and adopted a compound executive, has suffered the evils of it; and the public interest has been sacrificed, or it has languished under the inconveniences of an imbecile or irregular administration. In those states which have tried the project of executive councils, the weakness of them has been strongly felt and strikingly displayed; and in every instance in which they have been tried, (as in Pennsylvania and Georgia, for instance,) they were soon abandoned, and a single executive magistrate created, in accordance with the light afforded by their own experience, as well as by the institutions of their neighbours.

Unity increases not only the efficacy, but the responsibility of the executive power. Every act can be immediately traced and brought home to the proper agent. There can be no concealment of the real author, and, generally, none of the motives of public measures, when there are no associates to divide, or to mask responsibility. There will be much less temptation to depart from duty, and much greater solicitude for reputation, when there are no partners to share the odium, or to communicate confidence by their example. The eyes of the people will be constantly directed to a single conspicuous object; and, for these reasons, De Lolme[a] considered it to be a sound axiom of policy, that the executive power was more easily confined when it was one. "If the execution of the laws," he observes, "be intrusted to a number of hands, the true cause of public evils is hidden.

---

[a] *Const. of England*, p. 111.

Tyranny, in such states, does not always beat down the fences that are set around it, but it leaps over them. It mocks the efforts of the people, not because it is invincible, but because it is unknown." The justness of these reflections might be illustrated and confirmed by a review of the proceedings of the former council of appointment in this state. All efficient responsibility was there lost, by reason of the constant change of the members, and the difficulty of ascertaining the individual to whom the origin of a bad appointment was to be attributed.

(2.) The constitution requires,[a] that the president should be a natural born citizen, or a citizen of the United States at the time of the adoption of the constitution, and that he have attained to the age of thirty-five years, and have been fourteen years a resident within the United States. Considering the greatness of the trust, and that this department is the ultimately efficient power in government, these restrictions will not appear altogether useless or unimportant. As the president is required to be a native citizen of the United States, ambitious foreigners cannot intrigue for the office, and the qualification of birth cuts off all those inducements from abroad to corruption, negotiation, and war, which have frequently and fatally harassed the elective monarchies of Germany and Poland, as well as the Pontificate at Rome. The age of the president is sufficient to have formed his public and private character; and his previous domestic residence, is intended to afford to his fellow citizens the opportunity to attain a correct knowledge of his principles and capacity, and to have enabled him to acquire habits of attachment and obedience to the laws, and of devotion to the public welfare.

(3.) The mode of his appointment presented one of the most difficult and momentous questions that could have occupied the deliberations of the assembly which framed the constitution; and if ever the tranquillity of this nation is to

---

a Art. 2. sec. 5.

be disturbed, and its peace jeopardized, by a struggle for power among themselves, it will be upon this very subject of the choice of a president. This is the question that is eventually to test the goodness, and try the strength of the constitution; and if we shall be able, for half a century hereafter, to continue to elect the chief magistrate of the union with discretion, moderation, and integrity, we shall undoubtedly stamp the highest value on our national character, and recommend our republican institutions, if not to the imitation, yet certainly to the esteem and admiration of the more enlightened part of mankind. The experience of ancient and modern Europe has been unfavourable to the practicability of a fair and peaceable popular election of the executive head of a great nation. It has been found impossible to guard the election from the mischiefs of foreign intrigue and domestic turbulence, from violence or corruption; and mankind have generally taken refuge from the evils of popular elections in hereditary executives, as being the least evil of the two. The most recent and remarkable change of this kind occurred in France in 1804, when the legislative body changed their elective into an hereditary monarchy, on the avowed ground that the competition of popular elections led to corruption and violence. And it is a curious fact in European history, that on the first partition of Poland in 1773, when the partitioning powers thought it expedient to foster and confirm all the defects of its wretched government, they sagaciously demanded of the Polish diet, that the crown should continue elective.[a] This was done for the very purpose of keeping the door open for foreign intrigue and influence. Mr. Paley[b] condemns all elective monarchies, and he thinks nothing is gained by a popular choice worth the dissentions, tumults and interruptions of regular industry, with which it is inseparably attended. I am not called upon to question the wisdom or

---

[a] *Cox's Travels in Poland, Russia,* &c. vol. 1.
[b] *Principles of Moral and Pol. Philosophy*, 345.

policy of preferring hereditary to elective monarchies among the great nations of Europe, where different orders and ranks of society are established, and large masses of property accumulated in the hands of single individuals, and where ignorance and poverty are widely diffused, and standing armies are necessary to preserve the stability of the government. The state of society and of property in this country, and our moral and political habits, have enabled us to adopt the republican principle, and to maintain it hitherto with illustrious success. It remains to be seen whether the checks which the constitution has provided against the dangerous propensities of our system will ultimately prove effectual. The election of a supreme executive magistrate for a whole nation, affects so many interests, addresses itself so strongly to popular passions, and holds out such powerful temptations to ambition, that it necessarily becomes a strong trial to public virtue, and even hazardous to the public tranquillity. The constitution, from an enlightened view of all the difficulties that attend the subject, has not thought it safe or prudent to refer the election of a president directly and immediately to the people, but it has confided the power to a small body of electors, appointed in each state, under the direction of the legislature; and to close the opportunity as much as possible against negotiation, intrigue, and corruption, it has declared that congress may determine the time of choosing the electors, and the day on which they shall vote, and that the day of election shall be the same in every state.[a] This security has been still further extended, by the act of congress[b] directing the electors to be appointed in each state within thirty-four days of the day of election.

The constitution[c] directs that the number of electors in each state shall be equal to the whole number of senators and representatives which the state is entitled to send to congress, and according to the now existing apportionment

---

a Art. 2. sec. 4.   *b* Act of 1st March, 1792.
c Art. 2. sec. 2, 3.

of congress, the president is elected by 261 electors. And to prevent the person in office at the time of the election from having any improper influence on his re-election, by his ordinary agency in the government, it is provided, that no member of congress, nor any person holding an office of trust or profit under the United States, shall be an elector; and the constitution has in no other respect defined the qualifications of the electors.[a] These electors meet in their respective states, at the place appointed by the legislature thereof, on the first Wednesday in December in every fourth year succeeding the last election, and vote by ballot for president and vice-president, (for this last officer is elected in the same manner and for the same period as the president,) and one of whom at least shall not be an inhabitant of the same state with the electors. They name in their ballots the person voted for as president, and in distinct ballots, the person voted for as vice-president; and they make distinct lists of all persons voted for as president, and of all persons voted for as vice-president, and of the number of votes for each, which lists they sign, and certify and transmit, sealed, to the seat of the government of the United States, directed to the president of the senate. The act of congress of 1st March, 1792, sec. 2. directs that the certificate of the votes shall be delivered to the president of the senate before the first Wednesday in January next ensuing the election. The president of the senate, on the second Wednesday in February succeeding every meeting of the electors, in the presence of both houses of congress, opens all the certificates, and the votes are then to be counted. The constitution does not expressly declare *by whom* the votes are to be counted and the result declared. In the case of questionable votes, and a closely contested election, this power may be all important; and I presume, in the absence of all legislative provision on the subject, that the president of the senate counts the votes and deter-

---

a Art. 2. sec. 1.

mines the result, and that the two houses are present only as spectators, to witness the fairness and accuracy of the transaction, and to act only if no choice be made by the electors. The house of representatives, in such case, are to choose *immediately*, which, I presume, may be while the two houses are so together, though they may vote after they have retired, for the constitution holds their choice to be valid, if made before the fourth day of March following. And in the cases of the elections in 1801 and 1825, the house of representatives retired and voted, and the senate were admitted to be present as spectators. The person having the greatest number of votes for president is president, if such number be a majority of the whole number of electors appointed; but if no person have such majority, then, from the persons having the highest number, not exceeding three, on the list of those voted for as president, the house of representatives shall choose immediately by ballot the president. But in choosing the president, the votes shall be taken by states, the representation from each state having one vote. A quorum for this purpose shall consist of a member or members from two thirds of the states, and a majority of all the states shall be necessary to a choice. If the house of representatives shall not choose a president whenever the right of choice shall devolve upon them, before the fourth day of March next following, then the vice-president shall act as president, as in the case of the death or other constitutional disability of the president.[a]

The person having the greatest number of votes as vice-president, is vice-president, if such number be a majority of the whole number of electors appointed; and if no person have a majority, then, from the two highest numbers on the list, the senate shall choose the vice-president; a quorum for the purpose shall consist of two thirds of the whole number of senators, and a majority of the whole number is necessary to a choice; and no person constitutionally ineligi-

---

[a] *Amendments to the Constitution*, art. 12.

ble to the office of president, shall be eligible to that of vice-president of the United States.[a] The constitution does not specifically prescribe when or where the senate is to choose a vice-president, if no choice be made by the electors, and, I presume, the senate may elect by themselves, at any time before the fourth day of March following.

It is provided by law,[b] that the term of four years, for which a president and vice-president shall be elected, shall, in all cases, commence on the fourth day of March next succeeding the day on which the votes of the electors shall have been given.

In case of the removal of the president from office, or of his death, resignation, or inability to discharge the powers and duties of the office, the same devolve on the vice-president; and congress are authorized to provide, by law, for the case of the vacancy in the office, both of president and vice-president, declaring what officer should then act as president, and the officer so designated is to act until the office be supplied.[c] In pursuance of this constitutional provision, the act of congress of March 1st, 1792, sec. 9. declared, that in case of a vacancy in the office, both of president and vice-president, the president of the senate *pro tempore*, and in case there should be no president of the senate, then the speaker of the house of representatives, for the time being, should act as president, until the vacancy was supplied. The evidence of a refusal to accept, or of a resignation of the office of president or vice-president, is declared by the same act of congress, sec. 11. to be a declaration in writing, filed in the office of the secretary of state. And if the office should, by the course of events, devolve on the speaker, after the congress for which the last speaker was chosen had expired, and before the next meeting of congress, it might be a question who is to serve,

---

a *Amendments to the Constitution*, art. 12.
b *Act of Congress, March* 1, 1792.
c Art. 2. sec. 1.

and whether the speaker of the house of representatives, then extinct, could be deemed the person intended.

The mode of electing the president appears to be well calculated to secure a discreet choice, and to avoid all those evils which the partisans of monarchy have described, and the experience of other nations and past ages have too clearly shown, to be the consequence of popular elections. Had the choice of president been referred at once to the people at large, as one single community, there might have been reason to apprehend, and such no doubt was the sense of the convention, that it would have produced too violent a contest, and have been trying the experiment on too extended a scale for the public virtue, tranquillity, and happiness. But a still greater and more insuperable difficulty was, that such a measure would be an entire consolidation of the government of this country, and an annihilation of the state sovereignties, so far as concerned the organization of the executive department of the union. This was not to be permitted or endured, and it would, besides, have destroyed the balance of the union, and reduced the weight of the slave-holding states to a degree which they would have deemed altogether inadmissible. Had we imitated the practice of most of the southern states, and referred the choice of the president to congress, this would have rendered him too dependent upon the immediate authors of his elevation, to comport with the requisite energy of his own department; and it would have laid him under temptation to indulge in improper intrigue, or to form a dangerous coalition with the legislative body, in order to secure his continuance in office. All elections by the representative body are peculiarly liable to intrigues and coalitions for sinister purposes. The constitution has avoided all these objections, by confiding the power of election to a small number of select individuals in each state, chosen only a few days before the election, and solely for that purpose. This would seem, *prima facie*, to be as wise a provision as the wisdom of man could have devised, to avoid all opportunity for foreign or domestic intrigue. These electors assemble in separate and distantly detached bodies, and they are constituted in a manner best calculated to preserve them free from all inducements to disorder, bias, or corruption. There is no other mode of appointing the chief magistrate, under all the circumstances peculiar to our political condition, which appears to unite in itself so many unalloyed advantages. It must not be pronounced to be a perfect scheme of election, for it has not been sufficiently tried. The election of 1801 threatened the tranquillity of the union; and the difficulty that occurred in that case in producing a constitutional choice, led to the amendment of the constitution on this very subject; but whether the amendment be for the better or for the worse, may be well doubted, and remains yet to be settled by the lights of experience. The constitution says, that each state is to appoint electors in such manner as the legislature may direct; and in this and some other states, the electors have always been chosen by the legislature itself, in the mode prescribed by law. But it is to be presumed that there would be less opportunity for dangerous coalitions, and combinations for party, or ambitious, or selfish purposes, if the choice of electors was referred to the people at large, and this seems now to be the sense and expression of public opinion.

(4.) The president thus elected, holds his office for the term of four years, a period, perhaps, reasonably long for the purpose of making him feel firm and independent in the discharge of his trust, and to give stability and some degree of maturity to his system of administration. It is certainly short enough to place him under a due sense of dependence on the public approbation.

(5.) The support of the president is secured by a provision in the constitution, which declares,[a] that he shall, at stated times, receive for his services a compensation, that shall neither be increased nor diminished, during the period

---

[a] Art. 2. sec. 7.

for which he shall have been elected; and that he shall not receive, within that time, any other emolument from the United States, or any of them. This provision is intended to preserve the due independence and energy of the executive department. It would be in vain to declare that the different departments of government should be kept separate and distinct, while the legislature possessed a discretionary control over the salaries of the executive and judicial officers. This would be to disregard the voice of experience, and the operation of invariable principles of human conduct. A control over a man's living is, in most cases, a control over his actions. The constitution of Virginia considered it as a fundamental axiom of government, that the three great and primary departments should be kept separate and distinct, so that neither of them exercised the powers properly belonging to the other. But without taking any precautions to preserve this principle in practice, it made the governor dependent on the legislature for his annual existence and his annual support. The result was, as Mr. Jefferson has told us,[a] that during the whole session of the legislature, the direction of the executive was habitual and familiar. The constitution of Massachusetts discovered more wisdom, and it set the first example in this country, of a constitutional provision for the support of the executive magistrate, by declaring that the governor should have a salary of a fixed and permanent value, amply sufficient, and established by standing laws. Those state constitutions which have been made or amended since the establishment of the constitution of the United States, have generally followed the example which it has happily set them, in this and in many other instances; and we may consider it as one of the most signal blessings bestowed on this country, that we have such a wise fabric of government as the constitution of the United States constantly before our eyes, not only for our national protection and obedience, but for our local imitation and example.

---

[a] *Notes on Virginia*, p. 127.

Having thus considered the manner in which the president is constituted, it only remains for us to review the powers with which he is invested.

He is commander in chief of the army and navy of the United States, and of the militia of the several states, when called into the service of the union.*a* The command and application of the public force to execute the law, maintain peace, and resist foreign invasion, are powers so obviously of an executive nature, and require the exercise of qualities so characteristical of this department, that they have always been exclusively appropriated to it in every well organized government upon earth. In no instance, perhaps, did the enlightened understanding of Hume discover less acquaintance with the practical science of government, than when he gave the direction of the army and navy, as well as all the other executive powers, to one hundred senators, in his plan of a perfect commonwealth.*b* That of Milton was equally chimerical and absurd, when, in his " Ready and easy way to establish a free Commonwealth," he deposited the whole executive, as well as legislative power, in a single and permanent council of senators. That of Locke was equally unwise, for, in his plan of legislation for Carolina, he gave the whole authority, legislative and executive, to a small oligarchical assembly. Such specimens as these will well justify the observation of President Adams,*c* that " A philosopher may be perfect master of Descartes and Leibnitz, may pursue his own inquiries into metaphysics to any length you please, may enter into the inmost recesses of the human mind, and make the noblest discoveries for the benefit of his species; nay, he may defend the principles of liberty, and the rights of mankind, with great abilities and success, and, after all, when called upon to produce a plan of legislation, he may astonish the world with a signal absurdity."

---

a Art. 2. sec. 2.
b *Hume's Essays*, vol. 1. p. 526.
Defence of the American Constitutions, vol. 1. letter 54

The president has also the power to grant reprieves and pardons for offences against the United States, except in cases of impeachment. The Marquis Beccaria has contended, that the power of pardon does not exist under a perfect administration of law, and that the admission of the power is a tacit acknowledgment of the infirmity of the course of justice. And where is the administration of justice, it may be asked, that is free from infirmity? Were it possible, in every instance, to maintain a just proportion between the crime and the penalty, and were the rules of testimony, and the mode of trial, so perfect, as to preclude every possibility of mistake or injustice, there would be some colour for the admission of this plausible theory. But, even in that case, policy would sometimes require a remission of a punishment strictly due, for a crime certainly ascertained. The very notion of mercy implies the accuracy of the claims of justice. An inexorable government, says Mr. Yorke, in his Considerations on the law of Forfeiture,[a] will not only carry justice in some instances to the height of injury, but with respect to itself it will be dangerously just. The clemency of Massachusetts, in 1786, after an unprovoked and wanton rebellion, in not inflicting a single capital punishment, contributed by the judicious manner in which its clemency was applied, to the more firm establishment of their government. And this power of pardon will appear to be the more essential, when we consider, that under the most correct administration of the law, men will sometimes fall a prey to the vindictiveness of accusers, the inaccuracy of testimony, and the fallibility of jurors. Notwithstanding this power is clearly supported on principles of policy, if not of justice, English lawyers of the first class, and highest reputation,[b] have strangely concluded, that it cannot exist in a republic, because nothing higher is acknowledged than the magistrate. Instead of

---

[a] P. 101.
[b] *Yorke on Forf.* 100. *Blacks. Com.* vol. 4. 390.

falling into such an erroneous conclusion, it might fairly be insisted, that the power may exist with greater safety in free states, than in any other forms of government; because abuses of the discretion unavoidably confided to the magistrate in granting pardons, are much better guarded against by the sense of responsibility under which he acts. The power of pardon vested in the president is without any limitation, except in the single case of impeachments. He is checked in that case from screening public officers, with whom he might possibly have formed a dangerous or corrupt coalition, or who might be his particular favourites and dependents.

The president has also the power, by and with the advice and consent of the senate, to make treaties, provided two thirds of the senators present concur.[a]

Writers on government have differed in opinion as to the nature of this power, and whether it be properly, in the natural distribution of power, of legislative or executive cognizance. As treaties are declared by the constitution to be the supreme law of the land, and as, by means of them, new relations are formed, and obligations contracted, it might seem to be more consonant to the principles of republican government, to consider the right of concluding specific terms of peace as of legislative jurisdiction. This has generally been the case in free governments. The determinations respecting peace, as well as of war, were made in the public assemblies of the nation at Athens and Rome, and in all the Gothic governments of Europe, when they first arose out of the rude institutions of the ancient Germans. On the other hand, the preliminary negotiations which may be required, the secrecy and despatch proper to take advantage of the sudden and favourable turn of public affairs, seem to render it expedient to place this power in the hands of the executive department. The constitution of the United States has been influenced by the latter,

---

[a] Art. 2. sec. 2.

more than by the former considerations, for it has placed this power with the president, under the advice and control of the senate, who are to be considered for this purpose in the light of an executive council. The president is the constitutional organ of communication with foreign powers, and the efficient agent in the conclusion of treaties; but the consent of two thirds of the senators present is essential to give validity to his negotiations. To have required the acquiescence of a more numerous body, would have been productive of delay, disorder, imbecility, and, probably, in the end, a direct breach of the constitution. The history of Holland shows the danger and folly of placing too much limitation on the exercise of the treaty-making power. By the fundamental charter of the United Provinces, peace could not be made without the unanimous consent of the provinces; and yet, without multiplying instances, it is sufficient to observe, that the immensely important and fundamental treaty of Munster, in 1648, was made when Zealand was opposed to it; and the peace in 1661, when Utrecht was opposed. So feeble are mere limitations upon paper—mere parchment barriers, when standing in opposition to the strong force of public exigency.

The senate of the United States is a body of men most wisely selected for the deposit of this power. They are easily assembled, are governed by steady systematic views, feel a due sense of national character, and can act with promptitude and firmness.

The question, whether a treaty constitutionally made, was obligatory upon congress, equally as any other national engagement would be, if fairly made by the competent authority; or whether congress had any discretionary power to carry into effect a treaty requiring the appropriation of money, or other act to be done on their part, or to refuse it their sanction, was greatly discussed in congress in the year 1796, and again in 1816. The house of representatives, at the former period, declared, by resolution, that when a treaty depended for the execution of any of its stipulations on an act of congress, it was the right and duty of the house to deliberate on the expediency or inexpediency of carrying such treaty into effect. It cannot be mentioned, at this day, without equal regret and astonishment, that such a resolution passed the house of representatives on the 7th of April, 1796. But it was a naked abstract claim of right never acted upon; and congress shortly afterwards passed a law to carry into effect the very treaty with Great Britain, which gave rise to that resolution. President Washington, in his message to the house of representatives of the 30th of March, 1796, explicitly denied the existence of any such power in congress; and he insisted, that every treaty duly made by the president and senate, and promulgated, thenceforward became the law of the land.

If a treaty be the law of the land, it is as much obligatory upon congress as upon any other branch of the government, or upon the people at large, so long as it continues in force, and unrepealed. The house of representatives are not above the law, and they have no dispensing power. They have a right to make and repeal laws, provided the senate and president concur; but without such concurrence, a law in the shape of a treaty is as binding upon them as if it were in the shape of an act of congress, or of an article of the constitution, or of a contract made by authority of law. The argument in favour of the binding and conclusive efficacy of every treaty made by the president and senate, is so clear and palpable, that it has probably carried very general conviction throughout the community, and this may be now considered as the decided sense of public opinion. This was the sense of the house of representatives in 1816, and the resolution of 1796 would not now be repeated.

The president is the efficient power in the appointment of the officers of government. He is to nominate, and with the advice and consent of the senate, to appoint ambassadors, other public ministers and consuls, the judges of the Supreme Court, and all other officers whose appointments are not otherwise provided in the constitution; but congress may vest the appointment of inferior officers in the president alone, in the courts of law, or in the heads of departments.[a]

The appointment of the subordinate officers of government concerned in the administration of the law, belongs with great propriety to the president, who is bound to see that the laws are faithfully executed, and who is generally charged with the powers and responsibility of the executive department. The association of the senate with the president in the exercise of this power, is an exception to the general delegation of executive authority, and if he were not expressly invested with the exclusive right of nomination in the instances before us, the organization of this department would be very unskilful, and the government degenerate into a system of cabal, favouritism and intrigue. But the power of nomination is, for all the useful purposes of restraint, equivalent to the power of appointment. It imposes upon the president the same lively sense of responsibility, and the same indispensable necessity of meeting the public approbation or censure. This, indeed, forms the ultimate security that men in public stations will dismiss interested considerations, and act with a steady, zealous and undivided regard for the public welfare. The advice and consent of the senate, which are requisite to render the nomination effectual, cannot be attended, in the nature of the case, with very mischievous effects. Having no agency in the nomination, nothing but simply consent or refusal, the spirit of personal intrigue and personal attachment must be pretty much extinguished, from a want of means to gratify it. On the other hand, the advice of so respectable a body of men will add still further inducements to a coolly reflected conduct in the president, and will be at all times a check on his own misinformation or error.

The remaining duties of the president consist in giving information to congress of the state of the union, and in recommending to their consideration such measures as he shall

---

[a] Art. 2. sec. 2.

judge necessary or expedient. He is to convene both houses of congress, or either of them, on extraordinary occasions, and he may adjourn them in case of disagreement. He is to supply occasional vacancies that happen during the recess of the senate, by granting commissions, which shall expire at the end of their next session. He is to receive ambassadors and other public ministers, to commission all the officers of the United States, and take care that the laws be faithfully executed.^a

The propriety and simplicity of these duties speak for themselves. The power of receiving foreign ministers includes in it the power to dismiss them, since he alone is the organ of communication with them, the representative of the people in all diplomatic negotiations, and accountable to the community, not only for the execution of the law, but for the competent qualifications and conduct of foreign agents.

In addition to all the precautions which have been mentioned, to prevent abuse of the executive trust, in the mode of the president's appointment, his term of office, and the precise and definite limitations imposed upon the exercise of his power, the constitution has also rendered him directly amenable by law for mal-administration. The inviolability of any officer of government is incompatible with the republican theory, as well as with the principles of retributive justice. The president, as well as all other officers of the United States, may be impeached by the house of representatives for treason, bribery, and other high crimes and misdemeanors, and, upon conviction by the senate, removed from office.^b If, then, neither the sense of duty, the force of public opinion, nor the transitory nature of the seat, are sufficient to secure a faithful discharge of the executive trust, but the president will use the authority of his station to violate the constitution or law of the land, the house of

---

a Art. 2. sec. 2, 3.   *b* Art. 2. sec. 4.

representatives can arrest him in his career by resorting to the power of impeachment.

I have now finished a general survey of the office of president of the United States, and considering the nature and extent of the powers necessarily incident to that station, it was difficult to constitute the office in such a manner as to render it equally safe and useful, by combining in the structure of its powers a due proportion of energy and responsibility. The first is necessary to maintain a firm administration of the law; the second is equally requisite to preserve inviolate the liberties of the people. The authors of the constitution appear to have surveyed these two objects with profound discernment, and to have organized the executive department with consummate skill.

LECTURE XIV.

OF THE JUDICIARY DEPARTMENT.

As the judiciary power is intrusted with the administration of justice, it interferes more visibly and uniformly than any other part of government, with all the interesting concerns of social life. Personal security, and private property, rest entirely upon the wisdom, the stability, and the integrity of the courts of justice. In the survey which is to be taken of the judicial establishment of the United States, we will consider, (1.) The judges in relation to their appointment, the tenure of their office, and their support and responsibility. (2.) The structure, powers, and officers of the several courts.

The advantages of the mode of appointment of public officers by the president and senate, have been already considered. This mode is peculiarly fit and proper in respect to the judicial department. The just and vigorous investigation and punishment of every species of fraud and violence, and the exercise of the power of compelling every man to the punctual performance of his contracts, are grave duties, not of the most popular character, though the faithful discharge of them will certainly command the calm approbation of the judicious observer. The fittest men would probably have too much reservedness of manners, and severity of morals, to secure an election resting on universal suffrage. Nor can the mode of appointment by a large deliberative assembly, be entitled to unqualified approbation. There are too many occasions, and too much temptation for intrigue, party prejudice, and local interests, to permit such a body of men to act, in respect to such appointments, with a sufficiently single and steady regard for the general welfare. In ancient Rome, the prætor was chosen annually by the people, but it was in the *comitia* by centuries, and the choice was confined to persons belonging to the patrician order, until the close of the fourth century of the city, when the office was rendered accessible to the plebeians; and when they became licentious, says Montesquieu,[a] the office became corrupt. The popular elections did very well, as he observes, so long as the people were free, and magnanimous, and virtuous, and the republic was without corruption. But all plans of government which suppose the people will always act with wisdom and integrity, are plainly Utopian, and contrary to uniform experience. Government must be framed for man as he is, and not for man as he would be if he were free from vice. Without referring to those cases in our own country, where judges have been annually elected by a popular assembly, we may take the less invidious case of Sweden. During the diets which preceded the revolution in 1772, the states of the kingdom sometimes appointed commissioners to act as judges. The strongest party, says Catteau,[b] prevailed in the trials that came before them, and persons condemned by one tribunal were acquitted by another.

By the constitution of the United States,[c] " the judges both of the supreme and inferior courts are to hold their offices during good behaviour; and they are, at stated times, to receive for their services a compensation which shall not be diminished during their continuance in office." The tenure of the office, by rendering the judges independent, both of the government and people, is admirably fitted to produce the free exercise of judgment in the discharge of their trust. This principle, which has been the subject of so much deserved eulogy, was derived from the English constitution. The English judges anciently held their seats

---

[a] *Esprit des Loix*, liv. 8. c. 12.
[b] *View of Sweden*, ch. 8.
[c] Art. 3. sec. 1.

at the pleasure of the king, and so does the lord chancellor to this day. It is easy to perceive what a dangerous influence this must have given to the king in the administration of justice, in cases where the claims or pretensions of the crown were brought to bear upon the rights of a private individual. But, in the time of Lord Coke,[a] the barons of the exchequer were created during good behaviour, and so ran the commissions of the common law judges at the restoration of Charles II.[b] It was still, however, at the pleasure of the crown, to prescribe the form of the commission, until the statute of 12 and 13 Wm. III. c. 2. established by law the commissions of the judges to be *quamdiu se bene gesserint*. The excellence of this provision has recommended the adoption of it by other nations of Europe. It was incorporated into one of the modern reforms of the constitution of Sweden,[c] and it was an article in the French constitution of 1791, and in the French constitution of 1795, and it is inserted in the constitutional charter of Lewis XVIII. The same stable tenure of the judges is contained in a provision in the Dutch constitution of 1814, and it is a principle which likewise prevails in most of our state constitutions, and, in some of them, under modifications more or less extensive and injurious.

In monarchial governments, the independence of the judiciary is essential to guard the rights of the subject from the injustice of the crown; but in republics it is equally salutary, in protecting the constitution and laws, from the encroachments and the tyranny of faction. Laws, however wholesome or necessary, are frequently the object of temporary aversion, and sometimes of popular resistance. It is requisite that the courts of justice should be able, at all times, to present a determined countenance against all licentious acts; and to give them the firmness to do it, the judges ought to be confident of the security of their stations. Nor is an independent judiciary less useful as a check upon the

---

[a] 4 *Inst.* 117.   [b] 1 *Sid.* 2.
[c] *Catteau's View of Sweden*, ch. 5.

legislative power, which is sometimes disposed, from the force of passion, or the temptations of interest, to make a sacrifice of constitutional rights; and it is a wise and necessary principle of our government, as will be shown hereafter in the course of these lectures, that legislative acts are subject to the severe scrutiny and impartial interpretation of the courts of justice, who are bound to regard the constitution as the paramount law, and the highest evidence of the will of the people.

The provision for the permanent support of the judges is well calculated, in addition to the tenure of their office, to give them the requisite independence. It tends also to secure a succession of learned men on the bench, who, in consequence of a certain undiminished support, are enabled and induced to quit the lucrative pursuits of private business, for the duties of that important station. The constitution of the United States, on this subject, was an improvement upon all previously existing constitutions, in this or in any other country. It was provided in the constitution of Massachusetts, that permanent and honourable salaries should be established by law for the judges; but this was not sufficiently precise and definite, and the more certain provision in the constitution of the United States has been wisely followed in the subsequent constitutions of most of the individual states. The constitution of this state, as amended in 1821, is an exception to this remark, and it left the judicial department in a more dependent condition, and under greater disabilities than it found it, and greater than in any of those states in the union, or in any of those governments in Europe, whose constitutions have been recently reformed.

But though the constitution of the United States has rendered the courts of justice independent of undue influence from the other departments, it has made them amenable for any corrupt violation of their trust. The house of representatives, as we have already seen, is invested with the power of impeachment, and the judges may, by that process, be held to answer before the senate, and if convicted, they may be removed from office.

The federal judiciary being thus established on principles which are essential to maintain that department in a proper state of independence, and to secure the pure and vigorous administration of the law, the constitution proceeded to designate, with comprehensive precision, the objects of its jurisdiction. The judicial power extends[a] to all cases in law and equity arising under the constitution, the laws and treaties of the union; to all cases affecting ambassadors, other public ministers and consuls; to all cases of admiralty and maritime jurisdiction; to controversies to which the United States shall be a party; to controversies between two or more states; to controversies between a state, when plaintiff, and citizens of another state, or foreign citizens or subjects; to controversies between citizens of different states, and between citizens of the same state, claiming lands under grants of different states; and between a state, or citizens thereof, and foreign states; and between citizens and foreigners. The propriety and fitness of these judicial powers seem to result, as a necessary consequence, from the union of these states in one national government, and they may be considered to be requisite to its existence. The judicial power in every government must be co-extensive with the power of legislation. Were there no power to interpret, pronounce, and execute the law, the government would either perish through its own imbecility, as was the case with the articles of confederation, or other powers must be assumed by the legislative body, to the destruction of liberty. That the interpretation of treaties, and the cases of foreign ministers and maritime matters, are properly confided to the federal courts, appears from the close connexion those cases have with the peace of the union, the confusion that different proceedings in the separate states would tend to produce, and the responsibility which the United States are under to foreign nations for the conduct of all its members.

---

[a] Art. 3. sec. 2. *Amendments to the Constitution*, art. 11.

The other cases of enumerated jurisdiction are evidently of national concern, and they constitute one of the principal motives to union, and one of the principal cases of its necessity, which was the insurance of the domestic tranquillity. The want of a federal judiciary to embrace these important subjects, was once severely felt in the German confederacy, and disorder, license and desolation reigned in that unhappy country, until the establishment of the imperial chamber by the Emperor Maximilian, near the close of the fifteenth century; and that jurisdiction was afterwards the great source of order and tranquillity in the Germanic body.[a]

The judicial power, as it originally stood, extended to suits prosecuted *against* one of the United States by citizens of another state, or by citizens or subjects of any foreign state; but the states were not willing to submit to be arraigned as defendants before the federal courts, at the instance of private persons, be the cause of action what it may. The decision of the Supreme Court of the United States, in the case of *Chisholm* v. *The State of Georgia*,[b] decided in 1793, in which it was adjudged, that a state was sueable by citizens of another state, gave much dissatisfaction, and the legislature of Georgia carried their opposition to an open defiance of the judicial authority. The inexpediency of the power appeared so great, that congress, in 1794, proposed to the states an amendment to that part of the constitution, and it was subsequently amended in this particular under the provision in the fifth article. It was declared by the amendment,[c] that the judicial power of the United States should not be construed to extend to any suit in law or equity, commenced or prosecuted against one of the United States, by citizens of another state, or by citizens or subjects of any foreign state.

With these general remarks on the constitutional principles of the judicial department, and the objects of its au-

---

[a] *Robertson's Charles V.* vol. 1. 188. 395. 397.   [b] 2 *Dallas*, 419.
[c] *Amendments*, art. 11.

thority, we proceed to a particular examination of the several courts of the United States, as ordained by law.

(1.) The Supreme Court was instituted by the constitution, but it received its present organization from congress, for the constitution had only declared, in general terms, that there should be a Supreme Court with certain original and appellate powers. It consists of a chief justice, and six associate justices, any four of whom make a quorum; and it holds one term annually at the seat of government, commencing on the first Monday in February.[a] But though four of the judges are requisite for business in general, yet any one or more of them may make all necessary orders in a suit, preparatory to the hearing or trial, and the judge of the fourth circuit attends at the city of Washington on the first Monday of August annually, for the same purpose.

The Supreme Court has exclusive jurisdiction of all controversies of a civil nature, where a state is a party, except in suits by a state against one or more of its citizens, or against citizens of other states, or aliens, in which cases it has original, but not exclusive jurisdiction. It has also, exclusively, all such jurisdiction of suits, or proceedings against ambassadors, or other public ministers, or their domestics, or domestic servants, as a court of law can have or exercise, consistently with the law of nations; and original, but not exclusive jurisdiction, of all suits brought by ambassadors or other public ministers, or in which a consul or vice-consul shall be a party.[b] The Supreme Court was also clothed by the constitution[c] with appellate jurisdiction, under such exceptions and regulations as congress should prescribe; and, by the act of 1789, already referred to, appeals lie to this court from the circuit courts, and the courts of the several states. Final judgments and decrees, in civil

---

a *Acts of Congress of 29th of April,* 1802, *and February 24th,* 1807, sec. 5.

b *Act of Congress, September 24th,* 1789, sec. 13.

c Art. 3. sec. 2.

actions, and suits in equity in the circuit courts of the United States, whether brought there by original process, or removed there from the state courts, or by appeal from the district courts, in cases where the matter in dispute exceeds 2,000 dollars, exclusive of costs, may be re-examined, and reversed or affirmed in the Supreme Court.*a* Final judgments and decrees in the circuit courts, in cases of admiralty and maritime jurisdiction, and of prize or no prize, where the matter in dispute exceeds 2,000 dollars, exclusive of costs, may be reviewed on appeal in the Supreme Court; and in admiralty and prize cases, new evidence is admitted to be receivable on appeal in the Supreme Court.*b* This admission is conformable to the doctrine and usage of appellate courts of admiralty, permitting the parties, upon the appeal, to introduce new allegations and new proofs, and to add new counts to the libel.*c* So, also, a final judgment or decree in any suit in the highest court of law or equity of a state, may be brought up on error in point of law, to the Supreme Court of the United States, provided the validity of a treaty, or statute of, or authority exercised under the United States, was drawn in question in the state court, and the decision was against that validity; or provided the validity of any state authority was drawn in question, on the ground of its being repugnant to the constitution, treaties, or laws of the United States, and the decision was in favour of its validity; or provided the construction of any clause of the constitution, or of a treaty, or statute of, or commission held under the United States, was drawn in question, and the decision was against the title, right, privilege, or exemption, specially claimed under the authority of. the union.*d* Upon error from a decision in a state court, no other error can be assigned or regarded, than such as ap-

---

a Act of 1789, sec. 22.
b Act of Congress, March 2d, 1803, sec. 11.
c The Marianna Flora, 11 *Wheaton,* 38.
d Act of September 24th, 1789, sec. 25.

pears upon the face of the record, and immediately respects the questions of validity, or construction of the constitution, treaties, statutes, commissions, or authorities in dispute.

The Supreme Court is also armed with that superintending authority over the inferior courts, which ought to be deposited in the highest tribunal and dernier resort of the people of the United States. It has power to issue writs of prohibition to the district courts, when proceeding as courts of admiralty and maritime jurisdiction, and to issue writs of *mandamus* in cases warranted by the principles and usages of law, to any courts appointed, or persons holding office under the authority of the United States.[a] This court, and each of its judges, have power to grant writs of *ne exeat* and of injunction, but the former writ cannot be granted unless a suit in equity be commenced, and satisfactory proof be made that the party designs quickly to leave the United States; and no injunction can be granted to stay proceedings in a state court, nor in any case, without reasonable notice to the adverse party.[b] All the courts of the United States have power to issue writs of *scire facias*, *habeas corpus*, and all other writs not specially provided by statute, which may be necessary for the exercise of their respective jurisdictions, and agreeable to the principles and usages of law.[c] So the judges of the Supreme Court, as well as the judges of the district courts, may, by *habeas corpus*, relieve the citizens from all manner of unjust imprisonment occurring under or by colour of the authority of the United States.[d]

(2.) The circuit courts are established in each district (with one or two exceptions) of the seven great circuits into which the United States are divided. The first circuit is composed of the districts of Maine, New-Hampshire, Mas-

---

a *Act of 24th September*, 1789, sec. 13.
b *Act of Congress, March 2d*, 1793, sec. 5.
c *Act of 24th September*, 1789, sec. 14.
d Ibid.

sachusetts and Rhode-Island; the second circuit, of the districts of Connecticut, New-York and Vermont; the third circuit, of the districts of New-Jersey and Pennsylvania; the fourth circuit, of the districts of Maryland and Delaware; the fifth circuit, of the districts of Virginia and North-Carolina; the sixth circuit, of the districts of South-Carolina and Georgia; and the seventh circuit, of the districts of Kentucky, East and West Tennessee, and Ohio. In each district of these circuits, two circuit courts are annually held by one of the judges of the Supreme Court and the district judge of the district; but the Supreme Court may, in cases where special circumstances shall in their judgment render the same necessary, assign two of the judges of the Supreme Court to attend a circuit court, and when the district judge shall be absent, or shall have been counsel, or be interested in the cause, the circuit court may consist only of a judge of the Supreme Court.[a]

These circuit courts, thus organized, are vested with original cognizance, concurrent with the courts of the several states, of all suits of a civil nature at common law or in equity, where the matter in dispute exceeds 500 dollars, exclusive of costs, and the United States are plaintiffs, or an alien is a party, or the suit is between a citizen of the state where the suit is brought, and a citizen of another state. They have likewise exclusive cognizance, except in certain cases which will be hereafter mentioned, of all crimes and offences cognizable under the authority of the United States, exceeding the degree of ordinary misdemeanors, and of them they have concurrent jurisdiction with the district courts. But no person can be arrested in one district for trial in another, and no civil suit can be brought against an inhabitant of the United States out of his district; and the act of congress provides against the assumption of federal

---

[a] *Acts of March 2d*, 1793, sec. 1. *April 29th*, 1802, sec. 4. *February 24th*, 1807, sec. 2. *March 22d*, 1808, sec. 1. *March 30th*, 1820, sec. 1.

jurisdiction to be created by the assignment of promissory notes or other choses in action, except foreign bills of exchange. The circuit courts have also appellate jurisdiction from all final decrees and judgments in the district courts, where the matter in dispute, exclusive of costs, exceeds 50 dollars.*a* And if any suit be commenced in a state court against an alien, or by a citizen of the state in which the suit is brought against a citizen of another state, or against a citizen of the same state claiming lands under a grant from another state, and the matter in dispute exceeds 500 dollars, exclusive of costs, the defendant, on giving security, may remove the cause to the next circuit court.*b* The circuit courts have also original cognizance in equity and at law of all suits arising under any law of the United States relative to copyrights, and the rights growing out of inventions and discoveries.*c*

(3.) The district as well as the circuit courts, are derived from the power granted to congress by the constitution of constituting tribunals inferior to the Supreme Court.*d* The United States are at present divided into twenty-nine districts, which generally consist of an entire state; but in New-York, Pennsylvania, Virginia, North-Carolina and Tennessee, there are more districts than one. A court is established in each district, consisting of one judge, who holds annually four stated terms, and also special courts in his discretion.

The district courts have, exclusively of the state courts, cognizance of all lesser crimes and offences cognizable under the authority of the United States, and committed within their respective districts, or upon the high seas, and which are punishable by fine not exceeding 100 dollars, by imprisonment not exceeding six months, or when corporal

---

a *Act of September 28th*, 1789, sec. 11. 21, 22. *Act of 3d March*, 1803, sec. 11.
b *Act of 24th September*, 1789, sec. 12.
c *Act of February 15th*, 1819, sec. 1.
d Art. 1. sec. 8.

punishment, not exceeding thirty stripes, is to be inflicted. They have also exclusive original cognizance of all civil causes of admiralty and maritime jurisdiction, of seizures under impost, navigation or trade laws of the United States, where the seizures are made upon the high seas, or on waters within their districts navigable from the sea by vessels of ten or more tons burthen; and also of all other seizures made under the laws of the United States; and also of all suits for penalties and forfeitures incurred under those laws. They have also cognizance concurrent with the circuit courts, and the state courts, of causes where an alien sues for a tort committed in violation of the law of nations, or of a treaty of the United States; and of all suits at common law in which the United States are plaintiffs, and the matter in dispute amounts, exclusive of costs, to 100 dollars. They have jurisdiction, likewise, exclusive of the courts of the several states, of all suits against consuls or vice-consuls, except for offences above the magnitude which has been mentioned.[a] They have also cognizance of complaints, by whomsoever instituted, in cases of captures made within the waters of the United States, or within a marine league of its coasts.[b]

The judges of the district courts have also, in cases where the party has not had a reasonable time to apply to the circuit court, as full power to grant writs of injunction to operate within their respective districts, as is exercised by the judges of the Supreme Court, and to continue until the next circuit court.[c]

In addition to these general powers vested in the district courts, they have, in those cases where the districts are so situated as not to permit conveniently the presence of a judge of the Supreme Court, the powers of a circuit court superadded to their ordinary powers of a district court.

To guard against the inconvenience of a difference of

---

a *Act of 24th September*, 1789, sec. 10.
b *Act of April 20th*, 1818, sec. 7.
c *Act of February 13th*, 1807, sec. 1.

opinion between the circuit judge and the district judge, when holding together a circuit court, it is provided by law, that in all cases of appeal or error, from the district to the circuit court, judgment is to be rendered in conformity to the opinion of the judge of the Supreme Court, presiding in such circuit court. And in all other cases of a disagreement of opinion between the circuit and district judges, the point may be certified into the Supreme Court for its decision, but in no case shall imprisonment be allowed, or punishment inflicted, where the judges of the circuit court are divided in opinion upon the question.*a*

The district and territorial judges of the United States are required to reside within their respective jurisdictions; and no federal judge can act as counsel, or be engaged in the practice of the law.*b*

(4.) The state courts are, in some cases, invested by acts of congress, with the cognizance of cases arising under the laws of the United States. By the acts of March 8th, 1806, and April 21st, 1808, and March 3d, 1815, the county courts within, or adjoining the revenue districts, in certain parts of the states of New-York, Pennsylvania, and Ohio, are authorized to take cognizance of prosecutions for fines, penalties, and forfeitures, arising under the revenue laws of the United States; and the state or county courts adjoining any collection district, in relation to taxes or internal duties which may, at any time hereafter, be assessed, have cognizance of all suits for taxes, duties, fines, penalties, and forfeitures arising thereon.

In attending to this general survey of the organization of the judicial establishment of the United States, it will be perceived, that all the great features of the system are to be found in the act of congress which was passed in September, 1789, at the first session of the first congress under the present constitution. It has stood the test of ex-

---

a Act of April 29th, 1802, sec. 5, 6.
b Act of December 18th, 1812, sec. 1.

perience since that time, with very little alteration or improvement, and this fact is no small evidence of the wisdom of the plan, and of its adaptation to the interest and convenience of the country. The act of 1789 was the work of much profound reflection, and of great legal knowledge; and the system then formed and reduced to practice has been so successful and so beneficial in its operation, that the administration of justice in the federal courts has been constantly rising in influence and reputation.

The principal officers of the courts are attorneys and counsellors, clerks and marshals.

(1.) Attorneys and counsel are regularly admitted by the several courts, to assist the parties in their pleadings, and in the conduct of their causes, in those cases in which the parties do not appear and manage their own causes personally, as they are expressly permitted to do.[a] This privilege conceded to parties, though reasonable in itself, is upon the whole useless, and the necessity of a distinct profession to render the application of the law easy and certain to every individual case, has always been felt in every country under the government of written law. As property becomes secure, and the arts are cultivated, and commerce flourishes, and when wealth and luxury are introduced, and create the infinite distinctions and refinements of civilized life, the law will gradually and necessarily assume the character of a complicated science, requiring for its application the skill and learning of a particular profession. After the publication of the twelve tables, suitors at Rome were obliged to resort to the assistance of their patrons, and judicial proceedings became the study and practice of a distinct and learned body of men.[b] The division of advocates into attorneys and counsel has been adopted from the prevailing usage in the English courts. The business of the former is to carry on the practical and more mechanical parts of the suit, and of the

---

[a] Act of 24th September, 1789, sec. 35.
[b] Gravina, de Ortu et Prog. Jur. Civ. sec. 33. 40.

latter to draft or review and correct the special pleadings, to manage the cause at the trial, and also during the whole course of the suit, to apply established principles of law to the exigencies of the case. In the Supreme Court of the United States, the two degrees of attorney and counsel are kept separate, and no person is permitted to practise both as attorney and counsellor in that court. This was by a rule of the court in February, 1790; and when, afterwards, in August, 1801, the court declared that counsellors might be admitted as attorneys on taking the usual oath, this did not mean or imply, that if a counsellor was thus admitted an attorney, he could continue to act as counsellor. He must make his election between the two degrees. In all the other courts of the United States, as well as in the courts of this state, the same person can be admitted to the two degrees of attorney and counsel, and exercise the powers of each.

Besides the ordinary attorneys, the statute has directed,[a] that a meet person, learned in the law, be appointed to act as attorney general of the United States, and besides special and incidental duties, it is made generally his duty to prosecute and conduct all suits in the Supreme Court in which the United States are concerned, and to give his advice and opinion upon questions of law, when required by the president or the heads of the departments. Each judicial district has likewise a public officer to act as attorney for the United States in the district, and to prosecute all delinquents for crimes or offences cognizable under the authority of the United States, and to prosecute all civil actions within his district in which the United States are concerned.[b]

(2.) Clerks are appointed by the several courts, except that the clerk of the district court is *ex officio* clerk of the circuit court in such district. They have the custody of the seal and records, and are bound to sign and seal all pro-

---

a *Act of 24th September,* 1789, sec. 35.
b *Ibid.*

cess, and to record the proceedings and judgments of the courts. And this is a trust of so much importance, that, in addition to the ordinary oath of office, clerks are obliged to give security to the public for the faithful performance of their duty.^a To guard still further against abuse of office, all moneys paid into the circuit or district courts, or received by the officers, in cases pending therein, are required to be immediately deposited in bank; and no money can be drawn out of bank, except by an order of a judge, to be signed by him, and certified of record by the clerk. The clerks are likewise bound, at every regular session of the courts, to exhibit an account of all the moneys remaining in court.^b

(3.) Marshals are analagous to sheriffs at common law. They are appointed for each judicial district by the president and senate for the term of four years, but are removable at pleasure; and it is the duty of the marshal to attend the district and circuit courts, and to execute, within the district, all lawful precepts directed to him, and to command all requisite assistance in the execution of his duty. There are also various special duties assigned by statute to the marshals. The appointment of deputies is a power incidental to the office, and the marshal is responsible *civiliter* for their conduct, and they are removable not only at his pleasure, but they are also by statute made removable at the pleasure of the district or circuit courts.^c The act says, that the marshal shall be removable *at pleasure*, without saying by whom; and on the first organization of the government, it was made a question whether the power of removal, in the case of officers appointed to hold at pleasure, resided any where but in the body which appointed, and of course whether the consent of the senate was not requisite to remove. This was the construction given to the constitution while it was pending for ratification before the state con-

---

a *Act of 24th September*, 1789, sec. 7.
b *Act of March 3d*, 1817.
c *Act of 24th September*, 1789, sec. 27.

ventions, by the author of the *Federalist*. "The consent of the senate," the *Federalist* observes,[a] "would be necessary to displace as well as to appoint;" and he goes on to observe, that "those who can best estimate the value of a steady administration, will be most disposed to prize a provision which connects the official existence of public men with the approbation or disapprobation of that body, which, from the greater permanency of its own composition, will in all probability be less subject to inconstancy than any other member of the government." But the construction which was given to the constitution by congress, after great consideration and discussion, was different. In the act for establishing the treasury department,[b] the secretary was contemplated as being removable from office by the president. The words of the act are, "That *whenever the secretary shall be removed from office by the president of the United States,* or in any other case of vacancy in the office, the assistant shall act," &c. This amounted to a legislative construction of the constitution, and it has ever since been acquiesced in and acted upon, as of decisive authority in the case. It applies equally to every other officer of government appointed by the president and senate, whose term of duration is not specially declared. It is supported by the weighty reason, that the subordinate officers in the executive department ought to hold at the pleasure of the head of that department, because he is invested generally with the executive authority, and every participation in that authority by the senate was an exception to a general principle, and ought to be taken strictly. The president is the great responsible officer for the faithful execution of the law, and the power of removal was incidental to that duty, and might often be requisite to fulfil it.

This question has never been made the subject of judicial discussion; and the construction given to the constitu-

---

[a] No. 77. [b] September 2d, 1789. sec. 7.

tion in 1789, has continued to rest on this loose incidental declaratory opinion of congress, and the sense and practice of government since that time. It may now be considered as firmly and definitively settled, and I entertain no manner of doubt of the good sense and practical utility of the construction. It is, however, a striking fact in the constitutional history of our government, that a power so transcendent as that is, which places at the disposal of the president alone, the tenure of every executive officer appointed by the president and senate, should depend upon inference merely, and should have been gratuitously declared by the first congress, in opposition to the high authority of the *Federalist;* and should have been supported or acquiesced in by some of those distinguished men who questioned or denied the power of congress, even to incorporate a national bank.

The marshal is obliged to give security to the United States in 20,000 dollars, for the faithful performance of the duties of his office by himself and his deputies, and, together with his deputies, to take an oath of office.[a] By the common law, the death of the principal is a virtual repeal of the authority of the substitute or deputy; but to guard against any inconvenience which might arise from the operation of this principle, and to prevent the mischiefs of a vacancy in office, the act establishing the judicial courts has provided, that in case of the death of the marshal, his deputies shall continue in office, unless otherwise specially removed, and shall execute the same in the name of the deceased marshal, until another marshal be appointed and sworn. So, a marshal, when removed from office, or his term of office expires, may still execute all process in his hands, and he remains responsible for his prisoners until they are duly delivered over to his successor.[b] And with respect to the custody of the prisoners, under the laws of

---

a *Act of 24th September,* 1789, sec. 27.
b *Ibid.* sec. 28.

the United States, the marshal is directed to deliver his prisoners to the keeper of one of the gaols of the state in which he is marshal, in cases where the legislature of the state, in conformity with the recommendation of congress, have made it the duty of the gaolers to receive them; but where they have not, the marshal, under the direction of the district judge, is to provide his own place of security.[a]

---

[a] *Resolutions of Congress, September 23d,* 1789, *and March 3d,* 1792.

LECTURE XV.

OF THE ORIGINAL AND APPELLATE JURISDICTION OF THE SUPREME COURT.

HAVING taken a general view of the great departments of the government of the United States, I proceed to a more precise examination of its powers and duties, and of the degree of subordination under which the state governments are constitutionally placed.

It is to be observed that the constitution of the United States is an instrument containing the grant of *specific* powers, and the government of the union cannot claim any powers but what are contained in the grant, and given either expressly or by necessary implication. The powers vested in the state governments by their respective constitutions, or remaining with the people of the several states prior to the establishment of the constitution of the United States, continue unaltered and unimpaired, except so far as they are granted to the United States. We are to ascertain the true construction of the constitution, and the precise extent of the residuary authorities of the several states, by the declared sense and practice of the governments respectively, when there is no collision; and in all other cases where the question is of a judicial nature, we are to ascertain it by the decisions of the Supreme Court of the United States; and those decisions ought to be studied and universally understood, in respect to all the leading questions of constitutional law. The people of the United States have declared the constitution to be the supreme law of the land, and it is entitled to universal and implicit obedience. Every act of congress, and every act of the legislatures of the states, and every part of the constitution of any state, which is repugnant to the constitution of the United States, is necessarily void. This is a clear and settled principle of constitutional jurisprudence. The judicial power of the union is declared to extend to *all cases* in law and equity arising under the constitution; and to the judicial power it belongs, whenever a case is judicially before it, to determine what is the supreme law of the land. The determination of the Supreme Court of the United States must be final and conclusive, because the constitution gives to that tribunal the power to decide, and gives no appeal from the decision.

With respect to the judicial power, it may be generally observed, as the Supreme Court declared, in the case of *Turner* v. *The Bank of North America*,[a] that the disposal of the judicial power, except in a few specified cases, belongs to congress; and the courts cannot exercise jurisdiction in every case to which the judicial power extends, without the intervention of congress, who are not bound to enlarge the jurisdiction of the federal courts to every subject which the constitution might warrant. So again it has been decided,[b] that congress have not delegated the exercise of judicial power to the circuit courts, but in certain specified cases. The 11th section of the judicial act of 1789, giving jurisdiction to the circuit courts, has not covered the whole ground of the constitution, and those courts cannot, for instance, issue a *mandamus*, but in those cases in which it may be necessary to the exercise of their jurisdiction.

The original jurisdiction of the Supreme Court is very limited. It is confined by the constitution to those cases which affect ambassadors, other public ministers and consuls, and to those in which a state is a party;[c] and it has been made a question, whether this original jurisdiction of the Supreme Court was intended by the constitution to be exclusive. The judicial act of 1789 seems to have consi-

---

[a] 4 *Dallas*, 8.   [b] M'Intyre v. Wood, 7 *Cranch*, 504.
[c] Art. 3. sec. 2.

dered it to be competent for congress to vest concurrent jurisdiction, in those specified cases, in other courts; for it gave a concurrent jurisdiction, in some of those cases, to the circuit courts.[a] In the case of *The United States* v. *Ravara*,[b] this point arose in the Circuit Court for Pennsylvania district; and it was held that congress could vest a concurrent jurisdiction in other courts of those very cases over which the Supreme Court had original jurisdiction; and that the word original was not to be taken to imply exclusive cognizance of the cases enumerated. But the opinion of the Supreme Court of the United States, in *Marbury* v. *Madison*,[c] goes far towards establishing the principle of exclusive jurisdiction in the Supreme Court in all those cases of original jurisdiction. This last case was considered, in *Pennsylvania* v. *Kosloff*,[d] as shaking the decision in the case of *Ravara;* and yet the question was still left in doubt by the Supreme Court, in the case of *The United States* v. *Ortega*,[e] and a decision upon it was purposely waived.

Admitting this original jurisdiction of the Supreme Court may be shared by other courts in the discretion of congress, it has been decided, as we shall presently see, that this original jurisdiction cannot be enlarged, and that the Supreme Court cannot be vested, even by congress, with any original jurisdiction in other cases than those described in the constitution. It is the appellate jurisdiction of the Supreme Court that clothes it with most of its dignity and efficacy, and renders it a constant object of attention and solicitude on the part of the governments and the people of the several states.

(1.) The Supreme Court has appellate jurisdiction in certain cases over final decisions in state courts.

We have seen that, by the act of congress of the 24th of September, 1789, sec. 25. a final judgment or decree in any suit in the highest court of law or equity of a state, where

---

a *Act of Sept. 24th*, 1789, sec. 13. c 1 *Cranch*, 137.
b 2 *Dallas*, 297. d 5 *Serg. & Rawle*, 545.
e 11 *Wheaton*, 467.

is drawn in question the validity of a treaty, and the decision is against its validity; or where is drawn in question the construction of a treaty, and the decision is against the title, right, or privilege, set up or claimed under it, may be re-examined, and reversed or affirmed, in the Supreme Court of the United States, upon a writ of error; and, upon reversal, the cause may be remanded for final decision, or the Supreme Court may, at their discretion, if the cause shall have been once remanded before, proceed to a final decision of the same, and award execution. Under this authority, in the case of *Clerke* v. *Harwood*,[a] it was declared, that if the highest court in a state reverse the judgment of a subordinate court, and, on appeal to the Supreme Court of the United States, the judgment of the highest state court be in its turn reversed, it becomes a mere nullity, and the mandate for execution may issue to the inferior state court. But, in the case of *Fairfax* v. *Hunter*,[b] a writ of error from the Supreme Court of the United States, was awarded to the Court of Appeals of Virginia, upon a judgment in that court, against the right claimed under a construction of the treaties made with Great Britain in 1783 and 1794, and the judgment of the Court of Appeals was reversed, and the cause remanded, and the Court of Appeals below were required to cause the original judgment which had been reversed in that court, to be carried into due execution. The Court of Appeals, when the cause came back to them, resolved, that the appellate power of the Supreme Court of the United States did not extend to that court, and that so much of the act of congress as extended the appellate jurisdiction of the Supreme Court to that court, was not warranted by the constitution; and that the proceedings in the Supreme Court were *coram non judice* in relation to that court, and they, consequently, declined obedience to its mandate. A writ of error was awarded upon this refusal, and the cause came up again before the Supreme Court of

---

[a] 3 *Dallas*, 342.   [b] 7 *Cranch*, 603.

the United States, in a case in which the judgment of the court below drew in question, and denied the validity of the statute of the United States, authorizing an appeal from a state court.[a]

A graver question could scarcely have arisen in that court, or one involving considerations of higher importance and delicacy, or more deeply affecting the permanency and tranquillity of the American union. In the opinion which was delivered, the court observed, that the constitution unavoidably dealt in general language, and did not enter into a minute specification of powers, or declare the means by which those powers were to be carried into execution. This would have been a perilous and difficult, if not an impracticable task; and the constitution left it to congress, from time to time, to adopt its own means to effectuate legitimate objects, and to mould and model the exercise of its powers as its own wisdom, and the public interests, should require.

The judicial power of the United States is declared to extend to all cases arising under treaties made under the authority of the United States. It was an absolute grant of the judicial power in that case, and it was competent for the people of this country to invest the general government with that, or with any other powers they might deem proper and necessary; and to prohibit the states from the exercise of any powers which were, in their judgment, incompatible with the objects of the general compact. Congress were bound, by the injunctions of the constitution, to create inferior courts, in which to vest all that judicial jurisdiction which was exclusively vested in the United States, and of which the Supreme Court cannot take any other than an appellate cognizance. The whole judicial power must be at all times vested, either in an original or appellate form, in some courts created under the authority of the United States. The grant of the judicial power was absolute, and

---

[a] 1 *Wheaton*, 304. Martin v. Hunter.

it was imperative upon congress to provide for the appellate jurisdiction of the federal courts, in all the cases in which judicial power was exclusively granted by the constitution, and not given by way of original jurisdiction to the Supreme Court.

The court, in their examination of the judicial power, supposed that the constitution took a distinction between two classes of enumerated cases. It intended that the judicial power, either in an original or appellate form, should extend absolutely to *all cases* in law and equity arising under the constitution, the laws of the United States, and treaties made under their authority; and to all cases affecting ambassadors, other public ministers, and consuls; and to all cases of admiralty and maritime jurisdiction; because those cases were of vital importance to the sovereignty of the union, and they entered into the national policy, and affected the national rights, and the law and comity of nations. The original or appellate jurisdiction ought, therefore, to be commensurate with the mischiefs intended to be remedied, and the policy in view. But, in respect to another class of cases, the constitution seemed, *ex industria*, to drop the word *all*, and to extend the jurisdiction of the judiciary, not to all controversies, but to controversies in which the United States were a party, or between two or more states, or between citizens of different states, &c. and to leave it to congress to qualify the jurisdiction, original or appellate, in such manner as public policy might dictate. But, whatever weight might be due to that distinction, it was held to be manifest, that the judicial power was, unavoidably, in some cases, exclusive of all state authority, and, in all others, might be made so at the election of congress. The judicial act, throughout every part of it, and particularly in the 9th, 11th, and 13th sections, assumed, that in all the cases to which the judicial powers of the United States extended, congress might rightfully vest exclusive jurisdiction in their own courts. The criminal, and the admiralty and maritime jurisdiction, must be exclusive; and it was only in those cases where, previous to the constitution, state tribunals possessed jurisdiction independent of national authority, that they could now constitutionally exercise a concurrent jurisdiction.

The exercise of appellate iurisdiction was not limited by the constitution to the Supreme Court. Congress might create a succession of inferior tribunals, in each of which it might vest appellate, as well as original jurisdiction. The appellate jurisdiction of the Supreme Court, in cases where it had not original jurisdiction, was declared to be subject to such exceptions and regulations as congress might prescribe. It remained, therefore, entirely in the discretion of congress, to cause the judicial power to be exercised in every variety of form of appellate jurisdiction, and the appellate power was not limited to cases pending in the courts of the United States. If it had been limited to cases in those courts, it would necessarily follow, that the jurisdiction of the federal courts must have been exclusive of state courts, in all the cases enumerated in the constitution. If the judicial power of the United States extends to all cases arising under the constitution, laws and treaties of the union, and to all cases of admiralty and maritime jurisdiction, the state courts could not, consistently with the express grant in the constitution, entertain any jurisdiction in those cases without the right of appeal. If the state courts might entertain concurrent jurisdiction over any of those cases without control, then the appellate jurisdiction of the United States, as to such cases, would have no existence, which would be contrary to the manifest intent of the constitution. The appellate power of the federal courts must extend to the state courts, so long as the state courts entertain any concurrent jurisdiction over the cases which the constitution has declared shall fall within the cognizance of the judicial power. It is very plain, that the constitution did contemplate that cases within the judicial cognizance of the United States would arise in the state courts, in the exercise of their ordinary jurisdiction; and that the state courts would incidentally take cognizance of cases arising under the constitution, the laws, and the treaties of the

United States; and as the judicial power of the United States extended to all such cases, by the very terms of the constitution, it followed as a necessary consequence, that the appellate jurisdiction of the courts of the United States, must and did extend to state tribunals, and attach upon every case within the cognizance of the judicial power.

All the enumerated cases of federal cognizance are those which touch the safety, peace, and sovereignty of the nation, or which presume that state attachments, state prejudices, state jealousies, and state interests, might sometimes obstruct or control the regular administration of justice. The appellate power, in all these cases, is founded on the clearest principles of policy and wisdom, and is deemed requisite to fulfil effectually the great and beneficent ends of the constitution. It is likewise necessary, in order to preserve uniformity of decision throughout the United States, upon all subjects within the purview of the constitution, and the mischiefs of opposite constructions, and contradictory decisions in the different states, on all these points of general concern, would be deplorable.

The right of removal of a cause from a state court by a defendant, who is entitled to try his rights, and assert his privileges in the national forum, is also the exercise of appellate jurisdiction; and the right of removal of a cause may exist before or after judgment, in the discretion of congress. The Supreme Court, by a train of reasoning which appears to be unanswerable and conclusive, came to the decision, that the appellate power of the United States did extend to cases pending in the state courts, and that the 25th section of the judiciary act of 1789, authorizing the exercise of this jurisdiction in the specified cases by a writ of error, was supported by the letter and spirit of the constitution. The judgment of the Court of Appeals in Virginia, rendered on the mandate in the cause, and denying the appellate jurisdiction of the Supreme Court, was consequently reversed, and the judgment of the District Court in Virginia, which the Court of Appeals in Virginia had reversed, was affirmed.

Whether the Supreme Court had authority to issue the compulsory process of *mandamus* to the state courts, to enforce the judgment of reversal, was a question which the court did not think it necessary to discuss or decide, and one of the judges, in the separate opinion which he gave in the cause, seemed to think that the Supreme Court, in the exercise of its appellate jurisdiction, was supreme over the parties and over the case, but that it had no compulsory control over the state tribunals. The court itself gave no intimation of an opinion, whether it could or could not lawfully resort to compulsory or restrictive process, operating *in personam* upon the state tribunals; and it was no doubt deemed discreet not to assert more authority constitutionally vested in the court, than was necessary for the occasion. If the appellate jurisdiction be founded, as it no doubt was in that case, on a solid basis, it would seem to carry with it, as of course, all the coercive power incident to every such jurisdiction, and requisite to support it.

(2.) Another question which was largely discussed and profoundly considered by the Supreme Court, was touching its authority to issue a *mandamus*, when not arising in a case under its appellate jurisdiction, and when not required in the exercise of its original jurisdiction. In the case of *Marbury* v. *Madison*,[a] the plaintiff had been nominated by the president, and by and with the advice and consent of the senate, had been appointed a justice of the peace for the District of Columbia, and the appointment had been made complete and absolute by the president's signature of the commission, and the commission had been made complete by affixing to it the seal of the United States. The secretary of state, after all this, withheld the commission, and the withholding of it was adjudged to be a violation of a vested legal right, for which the plaintiff was entitled to a remedy by *mandamus*; and the only question was, whether the *mandamus* could constitutionally issue from the Supreme Court.

---

a 1 *Cranch*, 137.

The judicial act, sec. 13. authorized the Supreme Court to issue writs of *mandamus* in cases warranted by the principles and usages of law, to any courts appointed, or persons holding office under, the authority of the United States. There was no doubt that the act applied to the case, and gave the power, if the law was constitutional; but the court was of opinion that the act, in this respect, was not warranted by the constitution, because the issuing of a *mandamus* in this case would be an exercise of original jurisdiction not within the constitution, and congress had not power to give *original* jurisdiction to the Supreme Court in other cases than those described in the constitution. It had not authority to give to the Supreme Court appellate jurisdiction, where the constitution had declared that its jurisdiction should be original, nor original jurisdiction where the constitution had declared it should be appellate. To enable the court to issue a *mandamus*, it must be shown to be an exercise, or necessary to an exercise, of appellate jurisdiction.

(3.) The constitution gives to the Supreme Court original jurisdiction in those cases in which a state shall be a party; and in *Fowler* v. *Lindsey*,[a] the question arose, *when* a state was to be considered a party. The parties in that suit claimed title to lands under grants from different states. The plaintiff brought his ejectment in the Circuit Court of Connecticut, claiming title under a grant from that state, and under a claim that the lands lay within the jurisdiction of that state. The defendant claimed title under a grant from New-York, and on the ground that the lands lay within the rightful as well as actual jurisdiction of New-York. The court laid down this rule on the subject of the jurisdiction of the Supreme Court, on account of the interest that a state has in the controversy, that it must be a case in which a state is either nominally or substantially the party; and that it is not sufficient that the state may be consequentially affected,

---

a 3 *Dallas*, 411.

as being bound to make retribution to her grantee upon the event of eviction. Though there may be a controversy relative to soil or jurisdiction between two states, yet if that controversy occurs in a suit between two individuals, to which neither of the states is a party upon the record, it is not a case within the *original* jurisdiction of the Supreme Court, because the states may contest the right of soil in the Supreme Court at any time, notwithstanding a decision in the suit between the individuals. Nor will a decision as to the right of soil between individuals affect the right of the state as to jurisdiction, and that jurisdiction may remain unimpaired, though the state may have parted with the right of soil. In such a case, the Supreme Court would not allow an injunction on a bill, filed by the state of New-York against the state of Connecticut, to stay proceedings in the ejectment suit between individuals, though a general claim of soil and jurisdiction was involved in the private suit, because the state of New-York was not a party to the suit in the Circuit Court, nor interested in the decision.[a]

(4.) The appellate jurisdiction of the Supreme Court exists only in those cases in which it is affirmatively given. In the case of *Wiscart* v. *Dauchy*,[b] the Supreme Court considered, that its whole appellate jurisdiction depended upon the regulations of congress, as that jurisdiction was given by the constitution in a qualified manner. The Supreme Court was to have appellate jurisdiction, "with such exceptions, and under such regulations, as congress should make;" and if congress had not provided any rule to regulate the proceedings on appeal, the court could not exercise an appellate jurisdiction; and if a rule be provided, the court could not depart from it. In pursuance of this principle, the court decided in *Clarke* v. *Bazadone*,[c] that a writ of error did not lie to that court from a court of the United States

---

a 4 *Dallas*, 3. New-York v. Connecticut.
b 3 *Dallas*, 321.
c 1 *Cranch*, 212.

territory north west of the Ohio, because the act of congress had not authorized an appeal or writ of error from such a court. It was urged, that the judicial power extended to all cases arising under the constitution, and that where the Supreme Court had not original, it had appellate jurisdiction, with such exceptions, and under such regulations, as congress should make; and that the appellate power was derived from the constitution, and must be full and complete in all cases appertaining to the federal judiciary, where congress had not by law interfered and controlled it by exceptions and regulations. The court, however, adhered to the doctrine which they had before laid down; and proceeded upon the principle, that though the appellate powers of the court were given by the constitution, they were limited entirely by the judicial acts, which are to be understood as making exceptions to the appellate jurisdiction of the court, and to imply a negative on the exercise of such a power in every case, but those in which it is affirmatively given and described by statute. This was the principle also explicitly declared in the case of *The United States* v. *More*,^a and in the case of *Durousseau* v. *The United States*.^b In the first of those cases, the rule of construction was carried to the extent of holding that no appeal or writ of error lay in a criminal case from the circuit court of the district of Columbia, because the appellate jurisdiction, as to that district, applied by the terms of the statute to civil cases only. The rule was afterwards, in *Ex parte Kearney*,^c laid down generally, that the Supreme Court had no appellate jurisdiction from circuit courts, in criminal cases, confided to it by the laws of the United States.

(5.) The constitution says, that the judicial power shall extend to all cases arising under the constitution, laws, and treaties of the United States, and it has been made a question as to what was *a case* arising under a treaty. In

---

a 3 *Cranch*, 159.   *b* 6 *Cranch*, 307.   *c* 7 *Wheaton*, 38.

Owings v. *Norwood*,[a] there was an ejectment between two citizens of Maryland, for lands in that state; and the defendant set up an outstanding title in a British subject, which he contended was protected by the British treaty of 1794. The Court of Appeals decided against that title thus set up; and the Supreme Court of the United States held that not to be a case within the appellate jurisdiction of the court, because it was not a case arising under the treaty. The treaty itself was not drawn in question either directly or incidentally. The title in question did not grow out of the treaty, and as the claim was not under the treaty, the title was not protected by it; and whether the treaty was an obstacle to the recovery, was then a question exclusively for the state court.

(6.) The judicial act of 1789 required, that on error or appeal from a state court, the error assigned appear on the face of the record, and immediately respect some question affecting the validity or construction of the constitution, treaties, statutes, or authorities of the union. Under this act, it is not necessary that the record should state in terms, the misconstruction of the authority of the union, or that it was drawn in question; but it must show some act of congress applicable to the case, to give the Supreme Court appellate jurisdiction. The Court was so precise upon this point, that in *Miller* v. *Nicholls*,[b] notwithstanding it was believed that an act of congress, giving the United States priority in cases of insolvency, had been disregarded, yet as the fact of insolvency did not appear upon record, the court decided that they could not take jurisdiction of the case.

(7.) The appellate jurisdiction may exist, though a state be a party, and it extends to a final judgment in a state court, on a case arising under the authority of the union. The appellate powers of the federal judiciary over the state tribunals, was again, and very largely, discussed in the case

---

a 5 *Cranch*, 344.   *b* 4 *Wheaton*, 311.

of *Cohens* v. *Virginia*;[a] and the constitutional authority of the appellate jurisdiction of the Supreme Court was vindicated with great strength of argument, and clearness of illustration. The question arose under an act of congress instituting a lottery in the district of Columbia, and the defendant below was criminally prosecuted for selling tickets in that lottery, contrary to an act of the legislature of Virginia. Judgment was rendered against him in the highest court of the state in which the cause was cognizable, though he claimed the protection of the act of congress. A writ of error was brought upon that judgment into the Supreme Court of the United States, on the ground that the prosecution drew in question the validity of the statute in Virginia, as being repugnant to a law of the United States, and that the decision was in favour of the state law. It was made a great point in the case, whether the Supreme Court had any jurisdiction.

The court decided, that its appellate jurisdiction was not excluded by the character of the parties, one of them being a state, and the other a citizen of the state. Jurisdiction was given to the courts of the union in two classes of cases. In the first, their jurisdiction depended on the character of the cause, whoever might be the parties; and, in the second, it depended entirely on the character of the parties, and it was unimportant what might be the subject of controversy. The general government, though limited as to its objects, was supreme with respect to those objects. It was supreme in all cases in which it was empowered to act. A case arising under the constitution and laws of the union, was cognizable in the courts of the union, whoever might be the parties to that case. The sovereignty of the states was limited, or surrendered, in many cases, where there was no other power conferred on congress than a constructive power to maintain the principles established in the constitution. One of the instruments by which that duty might be peaceably per-

---

[a] 6 *Wheaton*, 264.

formed, was the judicial department. It was authorized to decide *all cases* of every description, arising under the constitution, laws, and treaties of the union; and from this general grant of jurisdiction, no exception is made of those cases in which a state may be a party. It was likewise a political axiom, that the judicial power of every well constituted government, must be coextensive with the legislative power, and must be capable of deciding every judicial question which grows out of the constitution and laws. The most mischievous consequences would follow, from the absence of appellate jurisdiction over a state court where a state was a party, for it would prostrate the government and laws of the union at the feet of every state. The powers of the government could not be executed by its own means, in any state disposed to resist its execution by a course of legislation. If the courts of the union could not correct the judgments of the state courts, inflicting penalties under state laws, upon individuals executing the laws of the union, each member of the confederacy would possess a *veto* on the will of the whole. No government ought to be so defective in its organization, as not to contain within itself the means of securing the execution of its own laws. If each state was left at liberty to put its own construction upon the constitutional powers of congress, and to legislate in conformity to its own opinion, and enforce its opinion by penalties, and to resist or defeat, in the form of law, the legitimate measures of the union, it would destroy the constitution, or reduce it to the imbecility of the old confederation. To prevent such mischief and ruin, the constitution of the United States, most wisely, and most clearly, conferred on the judicial department the power of construing the constitution and laws in every case, and of preserving them from all violation from every quarter, so far as judicial decisions could preserve them.

The case before the court was one in which jurisdiction depended upon the character of the cause, as it was a case arising under the law of the union. It was not an ordinary case of a controversy between a state and one of its citizens, for there the jurisdiction would depend upon the character of the parties. The court concluded, that the appellate power did extend to the case, though a state was a party, because it was a case touching the validity of an act of congress, and the decision of the state court was against its validity; and in all cases arising under the constitution, laws, and treaties of the union, the jurisdiction of the court may be exercised in an appellate form, though a state be a party.

The court observed, that the amendment to the constitution, declaring that the judicial power was not to be construed to extend to any suit in law or equity commenced or prosecuted against a state by individuals, did not apply to a writ of error, which was not a suit against a state within the meaning of the constitution; and the jurisdiction of the Supreme Court, in cases arising under the constitution, laws and treaties of the union, may be exercised by a writ of error brought upon the judgment of a state court. The United States are one nation and one people as to all cases and powers given by the constitution, and the judicial power must be competent not only to decide on the validity of the constitution or law of a state, if it be repugnant to the constitution or to a law of the United States, but also to decide on the judgment of a state tribunal enforcing such unconstitutional law. The federal courts must either possess exclusive jurisdiction in all cases affecting the constitution, and laws, and treaties of the union, or they must have power to revise the judgments rendered on them by the state tribunals. If the several state courts had final jurisdiction over the same cases arising upon the same laws, it would be a hydra in government, from which nothing but contradiction and confusion could proceed. Nothing can be plainer than the proposition, that the Supreme Court of the nation must have power to revise the decisions of local tribunals on questions which affect the nation, or the most important ends of the government might be defeated, and we should be no longer one nation for any efficient purpose. The doctrine would go to destroy the great fundamental principles on which the fabric of the union stands.

We have now finished the review of the most important points that have arisen in the jurisprudence of the United States, on the subject of the original and appellate jurisdiction of the Supreme Court. So far as the powers of that court, under the constitution, and under the 25th section of the judicial act of 1789, have been drawn in question, they have been maintained with great success, and with an equal display of dignity and discretion.

LECTURE XVI.

OF THE JURISDICTION OF THE FEDERAL COURTS IN RESPECT TO THE COMMON LAW, AND IN RESPECT TO PARTIES.

(1.) It has been a subject of much discussion, whether the courts of the United States have a common law jurisdiction, and, if any, to what extent.

In the case of the *United States* v. *Worrall*,[a] in the Circuit Court at Philadelphia, the defendant was indicted and convicted of an attempt to bribe the commissioner of the revenue; and it was contended, on the motion in arrest of judgment, that the court had no jurisdiction of the case, because all the judicial authority of the federal courts was derived, either from the constitution, or the acts of congress made in pursuance of it, and an attempt to bribe the commissioner of the revenue was not a violation of any constitutional or legislative prohibition. Whenever congress shall think any provision by law necessary to carry into effect the constitutional powers of the government, it was said, they may establish it, and then a violation of its sanctions will come within the jurisdiction of the circuit courts, which have exclusive cognizance of all crimes and offences cognizable under the authority of the United States. Congress had provided by law for the punishment of various crimes, and even for the punishment of bribery itself in the case of a judge, an officer of the customs, or an officer of the excise; but, in the case of the commissioner of the revenue, the act of congress did not create or declare the

---

[a] 2 *Dallas*, 384.

offence. The question then fairly and directly presented itself, what was there to render it an offence arising under the constitution or laws of the United States, and cognizable under their authority? A case arising under a law, must mean a case depending on the exposition of a law, in respect to something which the law prohibits or enjoins; and if it were sufficient, in order to vest a jurisdiction to try a crime, or sustain an action, that a federal officer was concerned and affected by the act, a source of jurisdiction would be opened which would destroy all the barriers between the judicial authorities of the states and the general government. Though an attempt to bribe a public officer be an offence at common law, the constitution of the United States contains no reference to a common law authority. Every power in the constitution was matter of definite and positive grant, and the very powers that were granted could not take effect until they were exercised through the medium of a law. Though congress had the power to make a law which would render it criminal to offer a bribe to the commissioner of the revenue, they had not done it, and the crime was not recognized either by the legislative or constitutional code of the union.

In answer to this view of the subject, it was observed, that the offence was within the terms of the constitution, for it arose under a law of the United States, and was an attempt by bribery to obstruct or prevent the execution of the laws of the union. If the commissioner of the revenue had accepted the bribe, he would have been indictable in the courts of the United States; and upon principles of analogy, the offence of the person who tempted it must be equally cognizable in those courts. The prosecution against Henfield for serving on board a French privateer against the Dutch, was the exercise of a common law power, applied to an offence against the law of nations, and a breach of a treaty which provided no specific penalty for such a case.

The court were divided in opinion on this question. In the opinion of the circuit judge, an indictment at common law could not be sustained in the Circuit Court. It was admitted that congress were authorized to define and punish the crime of bribery, but as the act charged as an offence in the indictment, had not been declared by law to be criminal, the courts of the United States could not sustain a criminal prosecution for it. The United States, in their national capacity, have no common law, and their courts have not any common law jurisdiction in criminal cases, and congress have not provided by law for the offence contained in the indictment, and until they defined the offence, and prescribed the punishment, he thought the court had not jurisdiction of it.

The district judge was of a different opinion, and he held that the United States were constitutionally possessed of a common law power to punish misdemeanors, and the power might have been exercised by congress in the form of a law, or it might be enforced in a course of judicial proceeding. The offence in question was one against the well-being of the United States, and from its very nature cognizable under their authority.

This case settled nothing, as the court were divided; but it contained some of the principal arguments on each side of this nice and interesting constitutional question.

In the case of *The United States* v. *Burr*, which arose in the Circuit Court in Virginia in 1807, the chief justice of the United States declared,[a] that the laws of the several states could not be regarded as rules of decision in trials for offences against the United States, because no man could be condemned or prosecuted in the federal courts on a state law. The expression, *trials at common law*, used in the 34th section of the judicial act, was not applicable to prosecutions for crimes. It applied to civil suits, as contradistinguished from criminal prosecutions, and to suits at common law, as contradistinguished from those which came before the court sitting as a court of equity and admiralty. He ad-

---

[a] Opinion delivered September 3d, 1807, and reported by Mr. Ritchie.

mitted, however, that when the judicial act, sec. 14. authorized the courts to issue writs not specially provided for by statute, but which were agreeable to *the principles and usages of law*, it referred to that generally recognised and long established law which formed the *substratum* of the laws of every state.

The case of *The United States* v. *Hudson & Goodwin*,^a brought this great question in our national jurisprudence for the first time before the Supreme Court of the United States. The question there was, whether the Circuit Court of the United States had a common law jurisdiction in cases of libel. The defendants had been indicted in the Circuit Court in Connecticut for a libel on the president of the United States, and the court was divided on the point of jurisdiction. A majority of the Supreme Court decided, that the circuit courts could not exercise a common law jurisdiction in criminal cases. Of all the courts which the United States, under their general powers, might constitute, the Supreme Court was the only one that possessed jurisdiction derived immediately from the constitution. All other courts created by the general government possessed no jurisdiction but what was given them by the power that created them, and could be vested with none but what the power ceded to the general government would authorize them to confer, and the jurisdiction claimed in that case had not been conferred by any legislative act. When a court is created, and its operations confined to certain specific objects, it could not assume a more extended jurisdiction. Certain implied powers must necessarily result to the courts of justice from the nature of their institution, but jurisdiction of crimes against the state was not one of them. To fine for contempt, to imprison for contumacy, to enforce the observance of orders, are powers necessary to the exercise of all other powers, and incident to the courts, without the authority of a statute. But to exercise criminal jurisdic-

---

a 7 *Cranch,* 32.

tion in common law cases was not within their implied powers, and it was necessary for congress to make the act a crime, to affix a punishment to it, and to declare the court which should have jurisdiction.

The general question was afterwards brought into renewed discussion in the Circuit Court of the United States for Massachusetts, in the case of *The United States v. Coolidge*.[a] Notwithstanding the decision in the case of *The United States v. Hudson & Goodwin*, the court in Massachusetts thought the question, in consequence of its vast importance, entitled to be reviewed and again discussed, especially as the case in the Supreme Court had been decided without argument, and by a majority only of the court. In this case, the defendant was indicted for an offence committed on the high seas, in forcibly rescuing a prize which had been captured by an American cruiser. The simple question was, whether the Circuit Court had jurisdiction to punish offences against the United States, which had not been previously defined, and a specific punishment affixed by statute. The judge who presided in that court did not think it necessary to consider the broad question whether the United States, as a sovereign power, had entirely adopted the common law. He admitted that the courts of the United States were courts of limited jurisdiction, and could not exercise any authorities not confided to them by the constitution and laws made in pursuance of it. But he insisted that when an authority was once lawfully given, the nature and extent of that authority, and the mode in which it should be exercised, must be regulated by the rules of the common law, and that if this distinction was kept in sight, it would dissipate the whole difficulty and obscurity of the subject.

It was not to be doubted that the constitution and laws of the United States were made in reference to the existence of the common law, whatever doubts might be entertained as to the question, whether the common law of England, in

---

[a] 1 Gallison, 488.

its broadest sense, including equity and admiralty as well as legal doctrines, was the common law of the United States. In many cases, the language of the constitution and laws would be inexplicable without reference to the common law; and the existence of the common law is not only supposed by the constitution, but it is appealed to for the construction and interpretation of its powers.

It was competent for congress to confide to the circuit courts jurisdiction of all offences against the United States, and they have given to it exclusive cognizance of most crimes and offences cognizable under the authority of the United States. The words of the 11th section of the judiciary act of 1789 were, that the circuit courts should have "exclusive cognizance of all crimes and offences cognizable under the authority of the United States, except where this act otherwise provides, or the laws of the United States shall otherwise direct." This means all crimes and offences to which, by the constitution of the United States, the judicial power extends, and the jurisdiction could not be given in more broad and comprehensive terms. To ascertain what are crimes and offences against the United States, recourse must be had to the principles of the common law taken in connexion with the constitution. Thus congress had provided for the punishment of murder, manslaughter, and perjury, under certain circumstances, but had not defined those crimes. The explanation of them must be sought in, and exclusively governed by, the common law; and upon any other supposition, the judicial power of the United States would be left in its exercise to arbitrary discretion. In a great variety of cases arising under the laws of the United States, the will of the legislature cannot be executed, unless by the adoption of the common law. The interpretation and exercise of the vested jurisdiction of the courts of the United States, as for instance, in suits in equity and in causes of admiralty and maritime jurisdiction, and in very many other cases, must, in the absence of positive law, be governed exclusively by the common law.

There are many crimes and offences, such as offences against the sovereignty, the public rights, the public justice, the public peace, and the public police of the United States, which are cognizable under its authority; and in the exercise of the jurisdiction of the United States over them, the principles of the common law must be applied in the absence of statute regulations. Treason, conspiracies to commit treason, embezzlement of public records, bribery, resistance to judicial process, riots and misdemeanors on the high seas, frauds and obstructions of the public laws of trade, and robbery and embezzlement of the mail of the United States, are offences at common law, and when directed against the United States, they are offences against the United States; and being offences, the circuit courts have cognizance of them, and can try and punish them upon the principles of the common law. The punishment must be fine and imprisonment, for it is a settled principle, that where an offence exists, to which no specific punishment is affixed by statute, fine and imprisonment is the punishment. The common law is then to be referred to, not only as the rule of decision in criminal trials in the courts of the United States, but in the judgment or punishment; and by common law be meant the word in its largest sense, as including the whole system of English jurisprudence.

It was accordingly concluded, that the circuit courts had cognizance of all offences against the United States, and what those offences were, depended upon the common law applied to the powers confided to the United States; and that the circuit courts having such cognizance, might punish by fine and imprisonment, where no punishment was specially provided by statute. The admiralty was a court of extensive criminal, as well as civil jurisdiction; and offences of admiralty jurisdiction were exclusively cognizable by the United States, and were offences against the United States, and punishable by fine and imprisonment, when no other punishment was specially prescribed.

This case was brought up to the Supreme Court, but it was not argued. A difference of opinion still existed among the members of the court, and under the circumstances, the court merely said, that they did not choose to review their former decision in the case of *The United States* v. *Hudson and Goodwin*, or draw it in doubt.ᵃ The decision was for the defendant, and consequently against the claim to any common law jurisdiction in criminal cases.

These jarring opinions and decisions of the federal courts, have not settled the general question as to the application and influence of the common law, upon clear and definite principles; and it may still be considered, in civil cases, as open for further consideration. The case of *Hudson and Goodwin* decided that the United States courts had no jurisdiction given them by the constitution or by statute, over libels; and the case of *Worrall* decided that they had no jurisdiction in the case of an attempt to bribe a commissioner of the revenue. If that were so, the common law certainly could not give them any. The cases were therefore very correctly decided upon the principle assumed by the court. But the subsequent case of *Coolidge* did not fall within that principle, because the offence there charged was clearly a case of admiralty jurisdiction, and the courts of the United States would seem to have had general and exclusive jurisdiction over the case. Mr. Du Ponceau, in his "Dissertation on the nature and extent of the jurisdiction of the courts of the United States," has ably examined the subject, and shed strong light on this intricate and perplexed branch of the national jurisprudence. He pursues the distinction originally taken in the circuit court in Massachusetts, and maintains, that we have not, under our federal government, any common law, considered as a source of *jurisdiction;* while on the other hand, the common law, considered merely as the *means or instrument* of exercising the jurisdiction, conferred by the constitution and laws of the union, does exist, and forms a safe and beneficial system of national jurisprudence. The courts cannot

---

ᵃ 1 *Wheaton*, 415.

derive their *right to act* from the common law. They must look for that right to the constitution and law of the United States. But when the general jurisdiction or authority is given, as in cases of admiralty and maritime jurisdiction, *the rules of action* under that jurisdiction, if not prescribed by statute, may, and must be taken from the common law, when they are applicable, because they are necessary to give effect to the jurisdiction.[a]

The principle assumed by the courts in the cases of *Worrall* and of *Hudson* v. *Goodwin*, is considered to be a safe and sound principle. The mere circumstance that the party injured by the offence under prosecution, was an officer of the government of the United States, does not give jurisdiction; for neither the constitution, nor the judicial acts founded upon it, gave the federal courts a general jurisdiction in criminal cases, affecting the officers of government, as they have in cases affecting public ministers and consuls. Because an officer was appointed under the constitution, that would not *of itself* render all cases in which they were concerned, or might be affected, cases arising under the constitution and laws, and cognizable by the judiciary. Such a wide construction would be transferring legislative power to the judiciary, and vest it with almost unlimited jurisdiction, for where is the act that might not, in some distant manner, be connected with the constitution or laws of the United States? It rests alone in the discretion of congress, to throw over the persons and character of the officers of the government, acting in their official stations, a higher protection than that afforded by the laws of the states; and when laws are made for that purpose, the federal courts will be charged with the duty of executing them.

This appears to be sound doctrine, and to be deduced from the cases which have been mentioned. There is

---

[a] *Cui jurisdictio data est, ea quoque concessa esse videntur, sine quibus jurisdictio explicari non potest.* Dig. 2. 1. 2.

much weight undoubtedly due to the argument of the Circuit Court in Massachusetts; and an attempt to bribe an officer of the government, or to libel an officer of the government, in relation to his official acts, would seem to be an offence against that government. They tend directly to weaken or pervert the administration of it; and if it once be admitted that such acts amount to an *offence against the United States*, they must of course be cognizable under its authority, and belong to the jurisdiction of the circuit courts. The great difficulty, and the danger is, in leaving it to the courts to say *what is an offence against the United States*, when the law has not specifically defined it. The safer course undoubtedly is, to confine the jurisdiction in criminal cases to *statute* offences duly defined, and to cases within the *express* jurisdiction given by the constitution. The admiralty jurisdiction of the federal courts is derived expressly from the constitution, and criminal cases belonging to that jurisdiction by the common law, and by the law of nations, might well have been supposed to be cognizable in the admiralty courts, without any statute authority. If the common law be a rule of decision in the exercise of the lawful jurisdiction of the federal courts, why ought it not to apply to criminal, as well as to civil cases, and upon the same principle, when jurisdiction is clearly vested? If congress should by law authorize the district or circuit courts to take cognizance of attempts to bribe an officer of the government in the exercise of his official trust, and should make no further provision, the courts would, of course, in the description, definition, prosecution, and punishment of the offence, be bound to follow those general principles and usages, which are not repugnant to the constitution and laws of the United States, and which constitute the common law of the land, and form the basis of all American jurisprudence. Though the judiciary of the United States cannot take cognizance of offences at common law unless they have jurisdiction over the person or subject matter, given them by the constitution or laws made in pursuance of it; yet, when the jurisdiction is once granted, the common law, under the correction of the constitution and statute law of the United States, would seem to be a necessary and a safe guide, in all cases, civil and criminal, arising under the exercise of that jurisdiction, and not specially provided for by statute. Without such a guide, the courts would be left to a dangerous discretion, and to roam at large in the trackless field of their own imaginations.

The Supreme Court of the United States, in *Robinson* v. *Campbell*,[a] went far towards the admission of the existence and application of the common law to civil cases in the federal courts. The judiciary act of 1789,[b] had declared, that the laws of the several states, except where the constitution, treaties, or statutes of the union, otherwise required, should be regarded as rules of decision in trials at common law in the courts of the United States, in cases where they applied. The subsequent act of May, 1792, confirmed the modes of proceeding then used in suits at common law in the federal courts, and declared, that the modes of proceeding in suits in equity should be according to the principles and usages of courts of equity. Under those provisions, the court declared, that the remedies in the federal courts at common law, and in equity, were to be, not according to the practice of state courts, " but according to the principles of common law and equity as distinguished and defined in that country from which we derived our knowledge of those principles."

In this view of the subject, the common law may be cultivated as part of the jurisprudence of the United States. In its improved condition in England, and especially in its improved and varied condition in this country, under the benign influence of an expanded commerce, of enlightened justice, of republican principles, and of sound philosophy, the common law has become a code of matured ethics, and enlarged civil wisdom, admirably adapted to promote and secure the freedom and happiness of social life. It has

---

a 3 *Wheaton*, 212.   *b* Sec. 34.

proved to be a system replete with vigorous and healthy principles, eminently conducive to the growth of civil liberty; and it is in no instance disgraced by such a slavish political maxim as that with which the Institutes of Justinian are introduced.[a] It is the common jurisprudence of the people of the United States, and was brought with them as colonists from England, and established here, so far as it was adapted to our institutions and circumstances. It was claimed by the congress of the United Colonies in 1774, as a branch of those " indubitable rights and liberties to which the respective colonies were entitled."[b] It fills up every interstice, and occupies every wide space which the statute law cannot occupy. Its principles may be compared to the influence of the liberal arts and sciences; *adversis perfugium ac solatium præbent; delectant domi, non impediunt foris; pernoctant nobiscum, peregrinantur, rusticantur.* To use the words of the learned jurist to whom I have already alluded,[c] " we live in the midst of the common law, we inhale it at every breath, imbibe it at every pore; we meet with it when we wake and when we lay down to sleep, when we travel and when we stay at home; and it is interwoven with the very idiom that we speak; and we cannot learn another system of laws, without learning, at the same time, another language."

II. The jurisdiction of the federal courts *ratione personarum*, and depending on the relative character of the litigant parties, has been the subject of much judicial discussion. The constitution gives jurisdiction to the federal courts of all suits between aliens and citizens, and between citizens of different states, and we have a series of judicial decisions on that subject.

---

a *Quod principi placuit, legis habet vigorem.* Inst. 1. 2. 6.

b *Declaration of rights of* 14th *October*, 1774, *Journals of Congress,* vol. 1. p. 28.

c *Du Ponceau on Jurisdiction,* p. 91.

In *Bingham* v. *Cabot*,[a] the Supreme Court held, that it was necessary to set forth the citizenship of the respective parties, or the alienage where a foreigner was concerned, by positive averments, in order to bring the case within the jurisdiction of the Circuit Court; and that if there was not a sufficient allegation for that purpose on record, no jurisdiction of the suit would be sustained. The same doctrine was maintained in *Turner* v. *Enville*,[b] and in *Turner* v. *The Bank of North America*;[c] and it was declared, that the Circuit Court was a court of limited jurisdiction, and had cognizance only of a few cases specially circumstanced, and that the fair presumption was, that a cause was without its jurisdiction till the contrary appeared. Upon that principle the rule was founded, making it necessary to set forth, upon the record of the Circuit Court, the facts or circumstances which gave jurisdiction, either expressly, or in such manner as to render them certain by legal intendment. It is necessary, therefore, where the defendant appears to be a citizen of one state, to show, by averment, that the plaintiff is a citizen of some other state, or an alien, or if the suit be upon a promissory note, by the endorsee, to show that the original payee was so, for it is his description, as well as that of the endorsee, which gives the jurisdiction.

The judiciary act of 1789, sec. 11. gives jurisdiction to the Circuit Court where an alien is a party, and it was decided, in *Mossman* v. *Higginson*,[d] that the jurisdiction was confined to the case of suits between citizens and foreigners, and did not extend to suits between alien and alien; and that if it appeared on record that the one party was an alien, it must likewise appear affirmatively, that the other party was a citizen. So, again, in *Course* v. *Stead*,[e] it was decided to the same effect. The principle is, that it must appear upon the record, that the character of the parties supports the jurisdiction; and the points in this case were re-as-

---

a 3 *Dallas*, 382.   b 4 *Dallas*, 7.   c 4 *Dallas*, 8.
d 4 *Dallas*, 12.   e 4 *Dallas*, 22.

serted in *Montalet* v. *Murray,*ᵃ and in *Hodgson* v. *Bowerbank,*ᵇ and in *Sullivan* v. *The Fulton Steam-Boat Company,*ᶜ In *Maxfield* v. *Levy,*ᵈ the question of jurisdiction arising from the character of the parties, was discussed in the Circuit Court in Pennsylvania, and the court animadverted severely upon an attempt to create a jurisdiction by fraud, contrary to the policy of the constitution, and the law. The suit was an ejectment between citizens of the same state, to try title to land; and to give jurisdiction to the Circuit Court, a deed was given collusively, and without any consideration, to a citizen of another state, for the sole purpose of making him a nominal plaintiff, in order to give the federal court jurisdiction. The court dismissed the suit, and observed, that the constitution and laws of the United States had been anxious to define by precise boundaries, and preserve with great caution, the line between the judicial authority of the union, and that of the individual states. No contrivance to defeat the law of the land, and create jurisdiction by fraud, could be tolerated.

The doctrine in the original case of *Bingham* v. *Cabot*, was again confirmed in *Abercrombie* v. *Dupuis,*ᵉ with some symptoms of reluctance; and it would seem, that the court was not entirely satisfied with the precise limits in which their jurisdiction had been circumscribed, and embarrassed, by their predecessors. But in *Strawbridge* v. *Curtiss,*ᶠ the limitation of the federal jurisdiction was considered as being still more close and precise. The Supreme Court declared, that where the interest was joint, and two or more persons were concerned in that interest, as joint plaintiffs, or joint defendants, each of them must be competent to sue, or liable to be sued, in the federal courts; and the suit was dismissed in this case, because some of the plaintiffs and defendants were citizens of the same state. The next case that arose on this subject was, whether a corporation was a

---

a 4 *Cranch*, 46.   b 5 *Cranch*, 303.   c 6 *Wheaton*, 450.
d 4 *Dallas*, 330.   e 1 *Cranch*, 343.   f 3 *Cranch*, 267.

citizen within the meaning of the constitution, and could sue in the federal courts in consequence of its legal character; and it was decided, in the cases of the *Hope Insurance Company* v. *Boardman*, and of the *Bank of the United States* v. *Deveaux*,ᵃ that a corporation aggregate was not, in its corporate capacity, a citizen, and that its right to litigate in the federal courts depended upon the character of the individuals who composed the body politic, and which character must appear by proper averments upon the record. But a corporate aggregate, composed of citizens of one state, may sue a citizen of another state in the Circuit Court of the United States.

With respect to the question on the peculiar right of the bank of the United States to sue in the federal courts, it was decided in reference to the first Bank of the United States, that no right was conferred on that bank by its act of incorporation, to sue in those courts. It had only the ordinary corporate capacity to sue, and be sued ; and being an invisible artificial being, a mere legal entity, and not a citizen, its right to sue must depend upon the character of the individuals of which it was composed. The constitution of the United States supposed apprehensions might exist, that the tribunals of the states would not administer justice as impartially as those of the nation, to parties of every description, and therefore it established national tribunals for the decision of controversies between aliens and a citizen, and between citizens of different states. The persons whom a corporation represents may be aliens or citizens, and the controversy is between persons suing by their corporate name for a corporate right, and the individual defendant. Where the members of the corporation are aliens or citizens of a different state from the opposite party, they come within the reason and terms of the jurisdiction of the federal courts. The court can look beyond the corporate name, and notice the character of the members, who are not con-

---

ᵃ 5 *Cranch*, 57. 61.

sidered to every intent as placed out of view and merged in the corporation. Incorporated aliens may sue a citizen, or the incorporated citizens of one state may sue a citizen of another state, in the federal courts, by their corporate name, and the controversy is substantially between aliens and a citizen, or between the citizens of one state and those of another. In that case, the president, directors and company of the bank of the United States averred, that they were citizens of Pennsylvania, and that the defendants were citizens of Georgia; and this averment not traversed or denied, was sufficient to sustain the suit in the Circuit Court. In suits by the present Bank of the United States, such an averment is not necessary, because the act incorporating the bank authorizes it to sue and be sued in the circuit courts of the United States, as well as in the state courts. Without such an express provision, it would have been difficult for the Bank of the United States ever to have sued in the federal courts, if the fact of citizenship of all the members was to be scrutinized, for there is probably few or no states, which have not some stockholder of the bank a resident citizen.[a] It was indispensable for congress to have provided specially for a jurisdiction over suits in which the bank was concerned, or no jurisdiction could well have been sustained. It was truly observed by the Supreme Court, that if the Bank of the United States could not sue a person who was a citizen of the same state with any one of its members, in the circuit courts, this disability would defeat the power.

A trustee who holds the legal interest, is competent to sue in right of his own character as a citizen or alien, as the case may be, in the federal courts, and without reference to the character or domicil of his *cestuy que trust*, unless he was created trustee for the fraudulent purpose of giving

---

[a] Osborn v. United States Bank, 9 *Wheaton*, 738. United States Bank v. Planter's Bank, 9 *Wheaton*, 904.

jurisdiction.[a] This rule equally applies to executors and administrators, who are considered as the real parties in interest; but it does not apply to the case of a general assignee of an insolvent debtor, and he cannot sue in the federal courts if his assignor could not have sued there. The 11th section of the judicial act will not permit jurisdiction to vest by the assignment of a *chose in action*, (cases of foreign bills of exchange excepted,) unless the original holder was entitled to sue, and whether the assignment was made by the act of the party, or by operation of law, makes no difference in the case.[b]

With respect to the district of Columbia, and to the territorial districts of the United States, they are not *states* within the sense of the constitution, and of the judicial act, so as to enable a citizen thereof to sue a citizen of one of the states in the federal courts. However extraordinary it might seem to be, that the courts of the United States, which were open to aliens, and to the citizens of every state, should be closed upon the inhabitants of those districts, on the construction that they were not citizens of a *state*, yet as the court observed, this was a subject for legislative, and not for judicial consideration.[c]

If the jurisdiction of the circuit court between citizens of different states has once vested, it is not devested by a subsequent change of domicil of one of the parties, and his removal into the same state with the adverse party, *pendente lite*.[d] The jurisdiction depends upon the state of things at the time the action is brought. So, an endorsee of a note

---

[a] Chappedelaine v. Decheneux, 4 *Cranch*, 306. 308. Browne v. Strode, 5 *Cranch*, 303. See also 5 *Cranch*, 91. and Childress v. Emory, 8 *Wheaton*, 642.

[b] Sere v. Pilot, 6 *Cranch*, 332.

[c] Hepburn v. Ellzey, 2 *Cranch*, 445. Corporation of New-Orleans v. Winter, 1 *Wheaton*, 91.

[d] Morgan v. Morgan, 2 *Wheaton*, 290.

who resides in one state, may sue his immediate endorser who resides in another state, though that immediate endorser and the maker be residents of the same state. The endorsement is a new contract between the parties to the record, quite distinct from the original note.[a]

The case of *Osborn* v. *The Bank of the United States*,[b] brought into view important principles touching the constitutional jurisdiction of the federal courts, where a state claimed to be essentially a party. The court decided, that the circuit courts had lawful jurisdiction, under the act of congress incorporating the national bank, of a bill in equity brought by the bank for the purpose of protecting it in the exercise of its franchises, which were threatened to be invaded under a law of the state of Ohio, and that as the state itself could not be made a party defendant, the suit might be maintained against the officers and agents of the state, who were intrusted with the execution of such laws.

As the amendment to the constitution prohibited a state to be made a party defendant by individuals of other states, the court felt the pressure and difficulty of the objection, that the state of Ohio was substantially a party defendant, inasmuch as the process of the court in the suit acted directly upon the state, by restraining its officers from executing a law of the state. The direct interest of the state in the suit was admitted, but the objection, if it were valid, would go in its consequences completely to destroy the powers of the union. If the federal courts had no jurisdiction, then the agents of a state, under an unconstitutional law of the state, might arrest the execution of any law of the United States. A state might impose a fine or penalty on any person employed in the execution of any law of the union, and levy it by a ministerial officer, without the sanction even of its own courts. All the various public officers of the Uni-

---

[a] Young v. Bryan; 6 *Wheaton*, 146. Mollan v. Torrance, 9 *Wheaton*, 537.

[b] 9 *Wheaton*, 738.

ted States, such as the carrier of the mail, the collector of the revenue, and the marshal of the district, might be inhibited, under ruinous penalties, from the performance of their respective duties. And if the courts of the United States cannot rightfully protect the agents, who execute every law authorized by the constitution, from the direct action of state agents in the collection of penalties, they could not rightfully protect those who execute any law. The court insisted that there was no such deplorable failure of jurisdiction, and that the federal judiciary might rightfully protect those employed in carrying into execution the laws of the union from the attempts of a particular state, by its agents, to resist the execution of those laws. It may use preventive proceedings, by injunction or otherwise, against the agents or officers of the state, and authorize proceedings against the very property seized by the agent; and the court concluded, that a suit brought against individuals for any cause whatever, was not a suit *against a state* in the sense of the constitution. The constitution contemplated a distinction between cases in which a state was interested, and those in which it was a party; and to be a party for the purpose of jurisdiction, it is necessary to be one upon record. The constitution only intended a party on record, and to be shown in the first instance by the simple inspection of the record, and that is what is intended in all cases where jurisdiction depends upon the party.

The question of jurisdiction depending upon the character and residence of parties, came again into discussion in the case of *The Bank of the United States* v. *The Planters' Bank of Georgia;*[a] and it was decided that the circuit courts had jurisdiction of suits brought by the Bank of the United States against a state bank, notwithstanding the state itself was a stockholder, together with private individuals who were citizens of the same state with some of the stockholders of the Bank of the United States. It was declared,

---

[a] 9 *Wheaton*, 904.

that the state of Georgia was not to be deemed a party defendant, though interested as a stockholder in the defence. The state, so far as concerned that transaction, was devested of its sovereign character, and took that of a private citizen.

We have now seen how far the courts of the United States have a common law jurisdiction; and it appears to have been wholly disclaimed in criminal cases; and the true distinction would seem to be, that all federal jurisdiction in civil and criminal cases, must be derived from the constitution and the laws made in pursuance of it; and that when the jurisdiction is vested, the principles of the common law are necessary to the due exercise of that jurisdiction. We have seen, likewise, with what caution, and within what precise limits, the federal courts have exercised jurisdiction in controversies between citizens and aliens, and between citizens of different states. In the next lecture, we shall enter upon a particular examination of the powers and claims of the federal courts, relative to admiralty and maritime jurisdiction.

LECTURE XVII.

OF THE DISTRICT AND TERRITORIAL COURTS OF THE UNITED STATES.

The district courts act as courts of common law, and also as courts of admiralty.

A distinction is made in England between the instance and the prize court of admiralty. The former is the ordinary admiralty court, but the latter is a special and extraordinary jurisdiction; and although it be exercised by the same person, it is in no way connected with the former, either in its origin, its mode of proceeding, or the principles which govern it. To constitute the prize court, or to call it into action in time of war, a special commission issues, and the court proceeds summarily, and is governed by general principles of policy and the law of nations. This was the doctrine of the English Court of King's Bench, as declared by Lord Mansfield in *Lindo* v. *Rodney*;[a] and though some parts of his learned and elaborate opinion in that case do not appear to be very clear and precise on the point concerning the difference in the foundation of the powers of the instance and of the prize court of admiralty, yet I should infer from it that the judge of the English admiralty requires a special commission, distinct from his ordinary commission, to enable him, in time of war, to assume the jurisdiction of prize. The practice continues to this day, of issuing a special commission, on the breaking out of hostili-

---

[a] *Doug.* 613. note.

ties, to the commissioners for executing the office of lord high admiral, giving them jurisdiction in prize cases.[a]

The division of the Court of Admiralty into two courts is said not to have been generally known to the common lawyers of England before the case of *Lindo* v. *Rodney;* and yet it appears, from the research made in that case, that the prize jurisdiction was established from the earliest periods of the English judicial history. The instance court is the ordinary and appropriate Court of Admiralty, and takes cognizance of the general subjects of admiralty jurisdiction, and it proceeds according to the civil and maritime law. The prize court has exclusive cognizance of matters of prize, and matters incidental thereto, and it proceeds to hear and determine according to the course of the admiralty and the law of nations. The distinction between these two courts, or rather between these two departments of the same court, is kept up throughout all the proceedings; and the appeals from the decrees of these two jurisdictions are distinct, and made to separate tribunals. The appeal from the instance court lies to delegates, but from the prize court it lies to the lords commissioners of appeals in prize causes, and who are appointed for that special purpose.

Such is the distinction in England between the instance and the prize court of admiralty; and in the case *Ex parte Lynch*, it was held, that the jurisdiction of the admiralty as a prize court, did not cease with the war, but extended to all the incidents of prize, and to an indefinite period after the war. It remains to see how far that distinction is known or preserved in the jurisdiction of our district courts.

It is said by a judge, who must be well acquainted with this subject, (for he was a register of a colonial court of admiralty before our revolution,) that this distinction between the instance and the prize court was not known to our admiralty proceedings under the colony administrations.[b] In

---

[a] Ex parte Lynch, 1 *Maddock's Rep.* 15.
[b] 1 *Peter's Adm. Rep.* 5, 6.

the case of *Jennings* v. *Carson*,[a] the District Court of Pennsylvania, in 1792, decided, that prize jurisdiction was involved in the general delegation of admiralty and maritime powers, and that congress, by the judiciary act of 1789, meant to convey to the district courts all the powers appertaining to admiralty and maritime jurisdiction, including that of prize. Prize jurisdiction was inherent in a court of admiralty, though it was of course a dormant power until called into activity by the occurrence of war.

But notwithstanding this early decision in favour of the plenary jurisdiction of the district courts as courts of admiralty, there was great doubt entertained in this country, about the year 1793, whether the district courts had jurisdiction, under the act of congress of 1789, as prize courts. The District Court of Maryland decided against the jurisdiction, and that decree was affirmed on appeal to the Circuit Court, on the ground that a prize cause was not a civil cause of admiralty jurisdiction, but rested on the *jus belli*, and that there was no prize court in existence in the United States. The same question was carried up to the Supreme Court of the United States, in February, 1794, in the case of *Glass* v. *The sloop Betsey*,[b] and was ably discussed. The Supreme Court put an end at once to all these difficulties about jurisdiction, by declaring that the district courts of the United States possessed all the powers of courts of admiralty, whether considered as instance or as prize courts.

In the case of *The Emulous*,[c] the Circuit Court in Massachusetts was inclined to think, that the admiralty, from time immemorial, had an inherent jurisdiction in prize, because if we examine the most venerable relicts of ancient maritime jurisprudence, we shall find the admiralty in possession of prize jurisdiction, independent of any known special commission. It seems to have always constituted an ordinary, and not an extraordinary branch of the admiralty powers; and it is to be observed, that Lord Mansfield leaves the

---

a 1 *Peters' Adm. Rep.* 1.   b 3 *Dallas*, 6.   c 1 *Gallison*, 563.

point uncertain, whether the prize and the instance jurisdictions were coeval in antiquity, or whether the former was constituted by special commission. Be that as it may, the equal jurisdiction of the admiralty in this country, as an instance and as a prize court, is now definitively settled; and if the prize branch of the jurisdiction of the admiralty be not known in time of peace, it is merely because its powers lie dormant, from the want of business to call them into action.

There is no pretence of claim on the part of courts of common law, to any share in the prize jurisdiction of the courts of admiralty. It is necessarily and completely exclusive; and we will first take a view of the jurisdiction and powers of the district courts in prize cases, and then of their ordinary admiralty jurisdiction. As prize questions are applicable to a state of war, and are governed chiefly by the rules of the law of nations, and the usages and practices of the maritime powers, I do not propose to enlarge on that subject. My object will be, to ascertain the exact jurisdiction of the District Court, in all its various powers and complicated character. I shall therefore treat of it, first, as an admiralty court; and under that description, I shall consider, (1.) Its character as a prize court. (2.) As a court of criminal jurisdiction in admiralty. (3.) The division line between the admiralty and the courts of common law. (4.) Its powers as an instance court of admiralty. I shall then next consider its jurisdiction as a court of common law, and clothed also with special powers over patents, and in cases of bankruptcy.

(1.) *As to the jurisdiction of the prize courts.*

The ordinary prize jurisdiction of the admiralty extends to all captures in war, made on the high seas. I know of no other definition of prize goods, said Sir William Scott, in the case of the *Two Friends*,[a] than that they are goods taken on the high seas, *jure belli*, out of the hands of the

---

[a] 1 Rob. 228.

enemy. The prize jurisdiction also extends to captures in foreign ports and harbours, and to captures made on land by naval forces, and upon surrenders to naval forces, either solely, or by joint operation with land forces.*a* It extends to captures made in rivers, ports, and harbours, of the captor's own country. But as to plunder or booty in a mere continental land war, without the presence or intervention of any ships or their crews, Lord Mansfield admitted, in *Lindo* v. *Rodney*, there was no case, or authority, or principle, to enable him to bring it within the cognizance of a prize court. The prize court extends also to all ransom bills upon captures at sea, and to money received as a ransom or commutation, on a capitulation to naval forces alone, or jointly with land forces.*b* The federal courts have asserted for the prize courts in this country, a jurisdiction equally as ample and extensive as any claimed for them in England. In the case of the *Emulous*,*c* though the court gave no opinion as to the right of the admiralty to take cognizance of mere captures made on the land, exclusively by land forces, yet it was declared to be very clear, that its jurisdiction was not confined to captures at sea. It took cognizance of all captures in creeks, havens, and rivers, and also of all captures made on land, where the same had been made by a naval force, or by co-operation with a naval force; and this exercise of jurisdiction was settled by the most solemn adjudications. A seizure may therefore be made in port, in our own country, as prize, if made while the property was water-borne. Had it been landed and remained on land, it would have deserved consideration, and no opinion was given, whether it could have been proceeded against as prize, under the admiralty jurisdiction, or whether, if liable to seizure and condemnation in our courts, the remedy ought not to have been pursued, by a process applicable to municipal confiscations.

---

a Lindo v. Rodney, *Doug.* 613. *note.*
b *Ships taken at Genoa*, 4 *Rob.* 388. Anthon v. Fisher, *Doug.* 649. *note.* Maisonnaire v. Keating, 2 *Gallison*, 525.
c 1 *Gallison*, 563.

It is understood in England, that the admiralty, merely by its own inherent powers, never exercises jurisdiction as to captures or seizures, as prize, made on shore, without the co-operation of naval forces. In the case of the *Ooster Eems*, cited by Sir Wm. Scott in the case of the *Two Friends*,[a] and decided by the highest authority, that of the lords commissioners of appeal, in 1784, it was held, that goods taken on shore as prize, where there had been no act of capture on the high seas, were not to be considered as prize, and that the prize courts had no jurisdiction in such a case. But, it is admitted, that if the jurisdiction has once attached, and the goods have been taken at sea, they may be followed on shore by the process of the prize court, and its jurisdiction over them still continues. In this respect, the prize court seems more extensive, and to hold a firmer jurisdiction, than the instance court; for, as to cases of wreck and derelict, if the goods are once on shore, or landed, the cognizance of the common law courts attaches.[b]

Though the prize be unwarrantably carried into a foreign port, and there delivered by the captors upon security, the prize court does not lose its jurisdiction over the capture, and the questions incident to it.[c] So, if the prize be lost at sea, the court may, notwithstanding, proceed to adjudication, and at the instance of the captors or the claimants.[d] It has jurisdiction, likewise, though the prize be actually lying within a foreign neutral territory. This is the settled law of the prize jurisdictions, both in England and in this country. The principle is, that the possession of the captor, though in a neutral country, is considered to be the possession of his sovereign, and *sub potestate curiæ*.[e] But, it is admitted, that if possession of the thing seized be actually as well as constructively lost, as by recapture, escape, or a

---

a 1 *Rob.* 238.
b The Two Friends, 1 *Rob.* 237, 238.
c The Peacock, 4 *Rob.* 185.
d The Susannah, 6 *Rob.* 48.
e *Vide supra*, p. 98.

voluntary discharge of the captured vessel, the jurisdiction of the prize court over the subject is lost. Though captured property be unjustifiably or illegally converted by the captors, the jurisdiction of the prize court over the case continues, but it rests in the sound discretion of the court, whether it will interfere in favour of the captors in such cases; and it is equally discretionary in all cases where the disposition of the captured vessel and crew has not been according to duty.[a] The prize court may always proceed *in rem*, whenever the prize, or the proceeds of the prize, can be traced to the hands of any person whatever; and this it may do, notwithstanding any stipulation in the nature of bail had been taken for the property. And it is a principle perfectly well settled, and constantly conceded and applied, that prize courts have exclusive jurisdiction, and an enlarged discretion as to the allowance of freight, damages, expenses, and costs, in all cases of captures; and as to all torts, and personal injuries, and ill treatments, and abuse of power, connected with captures *jure belli*, and the courts will frequently award large and liberal damages in those cases.

The prize courts may apply confiscation by way of penalty, for fraud and misconduct, in respect to property captured as prize, and claimed by citizens or neutrals.[b] They may decree a forfeiture of the rights of prize against captors guilty of gross irregularity or fraud, or any criminal conduct; and, in such cases, the property is condemned to the government generally.[c]

(2.) *As to the criminal jurisdiction of the admiralty.*

The ordinary admiralty and maritime jurisdiction, exclusive of prize cases, embraces all civil and criminal cases

---

[a] The Falcon, 6 *Rob.* 194. The Pomona, 1 *Dodson*, 25. L'Eole, 6 *Rob.* 220. La Dame Cecile, 6 *Rob.* 257. The Arabella and Madeira, 2 *Gallison*, 368.

[b] The Johanna Tholen, 6 *Rob.* 72. Oswell v. Vigne, 15 *East's Rep.* 70.

[c] Case of the George, 1 *Wheaton*, 408. 2 *Wheaton*, 278.

of a maritime nature; and though there does not seem to be any difficulty or doubt as to the proper jurisdiction of the prize courts, there is a great deal of unsettled discussion, respecting the civil and criminal jurisdiction of the district court as an instance court, and possessing, under the constitution and judicial act of 1789, admiralty and maritime jurisdiction.

The act of congress[a] gives to the district courts, exclusive of the state courts, and concurrently with the circuit courts, cognizance of all crimes and offences cognizable under the authority of the United States, and committed within their districts, or upon the high seas, where only a moderate corporal punishment, or fine or imprisonment, is to be inflicted. This is the ground of the criminal jurisdiction of the district courts; and it is given to them as district courts; and as it includes the minor crimes and offences committed on the high seas, and cognizable in the courts of admiralty under the English law, the district courts may be considered as exercising the criminal jurisdiction of a court of admiralty in those cases. The constitution of the United States declares, that the judicial power of the union shall extend to all cases of admiralty and maritime jurisdiction; and it has been supposed, that the federal courts might, without any statute, and under this general delegation of admiralty powers, have exercised criminal jurisdiction over maritime crimes and offences. But the courts of the United States have been reluctant to assume the exercise of any criminal jurisdiction in admiralty cases, which was not specially conferred by an act of congress. In the case of the *United States* v. *M'Gill*,[c] the defendant was indicted and tried in the Circuit Court at Philadelphia, for murder committed on the high seas, and the jurisdiction of the court was much discussed. One of the judges observed, that he had often decided, that the federal courts had a common law jurisdiction in criminal cases; but he considered, that the crime

---

a *Act of September 24th*, 1789, sec. 9. and 11.
b *Du Ponceau on Jurisdiction*, p. 59—61.
c 4 *Dallas*, 426.

charged (a mortal stroke having been given on the high seas, and the death in consequence of it happening on land) was not a case of admiralty and maritime jurisdiction, within the meaning of the constitution, or of the English admiralty law, and the prisoner, on account of this defect of jurisdiction, was acquitted. The other judge of the court gave no opinion, whether that case was one of admiralty and maritime jurisdiction, upon the general principles of the admiralty and maritime law; and he confined himself to the 8th section of the penal act of congress of April 30th, 1790; and the case charged was not, by that act, within the jurisdiction of the circuit court.

Afterwards, in the case of *The United States* v. *Bevans*,[a] the Supreme Court, on a case certified from the Massachusetts circuit, decided, that even admitting that the United States had exclusive jurisdiction of all cases of admiralty and maritime jurisdiction, and admitting that a murder committed on the waters of a state where the tide ebbs and flows, was a case of admiralty and maritime jurisdiction, yet that congress had not, by the 8th section of the act of 1790, ch. 9. "for the punishment of certain crimes against the United States," conferred on the courts of the United States jurisdiction over such murder. The act confined the federal jurisdiction to murder and other crimes and offences committed upon the high seas, or in any river, harbour, basin, or bay, out of the jurisdiction of any particular state; and the murder in question was committed on board a ship of war of the United States in Boston harbour, and within the jurisdiction of Massachusetts. There was no doubt of the competency of the powers of congress to confer such a jurisdiction in the case of a crime committed on board a ship of war of the United States, wherever the ship might be; but no such power had, to that extent, been as yet exercised by congress; and it must have followed of course, in that case, that the state courts had jurisdiction of the crime at common law, for it was committed within the territory of the state. It was ad-

---

[a] 3 *Wheaton*, 336.

mitted to be a clear point, that the state courts had cognizance of crimes and offences committed upon tide waters, in the bays and harbours within their respective territorial jurisdictions. And in the case of *The United States* v. *Willberger*,[a] it was decided, that the courts of the United States had no jurisdiction of the crime of manslaughter committed by the master upon one of the seamen on board a merchant vessel of the United States, lying at anchor in the river Tigris, within the empire of China, because the act of congress of the 30th of April, 1790, ch. 36. sec. 12. did not reach such a case, and was confined to the crime committed on the high seas. Upon the principle of this decision, the offender could not be judicially punished, except by the Chinese government; and it was said upon the argument in that case, that China disclaimed the jurisdiction. The law was defective upon this point, and a remedy was provided by the act of congress of 3d March, 1825, c. 67. which declared, that if any offence shall be committed on board of any vessel belonging to a citizen of the United States, while lying in a foreign port or place, the offence shall be cognizable in the circuit courts of the United States, equally as if it had been committed on board of such vessel on the high seas, provided that if the offender shall be tried and acquitted or convicted in the foreign state, he shall not be subject to another trial here. The act provided also for the punishment of many other crimes against the United States; but the crimes in any river, bay, &c. to be cognizable, must be committed out of the jurisdiction of any particular state, except it be conspiracies to defraud insurers; and it further provided, that the act was not to deprive the state courts of jurisdiction over the same offences.

It appears from these cases, that though the general cognizance of all cases of admiralty and maritime jurisdiction, as given by the constitution, extends as well to the criminal as to the civil jurisdiction of the admiralty, as known to the

---

a 5 *Wheaton,* 76.

English and maritime law when the constitution was adopted; yet that without a particular legislative provision in the case, the federal courts do not exercise criminal jurisdiction as courts of admiralty over maritime offences. In the case of *The United States* v. *Coolidge*,[a] it was insisted that the admiralty was a court of extensive criminal as well as civil jurisdiction, and that offences of admiralty jurisdiction were exclusively cognizable by the United States; and that a marine tort on the high seas, as for instance, the forcible rescue of a prize, was punishable by the admiralty, in the absence of positive law, by fine and imprisonment. The decision of the Supreme Court was otherwise;[b] and it seems now to be settled, that the federal courts, as courts of admiralty, are to exercise such criminal jurisdiction as is conferred upon them expressly by acts of congress, and that they are not to exercise any other. This limitation does not, however, apply to private prosecutions in the district court, as a court of admiralty or prize court, to recover damages for a marine tort. Such cases are cognizable in the admiralty by virtue of its general admiralty jurisdiction, and so it was held in the case of *The Amiable Nancy*.[c]

The civil jurisdiction of the English admiralty is according to the forms of the civil law, and before a single judge; but the criminal jurisdiction, in which all maritime felonies are tried, is in the court of admiralty sessions, before commissioners of oyer and terminer, being the judge of the court of admiralty, and three or four associates. It has cognizance of all crimes and offences committed at sea, or on the coasts out of the body of a county; and in that court, the proceedings are by indictment, and trial by jury, according to the course of the common law.[d] The criminal jurisdiction of the English admiralty received its present modification by the act of 28 Hen. VIII. c. 15.; but it had a very extensive criminal jurisdiction, coeval with the first exis-

---

[a] 1 *Gallison*, 488.
[b] 1 *Wheaton*, 415.
[c] 3 *Wheaton*, 546.
[d] 4 *Blacks. Com.* 265.

tence of the court. It proceeded by indictment and petit jury, before, and independent of, the statute of Hen. VIII.; and all criminal offences cognizable by the admiralty, and not otherwise provided for by positive law, are punishable by fine and imprisonment.*a* The better opinion, however, is, that the ancient common law, or primitive criminal jurisdiction of the English admiralty, has become obsolete, and has not been in exercise for the last one hundred years; and that no offence of a criminal nature can be tried there, which does not fall within the jurisdiction specially conferred by the statute of Hen. VIII.*b* There is, therefore, a very strong precedent for the doctrine of the Supreme Court of the United States, which refuses to the federal courts any criminal jurisdiction in admiralty cases not derived from statute. And to whatever extent the criminal jurisdiction of the admiralty may extend, the judiciary act of 1789 provides, that the trial of all issues in fact in the district courts, in all causes except civil causes of admiralty and maritime jurisdiction, shall be by jury.

(3.) *As to the division line between the jurisdiction of the admiralty, and of courts of common law.*

There has existed a very contested question, and of ancient standing, touching the proper division or boundary line between the jurisdiction of the courts of common law and the courts of admiralty. The admiralty jurisdiction in England originally extended to all crimes and offences committed upon the sea, and in all ports, rivers, and arms of the sea, as far as the tide ebbed and flowed. Lord Coke's doctrine was,*c* that the sea did not include any navigable waters within the body of a county; and Sir Matthew Hale supposed,*d* that prior to the statute of 35th Edw. III., the com-

---

a 4 *Rob. Rep.* 74. note.
b 2 *Bro. Civ. and Adm. Law*, appendix, No. 3. *Opinion of Law Officers of the Crown*, ibi.
c 4 *Inst.* 135.
d 2 *Hale's P. C.* ch. 3.

mon law and the admiralty exercised jurisdiction concurrently in the narrow seas, and in ports and havens within the ebb and flow of the tide. Under the statutes of 13 R. II. c. 5. and 15 R. II. c. 3., excluding the admiralty jurisdiction in cases arising upon land or water within the body of a county, except in cases of murder and mayhem, there have been long and vexatious contentions between the admiralty and the common law courts. On the sea shore, the common law jurisdiction is bounded by low water mark, and between high and low water mark, where the sea ebbs and flows, the common law and the admiralty have a divided or alternate jurisdiction.[a]

With respect to the admiralty jurisdiction over arms of the sea, and bays and navigable rivers, where the tide ebbs and flows, there has been great difference of opinion, and great litigation in the progress of the English jurisprudence. On the part of the admiralty, it has been insisted, that the admiralty continued to possess jurisdiction in all ports, havens, and navigable rivers, where the sea ebbs and flows below the first bridges. This seemed also to be the opinion of ten of the judges at Westminster, on a reference to them in 1713.[b] On the part of the common law courts, it has been contended, that the bodies of counties comprehended all navigable rivers, creeks, ports, harbours, and arms of the sea, which are so narrow as to permit a person to discern, and attest upon oath, any thing done on the other shore, and so as to enable an inquisition of facts to be taken.[c] In the case of *Bruce*, in 1812,[d] all the judges agreed, that the

---

[a] 1 *Blacks. Com.* 110. Constable's case, 5 *Co.* 106, 7. 2 *Lord Raym.* 1452. 2 *East's P. C.* 803. 4 *Blacks. Com.* 268.

[b] Cited in *Andrew's Rep.* 232.

[c] King v. Soleguard, *Andrew's Rep.* 231. The resolution of the judges in 1632, cited in 2 *Bro. Civ. and Adm. Law*, 78. 4 *Inst.* 140. *Hawkins' P. C.* c. 9. sec. 14. 2 *East's P. C.* 804. 5 *Wheaton's Rep.* 106. note. *Com. Dig.* tit. Adm. *E.* 7. 14. *Bacon*, tit. Adm. *A.*

[d] 2 *Leach*, 1093, case 353. 4th edit.

common law and the admiralty had a concurrent jurisdiction in bays, havens, creeks, &c., where ships of war floated.

The extent of the jurisdiction of the district courts, as courts of admiralty and maritime jurisdiction, was very fully examined, and with great ability and research, by the Circuit Court of the United States for Massachusetts, in the case of *De Lovio* v. *Boit*.[a] It was maintained, that in very early periods, the admiralty jurisdiction, in civil cases, extended to all maritime causes and contracts, and in criminal cases to all torts and offences, as well in ports and havens within the ebb and flow of the tide, as upon the high seas; and that the English admiralty was formed upon the same common model, and was coextensive in point of jurisdiction with the maritime courts of the other commercial powers of Europe. It was shown by an exposition of the ancient cases, that Lord Coke was mistaken, in his attempt to confine the ancient jurisdiction of the admiralty to the high seas, and to exclude it from the narrow tide waters, and from ports and havens. The court agreed with the admiralty civilians, that the statutes of 13 R. II. and 15 R. II., and 2 H. IV., did not curtail this ancient and original jurisdiction of the admiralty, and that consistently with those statutes, the admiralty might exercise jurisdiction over torts and injuries upon the high seas, and in ports within the ebb and flow of the tide, and in great streams below the first bridges; and also over all maritime contracts, as well as over matters of prize and its incidents. It appeared from an historical review of the progress of the controversy for jurisdiction, which lasted for two centuries, between the admiralty and the courts of common law, that the latter, by a silent and steady march, gained ground, and extended their limits, until they acquired concurrent jurisdiction over all maritime causes, except prize causes, within the cogni-

---

[a] 2 *Gallison*, 398.

zance of the admiralty. The common law doctrine was, that the sea, *ex vi termini*, was without the body of any county; but that all ports and havens, and all navigable tide waters, where one might see from one land to the other what was doing, were within the body of the county, and under the exclusive jurisdiction of the common law courts. On the sea shore or coast, high and low water mark determined what was parcel of the sea, and what was the line of division between the admiralty and the courts of law; and it was held, that it ought to be so considered by parity of reason, where the tide ebbs and flows, in ports and havens; and that the admiralty jurisdiction extends to all tide waters in ports and havens, and rivers beneath the first bridges. It was admitted, however, that the common law originally had jurisdiction on the high seas, concurrent with the admiralty; and that in cases manifestly within the admiralty jurisdiction, both civil and criminal, the common law now claimed concurrent jurisdiction.

The result of the examination in that case was, that the jurisdiction of the admiralty, until the statutes of Richard II., extended to all maritime contracts, and to all torts, injuries, and offences, on the high seas, and in ports and havens, as far as the ebb and flow of the tide; that the common law interpretation of those statutes abridged this jurisdiction to things wholly and exclusively done upon the sea, but that the interpretation was indefensible upon principle, and the decisions founded upon it inconsistent; that the admiralty interpretation of these statutes did not abridge any of its ancient jurisdiction, and *that* interpretation was consistent with the language and intent of the statutes, and analogous reasoning, and public convenience, and the decisions at common law on this subject, were not entitled to outweigh the decisions of the great civilians of the admiralty; that the vice-admiralty courts in this country under the colonial governments, exercised a most ample jurisdiction to the extent there claimed, over all maritime contracts, and over torts and injuries, as well in ports as upon the high seas; and that the constitution of the

United States, when it conferred not only admiralty, but *maritime* jurisdiction, added that word *ex industria*, to remove every latent doubt. This large and liberal construction of the admiralty powers of the district courts, and their extension to all maritime contracts, torts, and injuries, was recommended by the general equity and simplicity of admiralty proceedings, and the policy and wisdom of that code of maritime law which had embodied the enlightened reason of the civil law, and the customs and usages of the maritime nations, and regulates, by its decisions, the commercial intercourse of mankind.

It is understood, that this enlarged extension of the civil jurisdiction of the admiralty, as declared in the Circuit Court in Massachusetts, is a point now under review, and remains to be discussed, and definitively settled, in the Supreme Court. With respect to the criminal jurisdiction of the admiralty, we have already seen, that the courts of the United States do not assume any jurisdiction which is not expressly conferred by an act of congress; and the argument for the extension of the *civil* jurisdiction of the admiralty beyond the limits known and established in the English law, at the time of the formation of our constitution, is not free from very great difficulty.

It has been made a question, what were " cases of admiralty and maritime jurisdiction," within the meaning of the constitution of the United States. It is not in the power of congress to enlarge that jurisdiction beyond what was understood and intended by it when the constitution was adopted, because it would be depriving the suitor of the right of trial by jury, which is secured to him by the constitution in suits at common law; and it is well known, that in civil suits of admiralty and maritime jurisdiction, the proceedings are according to the course of the civil law, and without jury. If the admiralty and maritime jurisdiction of the district courts embraces all maritime contracts, then suits upon policies of insurance, charter parties, marine hypothecations, contracts for building, repairing, supplying, and navigating ships, and contracts between part owners of ships, must be tried in the admiralty by a single judge, to the exclusion of the trial by jury, and the state courts would be devested, at one stroke, of a vast field of commercial jurisdiction. The words of the judicial act of 1789, sec. 9. are, that the district courts shall have "*exclusive* original cognizance of all causes of admiralty and maritime jurisdiction, including all seizures under laws of impost, navigation, or trade, of the United States, where the seizures are made on waters which are navigable from the sea, by vessels of ten or more tons burthen, within their respective districts, as well as upon the high seas." But the act adds, by way of qualification to this designation of admiralty jurisdiction, these words, viz. "saving to suitors in all cases, the right of a common law remedy, where the common law is competent to give it."

The act of congress is rather ambiguous in its meaning, and leaves it uncertain whether it meant to consider seizures on tide waters in ports, harbours, arms, and creeks of the sea, as cases of admiralty and maritime jurisdiction, or as cases simply within the cognizance of the district courts, for the expression is *including*, that is, comprehending, either within the cognizance of the court, or within the class of cases of admiralty jurisdiction, all seizures under laws of impost, navigation and trade, on waters navigable from the sea by small vessels of ten tons burthen. This act has, however, been construed to put a construction upon the words "admiralty and maritime jurisdiction," conformable to the claims of the civilians, and in opposition to the claims of the common law tribunals, and there are a series of decisions in the Supreme Court of the United States to that effect.

In the case of the *United States* v. *Le Vengeance*,[a] a French privateer was libelled in the District Court of New-York, for an attempt to export arms from the United States to a foreign country contrary to law. She was adjudged to be forfeited to the United States. The decree, on appeal to the Circuit Court, was reversed. On a further appeal to

---

a 3 *Dallas*, 297.

the Supreme Court of the United States, it was contended, that this was a criminal case, both on account of the manner of prosecution, and the matter charged; and, therefore, that the decree of the District Court was final, and that it ought likewise to have been tried by a jury in the District Court; and that if it was even a civil suit, it was not a case of admiralty and maritime jurisdiction. To render it such, the cause must arise wholly upon the sea, and not in a bay, harbour, or water, within the precincts of any county of a state. But the Supreme Court decided, that it was a civil suit, not of common law, but of admiralty and maritime jurisdiction. The seizure was on the waters of the United States. The process was *in rem*, and did not, in any degree, touch the person, and no jury was necessary.

Afterwards, in the case of the *United States* v. *The schooner Sally*,[a] the vessel was libelled in the District Court, as forfeited for being concerned in the slave trade; and this was also held, on appeal, to be a case, not of common law, but of admiralty jurisdiction. So, in the case of the *United States* v. *The Schooner Betsey*,[b] it was held, that all seizures under the act of congress suspending commercial intercourse with a foreign country, and made on waters navigable from sea, by vessels of ten tons burthen, were civil causes of admiralty jurisdiction, being proceedings *in rem*, and not according to the course of the common law, and were to be tried without a jury. The court said, that the place of seizure being on navigable waters, decided the jurisdiction, and that the act of congress meant to make seizures on waters navigable from the sea, civil causes of admiralty and maritime jurisdiction. In this last case, the counsel for the claimant contended, that the seizure was made within the body of a county, for breach of a municipal law of trade, and that though it belonged to the jurisdiction of the District Court, it was not a case of admiralty cognizance. All seizures in England for violation of the,

---

a 2 *Cranch*, 406.   *b* 4 *Cranch*, 443.

laws of revenue, trade, or navigation, were tried by a jury in the Court of Exchequer, according to the course of the common law, and though a proceeding was *in rem*, it was not necessarily a proceeding or cause in the admiralty.

In the case of *The Samuel*,[a] where the vessel and cargo were seized and libelled, and condemned in the District Court of Rhode Island, for a breach of the non-importation laws of the United States, the same objection was made upon appeal to the Supreme Court, and it was again overruled on the authority of the preceding cases. The same objection was taken in the case of *The Octavia*,[b] and it was contended, that the word *including*, in the 9th section of the judicial act, ought not to be construed cumulatively, and that a suit might be a cause of admiralty and maritime jurisdiction, and yet triable under the common law proceeding by information, instead of the civil law process by libel. The objection was again overruled. The last case that brought up the same point for review and discussion, was *The Sarah*,[c] and the Supreme Court there recognised the marked and settled distinction between the common law and the admiralty jurisdictions of the district courts. In seizures made on land, the District Court proceeds as a court of common law, according to the course of the English Exchequer, on informations *in rem*, and the trial of issues of fact is to be by jury. But, in cases of seizures on waters navigable from the sea, by vessels of ten or more tons burthen, the court proceeds as an instance court of admiralty, by libel *in rem*, and the trial is by the court.

It may now be considered as the settled law of this country, that all seizures under laws of impost, navigation and trade, if made upon tide waters navigable from the sea, are civil cases of admiralty jurisdiction, and the successive judgments of the Supreme Court upon this point, are founded upon the judiciary act of 1789. If the act of congress declares them to be cases of admiralty jurisdiction, it is ap-

---

[a] 1 *Wheaton*, 9.   [b] *Ibid.* 20.   [c] 8 *Wheaton*, 391.

prehended that this is an extension of admiralty powers beyond the English practice. Cases of forfeiture for breaches of revenue law are cognizable in England in the exchequer upon information, though the seizure was made upon navigable waters, and they proceed there to try the fact on which the forfeiture arises by jury.[a] Informations are filed in the Court of Exchequer for forfeiture upon seizure of property, for breach of laws of revenue, impost, navigation, and trade. In the case of *The Attorney General v. Jackson*,[b] the seizure was of a vessel lying in port at Cowes, for breach of the act of navigation, and the proceeding was by information and trial by jury, according to the course of the common law. Lord Hale said,[c] that informations of that nature lay exclusively in the exchequer. Congress had a right, in their discretion, to make all such seizures and forfeitures cognizable in the district courts; but it may be a question whether they had any right to declare them to be cases of admiralty jurisdiction, if they were not so by the law of the land when the constitution was made. The constitution secures to the citizen trial by jury in all criminal prosecutions, and in all civil suits at common law, where the value in controversy exceeds 20 dollars. These prosecutions for forfeitures of large and valuable portions of property, under revenue and navigation laws, are highly penal in their consequences; and the government and its officers are always parties, and deeply concerned in the conviction and forfeiture. And if by an act of congress, or by judicial decisions, the prosecution can be turned over to the admiralty side of the district court, as being neither a criminal prosecution nor a suit at common law, the trial of the cause is then transferred from a jury of the country to the breast of a single judge. It is probable, however, that the judicial act of 1789 did not intend to do more than declare

---

a Attorney General v. Le Merchant, 1 *Anst.* 52.
b *Bunb.* 236.
c *Harg. Law Tracts,* 227.

the jurisdiction of the district courts over these cases; and that all prosecutions for penalties and forfeitures upon seizures under laws of impost, navigation and trade, were not to be considered of admiralty jurisdiction, when the case admitted of a prosecution at common law; for the act saves to "suitors in all cases the right of a common law remedy, where the common law was competent to give it." We have seen that it is competent to give it, because, under the vigorous system of the English law, such prosecutions *in rem* are in the exchequer according to the course of the common law, and it may be doubted whether the case of the *Le Vengeance*, on which all the subsequent decisions of the Supreme Court have rested, was sufficiently considered. There is, however, much colonial precedent for this extension of admiralty jurisdiction. The vice-admiralty courts in this country, when we were colonies, and also in the West Indies, obtained jurisdiction in revenue causes to an extent totally unknown to the jurisdiction of the English admiralty, and with powers quite as enlarged as those claimed at the present day.[a] But this extension of the jurisdiction of the American vice-admiralty courts beyond their ancient limits, to revenue cases and penalties, was much discussed and complained of on the part of this country at the commencement of the revolution.[b]

Whatever admiralty and maritime jurisdiction the district courts possess would seem to be *exclusive*, for the constitution declares that the judicial power of the United States shall extend to *all cases* of admiralty and maritime jurisdiction; and the act of congress of 1789 says, that the district courts shall have *exclusive* original cognizance of all civil causes of admiralty and maritime jurisdiction. It is certain, however, that the state courts take an extensive and unquestioned cognizance of maritime contracts, and on the ground

---

[a] See the form of the commissions of these vice-admiralty courts under the colonial establishments in a note to the case of De Lovio v. Boit, and in *Duponceau on Jurisdiction*, p. 158.

[b] *Journals of Congress*, vol. 1. p. 22. 29. 39.

that they are not cases, strictly and technically speaking, of admiralty and maritime jurisdiction. If, however, the claim of the district courts be well founded to the cognizance of all maritime contracts, wheresoever the same may be made, or whatever may be the form of the contract, it would seem that the jurisdiction of the state courts over those contracts could not be sustained. But I apprehend it may fairly be doubted whether the constitution of the United States meant by admiralty and maritime jurisdiction, any thing more than that jurisdiction which was settled and in active practice under the English jurisprudence when the constitution was made; and whether it had any retrospective or historical reference to the usages and practice of the admiralty, as it once existed in the middle ages, before the territories of the admiralty had been invaded and partly subdued by the bold and free spirit of the courts of common law, armed with the protecting genius and masculine vigour of trial by jury.

(4.) *As to the jurisdiction of the instance courts.*

According to the English jurisprudence, the instance court takes cognizance only of crimes committed, and things done, and contracts not under seal made *super altum mare*, and without the body of any county. This, of course, excludes all creeks, bays, and rivers, which are within the body of some county; and if the place be the sea coast, then the ebbing and flowing of the tide determines the admiralty. The cause must arise *wholly* upon the sea, and not within the precincts of any county, to give the admiralty jurisdiction. If the action be founded on a matter done partly on land and partly on water, as if a contract be made on land to be executed at sea, or be made at sea to be executed on land, the common law has the preference, and excludes the admiralty.[a] The admiralty has cognizance of maritime hypothecations of vessels and goods in foreign ports, for repairs done, or

---

[a] Com. Dig. tit. Adm. E. 1. 7. 10. 12. F. 1. 2. 4. 5. 3 *Black. Com.* 106, 107.

necessary supplies furnished;[a] and in the case of *Menetone v. Gibbons,*[b] it was admitted by the K. B. that the admiralty had entire jurisdiction in the case of an hypothecation bond, charging a ship with money taken up in a foreign port for necessaries, though the bond was under seal, and executed on land. The jurisdiction in such a case, depended on the subject matter, for here the contract was merely *in rem*, and there was no personal covenant for the payment of the money, and the admiralty jurisdiction in such a case was indispensable, as the courts of common law do not proceed *in rem*. If the admiralty has cognizance of the principal thing, it has also of the incident, though that incident would not of itself, and if it stood for a principal thing, be within the admiralty jurisdiction. Upon this principle it is, that goods taken by pirates and sold on land, may be recovered from the vendee, by suit in the admiralty.[c] Suits for seamen's wages are cognizable in the admiralty, though the contract may be made upon land; and this is intended for the ease and benefit of seamen, for they are all allowed to join in the suit, and all the persons on board below the rank of the master, are comprehended in the description of mariners.[d] This case of seamen's wages the courts of common law admit to be of admiralty jurisdiction; and this is an exception in favour of seamen, to the general rule that the admiralty has no jurisdiction of any matter arising on land, though it be of a maritime nature, as a charter party or policy of insurance. The District Court, as a court of admiralty, possesses a general jurisdiction in suits by material men, *in rem* and *in personam*. The proceeding *in personam*, is always maintainable by those men, but the proceeding *in rem*, is only when

---

[a] 1 *Salk.* 34. 1 *Lord Raym.* 152.
[b] 3 *Term Rep.* 267.
[c] *Com. Dig.* tit. Adm. F. 6. 3 *Blacks. Com.* 108.
[d] 1 *Salk.* 34. *Str.* 761. 937. 1 *Lord Raym.* 598. 3 *Lev.* 60. 4 *Inst.* 134. 142. *Com. Dig.* tit. Adm. E. 15.

there is a specific lien, as for repairs made, or necessaries furnished to a foreign ship, or to a ship in the ports of the state to which she does not belong.[a] The act of congress of July 20th, 1790, relative to seamen, section 6, has given a specific and summary relief for seamen, in the recovery of wages, by authorizing the district judge, or in his absence, a magistrate, to summon the master before him, and to attach the vessel as security for the wages.

We have now finished a general survey of the admiralty jurisdiction of the district courts, both in civil and criminal cases, and both as an instance and as a prize court. It would not be consistent with the plan of these elementary disquisitions, to give a detailed sketch of the course of proceeding, and of the peculiar practice in the admiralty courts. The proceedings are according to the course of the civil law, and are remarkable for their comprehensive brevity, celerity, and simplicity. Nothing can be more unlike in its process, pleadings, proof, trial, and remedy, than the practice of the courts of admiralty and of the courts of common law. For a knowledge of the admiralty practice, I would refer the student to *Clerke's Practice of the Court of Admiralty in England*, which is a work of undoubted credit; and in 1809, a new edition was published in this country by Mr. Hall, with an appendix of precedents. I would also refer him to the 2d volume of *Brown's Civil and Admiralty Law*, and to the Appendix to the 1st and 2d volumes of *Mr. Wheaton's Reports*, where he will find the practice of the instance and prize courts digested and summarily explained.

I proceed next to consider the jurisdiction of the District Court when proceeding as a court of common law. It extends to all minor crimes and offences, cognizable under the authority of the United States, and which are not strictly of admiralty cognizance; and to all seizures on land, and on waters not navigable from the sea; and to all suits for penalties and forfeitures there incurred; and to all suits

---

[a] *The General Smith*, 4 *Wheaton*, 438. *The Jerusalem*, 2 *Gallison*, 345.

by aliens for torts done in violation of the law of nations, or of a treaty; and to suits against consuls and vice-consuls; and to all suits at common law, where the United States sue, and the matter in dispute amounts to one hundred dollars.[a] It has jurisdiction likewise of proceedings to repeal patents obtained surreptitiously, or upon false suggestions. This is given by the act of congress of 21st February, 1793, chap. 11., and it is a jurisdiction that leads frequently to the most intricate, nice, and perplexed investigations, respecting the originality of inventions and improvements in complicated machinery. It was made a question in the District Court of New-York, in the case *Ex parte Wood*, whether the process to be awarded to repeal the patent, was not in the nature of a *scire facias* at common law, upon which issue of fact might be taken and tried by a jury. The district judge decided, that the proceeding was summary, upon a rule to show cause, and that no process of *scire facias* was afterwards admissible. But upon appeal to the Supreme Court of the United States,[b] the decree of the District Court was reversed, and the District Court was directed by *mandamus* to enter upon record the proceedings in the cause, antecedent to the granting of the rule to show cause why process should not issue to repeal the patent. The District Court was further directed to award process, in the nature of a *scire facias*, to the patentee, to show cause why the patent should not be repealed; and upon the return of the process, the Court was to proceed to try the cause upon the pleadings of the parties, and the issue of law or fact joined thereon, as the case might be; and that if the issue be an issue of fact, the trial thereof was to be by jury, according to the course of the common law.

This was a just and liberal decision of the Supreme Court, and it was observed, in the opinion which was pronounced,

---

[a] *Judiciary Act of September,* 1789. sec. 9.
[b] 9 *Wheaton,* 603.

that it was not lightly to be presumed, that congress, in this class of patent cases, placed peculiarly within their patronage and protection, involving some of the dearest and most valuable rights which society acknowledges, and the constitution itself meant to favour, would institute a new and summary process, which should finally adjudge upon those rights, without a trial by jury, without a right of appeal, and without any of those guards with which, in equity suits, it has fenced round the general administration of justice. The Supreme Court then went into an analytical examination of the 10th section of the act of 1793, on which the claim of summary jurisdiction rested, and vindicated the construction which they assumed, in opposition to that taken by the District Court.

The jurisdiction of the judges of the district courts, in cases of bankruptcy, has presented for consideration some extremely important and difficult questions on the point of jurisdiction. We have no bankrupt system in existence under the government of the United States; but there are some lingering traces of business yet arising and undetermined, under the bankrupt act of the year 1800; and we are in expectation, at every session of congress, of a revival of that, or some other analogous system and code of national bankrupt law. The question, which was not long since discussed and decided in the District Court of New-York in the case of *Comfort Sands*,[a] is worthy of some little examination.

The district judge observed, that, in England, the sole power of directing the execution, and controlling the administration of the bankrupt system, in all its departments, and in every stage of the proceeding, resided in the lord chancellor. He examined the provisions of the several English bankrupt acts, from 34th and 35th Hen. VIII. to 49th Geo. III. to show that, by them, the chancellor has authority to appoint the commissioners of bankrupts, to supersede

---

[a] *United States Law Journal*, vol. 1. p. 15.

their authority, to enlarge the time for the bankrupt to surrender, to punish for concealing him, to remove the assignees and appoint others, and to order them to pay dividends. Under this delegation of power, the whole administration of the bankrupt's effects is vested in the lord chancellor; though this administration was given immediately by the legislature to the commissioners. The chancellor, in virtue of his acknowledged power to appoint and remove, to create and annihilate these officers, possesses, in effect, the authority to control and direct them in all their acts, and thus effectually to exercise the whole jurisdiction. His power is adequate to every case, and to every emergency, that can arise in the course of the administration of the bankrupt system. He grants relief to all parties interested, the bankrupt as well as the creditor, in a summary way.

This jurisdiction of the English chancellor is not in the court of chancery, but in the individual who holds the great seal; and it is excercised summarily upon petition, and his judgment upon the petition is without appeal, unless the chancellor in his discretion allows a bill to be filed in order to found an appeal thereon. The judge, after giving this view of the jurisdiction of the lord chancellor of England, sitting in bankruptcy, proceeded to examine the several provisions of the bankrupt act of the United States of 1800, in order to show that upon the principles of construction adopted in England, the district judge had the same jurisdiction in cases of bankruptcy as is exercised by the lord chancellor. The same course of reasoning which sustains the jurisdiction of the one, would confer that of the other. He insisted that the jurisdiction here was given not to the District Court, but to the individual who happened to hold the office of district judge, and that, consequently, all his decisions in bankruptcy were without appeal, for appeals lie only from the decrees of the District Court.

The district judge accordingly proceeded to institute an inquiry, upon the petition of the bankrupt, into the execution of the commission of bankruptcy, and what the commissioners had done under it, and he made an order calling upon the assignees to account.

After this decision, an application was made to the Circuit Court of the United States to take cognizance of this case, and to injoin the bankrupt from further proceedings before the district judge; but that court held, that it had no jurisdiction in the case.

If the doctrine in this case be sound, and that the district judge had this plenary, absolute, uncontrollable and exclusive jurisdiction in all cases of bankruptcy, both in respect to the person and estate of the bankrupt, then it must be admitted that the bankrupt act of 1800 erected a tribunal of a most arbitrary character, and it is fortunate in that respect that the bankrupt act was speedily repealed. According to this decision, the state tribunals, such as the Court of Chancery and the Court of Errors of this state, which asserted and exercised concurrent jurisdiction between the bankrupt and his creditors, as in the case of *Codwise and others* v. *Sands and others*,[a] were all under a mistake, and the decrees of those courts respectively were null and void for want of jurisdiction. The weight of authority is, however, in favour of the concurrent jurisdiction of the state courts, and against any construction of the bankrupt act of 1800, which would vest such extravagant powers in the unchecked discretion of a single judge. There was nothing in that act which declared or intimated that the judge of the District Court, in executing the powers vested in the district judge, was not to be deemed to be acting judicially as a court. The act of congress was susceptible of a safer construction, and one better adapted to the genius and whole detail of our municipal institutions; and it is understood that the Circuit Court for the district of New-York has since admitted the right of appeal to that court, and also the concurrent jurisdiction of the state courts.

---

4 *Johnson's Rep.* 536.

With respect to the vast territories belonging to the United States, and which are not distinct political societies, known to the constitution as states, congress have assumed to exercise over them supreme powers of sovereignty. In the Michigan territory, congress have, by the acts of 7th of August, 1789, and January 14th, 1805, adopted the principles of the ordinance of the old confederation congress of the date of the 13th of July, 1787. This ordinance was formed upon sound and enlightened maxims of civil jurisprudence, and the judges appointed in that territory hold their offices during good behaviour. In the Arkansaw territory, a greater subjection is created to the will of the president of the United States. The governor and judges are appointed by the president and senate, but they are removeable at the pleasure of the president, and the judges subject to such removal, hold for four, and the governor for three years. The legislative power of the territory was originally vested in the governor, and the three judges of the superior court, by the act of March 2d, 1819. But a legislative assembly, to be composed of a council of nine members, appointed by the president and senate of the United States, and to continue in office for five years, and of a house of representatives to be chosen by the inhabitants biennially, was provided by the act of 21st of April, 1820, adopting the act of June 4th, 1812, c. 95. The Superior Court of that territory has exclusive cognizance of all capital offences, and the trial by jury is secured, together with many of the other great fundamental principles of civil liberty. The territorial legislatures both of Michigan and Arkansaw, are prohibited from interfering with the primary disposal of the soil by the United States, or from taxing lands belonging to the United States, or from taxing the lands of non-resident proprietors, higher than those of residents, or from interrupting the navigable waters flowing into the Mississippi and Missouri rivers, as common highways free to all the citizens of the United States.

In the organization of the territorial governments of East

and West Florida, by the act of congress of March 30th, 1822, the judges of the superior courts are appointed by the president and senate of the United States, and hold their offices for four years; but writs of error and appeal lie from their decisions to the Supreme Court of the United States, equally as from the circuit courts in the several states.

It would seem, from these various congressional regulations of the territories belonging to the United States, that congress have supreme power in the government of them, depending on the exercise of their sound discretion. Neither the District of Columbia, nor a territory, is *a state*, within the meaning of the constitution, or entitled to claim the privileges secured to the members of the union. This has been so adjudged by the Supreme Court.[a] Nor will a writ of error or appeal lie from a territorial court to the Supreme Court, unless there be a special statute provision for the purpose.[b] There is such a provision as to Florida, and there is a limited provision of that kind as to Arkansaw and Michigan, extending to cases in which the United States are concerned, and not extending further.[c] If, therefore, the government of the United States should carry into execution the project of colonizing the great valley of the Oregan to the west of the Rocky Mountains, it would afford a subject of grave consideration what would be the future civil and political destiny of that country. It would be a long time before it would be populous enough to be created into one or more independent states; and, in the mean time, upon the doctrine taught by the acts of congress, and even by the judicial decisions of the Supreme Court, the colonists would be in a state of the most complete subordination, and as dependent upon the will of congress as the people of this country would have been upon the king and parliament of Great Britain, if they could have sustained

---

a 2 *Cranch*, 445.   1 *Wheaton*, 91.
b 1 *Cranch*, 212.   8 *Cranch*, 159.
c *Act of 3d March*, 1805.

their claim to bind us in all cases whatsoever. Such a state of absolute sovereignty on the one hand, and of absolute dependence on the other, is not at all congenial with the free and independent spirit of our native institutions; and the establishment of distant territorial governments, ruled according to will and pleasure, would have a very natural tendency, as all proconsular governments have had, to abuse and oppression.

LECTURE XVIII.

OF THE CONCURRENT JURISDICTION OF THE STATE GOVERNMENTS.

The question how far the state governments have concurrent powers, either legislative or judicial, over cases within the jurisdiction of the government of the United States, has been much discussed. It will be my endeavour, in the course of the present lecture, to ascertain the just doctrine and settled distinctions applicable to this great and most important constitutional subject.

(1.) *As to the concurrent powers of legislation in the states.*

It was observed in the *Federalist*,[a] that the state governments would clearly retain all those rights of sovereignty which they had before the adoption of the constitution of the United States, and which were not by that constitution exclusively delegated to the union. The alienation of state power or sovereignty would only exist in three cases: Where the constitution in express terms granted an exclusive authority to the union; where it granted in one instance an authority to the union, and in another prohibited the states from exercising the like authority; and where it granted an authority to the union, to which a similar authority in the states would be absolutely and totally contradictory and repugnant.

In the judicial construction given from time to time to the constitution, there is no very essential variation from the contemporary exposition which was here laid down by the

---

[a] No. 32.

high authority of the *Federalist.* Judge Chase, in the case of *Calder* v. *Bull,*[a] declared, that the state legislatures retained all the powers of legislation which were not expressly taken away by the constitution of the United States; and he held, that no constructive powers could be exercised by the federal government. Subsequent judges have not expressed themselves quite so strongly in favour of state rights, and in restriction of the powers of the national government. In *Sturges* v. *Crowninshield,*[b] the chief justice of the United States observed, that the powers of the states remained, after the adoption of the constitution, what they were before, except so far as they had been abridged by that instrument. The mere grant of a power to congress did not imply a prohibition on the states to exercise the same power. Thus, congress are authorized to established uniform laws on the subject of bankruptcy, but the states may pass bankrupt laws, provided there be no act of congress in force establishing an uniform law on that subject. The states may legislate in the absence of congressional regulations. It is not the mere existence of the power, but its exercise, which is incompatible with the exercise of the same power by the states. It is not the right to establish these uniform laws, but their actual establishment, which is inconsistent with the partial acts of the states. But the concurrent power of legislation in the states did not extend to every case in which the exercise by the states had not been expressly prohibited. The correct principle was, that whenever the terms in which the power was granted to congress, or the nature of the power, required that it should be exercised exclusively by congress, the subject was as completely taken from the state legislatures, as if they had been expressly forbidden to act on it. In *Houston* v. *Moore,*[c] the same principles were laid down by Judge Washington in delivering the opinion of the court. He observed, that the power of the state governments to legislate on the subject

---

[a] 3 *Dallas,* 386.   [b] 4 *Wheaton,* 193.   [c] 5 *Wheaton,* 1.

of the state militia having existed prior to the formation of the constitution, and not being prohibited by that instrument, it remained with the states, subordinate, nevertheless, to the paramount power of the general government, operating upon the same subject. If congress, for instance, did not exercise the power of providing for organizing, arming and disciplining the militia, it was competent for the states to do it; but as congress had exercised its constitutional powers upon the subject of the militia as fully as was thought proper, the power of legislation over that subject by the states was excluded, except so far as it had been permitted by congress. The doctrine of the court was, that when congress exercised their powers upon any given subject, the states could not enter upon the same ground, and provide for the same objects. The will of congress may be discovered as well by what they have not declared, as by what they have expressed. Two distinct wills cannot at the same time be exercised, in relation to the same subject, effectually, and at the same time be compatible with each other. If they correspond in every respect, then the latter is idle and inoperative. If they differ, they must, in the nature of things, oppose each other so far as they do differ. It was, therefore, not true and constitutional doctrine, that in cases where the state governments have a concurrent power of legislation with the national government, they may legislate upon any subject on which congress have acted, provided the two laws are not in their operation contradictory and repugnant to each other.

Judge Story, in the opinion which he gave in this case, spoke to the same effect, and defined with precision the boundary line between the concurrent and residuary powers of the states, and the exclusive powers of the union. A mere grant of power in affirmative terms to congress, did not *per se* transfer an exclusive sovereignty on such subjects. The powers granted to congress were never exclusive of similar powers existing in the states, unless where the constitution has expressly in terms given an exclusive power to congress, or the exercise of a like power was prohibited to the states, or there was a direct repugnancy or incompatibility in the exercise of it by the states. This is the same description of the nature of the powers as that given by the *Federalist*. An example of the first class is to be found in the exclusive legislation delegated to congress over places purchased for forts, arsenals, &c.; and of the second class, in the prohibition of a state to coin money, or emit bills of credit; and of the third class, in the power to establish an uniform rule of naturalization, and in the delegation of admiralty and maritime jurisdiction. In all other cases, the states retain concurrent authority with congress, except where the laws of the states and of the union are in direct and manifest collision on the same subject, and then those of the union being the supreme law of the land, are of paramount authority, and the state laws, so far, and so far only as such incompatibility exists, must necessarily yield.

In the application of these general principles to the case before the court, it was observed, that the power given to congress to provide for organizing, arming, and disciplining the militia, was not exclusive. It was merely an affirmative power, and being not incompatible with the existence of a like power in the states, it might well leave a concurrent power in the latter. But when once congress have acted on the subject, and carried this power into effect, its laws for the organization, arming, and disciplining the militia, were supreme, and all interfering regulations of the states suspended. A state may organize, arm, and discipline its own militia, in the absence of, or subordinate to, the regulations of congress. This power originally existed in the states, and the grant of it to congress was not necessarily exclusive, unless a concurrent power in the states would be repugnant to the grant, and there was no such repugnancy in the nature of the power. But the question was, whether a state legislature had any concurrent power remaining after congress had provided in its discretion for the case. The conclusion was, that when once the legislature of the union has exercised its powers on a given subject, the state power over that same subject, which had before been concurrent, was by that exercise prohibited, and this was the opinion of the court.

These are sound expositions of the paramount powers of the general government, and the same doctrines had been previously declared in the Court of Errors of this state, in the steam boat case of *Livingston* v. *Van Ingen*.[a] "Our safe rule of construction and of action," as it was there observed,[b] "was this, that if any given power was originally vested in this state, if it had not been exclusively ceded to congress, or if the exercise of it has not been prohibited to the states, we might then go on in the exercise of power, until it came practically in collision with the exercise of some congressional power. When that happened to be the case, the state authority would so far be controlled, but it would still be good in all those respects in which it did not contravene the provision of the paramount law." A similar exposition of the concurrent jurisdiction of the states, was given by the Supreme Court of Pennsylvania, in *Moore* v. *Houston*.[c]

When the constitution of the United States was under the consideration of the state conventions, there was much concern expressed on the subject of the general power of taxation over all objects of taxation, vested in the national government; and it was supposed that it would be in the power of congress, in its discretion, to destroy in effect the concurrent power of taxation remaining in the states, and to deprive them of the means of supplying their own wants. All the resources of taxation might, by degrees, become the subjects of federal monopoly. The states must support themselves by direct taxes, duties, and excises, and congress may lay the same burthen, at the same time, on the same subject. Suppose the national tax should be as great as the article, whether it be land, or distilled spirits, or pleasure

---

[a] 9 *Johnson's Rep.* 507.   [b] 9 *Johnson's Rep.* p. 576.
[c] 3 *Serg. & Rawl.* 179.

carriages, for instance, will conveniently and prosperously bear, and the state should be obliged to lay a further tax for its own necessities; the doctrine, as I understand it, is, that the claim of the United States would be preferred, and must be first satisfied, because the laws of the United States, made in pursuance of the constitution, are the supreme law of the land. The author of the *Federalist*,[a] admits, that a state might lay a tax on a particular article, equal to what it would well bear, but the United States would still have a right to lay a further tax on the same article; and that all collisions in a struggle between the two governments for revenue, must and would be avoided by a sense of mutual forbearance. He no where, however, meets and removes the difficulty, in the case of a want of this mutual forbearance, where there is a concurrent tax laid on the same subject, and which will not bear both taxes. He says only, that the United States would have no right to abolish the state tax. This is not contended; but would not the United States have a right to declare, that their taxes were liens from the time they were imposed; and would they not, as of course, be entitled to be first paid; and must not the state collector, in all cases, stand by and wait until the national tax is collected, before he proceeds to collect his state tax out of the exhausted subject? Upon the doctrine of the federal courts, and upon the doctrine of 'the *Federalist* himself, this must be the case; and though the state legislatures have a concurrent jurisdiction in the case of taxation, except as to imposts, yet in effect, though not in terms, this concurrent power becomes a subordinate and dependent power. In every other case of legislation, the concurrent power in the states would seem to be a power entirely dependent, and subject to be taken away absolutely, whenever congress should choose to exercise their powers of legislation over the same subject. I do not mean

---

[a] No. 32. See also No. 31. 33. 34.

to be understood to question the validity, or to excite alarm at the existence of this doctrine. The national government ought to be supreme within its constitutional limits, for it is intrusted with the paramount interests and general welfare of the whole nation. Our great and effective security consists in the fact, that the constituents of the general and of the state governments are one and the same people; and the powers of the national government must always be exercised with a due regard to the interest and prosperity of every member of the union; for on the concurrence and good will of the parts, the stability of the whole depends. My object is, to discover what this concurrent power of legislation amounts to, and what is its value, and on what constitutional foundations it is supported.

It was observed by Mr. Hamilton, in the convention of this state in 1788,[a] that if the United States, and the state, should each lay a like tax on a specific article, and the individual should be unable to pay both, the party who first levied would hold the property. But this position must be received with some qualification. The United States have declared by law, that they were entitled, in respect to their debts, to priority of payment, in all cases whatsoever; and when it was said that this claim would interfere with the rights of the state sovereignties, and would defeat the measures they had a right to adopt, to secure themselves against delinquencies, the answer given in *Fisher* v. *Blight*[b] is, that "the mischief suggested, so far as it can really happen, was the necessary consequence of the supremacy of the laws of the United States, on all subjects to which the legislative power of congress extends." It would seem, therefore, that the concurrent power of legislation in the states, is not an independent, but a subordinate and dependent power, liable, in many cases, to be extin-

---

a *Debates in the New-York Convention,* printed by Francis Childs, p. 113.
b 2 *Cranch,* 397.

guished, and in all cases to be postponed, to the paramount or supreme law of the union, whenever the federal and the state regulations interfere with each other.

In *Weyman* v. *Southard*,[a] the question arose, how far the judicial process of the federal courts could be controlled by the laws of the several states. It was decided, that congress had exclusive authority to regulate proceedings and executions in the federal courts, and that the states had no authority to control such process; and, therefore, executions by *fieri facias* in the federal courts, were not subject to the checks created by the new Kentucky statute. It was, in that case, further observed, that the forms of execution, and other process in the federal courts, in suits at common law, except modes of proceeding, were to be the same as used in September, 1789, in the supreme courts of the states, subject only to alterations and additions by congress, and by the federal courts, but not to alterations since made in the state laws and practice. It was further observed, that the laws of the several states were to be regarded as rules of decision in trials at common law, in cases where they apply. This, however, did not mean to apply to the process and practice of the federal courts. As to them, the laws of the states were no rule of decision, and the direction was intended only as a legislative recognition of the principles of universal jurisprudence as to the operation of the *lex loci* in the trial and decision of causes.

(2.) *As to the concurrent power of the states in matters of judicial cognizance.*

In the 82d number of the *Federalist*, it is laid down as a rule, that the state courts retained all pre-existing authorities, or the jurisdiction they had before the adoption of the constitution, except where it was taken away either by an exclusive authority granted in express terms to the union, or in a case where a particular authority was granted to the union, and the exercise of a like authority was prohibited to

---

[a] 10 *Wheaton*, 1.

the states, or in the case where an authority was granted to the union, with which a similar authority in the states would be utterly incompatible. A concurrent jurisdiction in the state courts was admitted in all except those enumerated cases; but this doctrine was only applicable to those descriptions of causes of which the state courts had previous cognizance, and it was not equally evident in relation to cases which grew out of the constitution. Congress, in the course of legislation, might commit the decision of causes arising upon their laws, to the federal courts exclusively; but unless the state courts were expressly excluded by the acts of congress, they would, of course, take concurrent cognizance of the causes to which those acts might give birth, subject to the exceptions which have been stated. In all cases of concurrent jurisdiction, an appeal would lie from the state courts to the Supreme Court of the United States; and without such right of appeal, the concurrent jurisdiction of the state courts, in matters of national concern, would be inadmissible; because, in that case, it would be inconsistent with the authority and efficiency of the general government.

Such were the early and speculative views of the ablest commentators on the constitution, in relation to the judicial powers of the state courts. We will now examine a series of decisions in the federal courts, defining and settling the boundaries of the judicial authorities of the states.

In the case of *Martin* v. *Hunter*,[a] Judge Story, in delivering the opinion of the court, seemed to think, that it was the duty of congress to vest the whole judicial power of the United States in courts ordained and established by itself. But the general observation was subsequently qualified, and confined to that judicial power which was exclusively vested in the United States. The whole judicial power of the United States should be, at all times, vested either in an original or appellate form, in some courts created under its au-

---

[a] 1 Wheaton, 304.

thority. It was considered, that there was vast weight in the argument, that the constitution is imperative upon congress to vest all the judicial power of the United States, in the shape of original jurisdiction, in the supreme and inferior courts created under its own authority. At all events, it was manifest, that the judicial power of the United States is, unavoidably, in some cases, exclusive of all state authority, and, in all cases, may be made so, at the election of congress. No part of the criminal jurisdiction of the United States can, consistently with the constitution, be delegated to state tribunals. The admiralty and maritime jurisdiction is of the same exclusive cognizance; and it can only be in those cases where, previous to the constitution, state tribunals possessed jurisdiction independent of national authority, that they can now constitutionally exercise a concurrent jurisdiction. Congress, throughout the judicial act, and particularly in the 9th, 11th, and 13th sections, have legislated upon the supposition, that in all the cases to which the judicial powers of the United States extended, they might rightfully vest exclusive jurisdiction in their own courts.

State courts may, in the exercise of their ordinary, original, and rightful jurisdiction, incidentally take cognizance of cases arising under the constitution, the laws and treaties of the United States; yet, to all these cases, the judicial power of the United States extends by means of its appellate jurisdiction.

In *Houston* v. *Moore*[a] the same question came again under the consideration of the Supreme Court, and Judge Washington, in delivering the opinion of the court, observed, that he saw nothing unreasonable or inconvenient in the doctrine of the *Federalist*, on the subject of the concurrent jurisdiction of the state courts, so long as the power of congress to withdraw the whole, or any part of those cases, from the jurisdiction of the state courts, be, as he thought it

---

[a] 5 *Wheaton*, 1.

must be, admitted. The practice of the general government has been conformable to this doctrine, and, in the judicial act of 1789, the exclusive and concurrent jurisdiction conferred upon the courts by that act, were clearly distinguished and marked. The act shows, that, in the opinion of congress, a grant of jurisdiction generally, was not of itself sufficient to vest an exclusive jurisdiction. The judicial act grants exclusive jurisdiction to the circuit courts of all crimes and offences cognizable under the authority of the United States, except where the laws of the United States should otherwise provide; and this accounts for the proviso in the act of 24th of February, 1807, c. 75. and in the act of 10th of April, 1816, c. 44. concerning the forgery of the notes of the Bank of the United States, declaring, that nothing in that act contained should be construed to deprive the courts of the individual states of jurisdiction, under the laws of the several states, over offences made punishable by that act. There is a similar proviso in the act of 21st of April, 1806, c. 49. concerning the counterfeiters of the current coin of the United States. Without these provisoes, the state courts could not have exercised concurrent jurisdiction over those offences consistently with the judicial act of 1789. But these saving clauses restored the concurrent jurisdiction of the state courts, so far as, under state authority, it could be exercised by them. There are many other acts of congress which permit jurisdiction, over the offences therein described, to be exercised by state magistrates and courts. This was necessary, because the concurrent jurisdiction of the state courts over all offences was taken away, and that jurisdiction was vested exclusively in the national courts by the judiciary act, and it required another act to restore it. The state courts could exercise no jurisdiction whatever over crimes and offences against the United States, unless where, in particular cases, other laws had otherwise provided; and whenever such provision was made, the claim of exclusive jurisdiction to the particular cases was withdrawn, and the concurrent jurisdiction of the state courts, *eo instanti*, restored, not by way of grant from the national government, but by the removal of a disability before imposed upon the state tribunals.

In that case, the Supreme Court disclaimed the idea that congress could authoritatively bestow judicial powers on state courts and magistrates. "It was held to be perfectly clear, that congress cannot confer jurisdiction upon any courts but such as exist under the constitution and laws of the United States, although the state courts may exercise jurisdiction in cases authorized by the laws of the state, and not prohibited by the exclusive jurisdiction of the federal courts."

The Supreme Court, having thus declared the true foundation and extent of the concurrent jurisdiction of the state courts in criminal cases, proceeded to meet and solve a difficulty occurring on this subject of concurrent jurisdiction, whether the sentence of one jurisdiction would oust the jurisdiction of the other. The decision on this point was, that the sentence of either court, whether of conviction or acquittal, might be pleaded in bar of the prosecution before the other; as much so as the judgment of a state court, in a civil case of concurrent jurisdiction, might be pleaded in bar of an action for the same cause instituted in a circuit court of the United States.

There was another difficulty not so easily surmounted, and that was, whether, if a conviction of a crime against the United States be had in a state court admitted to have concurrent jurisdiction, the governor of the state would have the power of pardon, and in that way control the law and policy of the United States. Judge Washington, in speaking for the court, did not answer this question, but contented himself with merely observing, that he was by no means satisfied that the governor could pardon, but that if he could, it would furnish a reason for vesting the jurisdiction of criminal matters exclusively in the federal courts.

The conclusion, then, is, that in judicial matters, the concurrent jurisdiction of the state tribunals depends altogether upon the pleasure of congress, and may be revoked and extinguished whenever they think proper, in every case in which the subject matter can constitutionally be made cognizable in the federal courts; and that, without an express provision to the contrary, the state courts will retain a concurrent jurisdiction in all cases where they had jurisdiction originally over the subject matter. We will next see whether this state jurisdiction does not equally depend upon the volition of the state courts.

There are various acts of congress, in which duties have been imposed on state magistrates and courts, and by which they have been invested with jurisdiction in civil suits, and over complaints and prosecutions in penal and criminal cases for fines, penalties and forfeitures arising under laws of the United States. We have seen a very clear intimation given by the judges of the Supreme Court, that the state courts were not bound in consequence of any act of congress, to assume and exercise jurisdiction in such cases. It was merely permitted to them to do so as far as was compatible with their state obligations, and in some instances the state courts have acted in those cases, and in other instances they have declined jurisdiction, though expressly vested with it by the act of congress.

In the case of *Ferguson*,[a] an application was made to the Supreme Court of this state for the allowance of an *habeas corpus* to bring up the party alleged to be detained in custody by an officer of the army of the United States, on the ground of being an enlisted soldier, and the allegation was, that he was an infant, and so not duly enlisted. It was much discussed whether, the state courts had concurrent jurisdiction, by *habeas corpus*, over the question of unlawful imprisonment, when that imprisonment was by an officer of the United States, by colour or under pretext of the authority of the United States. The Supreme Court did not decide the question, and the motion was denied on other grounds; but subsequently, in the matter of *Stacy*,[b] the same court exercised jurisdiction in a similar case, by allowing and enforcing obedience to the writ of

---

[a] 9 *Johnson's Rep.* 239. [b] 10 *Johnson's Rep.* 328.

habeas corpus. The question was, therefore, settled in favour of a concurrent jurisdiction in that case, and there has been a similar decision and practice by the courts of other states.[a]

In the case of *The United States* v. *Dodge*,[b] the Supreme Court of this state held, that they had jurisdiction, and did sustain a suit on a bond for duties given to a collector of the United States customs. The suit was authorized by the judicial act of 1789, giving concurrent jurisdiction to the state courts in suits at common law, where the United States were plaintiffs. Afterwards, in the case of *The United States* v. *Lathrop*,[c] the same court discussed, very much at large, the question whether a state court had jurisdiction of an action in favour of the United States to recover a penalty or forfeiture for breach of a law of the United States, and when a suit for the penalty was by the act declared to be cognizable in a state court. It was decided that the court had no such jurisdiction, and that it could not even be conferred by an act of congress. The difference between this case and the one preceding, was, that *that* was a suit on a bond given to a collector of the customs for duties, and this was an action of debt for a penalty for breach of the excise law. They were both cases of debts due to the United States, but the one was a civil debt, and the other a penalty for breach of a revenue law, and this slight difference in the nature of the demand was considered to create a most momentous difference in its result upon the great question of jurisdiction. It was the opinion of the court, that congress could not

---

[a] Case of Lockington, before Tilghman, Chief Justice of Pennsylvania, November, 1813, 5 *Hall's Law Journal*, 92. Same case, 5 *Hall's Law Journal*, 301—330. A similar case in Maryland, 5 *Hall's Law Journal*, 486; and in South-Carolina, 5 *Hall's Law Journal*, 497. Commonwealth, v. Harrison, 11 *Mass. Rep.* 68. Case of Joseph Almeida in Maryland; case of Pool and others in Virginia, cited in *Sergeant's Constitutional Law*, p. 279. 280.

[b] 14 *Johnson's Rep.* 95.

[c] 17 *Johnson*, 4.

invest the state courts with jurisdiction of causes which they did not enjoy concurrently before the adoption of the constitution; and a pecuniary penalty for a violation of an act of congress was a punishment for an offence created under the constitution, and the state courts had no jurisdiction of the criminal offences or penal laws of the United States. The judicial act of 1789 was the true exposition of the constitution with respect to the concurrent jurisdiction of the state courts, and the exclusive jurisdiction of those of the United States; and by that act the exclusive cognizance of all crimes and offences cognizable under the authority of the United States, and of all suits for penalties and forfeitures, was given to the federal courts. The judicial act in no instance excluded the previously existing jurisdiction of the state courts, except in a few specified cases of a national nature; but their jurisdiction was excluded in all criminal cases, and with respect to offences arising under the acts of congress. In such cases, the federal jurisdiction was necessarily exclusive; but it was not so as to pre-existing matters within the jurisdiction of the state courts.

The doctrine seems to be admitted, that congress cannot compel a state court to entertain jurisdiction in any case. It only permits state courts which are competent for the purpose, and have an inherent jurisdiction adequate to the case, to entertain suits in the given cases; and they do not become inferior courts in the sense of the constitution, because they are not ordained by congress. The state courts are left to consult their own duty from their own state authority and organization; but if they do voluntarily entertain jurisdiction of causes cognizable under the authority of the United States, they do it upon the condition, that the appellate jurisdiction of the federal courts shall apply. Their jurisdiction of federal causes is, however, confined to civil actions for civil demands, or to enforce penal statutes; and they cannot hold criminal jurisdiction over offences exclusively existing as offences against the United States. Every criminal prosecution must charge the offence to have been committed against the sovereign whose courts sit in judgment upon the offender, and whose executive may pardon him.

We find a similar decision in one of the courts in the state of Ohio, in the case of the *United States* v. *Campbell*.^a That was an information filed by the collector of the revenue, to recover a penalty for breach of the excise law, and the court held it to be a criminal prosecution, and that one sovereign state could not make use of the municipal courts of another government to enforce its penal laws, and it was not in the power of congress to vest such a jurisdiction in the state courts. Upon the same principle, a state court in Virginia, in the case of *The State* v. *Feely*, decided, that it had no jurisdiction to punish by indictment stealing packets from the mail, as that was an offence created by act of congress.^b And in *Jackson* v. *Row*, the General Court of Virginia made the same decision precisely as that made by this state in the case of *Lathrop;* and it held, that the act of congress, authorizing such suits for penalties in the state courts, was not binding. It was decided in another case in Virginia,^c that congress could not give jurisdiction to, or require services of, a state court, or magistrate, as such, nor prosecute in the state courts for a public offence.^d

After these decisions in the states of Virginia, Ohio, and New-York, the act of congress of the 3d March, 1815, ch. 100. may be considered as essentially nugatory. That act vested in the state courts, concurrently with the federal courts, cognizance of all " complaints, suits, and prosecutions for taxes, duties, fines, penalties, and forfeitures, arising and payable under any act of congress passed, or to be passed, for the collection of any direct tax or internal duties ;" and it gave to the state courts and the presiding judge

---

a 6 *Hall's Law Journal*, 113.
b *Sergeant's Const. Law*, p. 272.
c *Ex parte Pool*.
d *Sergeant's Const. Law*, p. 272. 274.

thereof, the same power as was vested in the district judges, to mitigate or remit any fine, penalty, or forfeiture. And here the inquiry naturally suggests itself, can the state courts, consistently with those decisions, sustain a criminal prosecution for forging the paper of the Bank of the United States, or for counterfeiting the coin of the United States? These are cases arising under acts of congress declaring the offence: The state courts have exercised criminal jurisdiction over these offences, as offences against the state; but it is difficult to maintain the jurisdiction upon the doctrine of the Supreme Court of New-York in the case of *Lathrop;* and if it be entertained, there are difficulties remaining to be definitively cleared. These difficulties relate to the effect of a prosecution in one jurisdiction upon the jurisdiction of the concurrent court, and to the effect of the executive power of pardon of the crime under one government, upon the claim of concurrent jurisdiction.

LECTURE XIX.

OF CONSTITUTIONAL RESTRICTIONS ON THE POWERS OF THE SEVERAL STATES.

We proceed to consider the extent and effect of certain express constitutional restrictions on the authority of the separate states.

"No state," says the constitution,[a] "shall enter into any treaty, alliance, or confederation; grant letters of marque and reprisal; coin money; emit bills of credit; make any thing but gold and silver coin a tender in payment of debts; pass any bill of attainder, *ex post facto* law, or law impairing the obligation of contracts; or grant any title of nobility. No state shall, without the consent of congress, lay any imposts or duties on imports or exports, except what may be absolutely necessary for executing its inspection laws; nor lay any duty on tonnage, keep troops or ships of war in time of peace, enter into any agreement or compact with another state, or with a foreign power, or engage in war, unless actually invaded, or in such imminent danger as will not admit of delay."

Most of these prohibitions would seem to speak for themselves, and not to stand in need of exposition. I shall confine myself to those cases in which the interpretation and extent of some of these restrictions have been made the subject of judicial investigation.

(1.) *No state can pass any ex post facto law.*

In *Calder* v. *Bull*,[b] the question on the meaning of an *ex*

---

[a] Art. 1. sec. 10. [b] 3 *Dallas*, 386.

post facto law, within the prohibition of the constitution, was extensively discussed.

The legislature of Connecticut had, by a resolution or law, set aside a decree of the Court of Probates rejecting a will, and directed a new hearing before the Court of Probates, and the point was, whether that resolution was an *ex post facto* law prohibited by the constitution of the United States.

It was held, that the words *ex post facto laws* were technical expressions, and meant every law that made an act done before the passing of the law, and which was innocent when done, criminal; or which aggravated a crime, and made it greater than it was when committed; or which changed the punishment, and inflicted a greater punishment than the law annexed to the crime when committed; or which altered the legal rules of evidence, and received less or different testimony than the law required at the time of the commission of the offence, in order to convict the offender. The Supreme Court concluded, that the law or resolution of Connecticut was not within the letter or intention of the prohibition, and was, therefore, lawful. Afterwards, in *Fletcher* v. *Peck*,[a] it was observed, that an *ex post facto* law was one which rendered an act punishable in a manner in which it was not punishable when it was committed. This definition is distinguished for its comprehensive brevity and precision, and it extends equally to laws inflicting personal or pecuniary penalties, and to laws passed after the act, and affecting a person by way of punishment, either in his person or estate.

(2.) *No state can control the exercise of any authority under the federal government.*

The state legislatures cannot annul the judgments, nor determine the extent of the jurisdiction of the courts of the union. This was attempted by the legislature of Pennsylvania, and declared to be inoperative and void by the Su-

---

a 6 *Cranch*, 138.

preme Court of the United States, in the case of *The United States* v. *Peters*.[a] Such a power, as we have heretofore seen, necessarily resides in the supreme judicial tribunal of the nation. It has also been adjudged, that no state court has authority or jurisdiction to enjoin a judgment of the Circuit Court of the United States, or to stay proceedings under it. This was attempted by a state court in Kentucky, and declared to be of no validity by the Supreme Court of the United States, in *M'Kim* v. *Voorhies*.[b] No state tribunal can interfere with seizures of property made by revenue officers, under the laws of the United States; or interrupt by process of replevin, injunction, or otherwise, the exercise of the authority of the federal officers; and any intervention of state authority for that purpose is unlawful. This was so declared by the Supreme Court in *Slocum* v. *Mayberry*.[c] Nor can a state court issue a *mandamus* to an officer of the United States. This decision was made in the case of *M'Cluny* v. *Silliman*,[d] and it arose in consequence of the Supreme Court in Ohio sustaining a jurisdiction over the register of the land office of the United States in respect to his ministerial acts as register, and claiming a right to award a *mandamus* to that officer, to compel him to issue a final certificate of purchase. The principle declared by the Supreme Court was, that the official conduct of an officer of the government of the United States can only be controlled by the power that created him.

There is one case that may seem to be repugnant to this doctrine of the federal courts. In *Mills* v. *Martin*,[e] the Supreme Court of this state sustained an action of replevin for goods taken by a deputy marshal of the United States, under a warrant from a court martial composed of militia officers in the service of the United States. The court martial was organized and convened under acts of congress for the trial of such persons of

---

a 5 *Cranch*, 115.   b 7 *Cranch*, 279.   c 2 *Wheaton*, 1.
d 6 *Wheaton*, 598.   e 19 *Johnson*, 7.

the militia as had neglected or refused to rendezvous and enter the service of the United States, according to orders of the governor of this state, issued in compliance with the requisitions of the president of the United States; and it had assessed a fine upon the plaintiff, for having neglected or refused to enter the service of the United States as a soldier in the militia. The court held, that the rules and articles of war did not apply to the case of a delinquent who had never actually entered the service, nor did they apply in time of peace to militia men for delinquencies during war. Congress do not, by any existing laws, assume a right to subject the militia to martial law, except while they are in the actual service and pay of the United States. The court therefore gave a remedy against the assessment and process of the court martial, on the ground that the plaintiff was not amenable to a court martial of the United States, and that the court martial had no jurisdiction in the case. The whole proceeding was void, and the taking of the plaintiff's property a trespass. If a court of special and limited jurisdiction exceeds its authority, and takes cognizance of a case not within it, the proceeding is *coram non judice* and void. This was the doctrine of the court in that case, and it is apparently at variance with the principle laid down by the Supreme Court of the United States in the case of the *United States* v. *Peters*, that the power of determining the extent of the jurisdiction of the federal courts resides in the supreme judicial tribunal of the nation. It is also apparently at variance with the doctrine of the same court in *Slocum* v. *Mayberry*, where it was said, that a party supposing himself aggrieved by a seizure made by an officer of the United States, cannot replevy the property out of the custody of the seizing officer, or of the court having cognizance of the cause. If the officer had a right to seize under the laws of the United States, the question whether the forfeiture has been actually incurred, belongs exclusively to the federal courts, and cannot be drawn to another forum; and it depends upon the final decree of such courts, whether such seizure is to be deemed rightful or tortious. And if it be adjudged to be tortious, then the party may proceed by suit at common law, in the state courts, to recover damages for the illegal act.

The distinction which would appear to reconcile all these decisions, is this: if the officer of the United States who seized, or the court which awarded the process to seize, had jurisdiction of the subject matter, then the inquiry into the validity of the seizure belongs exclusively to the federal courts. But if there was no jurisdiction in the instance in which it was asserted, as the Supreme Court of this state held in the case of the court martial assuming cognizance over the delinquency of a member of the state militia, then the state courts have jurisdiction to protect the person and the property so illegally invaded; and it is to be observed, that the jurisdiction of the state court in Rhode Island was admitted by the Supreme Court of the United States in the case cited, and upon that very ground.

In the case of the *United States* v. *Barney*,[a] the district judge of Maryland carried to a great extent the exemption from state control of officers or persons in the service of the United States, and employed in the transportation of the mail. He held, that an innkeeper had no lien on the horses which he had fed, and which were employed in the transportation of the mail. The act of congress of March, 1790, prohibited all wilful obstruction of the passage of the mail; and a claim for debt would not justify the stopping of the mail, or the means necessary to transport it, either upon principles of common law or upon the statute. The judge stated in this case, that even a stolen horse found in the mail stage could not be seized; nor could the driver, being in debt, or having committed an offence, be arrested, in such a way as to obstruct the passage of the mail. But in a subsequent case in the Circuit Court of Pennsylvania,[b] it was held, that the act of congress was not to be so con-

---

a 3 *Hall's Law Journal*, 128.
b United States v. Hart, 1 *Peter's Rep.* 390.

strued as to endanger the public peace and safety. The carrier of the mail driving through a populous city with dangerous rapidity, and contrary to a municipal ordinance, may be stopped, and the mail temporarily detained by an officer of the city. So, if the officer had a warrant against a felon in the stage, or if the driver should commit murder in the street, and then place himself on the mail stage box, he would not be protected from arrest, though a temporary stoppage of the mail might be the consequence. The public safety in the one case, is of more moment than the public inconvenience which it might produce in the other.

But while all interference on the part of the state authorities with the exercise of the lawful powers of the national government, has been, in most cases, denied, there is one case in which any control by the federal over the state courts, other than by means of the established appellate jurisdiction, has equally been prevented. In *Diggs and Keith* v. *Wolcott*,[a] it was decided generally, that a court of the United States could not enjoin proceedings in a state court, and a decree of the Circuit Court of the United States for the district of Connecticut was reversed, because it had enjoined the parties from proceeding at law in a state court. This decision is not to be contested; and yet the district judge of the northern district of New-York, in the spring of 1823, in the case of *Lansing and Thayer* v. *The North River Steam Boat Company*, enjoined the defendants from seeking in the state courts, under the acts of the state legislature, the remedies which those acts gave them. This would appear to have been an unwarrantable assumption of the power of control over the jurisdiction of the state courts, and one in direct hostility to the doctrine of the Supreme Court of the United States. In the case of *Kennedy* v. *Earl of Cassillis*,[b] an injunction had been unwarily granted in the English Court of Chancery to restrain a party from proceeding in a suit in the Court of Sessions in Scotland, where

---

[a] 4 *Cranch*, 179. [b] 2 *Swanston*, 330.

the parties were domiciled. It was admitted, that the Court of Sessions was a court of competent jurisdiction, and an independent foreign tribunal, though subject to an appeal, like the Court of Chancery, to the House of Lords. If the Court of Chancery could in that way restrain proceedings in the Court of Sessions, the Sessions might equally enjoin proceedings in Chancery, and thus stop all proceedings in either court. Lord Eldon said, he never meant to go further with the injunction, than the property in England: and he, on motion, dissolved it *in toto*.

(3.) *No state can pass any law impairing the obligation of contracts.*

We come next to a prohibition of great moment, and affecting extensively and deeply the legislative authority of the states. There is no prohibitory clause in the constitution, which has given rise to more various and able discussion, or more protracted litigation, than that which denies to any state the right to pass any law impairing the obligation of contracts. I shall endeavour to give a full and accurate view of the judicial decisions defining and enforcing this prohibition.

The case of *Fletcher* v. *Peck*,[a] first brought this prohibitory clause into direct discussion. The legislature of Georgia, by an act of 7th of January, 1795, authorized the sale of a large tract of wild land, and a grant was made by letters patent in pursuance of the act, to a number of individuals, under the name of the Georgia Company. Fletcher held a deed from Peck for a part of this land, under a title derived from the patent; and in the deed Peck had covenanted, that the state of Georgia was lawfully seized when the act was passed, and had good right to sell, and that the letters patent were lawfully issued, and the title had not since been legally impaired. The action was for breach of covenant; and the breach assigned was, that the letters patent were void, for, that the legislature of Georgia, by act

---

[a] 6 *Cranch*, 87.

of 13th of February, 1796, declared the preceding act to be null and void, as being founded in fraud and corruption. One of the questions presented to the Supreme Court upon the case was, whether the legislature of Georgia could constitutionally repeal the act of 1795, and rescind the sale made under it.

The court declared, that when a law was in its nature a contract, and absolute rights have vested under that contract, a repeal of the law could not devest those rights, nor annihilate or impair the title so acquired. A grant was a contract within the meaning of the constitution. The words of the constitution were construed to comprehend equally executory and executed contracts, for each of them contains obligations binding on the parties. A grant is a contract executed, and a party is always estopped by his own grant. A party cannot pronounce his own deed invalid, whatever cause may be assigned for its invalidity, and though that party be the legislature of a state. A grant amounts to an extinguishment of the right of the grantor, and implies a contract not to re-assert that right. A grant from a state is as much protected by the operation of the provision of the constitution, as a grant from one individual to another, and the state is as much inhibited from impairing its own contracts, or a contract to which it is a party, as it is from impairing the obligation of contracts between two individuals. It was, accordingly, declared, that the estate held under the act of 1795, having passed into the hands of a *bona fide* purchaser for a valuable consideration, the state of Georgia was constitutionally disabled from passing any law whereby the estate of the plaintiff could be legally impaired and rendered void.

The next case that brought this provision in review before the Supreme Court, was that of *The State of New-Jersey* v. *Wilson.*[a] It was there held, that if the legislature should declare by law, that certain lands to be thereafter

---

[a] 7 *Cranch*, 164.

purchased for the use of the Indians, should not be subject to any tax, such a legislative act amounted to a contract which could not be rescinded by a subsequent legislature. In that case, the colonial legislature of New-Jersey, in 1758, authorized the purchase of lands for the Delaware Indians, and made that stipulation. Lands were accordingly purchased, and conveyed to trustees for the use of the Indians, and the Indians released their claim to other lands, as a consideration for this purchase. The Indians occupied these lands until 1803, when they were sold to individuals under the authority of an act of the legislature, and, in 1804, the legislature repealed the act of 1758, exempting those lands from taxation. The act of 1758 was held to be a contract, and the act of 1804 was held to be a breach of that contract, and void under the constitution of the United States.

The Supreme Court went again, and more largely, into the consideration of this delicate and interesting constitutional doctrine, in the case of *Terrett* v. *Taylor*.[a] It was there held, that a legislative grant, competently made, vested an indefeasible and irrevocable title. There is no authority or principle which could support the doctrine, that a legislative grant was revocable in its own nature, and held only *durante bene placito*. Nor can the legislature repeal statutes creating private corporations, or confirming to them property already acquired, under the faith of previous laws, and by such repeal vest the property in others, without the consent or default of the corporators. Such a proceeding would be repugnant to the letter and spirit of the constitution, and to the principles of natural justice.

But it was in the great case of *Dartmouth College* v. *Woodward*,[b] that the inhibition upon the states to impair by law the obligation of contracts, received the most elaborate discussion, and the most efficient and instructive application. It was there held, that the charter granted by the

---

a 9 *Cranch*, 43.   *b* 4 *Wheaton*, 518.

British crown to the trustees of Dartmouth College in 1769, was a contract within the meaning of the constitution, and protected by it; and that the college was a private charitable institution, not liable to the control of the legislature; and that the act of the legislature of New-Hampshire, altering the charter in a material respect, without the consent of the corporation, was an act impairing the obligation of the charter, and, consequently, unconstitutional and void.

The chief justice, in delivering the opinion of the court, observed, that the provision in the constitution never had been understood to embrace other contracts than those which respect property, or some object of value, and confer rights which may be asserted in a court of justice. Dartmouth College was a private eleemosynary institution, endowed with a capacity to take property for objects unconnected with government, and its funds were bestowed by individuals on the faith of the charter, and those funds consisted entirely of private donations. The corporation was not invested with any portion of political power, nor did it partake, in any degree, in the administration of civil government. It was the institution of a private corporation for general charity. The charter was a contract to which the donors, the trustees of the corporation, and the crown, were the original parties, and it was made on a valuable consideration, for the security and disposition of property. The legal interest in every literary and charitable institution is in trustees, and to be asserted by them, and they claim or defend in behalf of the religion, charity, and education, for which the corporation was created, and the private donations made. Contracts of this kind, creating these charitable institutions, are most reasonably within the purview and protection of the constitution. This contract remained unchanged by the revolution; and the duties, as well as the powers of the government, devolved on the people of New-Hampshire, but the act of that state which was complained of, transferred the whole power of governing the college, from trustees appointed according to the will of the founder expressed in the charter, to the executive of

New-Hampshire. The will of the state was substituted for the will of the donors, in every essential operation of the college. The charter was reorganized in such a manner as to convert a literary institution, moulded according to the will of its founders, and placed under the control of private literary men, into a machine entirely subservient to the will of government. This was, consequently, subversive of that contract, on the faith of which the donors invested their property; and the act of the legislature of New-Hampshire was, therefore, held to be repugnant to the constitution of the United States.

The same course of reasoning, and leading to the same conclusion, was adopted and expressed by some of the other judges.

In the opinion given by Judge Story, he added some new and interesting views of the nature of the contracts which the constitution intended to protect. He denied the power of the legislature to dissolve even the contract of marriage, without a breach on either side, and against the wishes of the parties. A dissolution of the marriage obligation, without any default or assent of the parties, may as well fall within the prohibition of the constitution, as any other contract for a valuable consideration. A man has as good a right to his wife, as to the property acquired under a marriage contract; and to devest him of that right without his default, and against his will, would be as flagrant a violation of the principles of justice, as the confiscation of his estate. The prohibitory clause he also considered to extend to other contracts besides those where the parties took for their own private benefit. A grant to a private trustee, for the benefit of a particular *cestui que trust*, or for any special private or public charity, cannot be the less a contract, because the trustee takes nothing for his own benefit. Nor does a private donation, vested in a trustee for objects of a general nature, thereby become a public trust, which the government may, at its pleasure, take from the trustee. Government cannot revoke a grant even of its own funds, when given to a private person, or to a corporation for special uses. It has no other remaining authority but what is judicial, to enforce the proper administration of the trust. Nor is a grant less a contract, though no beneficial interest accrues to the possessor. Many a franchise, whether corporate or not, may, in point of fact, be of no exchangeable value to the owners, and yet they are grants within the meaning and protection of the constitution. All incorporeal hereditaments, as immunities, dignities, offices, and franchises, are rights deemed valuable in law, and whenever they are the subjects of a contract or grant, they are just as much within the reach of the constitution as any other grant. All corporate franchises are legal estates. They are powers coupled with an interest, and corporators have vested rights in their character as corporators. Upon this doctrine it was insisted, that the trustees of Dartmouth College had rights and privileges under the charter, of which they could not be devested by the legislature without their consent. The act of the legislature did impair their rights, and vitally affect the interest of the college under the charter. If a grant of franchises be made to A. in trust for a special purpose, the grant cannot be revoked, and a new grant made to A., B., and C., for the same purpose, without violating the obligation of the first grant. If property be vested by grant in A. and B., for the use of a general charity, or private eleemosynary foundation, the obligation of that grant is impaired, when the estate is taken from their exclusive management, and vested in them in common with ten other persons.

I have thus stated the substance of the argument of the Supreme Court in this celebrated case, and it contains one of the most full and elaborate expositions of the constitutional sanctity of contracts to be met with in any of the reports. The decision in that case did more than any other single act, proceeding from the authority of the United States, to throw an impregnable barrier around all rights and franchises derived from the grant of government; and to give solidity and inviolability to the literary, charitable, religious, and commercial institutions of our country.

The same prohibitory clause in the constitution came again under discussion in the case of *Green* v. *Biddle*.ᵃ It was observed by the court, that the objection to a law, on the ground of its impairing the obligation of contracts, could never depend upon the extent of the change which the law effects in it. Any deviation from its terms, by postponing or accelerating the period of performance which it prescribes, imposing conditions not expressed in the contract, or dispensing with the performance of those which are expressed, however minute or apparently immaterial in their effect upon the contract, or upon any part or parcel of it, impairs its obligation. Upon this principle it is, that if a creditor agree with his debtor to postpone the day of payment, or in any other way to change the terms of the contract, without the consent of the surety, the latter is discharged, although the change was for his advantage.

The material point decided in this case was, that a compact between two states was a contract within the constitutional prohibition. The terms contract and compact were synonymous, and a contract is an agreement of two or more parties to do or not to do certain acts. The court declared, that the doctrine had been already announced and settled, that the constitution embraced all contracts executed and executory, and whether between individuals, or between a state and individuals; and that a state had no more power to impair an obligation into which she herself had entered, than she had to impair the contracts of individuals.

Another case that led to a very extensive inquiry into the operation and effect of the constitutional prohibition upon the states not to pass laws impairing the obligation of contracts, was that of *Sturges* v. *Crowninshield*.ᵇ The defendant was sued in one of the federal courts upon two promissory notes given in March, 1811, and he pleaded his discharge under an insolvent act of this state, passed in April, 1811. This insolvent act was retrospective, and dis-

---

a 8 *Wheaton*, 1.   *b* 4 *Wheaton*, 122.

charged the debtor upon his single petition, and upon his surrendering his property in the manner therein prescribed, without the concurrence of any creditor, from all his pre-existing debts, and from all liability and responsibility by reason thereof.

The chief justice, in the opinion which he delivered on behalf of the court, admitted, that until congress exercise the power to pass uniform laws on the subject of bankruptcy, the individual states may pass bankrupt laws, provided those laws contain no provision violating the obligation of contracts. It was admitted, that the states might by law discharge debtors from imprisonment, for imprisonment was no part of the contract, but only a means of coercion. It was also admitted, that they might pass statutes of limitation, for such statutes relate to the remedy, and not to the obligation of the contract. It was further stated by the court, that the insolvent laws of far the greater number of the states only discharged the person of the debtor, and left the obligation to pay in full force, and to this the constitution was not opposed. But a law which discharged the debtor from his contract to pay a debt by a given time, without performance, and released him, without payment, entirely from any future obligation to pay, impaired, because it entirely discharged, the obligation of that contract, and, consequently, the discharge of the defendant, under the act of 1811, was no bar to the suit.

The court held, that the obligation of a contract was not fulfilled by a *cessio bonorum*, for the parties had not merely in view the property in possession when the contract was made, but its obligation extended to future acquisitions, and to release them from being liable, impaired the obligation of the contract. There was a distinction, in the nature of things, between the obligation of a contract, and the remedy to enforce that obligation, and the latter might be modified, as the wisdom of the legislature should direct. But the constitution intended to restore and preserve public confidence completely. It intended to establish a great principle, that contracts should be inviolable.

The case in which this decision was made, was one in which the contract was existing when the law was passed; and the court said, that their opinion was confined to the case. A distinction has been taken between the case of a contract made before, and one made after, the passing of the act. It was taken by the Supreme Court of this state, in *Mather* v. *Bush*,^a and by the chief justice of Massachusetts, in *Blanchard* v. *Russell*,^b and was relied on as a sound distinction by the Court of Chancery of this state, in *Hicks* v. *Hotchkiss*.^c The doctrine of these cases is, that an insolvent act in force when the contract was made, did not, in the sense of the constitution, impair the obligation of that contract, because parties to a contract have reference to the existing laws of the country where it is made, and are presumed to contract in reference to those laws. It is an implied condition of every contract, that the party shall be absolved from its performance if the event takes place which the existing law declares shall dispense with the performance. The decision in *Sturges* v. *Crowninshield*, is supposed to be consistent with that distinction, when it establishes the principle, that an insolvent act discharging a debtor from his contract existing when the law passed, so that his future acquisitions could not be touched, is unconstitutional, and the discharge obtained under it void.

But the Supreme Court of the United States, in *M'Millan* v. *M'Neill*,^d went a step further, and held, that a discharge under a state insolvent law existing when the debt was contracted, was equally a law impairing the obligation of contracts, and equally within the principle declared in *Sturges* v. *Crowninshield*. This was a discharge under the insolvent law of a different government from that in which the contract was made. It remains yet to be settled, whether it be lawful for a state to pass an insolvent law

---

a 16 *Johnson's Rep.* 233.   b 13 *Mass. Rep.* 1.
c 7 *Johnson's Ch. Rep.* 297.   d 4 *Wheaton*, 209.

which shall be effectual to discharge the debtor from a debt contracted after the passing of the act, and contracted within the state making the law. The general language of the court would seem to reach even this case; but the facts in the cases decided do not cover this ground, and the cases decided are not authority to that extent. It will be perceived, that the power of the states over this subject is, at all events, exceedingly narrowed and cut down; and as the decisions now stand, the debt must have been contracted *after* the passing of the act, and the debt must have been contracted *within* the state, or else a discharge will not extinguish the remedy against the future property of the debtor.

And while on this point, it may not be amiss to observe, that the *cessio bonorum* of the Roman law, and which prevails at present in most parts of the continent of Europe, only exempted the person of the debtor from imprisonment. It did not release or discharge the debt, or exempt the future acquisitions of the debtor from execution for the debt. The English statute, commonly called the Lords' act,[a] went no further than to discharge the debtor's person; and it may be laid down as the law of Germany, France, Holland, Scotland, England, &c. that insolvent laws are not more extensive in their operation than the *cessio bonorum* of the civil law;[b] and indeed in many parts of Germany, as we are informed by Huberus and Heineccius,[c] a *cessio bonorum* does not even work a discharge of the debtor's person, and much less of his future property.

---

[a] 32 G. II. and 33 G. III.

[b] *Code*, 7. 71. 1. *Dig*. 42. 3. 4. & 6. *Voet ad Pand*. 42. 3. 8. *Heineccii Opera*, tom. 5. p. 620. tom. 6. 384. 387. *Code de Commerce*, No. 568. *Repertoire Universel et Raisonne de Jurisprudence, par Merlin*, tit. *Cession de Biens*. *Esprit des Loix*, tom. 1. 114. 16 *Johnson's Rep*. 244. note.

[c] *Hub. Prælec*. tom. 2. 1454. *Heinecc. Elem. Jur. Civ. secund. ord. Pand*. p. 6. l. 42. tit. 3. *Elem. Jus. Ger*. lib. 2. tit. 13. sec. 387.

(4.) *No state can pass naturalization laws.*

By the constitution of the United States, congress have power to establish an uniform rule of naturalization. It was held, in the Circuit Court of the United States at Philadelphia, in 1792, in *Collet* v. *Collet*,[a] that the state governments still enjoyed a concurrent authority with the United States upon the subject of naturalization, and that though they could not contravene the rule established by congress, or "exclude those citizens who had been made such by that rule, yet that they might adopt citizens upon easier terms than those which congress may deem it expedient to impose." But though this decision was made by two of the judges of the Supreme Court, with the concurrence of the district judge of Pennsylvania, it is obvious, that this opinion was hastily and inconsiderately declared. If the construction given to the constitution in this case was the true one, the provision would be, in a great degree, useless, and the policy of it defeated. The very purpose of the power was exclusive. It was to deprive the states individually of the power of naturalizing aliens according to their own will and pleasure, and thereby giving them the rights and privileges of citizens in every other state. If each state can naturalize upon one year's residence, when the act of congress requires five, of what use is the act of congress, and how does it become an uniform rule?

This decision of the Circuit Court may be considered, as in effect, overruled. In the same Circuit Court, in 1797, Judge Iredell intimated, that if the question had not previously occurred, he should be disposed to think, that the power of naturalization operated exclusively, as soon as it was exercised by congress.[b] And in the Circuit Court of Pennsylvania in 1814, it was the opinion of Judge Washington, that the power to naturalize was exclusively vested

---

a 2 *Dallas*, 294.
b United States v. Villato, 2 *Dallas*, 370.

in congress.[a] Afterwards, in *Chirac* v. *Chirac*,[b] the chief justice of the United States observed, that it certainly ought not to be controverted, that the power of naturalization was vested exclusively in congress. In *Houston* v. *Moore*,[c] Judge Story mentioned the power in congress to establish an uniform rule of naturalization, as one which was exclusive, on the ground of there being a direct repugnancy or incompatibility in the exercise of it by the states. The weight of authority, as well as of reason, may, therefore, be considered as clearly in favour of this latter construction.

(5.) *The states cannot impose a tax on the national bank, or its branches.*

The inability of the states to impede or control, by taxation or otherwise, the lawful institutions and measures of the national government, was largely discussed, and strongly declared, in the case of *M'Culloch* v. *The State of Maryland*.[d] In that case, the state of Maryland had imposed a tax upon the Branch Bank of the United States established in that state, and assuming the bank to be constitutionally created, and lawfully established in that state, the question arose on the validity of the state tax. It was adjudged that the state governments had no right to tax any of the constitutional means employed by the government of the union to execute its constitutional powers, nor to retard, impede, burden, or in any manner control the operations of the constitutional laws enacted by congress, to carry into effect the powers vested in the national government.

To define and settle the bounds of the restriction of the power of taxation on the states, and especially when that restriction was deduced from the implied powers of the general government, was a great and difficult undertaking; but it appears to have been, in this instance, most wisely

---

a Golden v. Prince, *Wharton's Digest*, tit. Constitutional Law, 26.
b 2 *Wheaton*, 269.
c 5 *Wheaton*, 49.
d 4 *Wheaton*, 316.

and most successfully performed. It was declared by the court, that it was not to be denied, that the power of taxation was to be concurrently exercised by the two governments; but such was the paramount character of the constitution of the United States, that it had a capacity to withdraw any subject from the action even of this power, and it might restrain a state from any exercise of it which may be incompatible with, and repugnant to, the constitutional laws of the union. The great principle that governed the case was, that the constitution and the laws made in pursuance thereof were supreme, and that they controlled the constitution and laws of the respective states, and could not be controlled by them. It was of the very essence of supremacy, to remove all obstacles to its action within its own sphere, and so to modify every power vested in subordinate governments as to exempt its own operations from their influence. A supreme power must control every other power which is repugnant to it. The right of taxation in the states extends to all subjects over which its sovereign power extends, and no further. The sovereignty of a state extends to every thing which exists by its own authority, or is introduced by its permission; but it does not extend to those means which are employed by congress to carry into execution their constitutional powers. The power of state taxation is to be measured by the extent of the state sovereignty, and this leaves to a state the command of all its resources, and the unimpaired power of taxing the people and property of the state. But it places beyond the reach of state power all those powers conferred on the government of the union, and all those means which are given for the purpose of carrying those powers into execution. This principle relieves from clashing sovereignty; from interfering powers; from a repugnancy between a right in one government to pull down what there is an acknowledged right in another to build up; from the incompatibility of a right in one government to destroy what there is a right in another to preserve. The power to tax would involve the power to destroy, and the power to destroy might defeat and render useless the power to create. There would be a plain repugnance in conferring on one government a power to control the constitutional measures of another, which other, with respect to those very measures, was declared to be supreme over that which exerts the control. If the right of the states to tax the means employed by the general government did really exist, then the declaration that the constitution and the laws made in pursuance thereof should be the supreme law of the land, would be empty and unmeaning declamation. If the states might tax one instrument employed by the government in the execution of its powers, they might tax every other instrument. They might tax the mail; they might tax the mint; they might tax the papers of the custom house; they might tax judicial process; they might tax all the means employed by the government, to an excess which would defeat all the ends of government.

The claim of the states to tax the Bank of the United States was thus denied and shown to be fallacious; and that there was a manifest repugnancy between the power of Maryland to tax, and the power of congress to preserve the institution of the branch bank. A tax on the operations of the bank, was a tax on the operations of an instrument employed by the government of the union to carry its powers into execution, and was consequently unconstitutional. A case could not be selected from the decisions of the Supreme Court of the United States superior to this one of *McCulloch and the State of Maryland*, for the clear and satisfactory manner in which the supremacy of the laws of the union have been maintained by the courts, and an undue assertion of state power overruled and defeated.

But the court were careful to declare that their decision was to be received with this qualification: that the states were not deprived of any resources of taxation which they originally possessed; and that the restriction did not extend to a tax paid by the real property of the bank, in common with the real property within the state; nor to a tax imposed upon the interest which the citizens of Maryland might hold in that institution in common with other property of the same description throughout the state.

The decision pronounced in this case against the validity of the Maryland tax, was made on the 7th of March, 1819, and it was on the 7th of February preceding, that the legislature of the state of Ohio imposed a similar tax, to the amount of 50,000 dollars annually, on the Branch Bank of the United States established in that state. Notwithstanding this decision, the officers of the state of Ohio proceeded to levy the tax, and that act brought up before the Supreme Court a renewed discussion and consideration of the legality of such a tax.[a] It was attempted to withdraw this case from the influence and authority of the former decision, by the suggestion that the Bank of the United States was a mere private corporation, engaged in its own business, with its own views, and that its great end and principal object were private trade and private profit. It was admitted, that if that were the case, the bank would be subject to the taxing power of the state, as any individual would be. But it was not the case. The bank was not created for its own sake, or for private purposes. It has never been supposed that congress could create such a corporation. It was not a private, but a public corporation, created for public and national purposes, and as an instrument necessary and proper for carrying into effect the powers vested in the government of the United States. The business of lending and dealing in money for private purposes, was an incidental circumstance, and not the primary object; and the bank was endowed with this faculty in order to enable it to effect the great public ends of the institution, and without which faculty and business the bank would want a capacity to perform its public functions. And if the trade of the bank was essential to its character as a machine for the fiscal operations of the government, that trade must be exempt from

---

[a] Osborn v. Bank of the United States, 9 *Wheaton*, 738.

state control, and a tax upon that trade bears upon the whole machine, and was, consequently, inadmissible, and repugnant to the constitution.

(6.) *The state governments have no jurisdiction in places ceded to the United States.*

The state governments may likewise lose all jurisdiction over places purchased by congress, by the consent of the legislature of the state, for the erection of forts, dock yards, light houses, hospitals, military academies, and other needful buildings.[a] The question which has arisen on this subject, was as to the effect of a proviso or reservation, usually annexed to the consent of the state, that all civil and criminal process issued under the authority of the state, might be executed on the lands so ceded, in like manner as if the cession had not been made. This point was much discussed in the Circuit Court of the United States in Rhode Island, in the case of the *United States* v. *Cornell*.[b] It was held, that a purchase of lands within the jurisdiction of a state, with the consent of the state, for the national purposes contemplated by the constitution, did, *ipso facto*, by the very terms of the constitution, fall within the exclusive legislation of congress, and that the state jurisdiction was completely ousted. What, then, is the true intent and effect of the saving clause annexed to the cessions? It does not imply the reservation of any concurrent jurisdiction or legislation, or that the state retained a right to punish for acts done within the ceded lands. The whole apparent object of the proviso was to prevent the ceded lands from becoming a sanctuary for fugitives from justice, for acts done within the acknowledged jurisdiction of the state; and such permission to execute process is not incompatible with exclusive sovereignty and jurisdiction. The acceptance of a cession, with this reservation, amounts to an agreement of the new sovereign, to permit the free exercise of such process, as being *quoad hoc* his own process. This construc-

---

[a] *Const.* art. 1. sec. 8.   [b] 2 *Mason.* 60.

tion has been frequently declared by the courts of the United States, and it comports entirely with the intention of the parties, and upon any other construction the cession would be nugatory and void. Judge Story doubted whether congress were even at liberty, by the terms of the constitution, to purchase lands, with the consent of a state, under any qualification of that consent, which would deprive them of exclusive legislation over the place. The courts of the United States have sole and exclusive jurisdiction over an offence committed within a ceded place, notwithstanding the ordinary reservation of the right to execute civil and criminal process of the state. That was no reservation of any sovereignty or jurisdiction.

Congress, in exercising powers of exclusive legislation over a ceded place or district, unite the powers of general, with those of local legislation. The power of local legislation carries with it, as an incident, the right to make that power effectual. Congress exercises that particular local power, like all its other powers, in its high character as the legislature of the union, and its general power may come in aid of these local powers. It is, therefore, competent for congress to try and punish an offender for an offence committed within one of those local districts, in a place not within such jurisdiction; or to provide for the pursuit and arrest of a criminal escaping from one of those districts, after committing a felony there; or to punish a person for concealing, out of the district, a felony committed within it. All these incidental powers are necessary to the complete execution of the principal power, and the Supreme Court, in *Cohens* v. *Virginia*,[a] held, that they were vested in congress.

It follows as a consequence, from this doctrine of the federal courts, that state courts cannot take cognizance of any offences committed within such ceded districts; and, on the other hand, that the inhabitants of such places cannot exer-

---

[a] 6 *Wheaton*, 426—429.

cise any civil or political privileges under the laws of the state, because they are not bound by those laws. This has been so decided in the state courts.^a But if, in any case, the United States have not actually purchased, and the state has not, in point of fact, ceded the place or territory to the United States, its jurisdiction remains, notwithstanding the place may have been occupied, ever since its surrender by Great Britain, by the troops of the United States, as a fort or garrison. The Supreme Court of this state accordingly held, in the case of *The People* v. *Godfrey*,^b that they had jurisdiction of a murder committed by one soldier upon another within Niagara fort. Nor would the purchase of the land by the United States, be alone sufficient to vest them with the jurisdiction, or to oust that of the state, without being accompanied or followed with the consent of the legislature of the state. This was so decided in the case of *The Commonwealth of Pennsylvania* v. *Young*.^c

(7.) *The construction of the power of congress to regulate commerce among the several states.*

I proceed next to examine the judicial decisions under the power given to congress to " regulate commerce with foreign nations, and among the several states;" and it will be perceived, that the questions arising under this power have been of the utmost consequence to the interests of the union, and the residuary claims and sovereignty of the states.

The first question that arose upon this part of the constitution was, respecting the power of congress to interrupt or destroy the commerce of the United States, by laying a general embargo, without any limitation as to time. By the act of congress of 22d December, 1807, an embargo was laid on all ships and vessels in the ports and harbours of the United States, and a prohibition of exportation from the United

---

a Commonwealth v. Clary, 8 *Mass. Rep.* 72. Same v. Young, 1 *Hall's Journal of Jurisprudence*, 53.
b 17 *Johnson*, 225.
c 1 *Hall's Journal of Jurisprudence*, 47.

States, either by land or water, of any goods, wares, or merchandise of foreign or domestic growth or manufacture. There were several supplementary acts auxiliary to this principal one, and intended more effectually to enforce it under certain specific exceptions. In the case of *The United States* v. *The Brigantine William*, in the District Court of Massachusetts, in September, 1808,[a] it was objected, that the act was unconstitutional, for that congress had no right, under the power to regulate commerce, thus to annihilate it, by interdicting it entirely with foreign nations. But the court decided, that the embargo act was within the constitutional provision. The power of congress was sovereign relative to commercial intercourse, qualified by the limitations and restrictions expressed in the constitution; and by the treaty making power of the president and senate, congress had a right to control or abridge commerce for the advancement of great national purposes. Non-intercourse and embargo laws are within the range of legislative discretion; and if congress have the power, for purposes of safety, of preparation, or counteraction, to suspend commercial intercourse with foreign nations, they are not limited as to the duration, more than as to the manner and extent of the measure.

A still graver question was presented for the consideration of the federal judiciary, in the case of *Gibbons* v. *Ogden*,[b] decided by the Supreme Court of the United States in February term, 1824. That decision went to declare, that several acts of the legislature of this state, granting to *Livingston* and *Fulton* the exclusive navigation of the waters of this state in vessels propelled by steam, were unconstitutional and void acts, and repugnant to the power given to congress to regulate commerce, so far as those acts went to prohibit vessels licensed under the laws of congress for carrying on the coasting trade from navigating the waters of this state.

---

[a] 2 *Hall's Law Journal*, 255.   [b] 9 *Wheaton*, 1.

It had been decided in the Court of Errors of this state, in 1812,[a] that five several statutes of this state, passed between the years 1798 and 1811, inclusive, and granting and securing to the claimants the sole and exclusive right of using and navigating boats by steam in the waters of this state, for a term of years, were constitutional and valid acts. According to the doctrine of the court in that case, the internal commerce of the state by land and water remained entirely and exclusively within the scope of its original sovereignty. It was considered to be very difficult to draw an exact line between those regulations which relate to external, and those which relate to internal commerce, for every regulation of the one will directly or indirectly affect the other. But it was supposed that there could be no doubt that the acts of the state which were then under consideration, were not within any constitutional prohibition, for not one of the restrictions upon state power, contained in the 9th and 10th sections of the 1st article of the constitution, appeared to apply to the case; nor was there any existing regulation of congress on the subject of commerce with foreign nations, and among the several states, which was deemed to interfere with the grant. It was declared to be a very inadmissible proposition, that a state was devested of a capacity to grant an exclusive privilege of navigating a steam boat within its own waters, merely because congress, in the plenary exercise of its power to regulate commerce, *might* make some future regulation inconsistent with the exercise of that privilege. The grant was taken, undoubtedly, subject to such future commercial regulations as congress might lawfully prescribe; and to what extent they might lawfully prescribe them, was admitted to be a question within the ultimate cognizance of the Supreme Court of the United States. The opinion of the court went no further than to maintain, that the grant to *Livingston* and *Fulton* was not within any constitutional prohibition upon the states, nor

---

[a] Livingston v. Van Ingen, 9 *Johnson's Rep.* 507.

was it repugnant or contradictory to any existing act of congress on the subject of commerce; and under those two restrictions, every state had a right to make its own commercial regulations. It was generally declared, that congress had not, in the understanding of the court, any direct jurisdiction over our interior commerce or waters, and that they had concurrent jurisdiction over our navigable waters only so far as might be incidental and requisite to the due regulation of commerce between the states and with foreign nations.

In this case, in 1812, the defendants, who objected to the validity of the state grant, did not set up any patent right, or any other right under any particular act of congress. They rested entirely on the objection, that the statutes conferring the exclusive privilege were absolutely unconstitutional and void. But afterwards, in the case of *Ogden* v. *Gibbons*,[a] the defendant set up, by way of right and title to navigate a steam boat upon the waters of this state, in opposition to the grant, that his boats were duly enrolled and licensed under the laws of the United States, at Perth Amboy, in the state of New-Jersey, to be employed in carrying on the coasting trade. The question in that case was, whether such a coasting license conferred any power to interfere with the grant; and it was decided in the Court of Chancery, and afterwards in the Court of Errors,[b] that the coasting license merely gave to the steam boat an American character for the purpose of revenue, and that it was not intended to decide a question of property, or to confer a right of property, or a right of navigation or commerce. The act of congress regulating the coasting trade, was never intended to assert any supremacy over state regulations or claims, in respect to internal waters or commerce. It was not considered by our courts as the exercise of the power of congress to regulate commerce among the states. The law concerning the coasting trade was passed on the 18th

---

[a] 4 *Johnson's Ch. Rep.* 150.   [b] 17 *Johnson*, 488.

of February, 1793, and it never occurred to any one during the whole period that the state laws were under consideration before the legislature, and in the councils of revision, and in the courts of justice, from 1798 down to and including the judicial investigations in 1812, that the coasting act of 1793 was a regulation of commerce among the states, prohibitory of any such grant. Such latent powers were never thought of, or imputed to it. The great objects and policy of the coasting act were, to exclude foreign vessels from commerce between the states, in order to cherish the growth of our own marine, and to provide that the coasting trade should be conducted with security to the revenue. The register and enrolment of the vessel were to ascertain the national character; and the license was only evidence that the vessel had complied with the requisites of the law, and was qualified for the coasting trade under American privileges. The license did not define the coasting trade. Free trade between the states then existed, subject to local and municipal regulations. The requisitions of the coasting act were restrictions upon the general freedom of that commerce, and not the grant of new rights. Steam vessels were subject to those regulations equally with any other vessels. If congress had intended that a coasting license should confer power and control, and a claim of sovereignty subversive of local laws of the states within their own jurisdictions, it was supposed they would have said so in plain and intelligible language, and not have left their claim of supremacy to be hidden from the observation and knowledge of the state governments, in the unpretending and harmless shape of a coasting license, obviously intended for other purposes.

It was, therefore, upon considerations like these, that the courts of justice in this state did not consider the grant to *Livingston* and *Fulton* as disturbed by a coasting license under the act of 1793. The courts in this state did not, either in this case of *Ogden* v. *Gibbons*, or in any of the cases which preceded it, deny to congress the power to regulate commerce among the states, by express and direct provisions, so as to control and restrict the exercise of the state grant. They only insisted, that without some such explicit provision, the state jurisdiction over the subject remained in full force. This cause was afterwards carried up by appeal to the Supreme Court of the United States, and the decree reversed, on the ground, that the grant was repugnant to the rights and privileges conferred upon a steam boat navigating under a coasting license.[a] The great question was fully and elaborately discussed; and though it would not be proper in this place to question the correctness of a final decision, yet it has always appeared to me, that some of the doctrines and expositions of the court would carry the powers of the general government, by construction, to a greater extent over the residuary claims and assumed rights of the states, than any decision which had hitherto been made.

In the construction of the power to regulate commerce, the court held, that the term meant, not only traffic but intercourse, and that it included navigation, and the power to regulate commerce was a power to regulate navigation. Commerce among the several states, meant commerce intermingled with the states, and which might pass the external boundary line of each state, and be introduced into the interior. It was admitted, that the power did not extend to that commerce which was completely internal, and carried on between different ports of the same state, and which did not extend to, or affect other states. The power was restricted to that commerce which concerned more states than one, and the completely internal commerce of a state was reserved for the state itself. The power of congress on this subject comprehended navigation within the limits of every state, and it might pass the jurisdictional line of a state, and be exercised within its territory, so far as the navigation was connected with foreign commerce, or with commerce among the several states. This power, like all

---

[a] Gibbons v. Ogden, 9 *Wheaton*, 1.

the other powers of congress, was plenary and absolute within its acknowledged limits. But, it was admitted, that inspection laws relative to the quality of articles to be exported, and quarantine laws, and health laws of every description, and laws for regulating the internal commerce of a state, and those which respect turnpike roads, ferries, &c. were component parts of an immense mass of legislation, not surrendered to the general government. Though congress may license vessels to sail from one port to another in the same state, the act is supposed to be necessarily incidental to the power expressly granted to congress, and it implies no claim of a direct power to regulate the purely internal commerce of a state, or to act directly on its system of police. The court construed the word *regulate* to imply full power over the thing to be regulated, and to exclude the action of all others, that would perform the same operation on the same thing.

After laying down these general propositions, and which (as I understand them) none of the judicial decisions in this state have ever controverted, the court proceeded to observe, that the acts of this state, granting exclusive privileges to certain steam-boats, were in collision with the acts of congress regulating the coasting trade, and that the acts of the state must, in that case, yield to the supreme or paramount law. If the law of congress was made in pursuance of the constitution, (and of which there could be no doubt,) the state laws must yield to the supremacy of it, even though they were enacted in pursuance of powers acknowledged to remain in the states. A license under the acts of congress for regulating the coasting trade, was an authority to carry on that trade. The words of the act of congress, directing the proper officer to grant to a vessel qualified to receive it, " a license for carrying on the coasting trade," was considered as conveying an explicit authority for that purpose. It was the legislative grant of a right, and it conferred all the right which congress could give in the case, and it was not intended to confer merely the national character. It was further held, that the power to regulate commerce extended to navigation, carried on by vessels exclusively employed in transporting passengers, and to vessels propelled by steam, as well as to vessels navigated by other means.

This is the substance of the argument of the Supreme Court of the United States in the steam-boat case. The only great point on which the Supreme Court of the United States, and the courts of this state, have differed, is in the construction and effect given to a coasting license. They did not differ in any general view of the powers of congress; and the Supreme Court expressly waived any inquiry or decision on the point, whether the exercise of the power assumed by the steam-boat laws, would have been illegal, provided there was no existing regulation of congress that came in collision with them. This was the very point and pith of the decision in *Livingston* v. *Van Ingen*. It was upon the assumption that there was no such regulation, that the decision in *Livingston* v. *Van Ingen* rested. I apprehend, that the steam-boat laws would never have been passed, and the decisions under them which have been complained of, would never have been made, if it had been clearly understood by the authorities of this state, that the coasting license act was the actual exercise of a power in congress repugnant to such a privilege, and if the opposition boats in that case had produced such a license. The formidable effect which has been given to a coasting license, was a perfect surprise upon the judicial authorities of this state; and none of the persons concerned in the former decisions in our state courts on this subject, ever entertained the idea, as I apprehend, that congress intended, by a coasting license, a grant of power that was to bear down all state regulations of internal commerce that stood in its way. The original and leading decision of *Livingston* v. *Van Ingen*, is not affected by this decision of the Supreme Court of the United States. None of the doctrines in that case are controverted by the Supreme Court, because, in that case, the opposition boats set up no license under the coasting act, and the whole controversy has turned and terminated upon the effect to be given to the coasting license.

But the decree of the Supreme Court seems to be broader than the facts in the case would warrant. The case related to a claim of right to steam-boat navigation between Elizabeth Town, in New-Jersey, and the city of New-York, by a licensed boat; and the court decided, that the Jersey boat had a right to navigate the waters of this state for the purpose of carrying on the coasting trade, any law of this state to the contrary notwithstanding. The decree went on to declare, that so much of the several laws of this state as prohibited vessels duly licensed from navigating the waters of this state by means of fire or steam, were repugnant to the constitution, and void. This language was too general and comprehensive for the case. The case related to a commerce between two states, which commenced in the one and terminated in the other, and the reasoning of the court did not go beyond the case. The decree, therefore, as I apprehend, could not have been intended to establish, that a steam-boat licensed under the coasting act, was not subject to the laws of the state in respect to mere internal commerce, or that the steam-boat privileges held under the laws of this state were not valid in respect to a purely domestic or internal commerce on the navigable waters of this state. The principle settled by the decision applies only to the case where the *termini* of the voyage or coasting trade rested in different states. The commerce or navigation protected by the coasting license must concern more states than one, in order to make it a commerce among the states. A vessel employed in the regular conveyance of goods, wares and merchandise, or of passengers, from one given port or place within this state to another, as for instance, between the cities of New-York and Albany, is as entirely employed in the internal commerce of the state, as it would be if the same vessel was employed in the same regular business between Albany and Troy, or upon the canal between Schenectady and Utica. A coasting license may, perhaps, reasonably imply a trading from port to port within the same state, as part and parcel of one continuous voyage between different states. But if a coasting license, founded on the power in congress to regulate commerce among the several states, be held to imply a right to navigate regularly and permanently between two ports or places within the same state, and to allow the vessel to be confined essentially, and for all business purposes, entirely to the waters of this state, then there would be no distinction between commerce among the several states, and a commerce confined entirely and exclusively within a state; and all state jurisdiction over its purely internal commerce would be utterly destroyed. This was never intended by the constitution, and it is what the Supreme Court itself appears to have disclaimed.

I have now finished the second general division of this course of lectures relating to the government and constitutional jurisprudence of the United States. Though I have considered the subject in a spirit of free and liberal inquiry, as the series of decisions in the federal courts have been brought under examination, I have uniformly felt, and it has been my invariable disposition to inculcate, a strong sentiment of deference and respect for the judicial authorities of the union. No point or question of any moment, touching the construction of the powers of the government, and which has received an authoritative determination, has been intentionally omitted. There are several important constitutional questions which remain yet to be settled; but if we recur back to the judicial annals of the United States for the last thirty years, we shall find that many of the most interesting discussions which had arisen, and which were of a nature to affect deeply the tranquillity of the nation, have auspiciously terminated.

The definition of direct taxes within the intendment of the constitution; the extent of the power of congress to regulate commerce with foreign nations and among the several states; the power to establish an uniform rule of naturalization, and uniform laws on the subject of bankruptcies; the power of congress over the militia of the states; their power of exclusive legislation over districts and ceded places; the mass of implied powers incidental to the express powers of congress, such as the power to institute and protect an incorporated bank, to lay a general and indefinite embargo, and to give to the United States, as a creditor, priority of payment, have all received elaborate discussion in the Supreme Court, and they have, to a certain extent, been ascertained and defined by judicial decisions. So, also, the extent of the constitutional prohibitions upon the states, not to pass *ex post facto* laws; and not to pass laws impairing the obligation of contracts; and not to impede or control by taxes, or grants, or any other exercise of power, the lawful authorities, or institutions, or rights and privileges depending on the constitution and laws of the United States, has been explored and declared by a series of determinations, which have contributed in an eminent degree to secure and consolidate the union, and to elevate the dignity and enlarge the influence of the national government.

The power of the president to remove all executive officers at his will and pleasure, has been settled, not indeed judicially, but perhaps as effectually, by the declared sense of the legislature, and the uniform acquiescence and practice of the government. The absolute and uncontrollable efficacy of the treaty-making power, has also been definitively established, after a struggle against it on the part of the house of representatives, which at one time threatened to disturb the very foundations of the constitution.

The comprehensive claims of the judicial power, as being co-extensive with all cases that can arise under the constitution, and laws, and treaties of the union, have been powerfully and successfully vindicated. The appellate jurisdiction of the Supreme Court, controlling and causing to bow to its supremacy, the highest courts of justice in the several states; the extensive sway of admiralty and maritime jurisdiction; the character of the parties necessary to give cognizance to the federal courts; the faith and credit which are to be given in each state to the records and judicial proceedings in every other state; the sovereignty of congress over all its territories, without the bounds of any particular state; and the entire and supreme authority of all the constitutional powers of the nation, when coming in collision with any of the residuary or asserted powers of the states, have all been declared (as we have seen in the course of these lectures) by an authority which claims our respect and obedience.

In the first ten or twelve years after the institution of the national judiciary, or from 1790 to 1801, the scanty decisions of the Supreme Court are almost all to be found in the third volume of Dallas' Reports. The first great and grave question which came before them, was that respecting the liability of a state to be sued by a private creditor; and it is a little remarkable, that the court, in one of its earliest decisions, should have assumed a jurisdiction which the author of the *Federalist* had a few years before declared to be without any colour of foundation. During the period I have mentioned, the federal courts were chiefly occupied with questions concerning their admiralty jurisdiction, and with political and national questions growing out of the revolutionary war, and the dangerous influence and action of the war of the French revolution upon the neutrality and peace of our country. It was during this portion of our juridical history, that the principles of the doctrines of expatriation, of *ex post facto* laws, of constitutional taxes, and of the construction and obligation of the treaty of 1783 upon the rights of British creditors, were ably discussed and firmly declared.

The reports of Mr. Cranch commence with the year 1801, and the nine volumes of those reports cover the business of a very active period down to the year 1815. The Supreme Court was occupied with many great and momentous questions, and especially during that portion of the time in which the United States had abandoned their neutral and assumed a belligerent character. It is curious to observe in those reports, the rapid cultivation and complete adoption of the law and learning of the English admiralty and prize courts, notwithstanding those courts had been the constant theme of complaint and obloquy in our political discussions for the fifteen years preceding the war. In the last three volumes of Mr. Cranch, the court was constantly dealing with great questions, embracing the rights and the policy of nations; and the prize and maritime law, not of England only, but of all the commercial nations of Europe, was suddenly introduced, and deeply and permanently interwoven with the municipal law of the United States. We perceive, also, in these volumes, the constant growth and accumulation of cases on commercial law generally, and relating to policies of insurance, negotiable paper, mercantile partnerships, and the various customs of the law merchant. The court was likewise busy in discussing and settling important principles growing out of the limited range of other matters of federal cognizance, and relating to the law of evidence, to frauds, trusts and mortgages. They were engaged also with the doctrine of the limitation of suits, the contract of sale, and with the more enlarged subjects of domicil, of the *lex loci*, of neutrality, and of the numerous points of international law.

By the time of the commencement of Mr. Wheaton's reports in 1816, the decisions of the Supreme Court had embraced so many topics of public and municipal law, and those topics had been illustrated by so much talent and learning, that, for the first time in the history of this country, we were enabled to perceive the broad foundations and rapid growth of a code of national jurisprudence. That code has been growing and improving ever since, and it has now become a solid and magnificent structure; and it seems destined, at no very distant period of time, to cast a shade over the less elevated, and perhaps we must add, the less attractive and ambitious systems of justice in the several states. The most interesting parts of Mr. Wheaton's reports are those which contain the examination of those great constitutional questions which we have been reviewing; and I cannot conceive of any thing more grand and imposing in the whole administration of human justice, than the spectacle of the Supreme Court sitting in solemn judgment upon the conflicting claims of the national and state sovereignties, and tranquillizing all jealous and angry passions, and binding together this great confederacy of states in peace and harmony, by the ability, the moderation, and the equity of its decisions.

There are several reasons why we may anticipate the still increasing influence of the federal government, and the continual enlargement of the national system of law in magnitude and value. The judiciary of the United States has an advantage over many of the state courts in the tenure of the office of the judges, and the liberal and stable provision for their support. The United States are, by these means, fairly entitled to command better talents, and to look for more firmness of purpose, greater independence of action, and brighter displays of learning. The federal administration of justice has a manifest superiority over that of the individual states, in consequence of the uniformity of its decisions, and the universality of their application. Every state court will naturally be disposed to borrow light and aid from the national courts, rather than from the courts of other individual states, which will probably never be so generally respected and understood. The states are multiplying so fast, and the reports of their judicial decisions are becoming so numerous, that few lawyers will be able or willing to master all the intricacies and anomalies of local law, existing beyond the boundaries of their own state. Twenty-four independent state courts of final jurisdiction over the same questions, arising upon the same general code of common and of equity law, must necessarily impair the symmetry of that code.

The danger to be apprehended is, that students will not have the courage to enter the complicated labyrinth of so many systems, and that they will, of course, entirely neglect them, and be contented with a knowledge of the law of their own state, and the law of the United States, and then resort for further assistance to the never failing fountains of European wisdom.

But though the national judiciary may be deemed preeminent in the weight of its influence, the authority of its decisions, and in the attraction of their materials, there are abundant considerations to cheer and animate us in the cultivation of our own local law. The judicial power of the United States is necessarily limited to national objects. The vast field of the law of property, the very extensive head of equity jurisdiction, and the principal rights and duties which flow from our civil and domestic relations, fall within the control, and we might almost say, the exclusive cognizance of the state governments. We look essentially to the state courts for protection to all these momentous interests. They touch, in their operation, every cord of human sympathy, and control our best destinies. It is their province to reward, and to punish. Their blessings and their terrors will accompany us to the fireside, and be " in constant activity before the public eye." The elementary principles of the common law are the same in every state, and equally enlighten and invigorate every part of our country. Our municipal codes can be made to advance with equal steps with that of the nation, in discipline, in wisdom, and in lustre, if the state governments (as they ought in all honest policy) will only render equal patronage and security to the administration of justice. The true interests and the permanent freedom of this country require, that the jurisprudence of the individual states should be cultivated, cherished, and exalted, and the dignity and reputation of the state authorities sustained with becoming pride. In their subordinate relation to the United States, they should endeavour to discharge the duty which they owe to the latter, without forgetting the respect which they owe to themselves. In the appropriate language of Sir William Blackstone, and which he applied to the people of his own country, they should be " loyal, yet free; obedient, and yet independent."

PART III.

OF THE VARIOUS SOURCES OF THE MUNICIPAL LAW OF THE SEVERAL STATES.

LECTURE XX.

OF STATUTE LAW.

MUNICIPAL law is a rule of civil conduct, prescribed by the supreme power in a state. It is composed of written and unwritten, or statute and common law. Statute law is the express written will of the legislature, rendered authentic by certain prescribed forms and solemnities.

It is a principle in the English law, that an act of parliament, delivered in clear and intelligible terms, cannot be questioned, or its authority controlled in any court of justice. " It is," says Sir William Blackstone, " the exercise of the highest authority that the kingdom acknowledges upon earth." When it is said in the books, that a statute contrary to natural equity and reason, or repugnant, or impossible to be performed, is void, the cases are understood to mean, that the courts are to give the statute a reasonable construction. They will not readily presume, out of respect and duty to the lawgiver, that any very unjust or absurd consequence was within the contemplation of the law. But if it should happen to be too direct and palpable in its direction to admit of but one construction, there is no doubt in the English law, as to the binding efficacy of the statute. The will of the legislature is the supreme law of the land, and demands irresistible obedience.^a

But while we admit this conclusion of the English law, we cannot but admire the intrepidity and powerful sense of justice which led Lord Coke, when chief justice of the K. B., to declare, as he did in *Doctor Bonham's* case,^b that the common law doth control acts of parliament, and adjudges them void when against common right and reason. The same sense of justice and freedom of opinion, led Lord Chief Justice Hobart, in *Day* v. *Savage*,^c to insist that an act of parliament made against natural equity, as to make a man judge in his own case, was void; and induced Lord Chief Justice Holt to say, in the case of the *City of London* v. *Wood*,^d that the observation of Lord Coke was not extravagant, but was a very reasonable and true saying. Perhaps what Lord Coke said in his reports, on this point, may have been one of the many things that King James alluded to, when he said, that in Coke's Reports there were many dangerous conceits of his own uttered for law, to the prejudice of the crown, parliament and subjects.^e

The principle in the English government, that the parliament is omnipotent, does not prevail in the United States. In this, and all other countries where there is a written constitution, designating the powers and duties of the legislative, as well as of the other departments of the government, an act of the legislature may be void as being against the constitution. It must conform, in the first place, to the constitution of the United States, and then to the subordinate constitution of its own state, and if it infringes the pro-

---

a 1 *Blacks. Com.* 91. 160. 185. *Christian's note to* 1 *Blacks. Com.* 41.
b 8 *Co.* 118.
c *Hob.* 87.
d 12 *Mod.* 687.
e *Bacon's Works*, vol. 6. p. 128.

visions of either, it is so far void. The courts of justice have a right, and are in duty bound, to bring every law to the test of the constitution, and to regard the constitution, first of the United States, and then of their own state, as the paramount or supreme law, to which every inferior or derivative power and regulation must conform. The constitution is the act of the people, speaking in their original character, and defining the permanent conditions of the social alliance; and there can be no doubt on the point with us, that every act of the legislative power, contrary to the true intent and meaning of the constitution, is absolutely null and void. The judicial department is the proper power in the government to determine whether a statute be or be not constitutional. The interpretation or construction of the constitution, is as much a judicial act, and requires the exercise of the same legal discretion, as the interpretation or construction of a law. To contend that the courts of justice must obey the requisitions of an act of the legislature, when it appears to them to have been passed in violation of the constitution, would be to contend, that the law was superior to the constitution, and that the judges had no right to look into it, and to regard it as the paramount law. It would be rendering the power of the agent greater than that of his principal, and be declaring, that the will of only one concurrent and co-ordinate department of the subordinate authorities under the constitution, was absolute over the other departments, and competent to control, according to its own will and pleasure, the whole fabric of the government, and the fundamental laws on which it rested. It would be perfectly idle to attempt to impose restraints upon the exercise of the legislative power, if the constitutional provisions were left without any power in the government to guard and enforce them. From the mass of powers necessarily vested in the legislature, and the active and sovereign nature of those powers; from the numerous bodies of which the legislature is composed, the popular sympathies which it excites, and its immediate dependence upon the people by the means of frequent periodical elections, it follows, that the legislative department of the government will have a decided superiority of influence. It is constantly acting upon all the great interests in society, and agitating its hopes and fears. It is liable to be constantly swayed by popular prejudice and passion, and it is difficult to keep it from pressing with injurious weight upon the constitutional rights and privileges of the other departments. An independent judiciary, venerable by its gravity, its dignity, and its wisdom, and deliberating with entire serenity and moderation, is peculiarly fitted for the exalted duty of expounding the constitution, and trying the validity of statutes by that standard. It is only by the free exercise of this power that courts of justice are enabled to repel assaults, and protect every part of the government, and every member of the community, from undue and destructive innovations upon their chartered rights.

It has accordingly become a settled principle in the legal polity of this country, that it belongs to the judicial power, as a matter of right and of duty, to declare every act of the legislature made in violation of the constitution, or of any provision of it, null and void. The progress of this doctrine, and the manner in which it has been discussed and established, is worthy of notice. It had been very ably examined in the *Federalist*,[a] and its solidity vindicated by unanswerable arguments; but it was not until the year 1792 that it seems to have received a judicial consideration.

In *Hayburn's case*, which came before the Circuit Court of the United States for the district of New-York, in April, 1791, the judges proceeded with the utmost delicacy and caution to declare an act of congress, assigning ministerial duties to the circuit courts, to be unconstitutional. The court laid down the position, that congress cannot constitutionally assign to the judicial power any duties which are not strictly judicial; and that the act in question was not

---

[a] No. 78.

obligatory upon the court. But they nevertheless proceeded voluntarily and *ex gratia* as commissioners to execute the duties of the act.

In Pennsylvania and North-Carolina, the circuit courts of the United States within those districts equally held the act not binding upon them, because the legislature had no right or power to assign to them duties not judicial; but they were not so accommodating as the Circuit Court of New-York, for they declined to act under the law in any capacity.[a]

In 1792, the Supreme Court of South-Carolina, in the case of *Bowman* v. *Middleton*,[b] went further, and set aside an act of the colony legislature, as being against common right and the principles of *magna charta*, for it took away the freehold of one man and vested it in another, without any compensation, or any previous attempt to determine the right. They declared the act to be *ipso facto* void, and that no length of time could give it validity. This was not strictly a question arising upon any special provision of the state constitution, but the court proceeded upon those great fundamental principles which support all government and property, and which have been supposed by many judges in England to be sufficient to check and control the regulations of an act of parliament. The next case in which the power of the judiciary to disregard or set aside a statute for being repugnant to the constitution, was one that came before Judge Paterson, at Philadelphia, in April, 1795.[c] He asserted the duty of the court, and the paramount authority of the constitution, in remarkably clear and decided language. That was a case of an act of Pennsylvania, which he held to be unconstitutional, and not binding. He insisted, that the constitution was certain and fixed, and contained the permanent will of the people, and was the supreme law, and paramount to the power of the legislature, and could only

---

a 2 *Dallas*, 410, 411, 412.   b 1 *Bay*, 252.
c Vanhorn v. Dorrance, 2 *Dallas*, 304.

be revoked or altered by the authority that made it; that the legislature was the creature of the constitution, and owed its existence to the constitution, and derived its power from the constitution, and all its acts must be conformable to it, or else they will be void.

The same question afterwards arose before the Supreme Court of South Carolina, in the case of *Lindsay* v. *The Charleston Commissioners;*[a] and the power of the legislature to take private property for necessary public purposes, as for a public street, was freely discussed; and though the judges were equally divided on the question whether it was a case in which the party was entitled to compensation, those who held him so entitled, held also, that the law was unconstitutional and inoperative, until the compensation was made. The judges, in exercising that high authority, claimed to be only the administrators of the public will, and the law was void, not because the judges had any control over the legislative power, but because the will of the people, declared in the constitution, was paramount to that of their representatives expressed in the law.

Hitherto, this question, as we have seen, was confined to one or two of the state courts, and to the subordinate, or circuit courts of the United States. But, in *Marbury* v. *Madison,*[b] the subject was brought under the consideration of the Supreme Court of the United States, and received a clear and elaborate discussion. The power and duty of the judiciary to disregard an unconstitutional act of congress, or of any state legislature, were declared in an argument approaching to the precision and certainty of a mathematical demonstration.

The question, said the chief justice, was, whether an act repugnant to the constitution, can become a law of the land, and it was one deeply interesting to the United States. The powers of the legislature are defined and limited by a

---

[a] 2 *Bay*, 38.   [b] 1 *Cranch*, 137.

written constitution. But to what purpose is that limitation, if those limits may at any time be passed? The distinction between a government with limited and unlimited powers is abolished, if those limits do not confine the persons on whom they are imposed, and if acts prohibited, and acts allowed, are of equal obligation. If the constitution does not control any legislative act repugnant to it, then the legislature may alter the constitution by an ordinary act. The theory of every government, with a written constitution, forming the fundamental and paramount law of the nation, must be, that an act of the legislature repugnant to the constitution is void. If void, it cannot bind the courts, and oblige them to give it effect; for this would be to overthrow, in fact, what was established in theory, and to make that operative as law which is not law. It is the province and the duty of the judicial department, to say what the law is; and if two laws conflict with each other, to decide on the operation of each. So, if the law be in opposition to the constitution, and both apply to a particular case, the court must either decide the case conformably to the law, disregarding the constitution, or conformably to the constitution, disregarding the law. If the constitution be superior to an act of the legislature, the courts must decide between these conflicting rules, and how can they close their eyes on the constitution and see only the law?

This great question may be regarded as now finally settled, and I consider it to be one of the most interesting points in favour of constitutional liberty, and of the security of property in this country, that has ever been judicially determined. We never had any doubt or difficulty in this state, in respect to the competency of the courts to declare a statute unconstitutional, when it clearly appeared to be so. Thus, in the case of *The People* v. *Platt*,[a] the Supreme Court held, that certain statutes affecting the right of Z. Platt, and his assigns, to the exclusive enjoyment of

---

[a] 17 *Johnson*, 195.

the river Saranac, were in violation of vested rights under his patent, and so far the court held them to be unconstitutional, inoperative, and void. The control which the judicial power of this state had, until the year 1823, over the passing of laws, by the institution of the *council of revision*, anticipated, in a great degree, the necessity of this exercise of duty. A law containing unconstitutional provisions, was not likely to escape the notice and objection of the council of revision; and the records of that body will show, that many a bill that had heedlessly passed the two houses of the legislature, was objected to, and defeated, on constitutional grounds. The records to which I refer are replete with the assertion of salutary and sound principles of public law and constitutional policy; and they will for ever remain a monument of the wisdom, firmness, and integrity of the council, and of the great value and benign influence of that institution.

A statute, when duly made, takes effect from its date when no time is fixed, and this is now the settled rule. It was so declared by the Supreme Court of the United States in *Matthews* v. *Zane*,[a] and it was likewise so adjudged in the Circuit Court in Massachusetts in the case of the brig *Ann*.[b] I apprehend, that the same rule prevails in the courts of this state, and that it cannot be admitted that a statute shall, by any fiction or relation, have any effect before it was actually passed. A retroactive statute would partake in its character of the mischiefs of an *ex post facto* law, as to all cases of crimes and penalties; and in every other case relating to contracts or property, it would be against every sound principle. It would come within the reach of the doctrine, that a statute is not to have a retrospective effect; and which doctrine was very much discussed in the case of *Dash* v. *Vankleeck*,[c] and shown to be founded, not only in English law, but on the principles of general jurisprudence.

---

[a] 7 *Wheaton*, 164.   [b] 1 *Gallison*, 62.   [c] 7 *Johnson*, 477.

The English rule formerly was, that if no period was fixed by the statute itself, it took effect by relation, from the first day of the session in which the act was passed, and which might be some weeks, if not months, before the act received the royal sanction, or even before it had ever been introduced into parliament.[a] This was an extraordinary instance of the doctrine of relation working gross injustice and absurdity; and yet we find the rule declared, and uniformly adhered to, from the time of Hen. VI.[b] All the judges agreed, in the case of *Partridge* v. *Strange*, in the 6 Edw. VI.[c] that the statute was to be accounted in law a perfect act from the first day of the session; and all persons were to be punished for an offence done against it after the first day of the session, unless a certain time was appointed when the act should take effect. In the case of *The King* v. *Thurston*,[d] this doctrine of carrying a statute back by relation to the first day of the session, was admitted in the K. B.; though the consequence of it was to render an act murder, which would not have been so without such relation. The case of the *Attorney General* v. *Panter*,[e] is another strong instance of the application of this rigorous and unjust rule of the common law, even at so late and enlightened a period of the law as the year 1772. An act for laying a duty on the exportation of rice *thereafter to be exported*, received the royal assent on the 29th of June, 1767, and on the 10th of June of that year, the defendants had exported rice. After the act passed, a duty of 115 pounds was demanded upon the prior exportation, and it was adjudged in the Irish Court of Exchequer to be payable. The cause was carried by appeal to the British House of Lords, on the ground of the palpable injustice of punishing the

---

a 4 *Inst.* 25.
b 33 *Hen. VI.* 18. *Bro. Exposition del Terms*, 33.
c 1 *Plow.* 79.
d 1 *Lev.* 91.
e 6 *Bro. P. C.* 553.

party for an act innocent and lawful when it was done; but the decree was affirmed, upon the opinion of the twelve judges, that the statute, by legal relation, commenced from the first day of the session. The K. B. also, in *Latless* v. *Holmes*,[a] considered the rule to be too well settled to be shaken, and that the court could not take notice of the great hardship of the case. The voice of reason at last prevailed, and by the statute of 33 Geo. III. c. 13. it was declared, that statutes are to have effect only from the time they receive the royal assent, and the former rule was abolished, in the words of the statute, by reason of " its great and manifest injustice."

There is a good deal of hardship in the rule as it now stands, both here and in England; for a statute is to operate from the very day it passes, if the law itself does not establish the time. It is impossible, in any state, and particularly in such a wide spread dominion as that of the United States, to have notice of the existence of the law, until some time after it has passed. It would be no more than reasonable and just, that the statute should not be deemed to operate upon the persons and property of individuals, or impose pains and penalties for acts done in contravention of it, until the law was duly promulgated. The rule, however, is deemed to be fixed beyond the power of judicial control, and no time is allowed for the publication of the law before it operates, when the statute itself gives no time. Thus, in the case of the brig *Ann*,[b] the vessel was libelled and condemned for sailing from Newburyport in Massachusetts, on the 12th of January, 1808, contrary to the act of congress of the 9th of January, 1808, though it was admitted the act was not known in Newburyport on the day the brig sailed. The court admitted, that the objection to the forfeiture of the brig was founded on the principles of good sense and natural equity; and that unless such time be allowed as would enable a party, with reasonable diligence,

---

a 4 *Term*, 660.   b 1 *Gallison*, 62.

to ascertain the existence of the law, an innocent man might be punished in his person and property, for an act which was innocent for aught he knew, or could, by possibility, have known, when he did it.

The code Napoleon[a] adopted the true rule on this subject. It declared, that laws were binding from the moment their promulgation could be known, and that the promulgation should be considered as known in the department of the imperial residence one day after that promulgation, and in each of the other departments of the French empire, after the expiration of the same space of time, augmented by as many days as there were distances of twenty leagues between the seat of government and the place.

If the statute be constitutional in its character, and has duly gone into operation, the next inquiry is respecting its meaning; and this leads us to a consideration of the established rules of construction, by which its sense and operation are to be understood.

There is a material distinction between public and private statutes, and the books abound with cases explaining this distinction in its application to particular statutes. It is sometimes difficult to draw the line between a public and private act, for statutes frequently relate to matters and things that are partly public and partly private. Generally speaking statutes are public, and a private statute may rather be considered as an exception to a general rule. It operates upon particular individuals, or upon private persons. It is said not to bind or include strangers in interest to its provisions, and they are not bound to take notice of a private act, even though there be no general saving clause of the rights of third persons. This is a safe and just rule of construction; and it was adopted by the English courts in very early times, and does great credit to their liberality

---

[a] Art. 1.

and spirit of justice.ᵃ It is supported by the opinion of Sir Matthew Hale in *Lucy* v. *Levington*,ᵇ where he lays down the rule to be, that though every man be so far a party to a private act of parliament, as not to gainsay it, yet he is not so far a party as to give up his interest. To take the case stated by Sir Matthew Hale, suppose a statute recites, *that whereas there was a controversy concerning land between A. and B., and enacts that A. shall enjoy it,* this would not bind the interest of third persons in that land, because they are not strictly parties to the act, but strangers, and it would be manifest injustice that the statute should affect them. This rule as to the limitation of the operation of private statutes, was adopted by the Supreme Court of this state, and afterwards by the Court of Errors, in *Jackson* v. *Catlin.*ᶜ Private statutes are likewise placed under another limitation. The courts of justice are bound, *ex officio*, to take notice of public acts without their being pleaded, for they are part of the general law of the land, which all persons, and particularly the judges, are presumed to know; but they are not bound to take notice of private acts, unless they be specially pleaded, and shown in proof, by the party claiming the effect of them.

The title of the act, and the preamble to the act, are, strictly speaking, no parts of it. They may serve to show the general scope and purport of the act, and the inducements which led to its enactment. They may, at times, aid in the construction of it; but generally they are very loosely and carelessly inserted, and are not safe expositors of the law. The title frequently alludes to the subject matter of the act only in general or sweeping terms, or it alludes only to a part of the multifarious matter of which the statute is composed. The title, as it was observed in *Fisher* v.

---

a 37 *Hen.* VI. 15. *Bro. Parliament,* pl. 27. *Boswell's case,* 25 and 26 *Eliz.* cited in *Barrington's case,* 8 *Co.* 138. *a.*

b 1 *Vent.* 175.

c 2 *Johnson's Rep.* 268. 8 *Johnson's Rep.* 520. S. C.

Blight,[a] when taken in connexion with other parts, may assist in removing ambiguities where the intent is not plain; for when the mind labours to discover the intention of the legislature, it seizes every thing, even the title, from which aid can be derived. So, the preamble may be resorted to in order to ascertain the inducements to the making of the statute; but when the words of the enacting clause are clear and positive, recourse must not be had to the preamble. Notwithstanding that Lord Coke[b] considers the preamble as a key to open the understanding of the statute, Mr. Barrington, in his *Observations on the Statutes*,[c] has shown, by many instances, that a statute frequently recites that which was not the real occasion of the law, or states that doubts existed as to the law, when, in fact, none had existed. The true rule is, as was declared by Mr. J. Buller in *Crespigny v. Wittenoom*,[d] that the preamble may be resorted to in restraint of the generality of the enacting clause, when it would be inconvenient if not restrained, or it may be resorted to in explanation of the enacting clause if it be doubtful. This is the whole extent of the influence of the title and preamble in the construction of the statute. The true meaning of the statute is generally and properly to be sought from the body of the act itself. But such is the imperfection of human language, and the want of technical skill in the makers of the law, that statutes often give occasion to the most perplexing and distressing doubts and discussions, arising from the ambiguity that attends them. It requires great experience, as well as the command of a perspicuous diction, to frame a law in such clear and precise terms as to secure it from ambiguous expressions, and from all doubt and criticism upon its meaning.

It is an established rule in the exposition of statutes, that the intention of the lawgiver is to be deduced from a view of the whole, and of every part of a statute, taken and

---

a 2 *Cranch*, 386.
c P. 300.
b *Co. Litt.* 79. a.
d 4 *Term*, 793.

compared together. The real intention, when accurately ascertained, will always prevail over the literal sense of terms. When the words are not explicit, the intention is to be collected from the occasion and necessity of the law, from the mischief felt, and the remedy in view; and the intention is to be taken or presumed, according to what is consonant to reason and good discretion. These rules, by which the sages of the law, according to Plowden,[a] have ever been guided in seeking for the intention of the legislature, are maxims of sound interpretation, which have been accumulated by the experience, and ratified by the approbation of ages.

The words of a statute are to be taken in their natural and ordinary signification and import; and if technical words are used, they are to be taken in a technical sense. A saving clause in a statute is to be rejected when it is directly repugnant to the purview or body of the act, and could not stand without rendering the act inconsistent and destructive of itself.[b] Lord Coke, in *Alton Wood's* case,[c] gives a particular illustration of this rule, by a case which would be false doctrine with us, but which serves to show the force of the rule. Thus, if the manor of Dale be by express words given by statute to the king, saving the right of all persons interested therein, or if the statute vests the lands of A. in the king, saving the rights of A., the interest of the owner is not saved, inasmuch as the saving clause is repugnant to the grant; and if it were allowed to operate, it would render the grant vain and nugatory. But there is a distinction in some of the books between a saving clause and a proviso in the statute, though the reason of the distinction is not very apparent. It was held by all the barons of the exchequer, in the case of *The Attorney General* v. *The Governor and Company of Chelsea Water Works*,[d] that where the proviso of an act of parliament was directly repugnant to the pur-

---

a *Plowd. Rep.* p. 205.   b *Plowd.* 565. 8 *Taunton*, 13—16.
c 1 *Co.* 47. a.   d *Fitzg.* 195. 4 *Geo.* II.

view of it, the proviso should stand and be held a repeal of the purview, because it speaks the last intention of the lawgiver. It was compared to a will, in which the latter part, if inconsistent with the former, supersedes and revokes it. But it may be remarked, upon this case in *Fitzgibbon*, that a proviso repugnant to the purview of the statute, renders it equally nugatory and void as a repugnant saving clause; and it is difficult to see why the act should be destroyed by the one and not by the other, or why the proviso and the saving clause, when inconsistent with the body of the act, should not both of them be equally rejected. There is also a technical distinction between a proviso and an exception in a statute. If there be an exception in the enacting clause of a statute, it must be negatived in pleading; but if there be a separate proviso, that need not.[a]

Several acts *in pari materia*, and relating to the same subject, are to be taken together, and compared in the construction of them, because they are considered as having one object in view, and as acting upon one system. This rule was declared in the case of *The Earl of Ailesbury v. Patterson*;[b] and the rule applies, though some of the statutes may have expired, or are not referred to in the other acts. The object of the rule is to ascertain and carry into effect the intention; and it is to be inferred, that a code of statutes relating to one subject, was governed by one spirit and policy, and was intended to be consistent and harmonious in its several parts and provisions. Upon the same principle, whenever a power is given by a statute, every thing necessary to the making of it effectual, or requisite to attain the end, is implied. *Quando lex aliquid concedit concedere videtur et id, perquod devenitur ad illud.*

Statutes are likewise to be construed in reference to the principles of the common law, for it is not to be presumed the legislature intended to make any innovation upon the common law, further than the case absolutely required.

---

a Abbott, J. 1 *Barn. & Ald.* 99.   *b Doug.* 27.

This has been the language of the courts in every age; and when we consider the constant, vehement and exalted eulogy which the ancient sages bestowed upon the common law, as the perfection of reason, and the best birthright and noblest inheritance of the subject, we cannot be surprised at the great sanction given to this rule of construction. It was observed by the judges, in the case of *Stowell* v. *Zouch*,[a] that it was good for the expositors of a statute to approach as near as they could to the reason of the common law; and the resolution of the barons of the exchequer, in *Heydon's* case,[b] was to this effect. For the sure and true interpretation of all statutes, whether penal or beneficial, four things are to be considered: What was the common law before the act; what was the mischief against which the common law did not provide; what remedy the parliament had provided to cure the defect; and the true reason of the remedy. It was held to be the duty of the judges to make such a construction as should repress the mischief, and advance the remedy.

In the construction of statutes, the sense which the contemporary members of the profession had put upon them, is deemed of some importance, according to the maxim that *contemporanea expositio est fortissima in lege*. Statutes that are remedial and not penal, are to receive an equitable interpretation, by which the letter of the act is sometimes restrained, and sometimes enlarged, so as more effectually to meet the beneficial end in view, and prevent a failure of the remedy. This may be illustrated in the case of the registry acts, for giving priority to deeds and mortgages, according to the dates of the registry. If a person claiming under a registered deed or mortgage, had notice of the unregistered prior deed when he took his deed, and procured the registry of it in order to defeat the prior deed, he shall not prevail with his prior registry, because that would

---

a *Plowd.* 365.   b 3 *Co.* 7.

be to counteract the intent and policy of the statutes, which were made to prevent and not to uphold frauds.

If an act be penal and temporary by the terms or nature of it, the party offending must be prosecuted and punished before the act expires. Though the offence be committed before the expiration of the act, the party cannot be punished after it has expired, unless a particular provision be made by law for the purpose.^a If a statute be repealed, and afterwards the repealing act be repealed, this revives the original act;^b and if a statute be temporary and limited to a given number of years, and before the expiration of the time it be continued by another act, it was formerly a question under which statute acts and proceedings were to be considered as done. In the case of *The College of Physicians*,^c it was declared, that if a statute be limited to seven years, and afterwards by another statute be made perpetual, proceedings ought to be referred to the last statute, as being the one in force. But this decision was erroneous, and contrary to what had been said by *Popham*, Ch. J. in *Dingley* v. *Moor*,^d and all acts, civil and criminal, are to be charged under the authority of the first act. Thus, in the case of *Rex* v. *Morgan*,^e on an indictment for perjury, in an affidavit to hold to bail, it was laid to have been taken by virtue of the statute of 12 Geo. I., which was a temporary law for five years, and which was afterwards, and before the expiration of it, continued by the act of 5 Geo. II., with some alterations. Lord Chief Justice Hardwicke said, that when an act was continued by a subsequent act, every body was estopped to say the first act was not in force; and as the act in question was not altered in respect to bail, the offence was properly laid to have been done against the first

---

a 1 *Wm. Blacks. Rep.* 451.   7 *Wheaton*, 551.
b 2 *Inst.* 686.
c *Littleton's Rep.* 212.
d *Cro. Eliz.* 750.
e *Str.* 1066.

act. In *Shipman* v. *Henbest*,[a] the King's Bench held, that if a statute be permitted even to expire, and be afterwards revived by another statute, the law derives its force from the first statute, which is to be considered as in operation by means of the revival. If, however, a temporary act be revived after it has expired, the intermediate time is lost, without a special provision reaching to the intermediate time.

If a statute inflicts a penalty for doing an act, the penalty implies a prohibition, and the thing is unlawful, though there be no prohibitory words in the statute. Lord Holt, in *Bartlett* v. *Viner*,[b] applied this rule to the case of a statute inflicting a penalty for making a particular contract, such as a simoniacal or usurious contract; and he held, that the contract was void under the statute, though there was a penalty imposed for making it. Whether any other punishment can be inflicted than the penalty given by the statute, has been made a serious question. The Court of K. B. in *Rex* v. *Robinson*,[c] laid down this distinction, that where a statute created a new offence, by making unlawful what was lawful before, and prescribed a particular sanction, it must be pursued, and none other; but where the offence was punishable at common law, and the statute prescribed a particular remedy, the sanction was cumulative, and did not take away the common law punishment, and either remedy might be pursued. The same distinction had been declared long before;[d] and the proper inquiry in such cases is, was the doing of the thing, for which the penalty is inflicted, lawful or unlawful before the passing of the statute. If it was no offence before, the party offending is liable to the penalty, and to nothing else.

---

a 4 *Term*, 109.
b *Carth.* 251. *Skinner*, 322.
c 2 *Burr.* 799.
d Castle's case, *Cro. J.* 644. Regina v. Wigg, 2 *Salk.* 460.

There are a number of other rules, of perhaps minor importance, relative to the construction of statutes, and it will be sufficient to observe, generally, that the great object of the maxims of interpretation, is to discover the true intention of the law; and whenever that intention can be indubitably ascertained, and it be not a violation of constitutional right, the courts are bound to obey it, whatever may be their opinion of its wisdom or policy. But it would be quite visionary to expect, in any code of statute law, such precision of thought and perspicuity of language, as to preclude all uncertainty as to the meaning, and exempt the community from the evils of vexatious doubts and litigious interpretations. Various and discordant readings, glosses, and commentaries, will inevitably arise in the progress of time, and, perhaps, as often from the want of skill and talent in those who comment, as in those who make the law. Though the French codes, digested under the revolutionary authority, are distinguished for sententious brevity, there are numerous volumes of French reports already extant, upon doubtful and difficult questions arising within a few years after those codes were promulgated.[a]

The Emperor Justinian, in one of the edicts which he published in confirmation of the authority of the Pandects, and prefixed to that work, expressly prohibited the civilians of his time, and those of all future ages, from writing any commentary upon his laws.[b] The history of Justinian's reign shows the folly and absurdity of this attempt to bar all future innovation. Greater changes took place in a few years in the laws and jurisprudence of Justinian, said Montesquieu, than in the three hundred years of the French mo-

---

[a] The *Journal du Palais, presentant la Jurisprudence de la Cour de Cassation, et des Cours Royales, sur l'application de tous les Codes Francais aux questions douteuses et difficiles*, had amounted in 1818 to fifty volumes and upwards.

[b] *Secunda Præfatio Digestorum*, sec. 21.

narchy immediately preceding his time; and those changes were so incessant and so trifling, that the inconstancy of the emperor can only be explained by having recourse to the secret history of Procopius, where he is charged with having sold equally his judgments and his laws.[a]

---

[a] *Grandeur des Romains et leur Decadence*, c. 20.

LECTURE XXI.

OF REPORTS OF JUDICIAL DECISIONS.

Having considered the nature and force of written law, and the general rules which are applied to the interpretation of statutes; we are next to consider the character of unwritten or common law, and the evidence by which its existence is duly ascertained.

The common law includes those principles, usages, and rules of action, applicable to the government and security of person and property, which do not rest for their authority upon any express and positive declaration of the will of the legislature. According to the observation of an eminent English judge,[a] statute law is the will of the legislature in writing, and the common law is nothing but statutes worn out by time, and all the law began by consent of the legislature.

This is laying down the origin of the common law rather too strictly. A great proportion of the rules and maxims which constitute the immense code of the common law, grew into use by gradual adoption, and received, from time to time, the sanction of the courts of justice, without any legislative act or interference. It was the application of the dictates of natural justice, and of cultivated reason, to particular cases. In the just language of Sir Matthew Hale,[b] the common law of England is " not the product of the wisdom of some one man, or society of men, in any one age; but of the wisdom, counsel, experience, and ob-

---

[a] Lord Chief Justice Wilmot, 2 *Wils. Rep.* 348. 351.
[b] *Preface to Rolle's Abridgment.*

servation, of many ages of wise and observing men." And his further remarks on this subject would be well worthy the consideration of those bold projectors, who can think of striking off a perfect code of law at a single essay. "Where the subject of any law is single, the prudence of one age may go far at one essay to provide a fit law; and yet, even in the wisest provisions of that kind, experience shows us, that new and unthought of emergencies often happen, that necessarily require new supplements, abatements, or explanations. But the body of laws, that concern the common justice applicable to a great kingdom, is vast and comprehensive, consists of infinite particulars, and must meet with various emergencies, and, therefore, requires much time, and much experience, as well as much wisdom and prudence successively, to discover defects and inconveniences, and to apply apt supplements and remedies for them; and such are the common laws of England, namely, the productions of much wisdom, time, and experience."

But though the great body of the common law consists of a collection of principles to be found in the opinions of sages, or deduced from universal and immemorial usage, and receiving progressively the sanction of the courts; it is, nevertheless, true, that with us the common law, as far as it is applicable to our situation and government, has been recognized and adopted, as one entire system, by the people of this state. It was declared to be a part of the law of the land, by an express provision in the constitution of 1777, and in the amended constitution of 1821.

The best evidence of the common law is to be found in the decisions of the courts of justice, contained in the numerous volumes of reports which crowd the lawyer's library; and in the treatises and digests of learned men, which have been multiplying from the earliest periods of the English history down to the present time. The reports of judicial decisions contain the most certain evidence, and the most authoritative and precise application of the rules of the common law. Adjudged cases become precedents for future cases resting upon analogous facts, and brought within the same reason; and the diligence of counsel, and the labour of judges, are constantly required in the study of the reports, in order to understand accurately their import, and the principles they establish. But to attain a competent knowledge of the common law in all its branches, has now become a very serious undertaking, and it requires steady and lasting perseverance, in consequence of the number of books which beset and encumber the path of the student.^a The grievance is constantly growing worse, for the number of periodical law reports and treatises which issue from the English and American press, is continually increasing; and if we wish to receive assistance from the commercial systems of other nations, and to become acquainted with the principles of the Roman law, as received and adopted in continental Europe, we are in still greater danger of being confounded, and our fortitude subdued, by the immensity and variety of the labours of the civilians.^b It is necessary that the student should exercise much discretion and skill, in the selection of the books which he is to peruse. To en-

---

a The number of volumes of English reports, exclusive of reports relating to the courts of admiralty, elections, settlement cases, and Irish reports, amount at present, it is said, to 364, and to render their contents accessible, the digested indexes of the modern reports amount to 33 volumes. The text books, or treatises, amount to 184 volumes, and the digests and abridgments to 67 volumes, making, in the whole, a copious library of 648 volumes, in addition to the statute law. See *Humphreys on Real Property*, p. 163. To these we may add upwards of 200 volumes of American reports, treatises, and digests.

b M. Camus annexed to his *Lettres sur la Profession d'Avocat*, a catalogue of select books for a lawyer's library, and which he deemed the most useful to possess and understand; and that catalogue, in the edition of 1772, included near 2,000 volumes, and many of them ponderous folios, and not one of them had any thing to do with the English statute or common law. It is now a complaint in France, that the crowd of reports of decisions encumber the law libraries; and M. Dupin, in his *Jurisprudence des Arrets*, edit. 1822, alludes to the immensity of such collections, and the great abuses to which that species of jurisprudence is subject.

counter the whole mass of law publications in succession, if practicable, would be a melancholy waste or misapplication of strength and time.

Lord Bacon, in the aphorisms annexed to his treatise *De augmentis Scientiarum*, speaks of the necessity of a revision and digest of the law, in order to restore it to a sound and profitable state, whenever there has arisen a vast accumulation of volumes, throwing the system into confusion and uncertainty. The evils resulting from an indigestible heap of laws, and legal authorities, are great and manifest. They destroy the certainty of the law, and promote litigation, delay, and subtilty. The professors of the law cannot afford the expense and time necessary to collect and digest the volumes, and they are obliged to rely too much on the second-hand authority of digests—*ipse advocatus, cum tot libros perlegere et vincere non possit, compendia sectatur—glossa fortasse aliqua bona.*[a] The period anticipated by Lord Bacon seems now to have arrived. The spirit of the present age, and the cause of truth and justice, require more simplicity in the system, and that the text authorities should be reduced within manageable limits; and a new digest of the whole body of the American common law, upon the excellent model of Comyn's Digest, and executed by a like master artist, retaining what is applicable, and rejecting every thing that is obsolete and inapplicable to our institutions, would be an immense public blessing.

A solemn decision upon a point of law, arising in any given case, becomes an authority in a like case, because it is the highest evidence which we can have of the law applicable to the subject, and the judges are bound to follow that decision so long as it stands unreversed, unless it can be shown that the law was misunderstood or misapplied in that particular case. If a decision has been made upon solemn

---

[a] Bacon's *Aphorisms, De accumulatione legum nimia,* Aph. No. 53—58. *De novis digestis legum,* Aph. No. 59—64. *De scriptoribus authenticis,* Aph. No. 78.

argument and mature deliberation, the presumption is in favour of its correctness; and the community have a right to regard it as a just declaration or exposition of the law, and to regulate their actions and their contracts by it. It would therefore be extremely inconvenient to the public if precedents were not duly regarded, and pretty implicitly followed. It is by the notoriety and stability of such rules, that professional men can give safe advice to those who consult them; and people in general can venture with confidence to buy, and to trust, and to deal with each other.[a] If judicial decisions were to be lightly disregarded, we should disturb and unsettle the great landmarks of property. If, however, any solemnly adjudged case can be shown to be founded in error, it is no doubt the right and the duty of the judges who have a similar case before them, to correct the error. But when a rule has been once deliberately adopted and declared, it ought not to be disturbed, unless by a court of appeal or review, and never by the same court, except for very cogent reasons; and if the practice were otherwise, it would be leaving us in a state of perplexing uncertainty as to the law.[b] The language of Sir William Jones[c] is exceedingly forcible on this point. " No man," says he, " who is not a lawyer, would ever know how to act; and no man who is a lawyer would, in many instances, know what to advise, unless courts were bound by authority as firmly as the Pagan deities were supposed to be bound by the decrees of fate."

Throughout the whole period of the year books, from the reign of Ed. III. to that of Hen. VII., the Judges were incessantly urging the sacredness of precedents, and that a counsellor was not to be heard who spoke against them, and that they ought to judge as the ancient sages taught. If we judge against former precedents, said Ch. J. Prisot,[d] it will be a bad example to the barristers and students at law, and

---

a 16 *Johnson*, 402.
c *Jones' Essay on Bailment*, p. 46.
b 20 *Johnson*, 722.
d 33 *Hen.* VI. 41.

they will not give any credit to the books, or have any faith in them. So the Court of King's Bench observed, in the time of James I.,[a] that the point which had been often adjudged ought to rest in peace. The inviolability of precedents was thus inculcated at a period which we have been accustomed to regard as the infancy of our law, with as much zeal and decision as at any subsequent period.

But I wish not to be understood to press too strongly the doctrine of *stare decisis*, when I recollect that there are one thousand cases to be pointed out in the English and American books of reports, which have been overruled, doubted, or limited in their application. It is probable that the records of many of the courts in this country are replete with hasty and crude decisions; and such cases ought to be examined without fear, and revised without reluctance, rather than to have the character of our law impaired, and the beauty and harmony of the system destroyed by the perpetuity of error. Even a series of decisions are not always conclusive evidence of what is law; and the revision of a decision very often resolves itself into a mere question of expediency, depending upon the consideration of the importance of certainty in the rule, and the extent of property to be affected by a change of it. Lord Mansfield frequently observed, that the certainty of a rule was often of much more importance in mercantile cases than the reason of it, and that a settled rule ought to be observed for the sake of property; and yet, perhaps, no English judge ever made greater innovations and improvements in the law, or felt himself less embarrassed with the disposition of the elder cases when they came in his way, to impede the operation of his enlightened and cultivated judgment. His successor, Lord Kenyon, acted like a Roman dictator, appointed to recall and reinvigorate the ancient discipline. He controlled or overruled several very important decisions of Lord Mansfield, as dangerous innovations, and on the ground that

---

[a] Cro. Jac. 527.

they had departed from the precedents of former times, and disturbed the land-marks of property, and had unauthorizedly superadded equity powers to a court of law. "It is my wish and my comfort," said that venerable judge, "to stand *super antiquas vias*. I cannot legislate, but by my industry I can discover what our predecessors have done, and I will tread in their footsteps." The English courts seem now to consider it to be their duty to adhere to the authority of adjudged cases, when they have been so clearly, and so often, or so long established, as to create a practical rule of property, notwithstanding they may feel the hardship, or not perceive the reasonableness of the rule. There is great weight in the maxim of Lord Bacon,[a] that *optima est lex, quo minimum relinquit arbitrio judicis; optimus judex, qui minimum sibi.* The great difficulty as to cases, consists in making an accurate application of the general principle contained in them to new cases, presenting a change of circumstances. If the analogy be imperfect, the application may be erroneous. The expressions of every judge must also be taken with reference to the case on which he decides; we must look to the principle of the decision, and not to the manner in which the case is argued upon the bench, otherwise the law will be thrown into extreme confusion.[b] The exercise of sound judgment is as necessary in the use, as diligence and learning are requisite in the pursuit, of adjudged cases.[c]

Considering the influence of manners upon law, and the force of opinion, which is silently and almost insensibly con-

---

[a] *Aphor.* 46, *Bacon's Works*, vol. 7. 448.

[b] *Best*, Ch. J. 2 *Bing.* 229.

[c] M. *Dupin*, in his *Jurisprudence des Arrets*, has given us many excellent rules and observations on the value, and on the abuse of the authority of reports of judicial decisions. He admits the force of them when correctly stated, and applied with discernment and sobriety; and that they have the force of law when there has been a series of uniform decisions on the same point, because they then become conclusive evidence of the law. The immense collection of reports by M. Merlin, in his *Repertoire*, and especially in his *Questions de Droit*, he would say, had the stamp of Papinian, if it were permitted to compare any lawyer to Papinian.

trolling the course of business and the practice of the courts, it is impossible that the fabric of our jurisprudence should not exhibit deep traces of the progress of society, as well as of the footsteps of time. The ancient reporters are going very fast not only out of use, but out of date, and almost out of recollection. The modern reports, and the latest of the modern, are the most useful, because they contain the last, and, it is to be presumed, the most correct exposition of the law, and the most judicious application of abstract and eternal principles of right to the refinements of property. They are likewise accompanied by illustrations best adapted to the inquisitive and cultivated reason of the present age. But the old reporters cannot be entirely neglected, and I shall devote the remainder of this lecture to a short historical review of the principal reporters prior to the present times. No one ought to read a book, said M. Lami,[a] (and the remark has peculiar application to law books,) unless he knows something of the author, and when he wrote, and the character of the work, and the character of the edition.

For the sake of perspicuity and convenient arrangement, we will divide the reports into two classes: those that preceded, and those that are subsequent to the year 1688. I select that period, because the distinction between the old and new law seems then to be more distinctly marked. The cumbersome and oppressive appendages of the feudal tenures were abolished in the reign of Charles II., and the spirit of modern improvement, and of commercial policy, began then to be more sensibly felt, and more actively diffused. The appointment of that great and honest lawyer, Lord Holt, to the station of chief justice of the King's Bench, gave a new tone and impulse to the vigour of the common law. The despotism of the Stuarts was abolished for ever, and the civil and political liberties of the English nation were more explicitly acknowledged and defined at the accession of the house of Orange. The old reporters will include all the reports from the year books down to

---

a Entretiens sur les Sciences, et sur la maniere d'etudier.

that period; and we will, in the first place, bestow upon those of them which are the most distinguished, a cursory glance and rapid review.

The eldest reports extant on the English law, are the Year Books, which consist of eleven parts or volumes, written in law French, and extend from the beginning of the reign of Edward II. to the latter end of the reign of Henry VIII., a period of about two hundred years. There are a few broken cases which may be gleaned from the old abridgments, and particularly from Fitzherbert, which go back to the reign of Henry III. The Year Books were printed by subscription in 1679; but they have never been translated, and they are not worth the labour and expense either of a new edition or of translation. The substance of the Year Books was afterwards included in the great abridgments of Statham, Fitzherbert, and Brooke, and those compilations superseded in a considerable degree the use of them. The Year Books were very much occupied with discussions touching the forms of writs, and the pleadings and practice in real actions, which have gone entirely out of use. In a late case in the C. B. the judges spoke with some sharpness of reproof against going back to the Year Books in search of a precedent in the case of levying a fine.[a] The great authenticity and accuracy of the Year Books arose from the manner in which they were composed. There were four reporters appointed to that duty, and they had a yearly stipend from the crown, and they used to confer together, and the reports being settled by so many persons of approved diligence and learning, deservedly carried great credit with them.[b] But so great have been the changes since the feudal ages, in the character of property, the business of civil life, and the practice of the courts, that the great mass of curious learning and technical questions contained in the Year Books, has sunk into oblivion; and it will be no cause of regret if that learning be destined never to be reclaimed. The Year Books have now become

---

a 2 *Taunton,* 201.   *b Preface to Plowden's Reports.*

nearly obsolete, and they are valuable only to the antiquary and historian, as a faithful portrait of ancient customs and manners.^a

The Year Books ended in the reign of Henry VIII., because persons were no longer appointed to the task of reporting, with the allowance of a fixed salary. Private lawyers then undertook the business of reporting for their own use, or for the purpose of publication. Many English lawyers have regretted that the practice of appointing public reporters, with a stipulated compensation, was not continued, as it would have relieved the profession from many hasty and inaccurate reports, which have greatly increased the uncertainty of the law. The reports of Dyer relate to the reigns of Henry VIII., Edward VI., Mary, and Elizabeth. They have always been held in high estimation, for Dyer presided as chief justice of the C. B. for upwards of twenty years, and was distinguished for learning, ability and firmness. His reports were afterwards enriched by marginal notes of Chief Justice Treby, and which are said by Mr. Justice Buller[b] to be good law. The work was compiled in law French, and published in an English translation in 1793, with the notes.

Plowden's Commentaries embrace the same period as the reports of Dyer. They bear as high a reputation for accuracy as any ancient book of reports, though Lord Coke said he had discovered four cases in Plowden which were erroneous.[c] Plowden gives the pleadings in those cases in which judgment was entered; and the arguments of counsel, and the decisions upon the bench very much at large. They were first published in 1578, and taken originally, as he says, for his private use. But he took great pains in ren-

---

a In a very recent case, in 1 *Barnewall & Cresswell*, 410, the Court of King's Bench decided a case chiefly upon the authority of a citation from the Year Book of 42 Edw. III.; but such a reference is extremely rare.

b 3 *Term*, 84.

c *Bacon's Works*, vol. 6. p. 122.

dering his work accurate, and he reported nothing but what had been debated and decided upon demurrer, or special verdict; and his reports were likewise submitted to the inspection of the serjeants and judges. The work is, therefore, distinguished for its authenticity and accuracy, and though not of so dramatic a character as much of the Year Books, it is exceedingly interesting and instructive, by the evidence it affords of the extensive learning, sound doctrine, and logical skill of the ancient English bar.

Lord Coke's reports, in 13 parts or volumes, are confined to the reigns of Elizabeth and James, and deservedly stand at the head of the ancient reports, as an immense repository of common law learning. The first eleven books of his reports contain about 500 cases, and were published in his lifetime, and he took care to report and publish only what he calls leading cases, and conducive to the public quiet. Lord Bacon said, that had it not been for Sir Edward Coke's reports, the law in that age would have been almost like a ship without ballast. Much of the various and desultory learning in these reports is law to this day, and the most valuable of the cases reported, have been selected and recommended to the attention of the American student by Professor Hoffman, of the university of Maryland, in his "Course of legal study." When these reports were published, between 1600 and 1615, there were no other prior reports, but the Year Books, Dyer, and Plowden. Lord Coke said, that he endeavoured, in his reports, to avoid obscurity, ambiguity, and prolixity. It is singular that he should have so egregiously failed in his purpose. The want of methodical arrangement and lucid order, is so manifest in his reports, and he abounds so greatly in extrajudicial *dicta* and desultory learning, that he is distinguished above most other reporters, for the very defects he intended to avoid. It is often very difficult to separate the arguments of counsel from the reasons and decision of the court, and to ascertain precisely the point adjudged. This, probably, gave occasion to Ireland and Manley's Abridgment of Lord Coke's Reports, in which they undertake to detach from the work all the collateral discussion and learning, and to give only " the very substance and marrow" of the reports. A work of this kind may be convenient in the hurry of research, but I believe no accurate lawyer would ever be content to repose himself upon such a barren account of a decision, without looking into the reason and authorities on which it was founded. With all their defects, Lord Coke's Reports are a standard work of that age, and they alone are sufficient to have discharged him of that great obligation of duty with which he said he was bound to his profession. When Coke's Reports were first published, they gave much offence to King James, as containing many doctrines which were deemed too free and injurious to the prerogative of the crown; and the king commanded Lord Coke to strike out the offensive parts, and he also referred the work to his judges to be corrected.[a] But Lord Coke was too independent in spirit, and he had too high a regard to truth and law, to gratify the king on this subject; and he was, for this and other causes, removed from the office of Chief Justice of the K. B.

Hobart's Reports of cases in the time of James I. were printed in 1646, and in a subsequent age they were revised and corrected by Lord Chancellor Nottingham. Like the reports of Lord Coke, they are defective in method and precision, and are replete with copious legal discussions. Hobart was chief justice of the C. B., and a very great lawyer. Judge Jenkins, the contemporary of Coke and Hobart, has given us, in the preface to his reports, an exalted eulogy on those distinguished men, and the biographical sketch of their characters is peculiarly animated and lively. Jenkins compiled his reports, or centuries, (as he quaintly terms them,) during the tumult of the civil wars under Charles I. and the commonwealth; and they resemble more a digest of decisions after the manner of Fitzherbert and Brooke, than regular reports of adjudged cases.

---

[a] *Lord Bacon's Works*, vol. 6. 121. 128. 132. 173.

From his intemperate language and hard fate, it is evident he was a zealous royalist, and had provoked the resentment of his enemies. He composed his work, as he says, when he was "broken with old age and confinement in prison, where his fellow subjects, grown wild with rage, had detained him for fifteen years, and that he was surrounded with an odious multitude of barbarians." He renders a just tribute of veneration to the memory of Lord Coke and Lord Hobart, as two men who had furnished surprising light to the professors of the law. They were judges of great authority and dignity, who, to the most accurate eloquence, joined a superlative knowledge of the laws, and consummate integrity, and whose names, he said, would flourish as long as the laws and the kingdom should endure. Lord Hobart, as he continues to observe, was adorned with the brightest endowments, and a piercing understanding, and he had always equity before his eyes. Lord Coke was a judge whom power could not break, nor favour bend. He enjoyed the smiles and frowns of the court by turns, and possessed an immense fortune which he had honestly acquired. The only thing objected to him as a fault was, that he was thought to go too great lengths with the republican party, but he admits that he died in the highest estimation.

Croke's Reports of decisions in the courts of law in the reigns of Elizabeth, James, and Charles, are a work of credit and celebrity among the old reporters. They commence about the time that Dyer ended, and were first published under the protectorate of Cromwell. From the character of the judge, his gravity, learning, diligence, and advantages, and from the precision and brevity of his cases, these reports have sustained their character in every succeeding age, and are, to this day, familiarly referred to, as an authentic depository of the rules of the common law.

The reports of Yelverton are a small collection of select cases in the latter part of the reign of Elizabeth, and the first ten years of the reign of James. He was a judge of the C. B. and one of the most eminent lawyers of that age, and which was truly the Augustan age of the old common law learning. These reports have been lately recommended to the notice of the American lawyer, by a new edition published in this country, and enriched with copious, valuable and accurate notes, by Mr. Metcalf.

In the reign of Charles II. the most distinguished of the reports are those of Chief Justice Saunders. They are confined to decisions in the K. B. for the space of six years, between the 18th and 24th years of the reign of Charles II., and contain the pleadings and entries in the cases decided, as well as the arguments of counsel, and the judgment of the court. They are recommended for the accuracy of the entries, and the concise, clear, and pointed method of decision; and are particularly valuable to the practising lawyer, as a book of precedents as well as of decisions. They have always been esteemed the most accurate and valuable reports of that age, and this is the character which has been repeatedly given of them by the judges in modern times.[a] A new edition of these reports was published in 1799 by Serjeant Williams, with very copious notes, which, in many instances, are distinct and elaborate essays on the subjects of which they treat. Lord Eldon has said, in reference to this edition, that to any one in a judicial situation, it would be sufficiently flattering to have it said of him, that he was as good a common lawyer as Serjeant Williams, and that no man ever lived, to whom the character of a great common lawyer more properly applied. I have no doubt of the merit of the edition, and of the great learning of the editor. The authorities, new and old, applicable to the subject, are industriously collected, and methodically arranged. But with all the praise justly due to the edition, it is liable to the great objection of making one of the old reporters the vehicle of voluminous dissertations. They introduce perplexity and confusion by their number and length. If such treatises were published by themselves, the student would know better where to find them; but when

---

[a] 3 *Burr.* 1730. 2 *Bos. & Pull.* 23.

appended to a plain reporter, they seem to be out of place. Notes would appear to be more appropriate, if they were confined simply and drily to the illustration of the case in the text, and to show, by a reference to other decisions, how far it might still be regarded as an authority, and when and where it had been confirmed, or questioned, or extended, or restricted, or overruled. The convenience and economy of the profession would certainly be well consulted by this course. This edition of Saunders so far surpasses in extent and variety of learning, the original work, as to become a new work of itself, which might properly be denominated Williams' notes; and the venerable simplicity of the reporter is obscured and lost, in the commentaries of the annotator.

The reports of Chief Justice Vaughan contain some very interesting cases. He was a grave and excellent judge, and his reports consist chiefly of his own arguments and opinions, delivered while he was chief justice, and they are distinguished for great variety of learning. The reports of Sir Thomas Jones, who was also chief justice in the reign of Charles II.; of Sir Creswell Levinz, who was a judge of the C. B.; of Sir Geffrey Palmer, who was attorney general under Charles II.; of Lord Chief Justice Pollexfen, whose reports consist of cases argued by him while he was at the bar; and of Sir Wm. Jones, who was for twenty-two years a judge, are all of them works of authority, though a considerable part of the discussions and decisions which they record, ceases at this day to excite much attention, or to be very applicable to the new and varied course of human affairs. And, indeed, it may be here observed, that a very large proportion of the matter contained in the old reporters, prior to the English revolution, has become superseded, and is now cast into the shade, by the improvements of modern times; by the disuse of real actions, and of the subtleties of special pleadings; by the cultivation of maritime jurisprudence; by the growing value and variety of personal contracts; by the spirit of commerce, and the enlargement of equity jurisdiction; by the introduction of more liberal and enlightened views of justice and public policy; and, in short, by the study and influence of the civil law.

In perusing the old reports, we cannot but be struck with the long, laborious, and subtle arguments, and the great delay which accompanied the investigation of points of law. Thus, for instance, the case of *Stowell* v. *Zouch*, in Plowden, was argued twice in the C. B., and then twice in the Exchequer Chamber, before all the judges of England. *Calvin's* case, in Coke, was argued first at the bar of the K. B. by counsel, then in the Exchequer Chamber, first by counsel, and then by all the judges. It was afterwards argued by counsel at two different times, and then by all the judges at the next term, upon four different days; and at another term thereafter by all the judges on four different days. So again, in *Manby & Richards* v. *Scott*, in Levinz, the case was argued at the bar three several times, by distinct counsel each time, and afterwards by all the judges at the bench. It was quite common in former times to have a case spoken to at two, and three, and four several times, and each time at a different term, before judgment was rendered. Indeed, so late as the time of Willes' reports, in the reign of George II. we find a case which was argued five times, and at five distinct terms, and the judgment was not rendered until the space of five years had elapsed from the first argument. It was not until the time of Lord Mansfield that such repeated arguments were disused, and great despatch and unexampled facility and vigour given to the administration of justice. There were some advantages attending these repeated discussions, which served as a compensation for the delay and expense attending them. They tended to dissipate shadows and doubts, and to unite the opinions on the bench, and prevent that constant division among the judges which has much weakened the authority of some of our American courts.

From the era of the English revolution, the reports increase in value and importance; and they deal more in points of law applicable to the great changes in property, and the commerce and business of the present times. I shall not undertake to speak critically of the particular merits of the modern reports, for this would lead me into too extensive details. Those of Lord Raymond and Serjeant Salkeld embrace the reigns of William and Mary, and Queen Anne; and during that period Lord Chief Justice Holt gave lustre to the jurisprudence of his country. The reports of Sir John Strange, of Lord Chief Baron Comyns, of Lord Chief Justice Willes, and part of the reports of Serjeant Wilson, occupy the reigns of George I. and II.; and they are all respectable, and the reports of Willes and Wilson, in particular, very accurate repositories of the judicial decisions of those reigns. The reports of Lord Raymond and of Serjeant Wilson are also peculiarly valuable to the pleader for the many useful entries and forms of pleadings which accompany the cases. From that period, the English reports are to be read and studied with profound attention. The reports of Burrow, Cowper, and Douglass, contain the substance of Lord Mansfield's judicial decisions, and they are among the most interesting reports in the English law. All the courts of law at Westminster have been filled with very eminent men since the time of the accession of George III.; and we need only refer to the Term Reports, and to East and his successors, as reporters to the King's Bench, and to Wilson, Henry Blackstone, Bosanquet & Puller, Taunton, and their successors in the C. B., for views and sketches of the English law in its most correct and cultivated state.

A still deeper interest must be felt by the American lawyer in the perusal of the judicial decisions of his own country. Our American reports contain an exposition of the common law, as received and modified in reference to the genius of our institutions. By that law we are governed and protected, and it cannot but awaken a correspondent attachment. But I need not undertake the invidious task of selection and discrimination among the numerous volumes of the reports of American decisions. Their relative character must be familiar to the profession, and it will be sufficient to advise the student to examine thoroughly, and to obtain the mastery of the principles of law, as expounded and declared by our more important tribunals, whether they be of federal or of state jurisdiction.

We have hitherto confined our attention to the reports of cases in the courts of common law. But the system of equity is equally to be found embodied in the reports of adjudged cases; and the maxims of the Court of Chancery are as fixed as those which govern other tribunals. That court is as much bound as a court of law, by a series of decisions applicable to the case, and establishing a rule. It has no discretionary power over principles and established precedents, and Chancery has grown to be a jurisdiction of so much strict technical rule, that it is said by a distinguished writer on equity doctrines, that there are now many settled rules of equity which require to be moderated by the rules of good conscience, as much as the most rigorous rules of law did before the chancellors interfered on equitable grounds.[a] A court of equity becomes in the lapse of time, by gradual and almost imperceptible degrees, a court of strict technical jurisprudence, like a court of law. The binding nature of precedents in a court of equity was felt and acknowledged by Lord Keeper Bridgman, in the reign of Charles II.;[b] and in the case of *The Earl of Montague* v. *Lord Bath*,[c] soon after the revolution, Lord Chief Justice Treby, who sat for the Lord Chancellor, declared, that the Court of Chancery was limited by the precedents and practice of former times, and that it was dangerous to extend its authority further. At this day, justice is administered in a court of equity upon as fixed and certain principles as in a court of law; and Lord Eldon has secured to himself a title to the reverence of his countrymen, for resisting the temptation so often pressed upon him, to make principles and precedents bend to the hardship of a particular case. In

---

a *Sugden's Letters to a Man of Property*, p. 4.
b 1 *Mod.* 307.
c 3 *Ch. Cas.* 95.

this country it is at least as important as in any other, that the administration of justice, both legal and equitable, should be stable and uniform; and especially if there be any weight in the opinion of an ancient English lawyer, that " variety of judgments, and novelty of opinions, were the two plagues of a commonwealth."[a]

We have no reports of chancery decisions until subsequent to the time of Lord Bacon. Anciently, the Court of Chancery administered justice according to what appeared to be the dictate of conscience as applied to the case, without any regard to law or rule; and great inconvenience and mischief must have been produced in the infancy of the court, by reason of the uncertainty and inconsistency of its decisions, flowing from the want of settled principles. The jurisdiction of the court was greatly enlarged in the time of cardinal Wolsey, who was chancellor under Henry VIII.; and he maintained his equitable jurisdiction with a high hand, and exercised his authority over every thing which could be a subject of judicial inquiry, and decided with very little regard to the common law. There was an extraordinary influx of business during his administration. This conduct in his judicial capacity was one of the grounds of accusation against him when he was impeached. Under his successor, Sir Thomas More, who was the first chancellor that ever had the requisite legal education, business rose again with rapidity, and to such extent as to require the assistance of a master of the rolls. He allowed injunctions so freely as to displease the common law judges, though he acted always with great ability and integrity.[b] To show how wonderfully business in chancery had increased by the time of Lord Bacon, we need only recur to the fact which he gives us himself,[c] that he made two thousand orders and decrees in a year; and yet we have not a single decision of his reported.

---

[a] *Pref. to Jenkins' Centuries.*
[b] *Reeves' History of the English Law,* vol. 4. p. 368—377.
[c] *Bacon's Works,* vol. 4. p. 530.

Those decisions, if well and faithfully reported, would doubtless have presented to the world a clear illustration and masterly display of many principles of equity since greatly considered and discussed; for even upon dry technical rules and points of law, he shed the illuminations of his mighty mind.

In West's Symboleography, a work published at the close of Elizabeth's reign, we have divers curious and authentic precedents of the process, and bills, and answers in chancery, prior to the time of Bacon. We have also, in the same work, a brief digest of the powers and jurisdiction of the court, from which it would appear, that equity was regarded in that day as a matter of arbitrary conscience, unencumbered by any rules or principles of law. No cases are cited to show what the authority was, but such as were gleaned from the Year Books, and the treatises of the Doctor and Student, and of the Diversity of Courts. It was not until after the restoration, that any report of adjudged cases in chancery were published. The volumes, entitled, " Reports of Cases taken and adjudged in the Court of Chancery in the reign of Charles I., Charles II., James II., William III., and Queen Anne," commence with the reign of Charles I., and contain the earliest adjudged cases in equity. But that work, and another contemporary work of the same character, entitled " Cases argued and adjudged in the High Court of Chancery," are both of them, in their general character, loose, meagre and inaccurate reports, of not much weight or authority. But the report of some cases decided by Lord Chancellor Cowper, in the third and last volume of the Reports in Chancery, and the great case of *the Duke of Norfolk*, and the case of *Bath and Montague*, at the conclusion of the Cases in Chancery, are distinguished exceptions to this complaint, and those great cases are fully and very interestingly reported. In the latter part of the reign of Charles II., Lord Chancellor Nottingham raised the character of the court to high reputation, and established both its jurisprudence and its jurisdiction upon wide and rational foundations. But we have but few reports of his decisions that are worthy of his fame. They are dispersed through several works of inferior authority. It is from his time, however, that equity became a regular and cultivated science, and the judicial decisions in chancery are to be carefully studied.

Vernon's Reports are the best of the old reports in chancery. They were published from his manuscripts, after his death, by order of Chancellor King, and were found to be quite imperfect and inaccurate. In 1806, Mr. Raithby favoured the profession with a new and excellent edition of Vernon, enriched by learned notes, and accurate extracts from the register's books, so that the volumes assumed a new dress and more unquestionable authenticity. Those reports include part of the judicial administration of Lord Nottingham, and the whole of the time of Lord Somers; but they give us nothing equal to the reputation of those great men. They bring the series of equity decisions down to the conclusion of Lord Chancellor Cowper's judicial life.

Precedents in Chancery is a collection of cases between 1689 and 1722; and the author of those reports, and of the first volume of Equity Cases Abridged, is generally supposed to be the same person. They are works which contain very brief cases in comparison with the voluminous details of modern reports; but they are of respectable authority.[a] Peere Williams' Reports extend from the beginning of the last century to the year 1735, and they embrace the period of the decisions of a succession of eminent men who presided in chancery in the former part of the last century. The notes of Mr. Cox to the fourth edition of these reports, gave to that edition the character of being the best edited book on the law. Even before his learning and industry had given new character and value to the reports of Peere Williams, they were regarded as one of the most perspicuous, useful and interesting repositories of equity law to be found in the language.

---

[a] 1 *Vesey*, J. 547. 3 *Vesey*, 285. 5 *Vesey*, 664.

Moseley's reports of cases during the time of Lord King, have received a various and contradictory character and treatment. Lord Mansfield said it was a book not to be quoted; but Lord Eldon, who is presumed to have been a better judge of the merits of the work, says, that Moseley is a book of considerable accuracy.[a] It is fortunate that we have even so imperfect a view of the decisions of Lord King, who was an eminent scholar, and to whom Mr. Locke bequeathed his papers and library.

Lord Talbot presided in chancery but a very few years. He was a pure and exalted character who died in the vigour of his age, and his loss was lamented as a great national calamity. The cases during his time, under the title of *Cases tempore Talbot*, are well reported, and have a reputation for accuracy.

Lord Hardwicke, the successor of Lord Talbot, held the great seal for upwards of twenty years, and the present wise and rational system of English equity jurisprudence, owes more to him than perhaps to any of his predecessors. His decisions are reported in the elder Vesey, and Atkyns, and partly in Ambler, and Dickens; and though none of them are eminent reporters, either for accuracy or precision in the statements of the cases, or in giving the judgment of the court,[b] yet the value of his opinions, and the great extent of his learning, and the solidity of his judgment, have been sufficiently perceived and understood. There is no judge in the juridical annals of England, whose judicial character has received greater and more constant homage. His knowledge of the law, said a very competent judge, was most extraordinary, and he was a consummate master of the profession.[c] His decisions at this day, and in our own courts, do undoubtedly carry with them a more command-

---

[a] 3 *Anst.* 861. 5 *Burr.* 2629. 1 *Merivale*, 92.

[b] *Buller. J. in* 6 *East*, 29. n. Sir J. *Mansfield, in* 5 *Taunton*, 64. 4 *Vesey*, 188. n. *Pref. to Eden's Reports.* 1 *Sch. & Lef.* 240.

[c] Lord Kenyon, 7 *Term*, 416.

ing weight of authority than those of any other judge; and the best editions of the elder Vesey and Atkyns will continue to fix the attention and study of succeeding ages.

Eden's Reports of the decisions of Lord Northington, the successor to Lord Hardwicke, are very authentic, and highly esteemed. They surpass in accuracy the reports either of Ambler or Dickens within the same period, and the authority of Lord Northington is very great, and it arose from the uncommon vigour and clearness of his understanding. The next book of reports of deserved celebrity is Brown, commencing with Lord Thurlow's appointment to the office of chancellor; and the high character of the court at that period, gave to those reports a very extensive authority and circulation, and for which they were indebted more to the reputation of the chancellor, than to any merit in the execution of the work. Cox's Cases in Chancery give us the decisions of Lord Kenyon while he was master of the rolls under Thurlow, as well as the decisions of the lord chancellor during the same period. They were intended as a supplement to the reports of Brown and the younger Vesey, so far as those reports covered the period embraced by these cases, and they are neat, brief, and perspicuous reports of unquestionable accuracy. A new and greatly improved edition has lately been published in New-York under the superintendance of one of the masters in chancery.

The reports of the younger Vesey extend over a large space of time, and contain the researches of Sir Richard Pepper Arden as master of the rolls, and the whole of the decisions of Lord Loughborough, and carry us far into the time of Lord Eldon. These reports are distinguished for their copiousness and fidelity. The same character is due to the reports of his successors; and though great complaints have been made at the delay of causes, arising from the cautious and doubting mind of the present venerable lord chancellor of England, it seems to be universally conceded, that he bestows extraordinary diligence in the investigation of immense details of business, and arrives in the end at a correct conclusion, and displays a most comprehensive and familiar acquaintance with equity principles. It must, nevertheless, be admitted, that the reports of Lord Eldon's administration in equity, amounting to perhaps thirty volumes, and replete with attenuated discussion, and loose suggestions of doubts and difficulties, are enough to task very severely the patience of the profession.

There are recent reports of decisions in other departments of equity, which are deserving of great attention. The character of those branches of the equity jurisdiction, is eminently sustained; and the reported decisions of Lord Redesdale and Lord Manners, in the Irish Court of Chancery, are also to be placed on a level, in point of authority, with the best productions of the English bench.

Upon our American equity reports, I have only to observe, that being decisions in cases arising under our domestic laws and systems, they cannot but excite a stronger interest in the mind of the student; and from their more entire application to our circumstances, they will carry with them the greater authority.

I have now finished a succinct detail of the principal reporters; and when the student has been thoroughly initiated in the elements of legal science, I would strongly recommend them to his notice. The old cases prior to the year 1688, need only be occasionally consulted, and the leading decisions in them examined. Some of them, however, are to be deeply explored and studied, and particularly those cases and decisions which have spread their influence far and wide, and established principles which lie at the foundations of English jurisprudence. Such cases have stood the scrutiny of contemporary judges, and been illustrated by succeeding artists, and are destined to guide and control the most distant posterity. The reports of cases since the middle of the last century, ought, in most instances, to be read in course, and they will conduct the student over an immense field of forensic discussion. They contain that great body of the commercial law, and of the law of contracts, and of trusts, which governs at this day. They are worthy of being studied even by scholars of taste and general literature, as being authentic memorials of the business and manners of the age in which they were composed. Law reports are dramatic in their plan and structure. They abound in pathetic incident, and displays of deep feeling. They are faithful records of those " little competitions, factions, and debates of mankind," that fill up the principal drama of human life; and which are engendered by the love of power, the appetite for wealth, the allurements of pleasure, the delusions of self-interest, the melancholy perversion of talent, and the machinations of fraud. They give us the skilful debates at the bar, and the elaborate opinions on the bench, delivered with the authority of oracular wisdom. They become deeply interesting, because they contain true portraits of the talents and learning of the sages of the law. We should have known but very little of the great mind and varied accomplishments of Lord Mansfield, if we had not been possessed of the faithful reports of his decisions. It is there that his title to the character of " founder of the commercial law of England," is verified. A like value may be attributed to the reports of the decisions of Holt, Hardwicke, Willes, Wilmot, De Grey, Camden, Thurlow, Kenyon, Sir William Scott, and many other illustrious names, which will be as immortal as the English law.

Nor is it to be overlooked as a matter of minor importance, that the judicial tribunals have been almost uniformly distinguished for their immaculate purity. Every person well acquainted with the contents of the English reports, must have been struck with the unbending integrity and lofty morals with which the courts were inspired. I do not know where we could resort, among all the volumes of human composition, to find more constant, more tranquil, and more sublime manifestations of the intrepidity of conscious rectitude. If we were to go back to the iron times of the Tudors, and follow judicial history down from the first page in Dyer to the last page of the last reporter, we should find the higher courts of civil judicature, generally, and with rare exceptions, presenting the image of the sanctity of a temple, where truth and justice seem to be enthroned and to be personified in their decrees.

LECTURE XXII.

OF THE PRINCIPAL PUBLICATIONS ON THE COMMON LAW.

The reports of adjudged cases are admitted to contain the highest and most authentic evidence of the principles and rules of the common law; but there are numerous other works of sages in the profession which contribute very essentially to facilitate the researches, and abridge the labour of the student. Those works acquire by time and their intrinsic value, the weight of authority; and the earlier text books are cited and relied upon as such, in the discussions at the bar and upon the bench, in cases where judicial authority is wanting.

One of the eldest of these treatises is Glanville's *Tractatus de Legibus Angliæ*, composed in the reign of Henry II. It is a plain, dry, perspicuous essay on the ancient actions, and the forms of writs then in use. It has become almost obsolete and useless for any practical purpose, owing to the disuse of the ancient actions; but it is a curious monument of the improved state of the Norman administration of justice. It is peculiarly venerable, if it be, as it is said, the most ancient book extant upon the laws and customs of England. It has been cited and commented upon by Lord Coke, Sir Matthew Hale, Sir Henry Spelman, Selden, Blackstone, and most of the eminent lawyers and antiquaries of the two last centuries. Mr. Reeves says, that he incorporated the whole of Glanville into his history of the English law.

Bracton wrote his treatise *De Legibus et Consuetudinibus Angliæ*, in the reign of Henry III., and he is said to have been a judge itinerant in that reign, and professor of law at

Oxford. He is a classical writer, and has been called by a perfect judge of his merits,[a] the father of the English law, and the great ornament of the age in which he lived. His work is a systematic performance, giving a complete view of the law in all its titles, as it stood at the time it was written; and it is filled with a copious and accurate detail of legal learning. It treats of the several ways of acquiring, maintaining, and recovering property, much in the manner of the institutes of Justinian. The style is clear and expressive, and sometimes polished; and it has been imputed to the influence of the civil and cannon law, which he had studied and admired; and the work evinces, by the freedom of the quotations, that he had drank deep at those fountains.

Sir William Jones says, he is certainly the best of our juridical classics, though he is perfectly aware that Bracton copied Justinian almost word for word. In the reign of Edward I. Bracton was reduced into a compendium by Thornton, which shows, says Selden,[b] how great the authority of Bracton was in the time of Edward I. He continued to be the repository of ancient English jurisprudence, and the principal source of legal authority, down to the time of the publication of the institutes of Lord Coke.

Staunforde, in his Pleas of the Crown, published about the time of Philip and Mary, bears strong testimony to the merits and to the authority of Bracton. It is stated in Plowden,[c] that neither Glanville nor Bracton were to be cited as authorities, but rather as ornaments to the discourse, and in several other books the same thing was said.[d] But Mr. Reeve, in his history of the English law,[e] justly vindicates the character of Bracton from such unmerited aspersion; and what is as much, and perhaps more to the purpose, the

---

[a] 4 *Reeve's History of the English Law*, 570.
[b] *Dissertation annexed to Fleta*, ch. 2. s. 1.
[c] P. 357, 358.
[d] 1 Show. 118.   11 St. Tri. 148.
[e] Vol. 4. p. 570, 571.

learned Selden, whose knowledge of English legal antiquities was unrivalled, declares, that this notion is founded in error. Glanville and Bracton are authors of great service to all who apply themselves to the study of the law, and are desirous of knowing its origin and progress from the very foundation.[a] They contain numberless things, said Selden, which in his day either remained entire, or were only partially abrogated; and they contain such information on ancient customs and laws, as to carry with them authority, as well as illustration. Lord Holt, in the great case of *Coggs v. Bernard*, made free use of Bracton, and spoke of him as an old author, but one full of reason and good sense.

Britton and Fleta, two treatises in the reign of Edw. I. were nothing more than appendages to Bracton, and from which they drew largely. The dissertation which Selden annexed to the edition of Fleta, printed in his time, is evidence of the high estimation in which the work was then held; and it is a little singular that President Henault, in his chronological abridgment of the History of France,[b] should refer to this ancient English treatise of Fleta as an historical authority.

Sir John Fortescue's treatise *De Laudibus Legum Angliæ*, was written in the reign of Henry VI. under whom he was chief justice, and afterwards chancellor. It is in the form of a dialogue between him and the young prince, and he undertakes to show, that the common law was the most reasonable, and the most ancient in Europe, and superior to the civil law. It displays sentiments of liberty, and a sense of a limited monarchy, remarkable in the fierce and barbarous period of the Lancastrian civil wars, and an air of probity and piety runs through the work. He insisted, for instance, that the conviction of criminals by juries, and without torture, was much more just and humane than the method of the continental nations; and that the privilege of

---

[a] *Selden's Dissertation*, ch. 1. sec. 8.
[b] Tom. 1. p. 258.

challenging jurors, and of bringing writs of attaint upon corrupt verdicts, and the usual wealth of jurors, afforded that security to the lives and property of English subjects, which no other country was capable of affording. He run a parallel, in many instances, between the common and the civil law, in order to show the superior equity of the former, and that the proceedings in courts of justice were not so dilatory as in other nations. Though some of the instances of that superiority which he adduces, such as the illegitimacy of ante-nuptial children, and the doctrine of feudal wardships, are of no consequence, yet the security of trial by jury, and the security of life and property by means of the mixed government of England, and the limitations of the royal prerogative, were solid and pre-eminent marks of superiority.

This interesting work of Fortescue has been translated from the Latin into English, and illustrated with the notes of the learned Selden; and it was strongly recommended, in a subsequent age, by such writers as Sir Walter Raleigh, and St. Germain. And while upon this author, we cannot but pause and admire a system of jurisprudence, which, in so uncultivated a period of society, contained such singular and invaluable provisions in favour of life, liberty, and property, as those to which Fortescue referred. They were unprecedented in all Greek and Roman antiquity, and being preserved in some tolerable degree of freshness and vigour, amidst the profound ignorance and licentious spirit of the feudal ages, they justly entitle the common law to a share of that constant and vivid eulogy which the English lawyers have always liberally bestowed upon their municipal institutions.

Littleton's Book of Tenures was composed in the reign of Edward IV. and it is confined entirely to the doctrines of the old English law, concerning the tenure of real estates, and the incidents and services relating thereto. In the first book, Littleton treats of the quantity of interest in estates, under the heads of fee simple, fee tail, tenant in dower, tenant by the curtesy, tenant for life, for years, and at will.

In the second book he treats of the several tenures and services by which lands were then held, such as homage, fealty, villenage, and knight service. In the third book he treats of divers subjects relative to estates, and their tenures, under the heads of parceners, joint-tenants, estates on condition, releases, warranty, &c. He explained the learning of that period on the subject of tenures and estates, with a felicity of arrangement, and perspicuity and precision of style, that placed him above all other writers on the law. No one ever attained a more decided and permanent reputation for accuracy and authority. Lord Coke says,[a] that Littleton's Tenures was the most perfect and absolute work, and as free from error as any book that ever was written on any human science. He said, he had known many of his cases drawn in question, but never could find any judgment given against any of them, which could not be affirmed of any other book in our law. The great excellence of Littleton is his full knowledge of the subject, and the neatness and simplicity of his manner. He cites but very few cases, but he holds no opinion, says his great commentator, but what is supported by authority and reason. A great part of Littleton is not now law, or is entirely obsolete with us; and particularly much of the matter in the chapters on estates in fee tail, copyholds, feudal services, discontinuance, attornment. remitter, confirmation, and warranty. But, even at this day, what remains concerning tenures, cannot be well understood without a general knowledge of what is abolished; and even the obsolete parts of Littleton can be studied with pleasure and profit, by all who are desirous to trace the history and grounds of the law. It has been supposed by Mr. Butler, that Littleton's treatise would still be a proper introduction to the institutes of the English law on the subject of real estates.

Perkins' Treatise of the Laws of England, written in the reign of Henry VIII. has always been deemed a valuable

---

[a] *Preface to Coke's Littleton.*

book for the learning and ingenuity displayed in it relating to the title and conveyance of real property. Coke said it was wittily and learnedly composed; and Lord Mansfield held it to be a good authority in point of law. So great was its popularity with the profession, that it had gone through thirteen editions when it was translated from the law French into English in 1757. It treats of grants, deeds, feoffments, exchange, dower, curtesy, devises, surrenders, reservations, and conditions; and it abounds with citations, and supports the positions laid down by a reference to the Year Books, or Fitzherbert's Abridgment.

The Dialogue between a Doctor of Divinity and a Student in Law, was also written in the reign of Henry VIII., and discusses in a popular manner many principles and points of the common law. The seventeenth edition of this work was published in 1787, and dedicated to the younger students and professors of law. It has always been considered by the courts, and the best of the juridical writers, as a book of merit and authority. The form of writing by dialogue was much in use among the ancients, and some of the finest treatises of the Greeks and Romans were written in that form, and particularly the remains of the Socratic school in the writings of Xenophon and Plato, and the rhetorical and philosophical treatises of Cicero. The three most interesting productions, in the form of dialogue, on the English law, are Fortescue, already mentioned, this work of St. Germain, and the elegant and classical work entitled Eunomus, or Dialogues concerning the Law and Constitution of England, by Mr. Wynne.

But the legal productions of the preceding ages were all surpassed in value and extent in the reigns of Elizabeth and James, by the results of the splendid talents and immense erudition of Bacon and Coke. The writings of Lord Bacon on the municipal law of England are not to be compared in reputation to his productions in metaphysical and moral science; but it is, nevertheless, true, that he shed light and learning, and left the impression of profound and original thought on every subject which he touched. It was the course of his life to connect law with other studies, and, therefore, he admitted, that his arguments might have the more variety, and perhaps the greater depth of reason. His principal law tracts are, his Elements of the Common Law, containing an illustration of the most important maxims of the common law, and of the use of the law in its application to the protection of person, property and character, and his Reading upon the Statute of Uses. Lord Bacon seems to have disdained to cite authorities in his law treatises; and in that respect he approved of the method of Littleton and Fitzherbert, and condemned that of Perkins and Staunford.ᵃ He admits, however, that in his own private copy, he had all his authorities quoted, and that he did sometimes " weigh down authorities by evidence of reason;" and that he intended rather to correct the law than sooth received error, or endeavour to reconcile contradictions by unprofitable subtlety. He made a proposal to King James for a digest of the whole body of the common and statute law of England; and if he had been encouraged and enabled to employ the resources of his great mind on such a noble work, he would have done infinite service to mankind, and have settled in his favour the question, which he said would be made with posterity, whether he or Coke was the greater lawyer. The writings of Lord Bacon are distinguished for the perspicuity and simplicity with which every subject is treated.

Lord Coke's Institutes have had a most extensive and permanent influence on the common law of England. The first volume is a commentary upon Littleton's Tenures; and notwithstanding the magnitude of the work, it has reached seventeen editions. Many of the doctrines which his writings explain and illustrate, have become obsolete, or have been swept away by the current of events. The influence of two centuries must inevitably work a great revolution in the laws and usages, as well as in the manners and taste of a na-

---

a Preface to his Law Tracts.

tion. Perhaps every thing useful in the institutes of Coke may be found more methodically arranged, and more interestingly taught, in the modern compilations and digests; yet his authority on all subjects connected with the ancient law, is too great and too venerable to be neglected. The writings of Coke, as Buller has observed,[a] stand between and connect the ancient and the modern law—the old and the new jurisprudence. He explains the ancient system of law as it stood in his day, and he points out the leading circumstances of the innovation which was begun. We have in his works the beginning of the disuse of real actions; the tendency of the nation to abolish the military tenures; the rise of a system of equity jurisdiction; and the outlines of every point of modern law.

The second part of the Institutes of Coke is a commentary upon the ancient statutes, beginning with magna charta, and proceeding down to the reign of Henry VIII.; and his commentaries upon the ancient statutes consisted, as he himself declared, of the authentic resolutions of the courts of justice, and were not like the glosses of the civilians upon the text of the civil law, which contain so many diversities of opinion as to increase rather than to resolve doubts and uncertainties. His commentary upon magna charta, and particularly on the celebrated 29th chapter, is deeply interesting to the lawyers of the present age, as well from the value and dignity of the text, as the spirit of justice and of civil liberty which pervades and animates the work. In this respect, Lord Coke eclipses his contemporary and great rival Lord Bacon, who was as inferior to Coke in a just sense and manly vindication of the freedom and privileges of the subject, as he was superior in general science and philosophy. Lord Coke, in a very advanced age, took a principal share in proposing and framing the celebrated *Petition of Right*, containing a parliamentary sanction of those consti-

---

[a] *Pref. to Co. Litt.*

tutional limitations upon the royal prerogative, which were deemed essential to the liberties of the nation.

The third and fourth parts of the Institutes treat of high treason and the other pleas of the crown, and the history and antiquities of the English courts. The harshness and severity of the ancient criminal code of England is but ill suited to the taste and moral sense of the present age; and those parts of the institutes are of very inconsiderable value and use, except it be to enlighten the researches of the legal antiquary. In this respect, Coke's Pleas of the Crown are inferior to the work under that title by Staunforde, who wrote in the age of Philip and Mary, and was the earliest writer who treated didactically on that subject. Staunforde wrote in law French; but Lord Coke, more wisely and benevolently, wrote in English, because, he said, the matter of which he treated concerned all the subjects of the realm.

Before we quit the period of the old law, we must not omit to notice the grand abridgments of Statham, Fitzherbert, and Brooke. Statham was a baron of the Exchequer in the time of Edward IV. His abridgment of the law was a digest of most titles of the law, and comprising under each head adjudged cases from the Year Books, given in a concise manner. The cases were strung together without regard to connexion of matter. It is doubtful whether it was printed before or after Fitzherbert's work, but the latter entirely superseded it. Fitzherbert was published in the reign of Henry VIII. and came out in 1514, and was a work for that period of singular learning and utility. Brooke was published in 1573, and in a great degree superseded the others. These two last abridgments contain the substance of the Year Books regularly digested; and by the form and order which they gave to the rude materials before them, and the great facility which they afforded to the acquisition of knowledge, they must have contributed very greatly and rapidly to the improvement of legal science. Even those exceedingly laborious abridgments were in their turn to be superseded by the abridgments of Rolle, and his successors. Dr. Cowell, who was contemporary with Coke, published in Latin an Institute of the Laws of England, after the manner of Justinian's Institutes. His work was founded upon the old feudal tenures, such as the law of wards and liveries, tenures *in capite*, and knight service. While the writings of Lord Coke have descended with fame and honour to posterity, it was the fate of the learned labours of Dr. Cowell, to pass unheeded and unknown, into irreclaimable oblivion. And, with respect to all the preceding periods, Reeves' History of the English Law contains the best account that we have of the progress of the law, from the time of the Saxons to the reign of Elizabeth. It covers the whole ground of the law included in the old abridgments, and it is a work deserving of the highest commendation. I am at a loss which most to admire, the full and accurate learning which it contains, or the neat, perspicuous, and sometimes elegant style in which that learning is conveyed.

The treatise of Sir Henry Finch, being a discourse in four books on the maxims and positive grounds of the law, was first published in French in 1613, and we have the authority of Sir William Blackstone for saying, that his method was greatly superior to all the treatises that were then extant. His text was weighty, concise, and nervous, and his illustrations apposite, clear, and authentic. But the abolition of the feudal tenures, and the disuse of real actions, have rendered half of his work obsolete.

Shepherd's Touchstone of Common Assurances was the production of Mr. Justice Doddridge in the reign of James I. It is a work of great value and authority, touching the common law modes of conveyance, and those derived from the statute of uses. It treats also copiously of the law of uses and devises; but the great defect of the book is the want of that lucid order and perspicuous method which are essential to the cheerful perusal and ready perception of the merits of such a work. The second volume of *Collectanea Juridica* has an analysis of the theory and practice of conveyancing, which is only a compendious abridgment of the Touchstone; and there is a very improved edition of it by Mr. Preston, who has favoured the profession with several excellent tracts on the law of real property.

Rolle's Abridgment of the Law was published soon after the restoration, with an interesting preface by Sir Matthew Hale. It brings down the law to the end of the reign of Charles I., and though it be an excellent work, and, in point of method, succinctness, and legal precision, a model of a good abridgment, Sir Matthew Hale considered it an unequal monument of the fame of Rolle, and that it fell short of what might have been expected from his abilities and great merit. It is also deemed, by Mr. Hargrave, a great defect in Viner's very extensive abridgment, that he should have attempted to engraft it on such a narrow foundation as that of Rolle's work. Rolle was chief justice of England under the protectorate of Cromwell, and under the preceding commonwealth; but as his abridgment was printed in the reign of Charles II. he has no other title annexed to his name than that of Serjeant Rolle, and his republican dignity was not recognised.

Since the period of the English revolution, the new digests have superseded the use of the former ones; and Bacon, Viner, Comyns, and Cruise, contain such a vast accession of modern law learning, that their predecessors have fallen into oblivion. Viner's abridgment, with all its defects and inaccuracies, is a convenient part of every lawyer's library. We obtain by it an easy and prompt access to the learning of the Year Books, and the old abridgments, and the work is enriched with many reports of adjudged cases not to be found elsewhere; but, after all that can be said in its favour, it is an enormous mass of crude undigested matter, and not worth the labour of the compilation. The digest of Lord Chief Baron Comyns is a production of a vastly higher order and reputation, and it is the best digest extant upon the entire body of the English law. Lord Kenyon held his opinion alone to be of great authority, for he was considered by his contemporaries as the most able lawyer in Westminster Hall.[a] The

---

[a] 3 *Term*, 64. 631.

title Pleader has often been considered as the most elaborate and useful head of the work, but the whole is distinguished for the variety of the matter, its lucid order, the precision and brevity of the expression, and the accuracy and felicity of the execution. Bacon's Abridgment was composed chiefly from materials left by Lord Chief Baron Gilbert. It has more of the character of an elementary work than Comyns' Digest. The first edition appeared in 1736, and was much admired, and the abridgment has maintained its great influence down to the present time, as being a very convenient and valuable collection of principles, arising under the various titles in the immense system of the English law. And in connexion with this branch of the subject, it will be most convenient, though a little out of the order of time, to take notice of Cruise's recent and very valuable Digest of the Laws of England respecting real property. It is by far the most perfect elementary work of the kind, which we have on the doctrine of real property, and it is distinguished for its methodical, accurate, perspicuous, and comprehensive view of the subject. All his principles are supported and illustrated by the most judicious selection of adjudged cases. They are arranged with great skill, and applied in confirmation of his doctrines with the utmost pertinency and force.

The various treatises of Lord Chief Baron Gilbert are of high value and character, and they contributed much to advance the science of law in the former part of the last century. His treatise on Tenures deserves particular notice, as having explained upon feudal principles several of the leading doctrines in Littleton and Coke; and it is a very elementary and instructive essay upon that abstruse branch of learning. His essay on the Law of Evidence is an excellent performance, and the groundwork of all the subsequent collections on that subject, and it still maintains its character, notwithstanding the law of evidence, like most other branches of the law, and particularly the law of commercial contracts, has expanded with the progress and the exigencies of society. His treatise on the Law of Uses and Trusts is another work of high authority, and it has been rendered peculiarly valuable by the revision and copious notes of Mr. Sugden.

The treatises on the Pleas of the Crown, by Sir Matthew Hale and Sergeant Hawkins, appeared early in the last century, and they contributed to give precision and certainty to that most deeply interesting part of jurisprudence. They are both of them works of great authority, and have had great sanction, and been uniformly and strongly recommended to the profession. Sir Martin Wright's Introduction to the Law of Tenures is an excellent work, and the value of it cannot be better recommended than by the fact, that Sir William Blackstone has interwoven the substance of that treatise into the second volume of his commentaries. Dr. Wood published in 1722 his Institute of the Laws of England. His object was to digest the law, and to bring it into better order and system. By the year 1754, his work had passed through eight folio editions, and thereby affording a decisive proof of its value and popularity. It was greatly esteemed by the lawyers of that age; and an American judge,[a] (himself a learned lawyer of the old school,) has spoken of Wood as a great authority, and of weight and respect in Westminster Hall.

But it was the fate of Wood's Institutes to be entirely superseded by more enlarged, more critical, and more attractive publications, and especially by the Commentaries of Sir William Blackstone, who is justly placed at the head of all the modern writers who treat of the general elementary principles of the law. By the excellence of his arrangement, the variety of his learning, the justness of his taste, and the purity and elegance of his style, he communicated to those subjects which were harsh and forbidding in the pages of Coke, the attractions of a liberal science, and the embellishments of polite literature. The second and third volumes of the commentaries are to be thoroughly

---

[a] M'Kean, Ch. J. 1 Dallas. p. 357.

studied and accurately understood. What is obsolete is necessary to illustrate that which remains in use, and the greater part of the matter in those volumes is law at this day, and on this side of the Atlantic.

I have necessarily been obliged to omit the mention of many valuable works upon law, as my object in the present lecture was merely to select those which were the most useful or distinguished. With respect to the more modern didactic treatises on various heads of the law, and which have multiplied exceedingly within the period of the present generation, I will take notice of a few of those which relate to the law of real property, and are deemed the most important. The numerous works, both foreign and domestic, on various branches of the law of personal rights and commercial contracts, I may have occasion to refer to hereafter, as the subjects of which they treat pass under consideration in the course of these lectures. I cannot take any critical notice of them at present, without going too far from the general purpose of this inquiry, and many of them are not sufficiently matured by time to become of much authority.

Sanders' Essay on Uses and Trusts is a comprehensive and systematic treatise, but it wants that fulness of illustration, and neat and orderly arrangement, requisite in the discussion of so abstruse and complicated a branch of the law. The learned Mr. Butler has given a very elaborate note on the same subject;[a] and there is an excellent summary of the law of uses and trusts in Cruise's Digest, arranged with his customary skill, and supported by an accurate analysis of adjudged cases, which are apposite and pertinent to the inquiry.

Sugden's Practical Treatise on Powers is the best book we have on that very abstruse title in the law. It was regarded by the author as his favourite performance, and he is entitled to the gratitude of the student for his masterly

---

[a] Note 231 to lib. 3. *Co. Litt.*

execution of the work. It is perspicuous, methodical, and accurate. Mr. Sugden's Treatise on the Law of Vendors and Purchasers, is also a correct and useful collection of equity principles on a subject extremely interesting, and of constant forensic discussion. Roberts on Fraudulent Conveyances covers a very important head in the jurisprudence of the courts of equity. He has collected the cases arising under the statutes of 13 and 27 Elizabeth, respecting conveyances that are deemed fraudulent in respect to creditors and purchasers; and though the treatise is written in bad taste, it is a useful digest of the law on that subject. Powell's essay upon the learning of devises contains a systematical and valuable view of an important branch of the law concerning title to real property, and it is enlivened with some spirited discussions; but neither that essay, nor the one of his upon mortgages, are to be compared to the clear, succinct and masterly analysis of the cases under similar titles in the great work of Mr. Cruise. Fearne's Essay on Contingent Remainders and Executory Devises is a performance of very superior character. It is eminently distinguished for the ability and perspicuity with which it unfolds and explains the principles of the most intricate parts of the law. Mr. Preston's recent essays on Estates and Abstracts of Title are so admirably executed, and contain such sound and clear views of the law of real property, that they have already attained the distinction and authority of works of established reputation.

I have thus attempted, for the assistance of the student, to unfold, in this and the preceding lecture, the principal sources from which we derive the evidence and rules of the common law. There is another source still untouched, from which a great accession of sound principles, particularly on the subject of personal contracts, has been received, to enlarge, improve, and adorn our municipal codes. I allude to the body of the civil law, contained in the Institutes, Digest and Code of Justinian; and our attention will be directed to that subject in the next lecture.

LECTURE XXIII.

OF THE CIVIL LAW.

The great body of the Roman or civil law was collected and digested by order of the Emperor Justinian, in the former part of the sixth century. That compilation has come down to modern times, and the institutions of every part of Europe have felt its influence, and it has contributed largely, by the richness of its materials, to their character and improvement. With some of the European nations, and in the new states in Spanish America, in the province of Lower Canada, and in one of these United States,[a] it constitutes the principal basis of their unwritten or common law. It exerts a very considerable influence upon our own municipal law, and particularly on those branches of it which are of equity and admiralty jurisdiction, or fall within the cognizance of the surrogate's or consistorial courts. The Roman law is blended with that of the Dutch, and carried into their Asiatic possessions; and when the island of Ceylon passed to the hands of the English, justice was directed to be administered according to the former system of laws in the Dutch courts; and Van Leeuwen's Commentaries on the Roman Dutch Law were translated into English in 1820, expressly for the benefit of the English judiciary in that island.

The history of the venerable system of the civil law is peculiarly interesting. It was created and gradually ma-

---

[a] See the *Civil Code of the State of Louisiana*, as reported in 1823.

tured on the banks of the Tiber, by the successive wisdom of Roman statesmen, magistrates and sages; and after governing the greatest people in the ancient world, for the space of thirteen or fourteen centuries, and undergoing extraordinary vicissitudes after the fall of the western empire, it was revived, admired and studied in modern Europe, on account of the variety and excellence of its general principles. It is now taught and obeyed, not only in France, Germany, Holland, and Scotland, but in the islands of the Indian Ocean, and on the banks of the Mississippi and the St. Lawrence. So true, it seems, are the words of D'Aguesseau, that "the grand destinies of Rome are not yet accomplished; she reigns throughout the world by her reason, after having ceased to reign by her authority."

My design in the present lecture is to make a few general observations on the history and character of the civil law, in order to excite the curiosity and direct the attention of the student to the proper sources of information on the subject. The acquaintance which I have with that law is necessarily very imperfect; and I am satisfied that no part of it can be examined, and no one period of its history can be touched by a person not educated under that system, without finding himself at once admonished of the difficulty and delicacy of the task, by reason of the overwhelming mass of learning and criticism which press upon every branch of the inquiry.

That part of the Roman jurisprudence which has been denominated the ancient, embraced the period from the foundation of the city by Romulus, to the establishment of the twelve tables.

The fragment of the Enchiridion inserted in the Pandects,[a] is the only ancient history of the first ages of the Roman law now extant. It was composed by Pomponius in the second century of the Christian era, and rescued from oblivion by Justinian; and Bynkershoeck[b] has republished

---

a *Dig.* lib. 1. tit. 2. *De origine juris.*
b *Prætermissa ad leg.* 2 D. *De origine juris. Opera*, tom. 1. 301.

it, and endeavours to restore the integrity of the original text by emendations and a critical commentary. From this fragment we learn that Sextus or Caius Papirius, who was a pontifex maximus about the time of the expulsion of Tarquin, made a collection of the *leges regiæ*, or laws and usages of the Romans under their kings, and which was known by the name of the *Jus Civile Papirianum*. Very few, if any, fragments of this original collection by Papirius now remain, though efforts have been made to restore, if possible, some portion of these early Roman laws.^a Such a work was evidence of great progress in jurisprudence under the kings, and it must have contained an account, which would have been at the present day most deeply interesting and curious, of the primitive institutions of a city destined to become the mistress of the world.^b

The genius of the Roman government and people had displayed itself by the time of the expulsion of their kings, and the foundations of their best institutions and discipline had been laid. Romulus divided the people into tribes and curiæ, and instituted the patrician order and the Roman senate, which last body became in process of time the most powerful and majestic tribunal in all antiquity. The general assemblies of the people were a part of the primitive government, and a very efficient portion of the legislative power, and they met in their curiæ or parishes, and the vote of every citizen belonging to the curiæ was equal in these *comitia curiata*. The fecial and other colleges established by Numa, bound the Romans to religious disci-

---

a Heinecc. Antiq. Rom. Jur. Proœm. sec. 1 and 2.

b Mr. *Gibbon*, in his History, vol. 8. p. 5. note, denies altogether the fact of any such original compilation by Papirius. I am incompetent to decide such a question. It is cited as an original and authentic work by Pomponius, who had infinitely better means of knowledge than any modern writer; and it is assumed to be so by such master critics as Bynkershoeck and Heineccius, and yet the singular learning and acuteness of Gibbon give almost overbearing weight to his critical opinions.

pline.ᵃ Servius Tullius divided the people into six classes and one hundred and ninety-three centuries, and this was a most important change in the Roman polity. The first class contained the patricians, knights, and rich citizens, and 98 centuries; and when the people assembled by centuries in their *comitia centuriata*, (as they generally did thereafter, when called by the consuls or senate,) they voted by centuries, and the first class containing a majority of all the centuries, if unanimous, dictated the laws. This arrangement threw the powers of government into the hands of the patrician order, and of men of property.

After the establishment of the republic, all the higher magistrates were elected in the *comitia centuriata*, which were convoked by the consuls, and they presided in them, counted the votes, and declared the result; and their resolutions were *leges* of the highest authority, and binding on the whole community. After the institution of tribunes, they convoked the assemblies of the people by tribes, and there all the people met on an equality, and voted *per capita*, and the *comitia tributa* were the same in effect and substance as the *comitia curiata*. They elected the subordinate magistrates, and enacted *plebiscita*, binding on the plebeians alone, until the Hortensian law made the decrees of the people in their *comitia tributa* binding equally on patricians and plebeians.ᵇ

As the whole administration of justice, civil and criminal, had been transferred from the kings to the consuls, it soon became necessary to control the exercise of this formidable power. This was done by the Valerian law, proposed by the consul Valerius, and granting to persons accused of crimes a right of appeal from the judgment of the consuls to the people. It then became an established principle in the Roman constitution, that no capital punishment could be

---

a Numa religionibus et divino jure populum devinxit. Tac. Ann. 3. 26.

b Dig. 1. 2. 2. 8. *Gravina de ortu et prog. jur. civ.* sec. 28.

inflicted upon a Roman citizen without the vote of the people, though the consuls retained the power of inflicting very severe imprisonment.[a] The Valerian law became an imperfect *palladium* of civil liberty, and was in some respects analogous to the *habeus corpus* act in the English law, but the appointment of a dictator was a suspension of the law.

As the royal laws collected by Papirius had ceased to operate, except indirectly by the force of usage; and as the Romans for twenty years after the expulsion of Tarquin had been governed without any known public rules,[b] they began to suffer the evils of uncertain and unsteady laws. The call for written law was a long time resisted on the part of the magistrates and senate; but it was at last complied with, and a commission of three persons, by the joint consent of the senate and tribunes, was instituted to form a system of law. This commission gave birth to the twelve tables, which form a distinguished era in the history of the Roman law, and constitute the commencement of what has been called the middle period of the Roman jurisprudence.[c]

---

[a] *Dig.* 1. 2. 2. 16.

[b] *Incerto magis jure et consuetudine quam per latam legem.* Dig. 1. 2. 3.

[c] The *Enchiridion* of Pomponius says, that the deputies were commissioned to seek laws from the Grecian cities; *(Dig.* 1. 2. 2. 4.) and the original historians, Livy (b. 3. ch. 31, 32.) and Dionysius of Halicarnassus, *(Antiq. Rom.* b. 10.) say, that the deputation was sent to Athens to learn the laws and institutions of Greece. Gravina, *(De ortu et prog. jur. civ.* sec. 32. and *De jure nat. gent. et* XII *tabularum,* sec. 28.) Heineccius, *(Hist. Jur. civ.* sec. 24. and *Antiq. Rom. Jur. Proœm.* sec. 3.) Voet, *(Com. ad Pand.* 1. 2. 1.) Dr. Taylor, *(Hist. of the Roman Law,* p. 8) and the generality of modern writers on Roman history and law, assume it to be a conceded fact, on the authority of Livy, Dionysius, Cicero, Pliny, and others, that the embassy went to Athens. Tacitus *(Ann.* 3. 27.) observes generally, *accitis quæ usquam egregia,* and the deputies must have visited at least the Grecian cities in lower Italy. A learned French writer has, however, written three dissertations to prove that there was no

The twelve tables were ratified by the consent equally of the patricians and plebeians, and they consisted partly of entire laws transcribed from the institutions of other nations, partly of such as were altered and accommodated to the manners of the Romans, partly of new provisions, and partly of the laws and usages of their ancient kings.* They

---

such thing as a Grecian embassy. Dr. Taylor has referred to them, but they failed to convince him. Mr. Gibbon (*Hist.* vol. 8. p. 8.) is also decidedly of opinion that the deputation never visited Athens, and he gives very plausible reasons for his belief; but I think the weight of the opinion of Cicero alone is not easily to be surmounted; and he says *(De Legg.* b. 2. ch. 23. and 25.) that the regulations in the twelve tables concerning funerals, were translated from the laws of Solon, and the decemviri had adopted almost the very words of Solon.

a *Gravina de Ortu et Prog. J. C.* sec. 32. Fragments of the twelve tables were collected, and distributed with great accuracy under their original and proper divisions, by J. Gothofred, in a work entitled *Quatuor Fontes Juris Civilis*, printed in 1653; and his collection, Heineccius says, (*Antiq. Jur. Rom. Proœm.* sec. 5.) is to be preferred to that of all others. His collection, distribution and interpretation of the tables has been followed by Gravina, who has inserted the originals, with a paraphrase, at the conclusion of his treatise *de Jure Naturali Gentium et XII Tabularum.* He has also given a copious commentary upon that collection. They were redigested and inserted at length in the voluminous *L'Histoire Romaine* of the Jesuits Cotrou and Rouille, and copied from them into Hooke's Roman History, b. 2. ch. 27. A summary of this curious and celebrated code, which had such permanent influence on Roman jurisprudence, and is so constantly alluded to by Roman jurists, will not be unacceptable to the American student.

The 1st table related to *law suits*, and regulated the right of citation of the defendant before the prætor. He was allowed to give bail for his appearance, and if old or infirm, the plaintiff was to provide him with a jumentum or open carriage. (But even this provision was reprobated in after ages for its severity. *A. Gell. Noct. Att.* 20. 1.) The prætor was to decide the cause promptly by day light, and if the accuser wanted witnesses, he was allowed to go before his adversary's house, and to repeat his demand for three days together, by loud outcry.

The 2d table related to *robbery, theft, trespass, and breaches of trust.*

were written in a style exceedingly brief, elliptical and obscure, and they show the great simplicity of Roman manners, and are evidence of a people under a rugged police, and very

---

It allowed the right to kill a robber by night. It inflicted corporal punishment and slavery on conviction of robbery, unless the parties settled with each other. Slaves guilty of robbery were to be thrown down the Tarpeian Rock. Thefts and trespasses were punished by a pecuniary mulct. Trespasses by night on harvests or cornfields were punished capitally, as victims devoted to Ceres. No term of prescription gave a right to stolen goods, nor any right of a foreigner to the goods of a Roman citizen. Breaches of trust were punished with the forfeiture of double the value of the deposit.

The 3d table related to *loans, and the right of creditors over their debtors*. It prohibited more than one per cent. interest for money, and the debtor was to have thirty days after judgment to pay his debt; and if he did not then pay or give security, his creditor had a right to seize him, and load him with chains of a certain weight, and maintain him on a prescribed scanty allowance; and if he failed to pay after being sixty days in prison, he was to be brought before the people on three market days, and the debt proclaimed, and if there were several creditors, he might at their election be sold beyond the Tiber, or his body cut into pieces. (Mr. Gibbon, *Hist.* vol. 8. 92. takes this law in the literal sense, and so does Gravina, *de Jure Nat. Gent. et XII Tab.* sec. 72.; and he adopts the argument of Sextus Cæcilius in *A. Gell. Noct. Att.* 20. 1. who maintained, that the law was only cruel in appearance, and that he had never read or heard of its being executed, for its extreme severity prevented the creation of debt. Montesquieu well observes, that upon such reasoning the most cruel laws would be best, and he thinks the better construction to be, that the law only related to the division of the debtor's property. *Esprit des Loix*, b. 29. ch. 2. Bynkershoeck, *Observ. Jur. Rom.* lib. 1. c. 1. and Heineccius, *Antiq. Rom.* lib. 3. tit. 30. sec. 4. are of the same opinion. Gravina, *ibid* sec. 21. says, there are grounds to conclude that the *leges regiæ*, with the exception of such as related to regal domination, were incorporated into the three first of these twelve tables.)

The 4th table related to *the rights of fathers and families*. It gave to fathers the power of life and death and of sale over their children, and the right to kill immediately a child born deformed. On the other hand, and as some compensation for these atrocious provisions, it declared, that if a father neglected to teach his son a

considerably advanced in civilization. They contain a great deal of wisdom and good sense, intermixed with folly, injustice, and cruelty. They were engrossed on tables of

---

trade, he was not obliged to maintain his father when in want; nor was an illegitimate child bound to maintain his father.

The 5th table related to *inheritances and guardianships*. It declared, that if the father died intestate, and had no children, his nearest relations were to be his heirs; and if he had no relations, a man of his own name was to be his heir. He had the right to appoint guardians to his children. If a freedman died intestate and without heirs, his effects went to the family of his patron. The heirs were to pay the debts of the ancestor in proportion to their share of his estate. It also provided, in the case of lunatics and prodigals, that the relations, and if none, that one of the name was to have the care of the person and estate.

The 6th table related to *property and possession*. It declared, that the title of goods should not pass on sale and delivery, without payment. Two years possession amounted to a right of prescription for lands, and one year for moveables. It likewise declared, that in litigated cases, the presumption should always be on the side of the possessor; and that in disputes about liberty and slavery, the presumption should always be on the side of liberty.

The 7th table related to *trespasses and damages*. It provided, that compensation be made for trespasses; and that for arson or maliciously setting fire to a house, or to grain near it, the offender was to be scourged and burnt to death. The *lex talionis* was applied to losses of limb, unless the injured party accepted some other satisfaction. A pecuniary fine of three hundred pounds of brass was declared for dislocating a bone, and twenty-five asses of brass for a common blow with the fist. (It is related in the *Noct. Att.* 20. 1. that one Lucius Neratius, in after times, when the city became wealthy, and such a fine insignificant, amused himself by striking freemen in the face as he met them in the street, and then ordering his servant, who followed him for the purpose with a bag of brass money, to count out and tender the twenty-five pieces as the compensation fixed by law.) It was provided also by this table, that slanderers by words or verses should be beaten with a club. False witnesses were to be thrown headlong from the capitol, and parricides were to be sewed up in a sack and thrown into the Tiber. Whoever wilfully killed, or poisoned, or prepared poison for a freedman, or used magical words to hurt him, was punishable as a homicide. Guardians and patrons

wood, or brass, or ivory, and were destroyed when the city was burnt by the Gauls. They were afterwards collected, and existed entire in the third century; but did not, as Hei-

---

who acted fraudulently in their trust, were to be fined and held odious.

The 8th table related to *estates in the country*. It required a space of two and a half feet to be left between every house; and it allowed societies or private companies to make their own by-laws, not being inconsistent with the public law. The prætor was to assign abitrators in cases of disputes about boundaries; and it provided redress for nuisances to fields by the shade of trees, or by water courses. It required roads to be eight feet wide, and double at corners. It allowed travellers to drive over the adjoining lands, if the road was bad.

The 9th table was concerning *the common rights of the people*. It prohibited all special privileges to any person, and it restored debtors who had been redeemed from slavery to their former rights. It made bribery in a judge or arbitrator, or the holding seditious assemblies in the city by night, or delivering up a Roman citizen to a foreigner, or soliciting a foreigner to declare himself against Rome, capital offences. It declared that all causes relating to the life, liberty or rights of a Roman citizen, should be tried in the *comitia centuriata*. The people were to choose quæstors to take cognizance of capital cases.

The 10th table related to *funerals*. It prohibited the dead to be interred or burnt within the city, or within sixty feet of any house. It prohibited all excessive wailings at funerals, and women from tearing their faces or making hideous outcries on such occasions. It regulated and limited the expense of the funeral piles, and all costliness at funerals, such as the dress of the deceased, the players upon the flute, the perfumed liquors, the gold thread, the crown, festoons, &c.

The 11th table made part of the *jus sacrum*, or pontifical law. All the other tables related to civil rights, but this related to *religion and the worship of the gods*. It required all persons to come with purity and piety to the assemblies of religion; and no person was to worship any new or foreign gods in private, unless authorized by public authority. Every one was to observe his family festivals, and the rights used in his own family, and by his ancestors, in the worship of his domestic deities. Honour was to be paid to those heroes and sages whom their merit had raised to heaven. The commendable

neccius supposes, survive the sixth century of the Christian era. This code obtained, in the subsequent ages of the republic, from the most distinguished philosophers, historians, and statesmen, the blind tribute of patriotic veneration, and the most extravagant eulogy, as being a system inculcating the soundest principles of philosophy and civil polity, and surpassing in value the jurisprudence of Solon and Lycurgus, and the ten books of the laws of Plato, and whole libraries of Grecian philosophy.ᵃ As Rome increased in territory, wealth, arts, and refinement, her laws were progressively enlarged and improved, and adapted to the progress of society, and its increasing wants and vices. The obligation of the twelve tables was gradually diminished or destroyed by the multitude of new regulations, and the history of the Roman law, from the time of the twelve tables to the reign of Hadrian, is eminently instructive.

After many struggles, the patricians were obliged, by the *lex Horatia*, to submit to the authority of the *plebiscita*,

---

virtues were to be ranked among the gods, and to have temples erected to them, but no worship was to be paid to any vice. The sacrifices to the gods by the priests were to be the fruits of the earth and young animals, and with the most authorized ceremonies. No one was to be initiated in any mysteries but those of Ceres. Stealing of what was devoted to the gods, and incest, were declared to be capital crimes.

The 12th table related to *marriage, and the rights of husbands.* It prescribed freedom of divorce at the pleasure of the husband; and it allowed the husband, with the consent of his wife's relations, to put her to death when taken in adultery or drunkenness; and it declared it to be unlawful for patricians to intermarry with plebeians.

a *Cic. de Orat.* b. 1. c. 43. 44. *De Legg.* 2. sec. 23. *Livy's Hist.* 3. 34. *Tacit. Ann.* 3. 27. *A. Gell. Noct Att.* 20. 1. In the newly discovered treatise of Cicero *De Republica*, lib. 2. c. 36, 37. he insists, that the ten first tables were composed with the greatest equity and prudence, but he declares that the two last tables added by the decemvirs, were iniquitous laws, and that the law prohibiting marriages between plebeians and senatorial families was a most infamous law.

enacted by the plebeians alone in their *comitia tributa*, as being of equal force with the *leges*, passed at the instance of a consular or senatorial magistrate, by the whole aggregate body of the people, patricians and plebeians. The senate also frequently promulgated laws under the name of *senatus consulta*, by their own authority.[a] A *senatus consultum* was allowed to continue in force only one year, unless ratified by the common course of *rogatio ad populum*; and the tribunes could, at any time, by their *veto*, put a negative upon any projected decree of the senate. That body likewise assumed the right to dispense with laws, though, by a law proposed by the tribune Caius Cornelius, the senate could not exercise their dispensing power, unless 200 senators were present. Within a very few years after the adoption of the twelve tables, the prohibition of marriages between the patricians and plebeians was abolished; but the patricians had the address to retain the management and control of the whole administration of justice. This was effected in several ways. It was effected by the institution of legal forms of judicial proceeding called *legis actiones*, and by means of the *pontifices* who regulated the calendar, and assumed the power of fixing the lawful days of business, the *dies fasti et nefasti*. These judicial forms and solemnities gave order and uniformity to the administration of justice; but they were mysteries of jurisprudence, confined to the learned of the patrician order, and locked up in the pontifical archives. They could not be changed at the pleasure of the people, and the right to interpret them belonged to the pontifical college.[b] They remained confused and undigested until Appius Claudius Cœcus, a member of the pontifical fraternity, reduced them into one collection, which his scribe Cnæus Flavius surreptitiously published, to

---

[a] *Inst.* 1. 2. 4. *Dig.* 1. 2. 9.
[b] *Dig.* b. 1. tit. 2. *De Orig. Jur.* sec. 6. Gravina says, *De Ortu et Prog. J. C.* sec. 33. that they were established by the policy of the ancient lawyers.

the great satisfaction of the people. It acquired the title of the *Jus civile Flavianum;* and a second collection of these legal precedents afterwards appeared, and was called the *Jus civile Ælianum.*ᵃ This Roman science of special pleading became a subject of ridicule by Cicero, as being a cunning and captious verbal science; and these forms were expressly abolished by the Emperor Constantine as insidious.ᵇ

The edicts of the prætor became another very important means of the increase and improvement of the Roman law. The judicial decisions of the prætors, or *edicta prætorum,* became of great consequence. They were called *jus honorarium,* or patrician law derived from the honour of the prætor.ᶜ There had been, from the foundation of the city, a magistrate called *præfectus urbis,* to administer justice in the absence of the king or consul; and after the plebeians obtained a share in the consular dignity, the patricians created a permanent city prætor, and they confined his province to the administration of justice, and such a magistrate was indispensable, as the consuls were engaged in foreign and executive duties.ᵈ The prætor was at first a patrician, and elected in the *comitia centuriata,* though the office in time became accessible to plebeians. Business soon required a second prætor to preside over the causes of foreigners, called *prætor peregrinus,* and prætors were afterwards allotted to the provinces as the empire widened. Under Augustus, the prætors had multiplied to sixteen; and in the time of Pomponius, there were eighteen, and one of them judged *de fidei commissa.*ᵉ Every prætor, on entering into office, establish-

---

a *Dig.* 1. 2. 7. *Livy's Hist.* 9. 46. *Gravina de Ortu Jus. Civ.* sec. 33. and *de Jur. Nat. et XII. Tab.* sec. 79, 80.

b *Legulejus quidam cautus et acutus præco actionum, cantor fabularum, auceps syllabarum. Cic. de Orat.* 1. 55. See also *Cod.* 2. 58. *De formulis et impretrationibus actionum sublatis.*

c *Dig.* 1. 1. 7. and 1. 2. 10.

d *Dig.* 1. 2. sec. 26. 28.

e *Dig.* 1. 2. 32.

ed and published certain rules and forms, as the principle and method by which he proposed to administer justice for the year. He had no power to alter these rules, and this *jus prætorium vel honorarium*, tempered the ancient law by the spirit of equity and public utility, and it was termed the living interpreter of the civil law.[a] But as the prætor was apt to vary from his annual edict, and to change it according to circumstances, which opened the way to many frauds, it was provided by a law, enacted at the instance of the tribune Caius Cornelius, that the prætor should adhere to his edicts promulgated on the commencement of his magistracy. These prætorian edicts were studied as the most interesting branch of the Roman law, and they became a substitute for the knowledge of the twelve tables, which fell into neglect, though they had once been taught as a *carmen necessarium*, and regarded as the source of all legal discipline.[b]

The opinions of lawyers, called the *responsa*, or *interpretationes prudentum*, composed another and very efficient source of the ancient Roman jurisprudence.

The most ancient interpreters were the members of the college of *pontifices*, composed of men of the first rank and knowledge. Civil statesmen, and eminent private citizens, followed their example, and sometimes debated in the forum. Their answers to questions put, were gradually adopted by the courts of justice, by reason of their intrinsic equity and good sense; and they became incorporated into the body of the Roman common law, under the name of *fori disputationes*, and *jus civile*, or *responsa prudentum*.[c] This business, undertaken gratuitously by persons of the highest distinction, grew into a public profession, and law became a regular science, taught openly in private houses as in schools. The names of the principal lawyers who became, in this way,

---

a *Dig.* 1. 1. 7. and 8.
b *Cic. de Legg.* b. 1. c. 5. and b. 2. c. 23. *Gravina de Ortu et Prog. J. C.* sec. 38.
c *Dig.* 1. 2. 5.

public professors of the law, are to be found in the work of Pomponius,[a] and in the writings of Cicero, Horace, Tacitus, and the other authors of the classical ages. Their opinions were preserved by their successors, and fragments of them are, no doubt, dispersed in different parts of the pandects, without the sanction of their names.[b] Cicero speaks of this employment of distinguished jurists with the greatest encomiums, and as being the grace and ornament, and most honourable business of old age. The house of such a civilian becomes a living oracle to the whole city, and this very accomplished orator and statesman fondly anticipated such a dignified retreat and occupation for his declining years.[c] The philosophy, and policy, and wisdom of Greece, were collected together, says Gravina,[d] by the Roman civilians, and all that was useful introduced into the Roman law; and if it were really true that the twelve tables were not drawn by the rough agents who compiled them directly from Grecian fountains, we are assured that the omission was abundantly supplied in after ages; and the institutions of Greece

---

a *Dig.* 1. 2.

b In the times of the republic, the practice of the law was gratuitous, and highly honorary. All employment for hire was prohibited by a law enacted in the year of the city 550, at the instance of the Tribune Marcus Cincius. The profession at length became a business of gain, and was abused until Augustus revived the Cincian law with additional sanction by a decree of the senate. But as a reasonable compensation was necessary to advocates who devoted their time and talents to the profession, the compensation was allowed and regulated by a decree of the senate in the time of Claudius; (*Tacit. Ann.* b. 11. c. 5, 6, 7.) and, afterwards, according to the law of the *Pandects*, b. 50. tit. 13. c. 1. sec. 5. 10. 12. the judges in the provinces were to determine on, and allow a reasonable charge to the advocate.

c *Cic. de Orat.* 1. 45. See also *Quinctilian's Inst.* lib. 12. c. 11. where he alludes to Cicero, and strongly approves of this employment of the orator when he retires from practice at the bar.

d *Orig. Jur. Civ.* b. 1. *Proem.*

were studied by more enlightened statesmen, and contributed to perfect and adorn the Roman law.

In the Augustan age, the body of the Roman law had grown to immense magnitude.[a] It was composed of the *leges*, or will of the whole Roman people declared in the *comitia centuriata*; the *plebiscita*, enacted in the *comitia tributa*; the *senatus consulta*, promulgated by the single authority of the senate; the *legis actiones*; the *edicta magistratuum*; the *responsa prudentum*; and, subsequent to the age of Cicero, is to be added the *constitutio principis*, or ordinances of the Roman emperors.[b] The Roman civilians began very early to make collections and digests of the law. The book of Sextus Ælius contained the laws of the twelve tables, the forms of actions, and the *responsa prudentum*. Publius Mucius, Quintus Mucius, Brutus, and Manilius, all left volumes upon law, and the three books of the latter existed in the time of Pomponius as monuments of his fame.[c] Servius Sulpicius left behind him nearly 180 volumes upon the civil law. Many distinguished scholars arose under his discipline, who wrote upon jurisprudence; and Aufidius Namusa digested the writings of ten of those scholars into 140 books. Antistius Labeo, under Augustus, surpassed all his contemporaries, and he compiled 400 volumes, many of which, Pomponius says, he possessed.[d] The noble design of reducing the civil law into a convenient digest, was conceived by such great men as Cicero, Pompey, and Julius Cæsar; though it is certain that no systematic, accessible, and authoritative treatise on the civil law, appeared during the existence of the republic; and Cicero says, that the law lay scattered and dissipated in his time.[e] The Roman juris-

---

a *Immensus aliarum super alias acervatarum legum cumulus.* Livy, 3. 34.

b *Dig.* 1. 1. 7. and 1. 2. 12.

c *Dig.* 1. 2. 36. and 39.

d *Dig.* 1. 2. sec. 41. 43, 44. 46, 47.

e *Cic. de Orat.* lib. 2. c. 33. *Suet. J. Cæsar*, sec. 44. *Heineccii Elementa Juris Inst. Proæm.* sec. 2. Dr. Taylor's *Elements of the Civil Law*, 14.

prudence was destined to continue for several centuries under the imperial government, a shapeless and enormous mass, receiving continual accumulations, but it was fortunately cultivated under the emperors by a succession of illustrious men, equally distinguished for their learning, wisdom, and probity.

Before the time of Augustus, the *responsa prudentum* were given *viva voce*, and they had not the force of any authority in the forum, and the business was free to all persons. The character of these *responsa* was abused and discredited by the crude opinions of pretenders, and Augustus restrained the profession of the jurisconsults to such as he should select as most worthy, and they were to be first approved of and commissioned by him. They then began to give their opinions in writing, with their reasons annexed.[a] This raised their influence, and reduced the prætors to a state of comparative dependence upon those living oracles of law, who were under the influence of the emperor, and who obtained by their means the control of the administration of the law.[b] Heineccius says that Augustus instituted this college of civilians, in order that he might covertly assume legislative power, and adapt the republican jurisprudence to the change in the government. He likewise instituted a cabinet council, which was called the *consistory* by succeeding princes. It was composed of the consuls, several other magistrates, and a certain number of senators chosen by lot.[c] Ulpian was a member of this royal council under Alexander Severus. It was the imperial legislature. The power of the *comitia* was transferred to this shadow of a Roman senate, for the old constitutional senate not being able conveniently to govern all the provinces, (according to

---

a *Dig.* 1. 2. 47. *Heinecc. Hist. Jur. Civ.* lib. 1. sec. 157, 158. 180.

b *Gravina de Ortu. et Prog.* sec. 42. *Heinecc. Antiq. Rom.* lib. 1. tit. 2. sec. 39.

c *Gravina de Romano Imperio*, sec. 17.

the courtly language of the Pandects,[a]) gave to the prince the right to make laws. The judgments of the prince were called imperial constitutions, and they were usually enacted and promulgated in three ways: 1st. By rescript, or letter in answer to petitions, or to a distant magistrate.[b] 2d. By decrees passed by the emperor on a public hearing in a court of justice; and Paulus collected six books of those decrees, and from which he for the most part dissented.[c] 3d. By edict, or mere voluntary ordinances. Gravina says, that these imperial constitutions proceeded not as from a single individual, but as from the oracle of the republic by the voice of the senators, who were consulted, and were the visible representatives of the majesty of the commonwealth.[d] Many of these imperial ordinances were suggested by the best of the civilians, and do great honour to their authors; and with regard to private and personal rights, the Romans enjoyed to a very great degree, under the emperors, the benefit of their primitive fundamental laws, as they existed in the times of the republic. The profession of the law was held in high estimation under the emperors, and Hadrian took off the restriction of Augustus, and gave the privilege of being a public interpreter of the law to the profession at large.[e] It was restored by the Emperor Severus, and the *responsa prudentum* assumed an air of great importance. Though in the first instance they were received as mere opinions, they gradually assumed the weight of authority. The opinions were sent in writing to the judges, and in the time of Justinian, they were bound to determine according to those opinions.[f] These *responsa* (of which many are preserved in the Pandects) were not of the same authori-

---

a *Dig.* 1. 2. sec. 11.
b *Code* 1. 14. 3. Gravina de Ortu. et Prog. sec. 123, 124.
c *Gravina, ibid.* sec. 122. *De Romano Imperio,* sec. 20.
d *Gravina de Romano Imperio, ibid.*
e *Dig.* 1. 2. 2. 47.
f *Inst.* 1. 2. 8.

ty as the constitutional *leges*, but they were law for the case, and they were applied to future cases under the character of principles of equity, and not of precepts of law. In the ages immediately preceding Justinian, the civil law was in a deplorable condition, by reason of its magnitude and disorder; and scarcely any genius, says Heineccius, was bold enough to commit himself to such a labyrinth. As a remedy for the evil, the Emperors Theodosius and Valentinian confirmed by decree the writings of Papinian, Paulus, Gaius, Ulpian, and Modestinus, by name, and directed that they alone be permitted to be cited in the courts of justice, with the exception of such extracts as they had transferred into their books from the ancient lawyers, and with some other qualified exceptions in favour of Scævola, Sabinus, Julianus, and Marcellus. The opinion of the majority of these five legislative characters was to govern; and where there was in any case an equal division of opinion, that of Papinian was to be preferred.^a

The first authoritative digest of the Roman law which actually appeared, was the Perpetual Edict, compiled by Salvus Julianus under the orders of the Emperor Hadrian, and of which nothing now remains but some fragments collected and arranged by Gothofred, and published along with the body of the civil law. Hadrian was the first emperor who dispensed with the ceremony of the *senatus consulta*, and promulgated his decrees upon his sole authority.^b The prætorian edicts had been so controlled under the government of the emperors by the opinions of the civilians, that they lost the greater part of their ancient dignity, and Hadrian projected the design of reducing the whole Roman law into one regular system. All that he, however, lived to

---

a Heinecc. Antiq. Rom Jur. lib. 1. tit. 2. sec. 41. *Histor. Jur. Civ.* lib. 1. sec. 378. Heineccius says, that Papinian was every where called *Juris asylum et Doctrinæ legalis thesaurus*, and he far surpassed all his brethren, *omnes longo post se intervallo reliquerit*.

b Gibbon's History, vol. 8. p. 16.

perform, was, to procure the compilation of those edicts of the prætors which had stood the test of experience, on account of their authority and equity, and had received the illustrations of civilians.[a] Many able professors undertook from time to time a digest of the civil law. Papirius Justus collected some of the imperial constitutions into twenty books, and Julius Paulus compiled six books of decrees or imperial decisions. Gregorius made a collection of a higher character, and he digested into order the chief, if not the whole of the imperial edicts from Hadrian down to the reign of Dioclesian and his colleagues, and which was called the *Gregorian Code*, and attained great authority in the forum. Hermogenes continued this collection under the name of the *Hermogenian Code*.[b] Theodosius the younger appointed a committee of eight civilians to reduce the imperial constitutions, from the time of Constantine, into a methodical compendium; and this *Theodosian code* became a standard work throughout the empire, and it was published in six folio volumes in 1665, with a vast and most learned commentary by Gothofrede. Another century elapsed before Justinian directed Tribonian, who was an eminent lawyer and magistrate, to unite with him a number of skilful civilians, and to assume the great task of collecting the entire body of the civil law, which had been accumulating for fourteen centuries, into one systematic code. Whether the Roman law at that period exceeded or fell short of the number of volumes in which the English law is now embodied, it is not easy to determine. Tribonian represented to the emperor, that when he and his learned associates undertook the business of digesting the civil law, he found it dispersed in two thousand volumes, and in upwards of three millions of small tracts or fragments,[c] detached from the writings of the sages, which it was necessary to read and un-

---

a *Gravina de Ortu et Prog. Jur. Civ.* sec. 38.
b *Heinecc. Hist. Jur. Civ.* lib. 1. sec. 368—372.
c *Duo pene millia librorum esse conscripta, et plus quam trecentiens decem millia versuum a veteribus effusa. Secund. Præf. ad Dig.* sec. 2.

derstand in order to make the selections. The size of these volumes, and the exact quantity of matter in these small pieces or texts, we cannot ascertain. It is, however, a fact beyond all doubt, that the state of the Roman law rendered a revision indispensable. Justinian himself assures us,[a] that it lay in such great confusion, and was of such infinite extent, as to be beyond the power of any human capacity to digest.

The compilations made under Justinian, and which constitute the existing body of the civil law, consist of the following works, and which I shall mention in the order in which they were originally published.

(1.) The Code, in twelve books, is a collection of all the imperial statutes that were thought worth preserving from Hadrian to Justinian. In the revision of them, the direction to Tribonian, and his nine learned associates, was, that they should extract a series of plain and concise laws, omitting the preambles, and all other superfluous matter, and they were likewise intrusted with the great and hazardous power to extend, or limit, or alter the sense, in such manner as they should think most likely to facilitate their future use and operation.[b]

(2.) The Institutes, or Elements of the Roman Law, in four books, were collected by Tribonian and two associates. They contain the fundamental principles of the ancient law in a small body, for the use and benefit of students at law. This work was particularly adapted to the use of the law schools at Berytus, Rome, and Constantinople, which flourished in that age, and shed great lustre on the Roman jurisprudence. It is such an admirable compendium of the elements of the civil law, that it has in modern times passed through numerous editions, and received the most copious and laborious illustrations. It has been a model for every modern digest of municipal law. The institutes were

---

a *Prima Præf. ad Dig.* sec. 1.
b *Præf. primus ad Cod.* sec. 2.

compiled chiefly from the writings of Gaius; and a discovery by Mr. Niebuhr so late as 1816, of a re-written manuscript of the entire Institutions of Gaius, has given increased interest to the Institutes of Justinian.^a

(3.) The Digest, or Pandects, is a vast abridgment in fifty books of the decisions of prætors, and the writings and opinions of the ancient sages of the law. This is the work which has principally excited the study, and reflections, and commentaries of succeeding ages. It is supposed to contain the embodied wisdom of the Roman people in civil jurisprudence for near 1200 years, and the European world has ever since had recourse to it for authority and direction upon public law, and for the exposition of the principles of natural justice. The most authentic and interesting information concerning the compilation of the Pandects, is to be found in the ordinances of Justinian, prefixed, by way of prefaces, to the work itself.

In the first ordinance addressed by Justinian to his quæstor Tribonian, he directs him and his associates to read and correct the books which had been written by authority upon the Roman law, and to extract from them a body of jurisprudence in which there should be no two laws contradictory or alike, and that the collection should be a substitute for all former works; that the compilation should be made in fifty books, and digested upon the plan of the perpetual edict, and contain all that is worth having in the Roman law for the preceding 1400 years, so that it might thereafter be regarded as the temple and sanctuary of justice. He directed, that the selection be made from the civilians, and the laws then in force, with such discretion and sagacity as to produce in the result a perfect and immortal work. And, in the anticipation of the result, he declared, that no commentaries were to be made upon the digest, as

---

a See an account of that discovery in *N. A. Review* for April, 1821.

it had been found that the contradictions of expositors had disturbed the whole body of the ancient law.

In about three years after the publication of this first ordinance, Justinian issued another upon the completion of the work. In that latter ordinance, addressed to the senate and people, he declared that he had reduced the jurisprudence of the empire within reasonable limits, and within the power of all persons to possess at a moderate price, and without the necessity of expending a fortune in acquiring useless volumes of laws. He stated, that in the compilation of the Pandects, Tribonian and his associates had drawn from authors of such antiquity, that their names were unknown to the learned of that age. If defects should be discovered, recourse must be had to the emperor, and he pointedly prohibited all persons to have any further recourse to the ancient laws, or to institute any comparison between them and the new compilation. And to prevent the system from being disfigured and disordered by the glosses of interpreters, he declared, that no citations were to be made from any other books than the Institutes, the Pandects, and the Code; and that no commentaries were to be made upon them, upon pain of being subjected to the charge of the *crimen falsi*, and to have the commentaries destroyed.

The Pandects are supposed to have been compiled with too much haste, and they were very defective in precision and methodical arrangement. The emperor allowed ten years, and Tribonian and his sixteen colleagues finished the work in three years. It is said that the Pandects were composed of the writings of forty civilians, the principal part of whom lived under the latter Cæsars, and the doctrines only, and not the names of the more ancient sages, were preserved. If the work had been executed with the care and leisure that Justinian intended, it would have been an incomparable monument of human wisdom. There are, as it is, a great many contradictory doctrines and opinions in the compilation on the same subject, and too much of that very uncertainty which Justinian was so solicitous to avoid. But with all its errors and imperfections, the Pandects are the greatest repository of sound legal principles, applied to the private rights and business of mankind, that has ever appeared in any age or nation. Justinian has given it the venerable appellation of the temple of human justice. The excellent doctrines, and the enlightened equity which pervade the work, were derived from the ancient sages, who were generally men of distinguished virtue and patriotism, and sustained the most unblemished character, and had been frequently advanced to the highest offices in the administration of the government. The names of Gaius, Scævola, Papinian, Ulpian, Paulus, and Modestinus, may be selected from a multitude of civilians, as models of exalted virtue, and of the most cultivated and enlightened human reason. It is owing to their writings that the civil law, for the purity and vigour of its style, almost rivals the productions of the Augustan age.

(4.) The novels of Justinian are a collection of new imperial statutes, which constitute a part of the body of the civil law. Those ordinances were passed subsequent to the date of the code, and had been required in the course of a long reign, and by the exigencies of succeeding times. They were made to supply the omissions and correct the errors of the preceding publications; and they are said by competent judges to show the declining taste of the age, and to want much of that brevity, dignity, perspicuity, and elegance which distinguished the juridical compositions of the ancients. Some of these novels are of great utility, and particularly the 118th novel, which is the groundwork of the English and our statute of distribution of intestates' effects.ᵃ The institutes and pandects were afterwards trans-

---

a *Sir William Blackstone, Com.* vol. 2. 516. does not seem willing to admit that the statute of distributions was taken from the civil law; but when Lord Holt and Sir Joseph Jekyll declare, (1 *P. Wm.* 27. *Prec. in Chan.* 593.) that the statute was penned by a civilian, and is to be governed and construed by the rules of the civil law; and when we compare the provisions in the English statute and the Roman novel, the conclusion seems to be very fair and very strong, that the one was borrowed essentially from the other.

lated into Greek, and the novels were generally composed in that language, which had become the vernacular tongue of the eastern empire; and as evidence of the universality of that tongue, Justinian declared that one of his constitutions was composed in the Greek language, for the benefit of all nations.[a]

When the body of the civil law as contained in the Institutes, the Pandects, and the Code, was ratified and confirmed by Justinian, it became exclusively the law of the land; and the various texts from which the compilation was made, fell speedily into oblivion; and all of them, except the Theodosian code and fragments of the other parts, disappeared in the wreck of the empire. The great work itself was in danger of being involved in the general destruction which attended the irruption of the northern barbarians into the southern provinces of Europe. The civil law maintained its ground a long time at Ravenna and in the Illyrian borders; but all Italy passed at length under the laws as well as under the yoke of the barbarians:—*belluinas, atque ferinas immanesque Longobardorum leges accepit.*[b] There was but one circumstance that could give any thing like compensation to the inhabitants of Europe for the absence or silence of the civil law during the violence and confusion of the feudal ages; and that circumstance was the redeeming spirit of civil and political liberty, which pervaded the Gothic institutions, and tempered the fierceness of military governments, by the bold outlines and rough sketches of popular representation. It was an indelible and foul blot on the character of the civil law, as digested under Justinian, that it expressly avowed and inculcated the doctrine of the absolute power of the emperor, and that all the right and power of the Roman people was transferred to him.[c] This

---

a *Inst.* 3. 8. 3.

b *Gravina de Ortu et Prog Jur. Civ.* sec. 139.

c *Inst.* 1. 2. 6. *Prima præf. ad Dig.* sec. 7. *Præf. secund. ad Dig.* sec. 18. 21.

had not been until then the language of the Roman laws; and Gravina, with much indignation, charges the introduction of the *lex regia* to the fraud and servility of Tribonian.[a] Be that as it may, the claim of despotism became afterwards a constitutional principle of imperial legislation. It has been made a question, whether the Pandects were for many ages so entirely lost to the western parts of Europe as has been generally supposed. It is certain, however, that about the time of the assumed discovery or exhibition of a complete copy of them at Amalphi in Italy, near the middle of the twelfth century, the study of the civil law revived throughout Italy and western Europe with surprising ardour and rapidity. The impression which the science of law in so perfect a state of cultivation made upon the progress of society, and the usages of the feudal jurisprudence, was sudden and immense.[b] In defiance of the command of Justinian to abstain from all notes or comments upon his laws, the civil law, on its revival, was not only publicly taught in most of the universities of Europe, but it was overloaded with the commentaries of civilians. From among the number of distinguished names, I would respectfully select Vinnius on the Institutes, Voet on the Pandects, and Perezius on the Code, together with the treatises on the civil law which abound in the works of Bynkershoeck, Heineccius, and Pothier, as affording a mass of instruction and criticism, most worthy of the attention and diligent examination of the student.

The civil law was introduced and taught, in the first instance, in England, with the same zeal as on the continent; but the rivalship, and even hostility, which soon afterwards arose between the civil and common law; between the two universities, and the law schools or colleges at Westminster; between the clergy and laity—tended to check the progress of the system in England, and to confine its influ-

---

a *De Romano Imperio*, sec. 23, 24.
b *Esprit des Loix*, liv. 28. ch. 42.

ence to those courts which were under the more immediate superintendence of the clergy.^a The ecclesiastical courts, and the Court of Chancery, accordingly adopted the canon and Roman law, and the court of admiralty, which was constituted about the time of Edw. I. also supplied the defects of the laws of Oleron from the civil law, which was generally applied to fill up the chasms that appeared in any of the municipal institutions of the modern European nations.^b A national prejudice was early formed against the civil law, and it was too much cultivated by English lawyers. Lord Coke mentions, by way of reproach, that William De la Pole, Duke of Suffolk, in the reign of Hen. VI. endeavoured to bring in the civil law, which gave occasion to Sir John Fortescue to write his work in praise of the English law; and the same charge was made one of the articles of impeachment against Cardinal Wolsey.^c But the more liberal spirit of modern times has justly appreciated the intrinsic merit of the Roman system. Sir Matthew Hale, according to the account of Bishop Burnet,^d frequently said, that the true grounds and reasons of law were so well delivered in the digest, that a man could never well understand law as a science without first resorting to the Roman law for information, and he lamented that it was so little studied in England. And in *Lane* v. *Cotton*,^e that strict English lawyer, Lord Holt, admitted, that the laws of all nations were raised out of the ruins of the civil law, and that the principles of the English law were borrowed from that system, and grounded upon the same reason.

The value of the civil law is not to be found in questions which relate to the connexion between the government and the people, or in provisions for personal security

---

a Blacks. Com. vol. 1. *Introductory Lecture. Reeve's Hist. of the English Law,* vol. 1. 81, 82. *Millar's Historical View of the English Government,* b. 2. c. 7. sec. 3.

b 3 *Reeve's Hist.* 198.

c 3 *Inst.* 208.

d Life of Sir M. Hale, p. 24.

e 12 *Mod.* 482.

in criminal cases. In every thing which concerns civil and political liberty, it cannot be compared with the free spirit of the English and American common law. But upon subjects relating to private rights and personal contracts, and the duties which flow from them, there is no system of law in which principles are investigated with more good sense, or declared and enforced with more accurate and impartial justice. I prefer the régulations of the common law upon the subject of the paternal and conjugal relations, but there are many subjects in which the civil law greatly excels. The rights and duties of tutors and guardians are regulated by wise and just principles. The rights of absolute and usufructuary property, and the various ways by which property may be acquired, enlarged, transferred, and lost, and the incidents and accommodations which fairly belong to property, are admirably discussed in the Roman law, and the most refined and equitable distinctions are established and vindicated. Trusts are settled and pursued through all their numerous modifications and complicated details, in the most rational and equitable manner. So, the rights and duties flowing from personal contracts, express and implied, and under the infinite variety of shapes which they assume in the business and commerce of life, are defined and illustrated with a clearness and brevity without example. In all these respects, and in many others which the limits of the present discussion will not permit me to examine, the civil law shows the proofs of the highest cultivation and refinement; and no one who peruses it can well avoid the conviction, that it has been the fruitful source of those comprehensive views and solid principles, which have been applied to elevate and adorn the jurisprudence of modern nations.

The Institutes ought to be read in course, and accurately studied, with the assistance of some of the best commentaries with which they are accompanied. Some of the titles in the Pandects, have also been recommended by Heineccius to be read and re-read by the indefatigable student. The whole body of the civil law will excite never failing curiosity, and receive the homage of scholars, as a singular monument of human wisdom. It fills such a large space in the eye of human reason; it regulates so many interests of man as a social and civilized being; it embodies so much thought, reflection, experience, and labour; it leads us so far into the recesses of antiquity, and it has stood so long "against the waves and weathers of time," that it is impossible, while engaged in the contemplation of the system, not to be struck with the awe and veneration which are felt in the midst of the solitudes of a majestic ruin.

END OF VOLUME I.

www.ingramcontent.com/pod-product-compliance
Lightning Source LLC
Chambersburg PA
CBHW030329240426
43661CB00052B/1577